Anders Å

UKRAINE

What Went Wrong and How to Fix It

Anders Åslund

UKRAINE

What Went Wrong and How to Fix It

Peterson Institute for International Economics

Washington, DC
April 2015

Anders Åslund is a leading specialist on economic policy in Eastern Europe, especially Russia and Ukraine. Since 2006, he has been a senior fellow at the Peterson Institute for International Economics. He also teaches at Georgetown University.

He has been deeply engaged in Ukraine since 1985, having served as an economic advisor to its government in 1994–97. In 2004 he cochaired a United Nations Blue Ribbon Commission for Ukraine and a similar International Commission of Independent Experts in 2009. He was one of the founders of the Kyiv School of Economics and cochaired its board of directors (2003–12).

He is the author of 14 books, including *How Capitalism Was Built: The Transformation of Central and Eastern Europe, Russia, the Caucasus and Central Asia* (2007, 2013), *How Ukraine Became a Market Economy and Democracy* (2009), and *Russia's Capitalist Revolution: Why Market Reform Succeeded and Democracy Failed* (2007). He has also edited 16 books, including *Economic Reform in Ukraine: the Unfinished Agenda* (2000), *Revolution in Orange* (2006), and *The Great Rebirth: Lessons from the Victory of Capitalism over Communism* (2014).

Åslund was the director of the Russian and Eurasian Program at the Carnegie Endowment for International Peace, founding director of the Stockholm Institute of Transition Economics, and professor at the Stockholm School of Economics. He earned his doctorate from the University of Oxford.

PETERSON INSTITUTE FOR INTERNATIONAL ECONOMICS
1750 Massachusetts Avenue, NW
Washington, DC 20036-1903
(202) 328-9000   FAX: (202) 659-3225
www.piie.com

Adam S. Posen, *President*
Steven R. Weisman, *Vice President for Publications and Communications*

Cover Design by Peggy Archambault
Cover Photo by ©Oleg Pereverzev/Demotix/Corbis
Printing by Versa Press

Printed in the United States of America
17   16   15   5   4   3   2

Library of Congress Cataloging-in-Publication Data
Åslund, Anders, 1952–
  Ukraine : what went wrong and how to fix it / Anders Åslund.
      pages cm
  "January 2015."
  Includes bibliographical references.
  ISBN 978-0-88132-701-4
1. Ukraine—Politics and government—1991–
2. Ukraine—Economic policy—1991–
3. Ukraine—Military policy. 4. Ukraine—Social policy. 5. Political corruption—Ukraine.
6. Social change—Ukraine. 7. Crisis management in government—Ukraine.
8. Yanukovych, Viktor. I. Title.
  DK508.848.A53 2015
  947.7086—dc23

2014042507

This publication has been subjected to a prepublication peer review intended to ensure analytical quality. The views expressed are those of the author. This publication is part of the overall program of the Peterson Institute for International Economics, as endorsed by its Board of Directors, but it does not necessarily reflect the views of individual members of the Board or of the Institute's staff or management.

The Peterson Institute for International Economics is a private, nonprofit institution for the rigorous, intellectually open, and indepth study and discussion of international economic policy. Its purpose is to identify and analyze important issues to make globalization beneficial and sustainable for the people of the United States and the world, and then to develop and communicate practical new approaches for dealing with them. The Institute is widely viewed as nonpartisan. Its work is funded by a highly diverse group of philanthropic foundations, private corporations, and interested individuals, as well as income on its capital fund. About 35 percent of the Institute's resources in its latest fiscal year were provided by contributors from outside the United States. A list of all financial supporters for the preceding four years is posted at http://piie.com/supporters.cfm.

Contents

Tables

Figures

Box

Preface

After the collapse of the Soviet Union, all of its former republics had to build new political and economic structures. Ukraine has experienced one of the most difficult and prolonged transitions because of its hesitation to break fully from the old system, including persistent widespread corruption. Given its geography, Ukraine's leaders tried to keep good relations with both Russia and the European Union, without opting fully for either in economic terms.

How Ukraine descended to the depths of economic and political dysfunction from these hesitations, and what it should do to pursue successful development, is the subject of this important study by Dr. Anders Åslund, one of the world's leading experts on the transition of one-time communist states to market economic systems and political freedom. Dr. Åslund also explains how Ukraine's worsening economic problems have been inextricably tied to political tensions with Russia, even before Russia directed military forces to annex Crimea in 2014, and of course all the more so since that invasion.

In this study, Dr. Åslund, a longtime senior fellow at the Peterson Institute for International Economics, lays out a sweeping agenda for political and economic reform for a country that he has studied for many years. His 2009 book, *How Ukraine Became a Market Economy and Democracy,* won wide acclaim for its analysis of the sources of difficulties in the only partial Ukrainian transition. In this new book, he explains why incremental measures toward liberalizing the economy, eliminating corruption, and removing wasteful subsidies and regulations will not address the grave nature of Ukraine's underlying problems. Dr. Åslund contends that only a radical program of reform will address Ukraine's deep-rooted dysfunction and strengthen its economy. So doing would enable Ukraine to stand up to Russian-backed pressure, thereby stabilizing its situation, as well as improving its longer-term prospects. In addition, Dr. Åslund calls on the West to supply vital economic assistance to pave the way for reform. In the fall of 2013, the country's record of fiscal and international deficits caught up with the leadership in Kyiv. Faced with a run on international currency reserves and sharply contracting economic output, then-president Viktor Yanukovych equivocated where to turn. Should Ukraine ask the European Union for help—or Russia, which feared Ukraine shifting orientation to the West? Increasingly, as Dr. Åslund documents, the Ukrainian population doubted Yanukovych's leadership.

After first choosing to pursue a deeper relationship with the European Union, Yanukovych changed his mind under pressure from Moscow. That reversal provoked an uprising that focused not only on that decision but also on the corruption and poor economic policies that had strangled the Ukrainian economy for years. As protests mounted, and police actions sought to counter them, the parliament voted Yanukovych out of power in late February 2014. This was a democratic breakthrough that gave rise to hope for an economic breakthrough as well. A presidential election in May installed Petro Poroshenko as president and parliamentary elections in October offered more hope for improvement (both elections deemed free and fair by the Organization for Security and Cooperation in Europe). Given the difficult security situation, as well as domestic political resistance to reform, Dr. Åslund importantly offers a clear list of policy priorities in this volume.

The Peterson Institute for International Economics is grateful to the Smith Richardson Foundation for its support of this study. The Institute is a private, nonprofit institution for rigorous, intellectually open, and indepth study and discussion of international economic policy. Its purpose is to identify and analyze important issues to make globalization beneficial and sustainable for the people of the United States and the world, and then to develop and communicate practical new approaches for dealing with them. The Institute is widely viewed as nonpartisan.

The Institute's work is funded by a highly diverse group of philanthropic foundations, private corporations, and interested individuals, as well as income on its capital fund. About 35 percent of the Institute resources in our latest fiscal year were provided by contributors from outside the United States. A list of all our financial supporters for the preceding year is posted at http://www.piie.com/supporters.cfm. Dr. Åslund has been a paid consultant to investors in Ukraine on the macroeconomic and policy outlook there over a period of years. His advice has not involved disclosure of market sensitive information or evaluation of any specific assets that these investors hold or intend to acquire or sell. His advice has been uniformly consistent with his publicly stated policy opinions about Ukraine.

The Executive Committee of the Institute's Board of Directors bears overall responsibility for the Institute's direction, gives general guidance and approval to its research program, and evaluates its performance in pursuit of its mission. The Institute's President is responsible for the identification of topics that are likely to become important over the medium term (one to three years) that should be addressed by Institute scholars. This rolling agenda is set in close consultation with the Institute's research staff, Board of Directors, and other stakeholders.

The President makes the final decision to publish any individual Institute study, following independent internal and external review of the work. Interested readers may access the data and computations underlying Institute publications for research and replication by searching titles at www.piie.com.

The Institute hopes that its research and other activities will contribute to building a stronger foundation for international economic policy around the world. We invite readers of these publications to let us know how they think we can best accomplish this objective.

Adam S. Posen
President
February 2015

Acknowledgments

Since 1985, I have followed the Ukrainian economy closely, with my engagement becoming more intense when hope for positive change arose. I have experienced many unforgettable moments with many friends but also numerous sad insights.

From 1994 to 1997, I worked as an economic advisor to President Leonid Kuchma and codirected the Soros International Economic Advisory Group together with Professors Georges de Ménil and Marek Dabrowski. We summarized our insights in a conference volume (Åslund and De Ménil 2000). I also assisted with setting up the graduate economic school, the Kyiv School of Economic, whose board I cochaired for nine years.

In 2004, Ukraine was all too obviously approaching a breaking point. The economy boomed as never before or since, but the wealth was concentrated to the few at the top. Kálmán Mizsei, assistant secretary general of the United Nations, suggested that I cochaired a blue ribbon commission on a reform program for the next president of Ukraine. I did so together with Professor Oleksandr Paskhaver and a commission of 20 people, half Ukrainian policy intellectuals, half foreigners with great insights into the Ukrainian economy. We produced a substantial report (Blue Ribbon Commission for Ukraine 2005).

The Orange Revolution did take place and our favored friends formed a government, but reform fell by the wayside. Michael McFaul and I coedited a book about the Orange Revolution (Åslund and McFaul 2006). In 2009, I published a monograph about Ukraine's economic and political development since independence in 1991 (Åslund 2009).

In 2008, financial crisis hit Ukraine once again. My friends asked me to assist Prime Minister Yulia Tymoshenko with her negotiations with the International Monetary Fund (IMF), which I was happy to do. Ukraine got through the crisis, though political stalemate made structural reforms impossible. As the next presidential elections approached, Paskhaver and I were asked to repeat our reform commission of 2004–05. We did so with a similar group of 20 people, half Ukrainians, half foreign specialists (Åslund and Paskhaver 2010). The Ministries for Foreign Affairs of Sweden and the Netherlands provided matching financing.

When Viktor Yanukovych won the presidential elections in February 2010, we did not expect that our reform program would make much headway, but to our surprise he adopted a similar program in June and quickly concluded an IMF program and adopted several desirable laws. Alas by October 2010, the show was over and no more reforms were forthcoming. I kept my distance from the government, which I quickly recognized as predatory.

In August 2013, Yanukovych declared that he wanted to sign the European Association Agreement at the Eastern Partnership Summit in Vilnius on November 28–29, and as a result Russia imposed quite severe trade sanctions on Ukraine. I put other work aside and focused on Ukrainian developments at the Peterson Institute for International Economics, where I have the advantage of being employed as a free intellectual and able to quickly change my agenda. I wrote multiple blog pieces as events evolved.

After the ouster of Yanukovych in the spring of 2014, major reforms appeared possible. Time was short and I had a pretty clear idea what Ukraine needed. I decided to write this book as fast as possible under the auspices of the Peterson Institute. I was happy to receive Peterson Institute President Adam Posen's full support for this work, and Smith Richardson Foundation kindly offered the Institute a generous grant for me to do this work. On July 3, 2014, I started writing this book, and I completed it over the next six months.

In mid-September I spent one intense week in Kyiv around Victor Pinchuk's always enlightening annual Yalta European Strategy, though this time it took place in Kyiv rather than at the Livadia Palace in Yalta because of the Russian annexation of Crimea. Then and in other contexts, I pursued substantial conversations with Victor and Elena Pinchuk, Prime Minister Arseniy Yatsenyuk, Governor of the National Bank of Ukraine Valeriya Hontareva, former President Leonid Kuchma, former Ministers of Economy Pavlo Sheremeta and Roman Shpek, former Deputy Prime Minister Hryhoriy Nemyria, head of the State Fiscal Service Ihor Bilous, former ministers of finance Viktor Pynzenyk and Ihor Mityukov, deputy chief of staff of President Poroshenko for economic reform Dmytro Shymkiv, the president's representative in the Cabinet of Ministers Oleksandr Danilyuk, Chrystia Freeland, Daniel Bilak, Oleksandr Paskhaver, Oleksander Savchenko, Thomas Weihe, Ivanna Klympush-Tsinsadze, Mykola Honchar, Irina Akimova, and Ihor Koliushko. I also talked with my old friends from the business community, Aivaras Abromavičius, Carl Sturén, Fredrik Svinhufvud, Yulia Chebotareva, Tomas Fiala, Natalie Jaresko, Olena Bilan, Maxim Timchenko, Ruben Beliaev, Ivan Yuryk, and Steven Fisher. I benefited from meetings with US Ambassador Geoffrey Pyatt, Swedish Ambassador Andreas von Beckerath, his predecessor Ambassador Stefan Gullgren, EU Ambassador Jan Tombinski and EU representative Kálmán Mizsei.

At various meetings in Washington, I have learned a great deal from talking with visitors from Ukraine, such as Minister of Education Serhiy Kvit, CEO of Naftogaz Ukrainy Andriy Kobolyev and his deputy Yuriy Vitrenko, Jock Mendoza-Wilson, various parliamentarians, notably Hanna Hopko and Serhiy Leshchenko, Markian Bilinskiy, George Logush, various journalists, and battalion commanders.

In Washington, our steady group of Ukraine associates has included Nadia Diuk, Paula Dobriansky, Katie Fox, Paul Gregory, John Herbst, Laura Jewett, David Kramer, Nadia and Robert McConnell, Stephen Nix, Irina Paliashvili, Steven Pifer, Roman Popadiuk, Morgan Williams, and Damon Wilson. I have also interacted extensively with the US government, the International Monetary Fund, the World Bank, and the US Congress, and most recently testified before the Helsinki Committee at the invitation of Cochairman Senator Benjamin Cardin. Lawrence Summers, David Lipton, Robert Zoellick, Poul Thomsen, Christopher Smart, and Rory MacFarquhar have been invaluable interlocutors.

Among journalists, I would particularly like to mention the editor-in-chief of *Kyiv Post*, Brian Bonner, the editor of the Project Syndicate, Kenneth Murphy, the *Ukrainskaya pravda* journalists Olena Prytula and Pavel Sheremet, as well as Judy Miller, Neil MacFarquhar of the *New York Times*, and Michael Birnbaum of the *Washington Post*.

In May, Minister of Economy Pavlo Sheremeta invited Daron Acemoglu, Kakha Bendukidze, Oleh Havrylyshyn, Basil Kalymon, and me to assist him with advice. As Sheremeta resigned in August and poor Kakha passed away last November, we invited Ivan Mikloš, Mikuláš Dzurinda, and Andrius Kubilius to join our circle, which they kindly did, as independent supporters of economic reform in Ukraine. Our group spent a few intense days in January 2015, which provided me with a catching-up opportunity and gave us substantial conversation with the new government appointed in December.

Several people kindly read my manuscript and provided useful comments, notably Aivaras Abromavičius, Daron Acemoglu, Daniel Bilak, Simon Commander, Basil Kalymon, Alexander Pankov, Tamara Sulukhia, Paolo Belli, Eugeniu Osmochescu, Lalita Moorty, Anastasia Golovach, Oleksyii Balabushko, Yadviga Semikolenova, and Iryna Scherbyna.

On October 16, the Peterson Institute organized a study group to discuss my book manuscript, and I greatly enjoyed the comments from Edward Chow, William Cline, John Earle, Vadim Grishin, Anne Krueger, Matthew Malloy, Michael Mandelbaum, Valerie Rouxel-Laxton, Brad Setser, John Sullivan, György Szapáry, Hung Tran, and Ángel Ubide.

I have benefitted enormously from the keen and intelligent work of my two research assistants, Vitaliy Shpak and Vijay Khosa.

I am indebted to the publications department of the Peterson Institute for producing this book so fast—Steve Weisman, Madona Devasahayam, and Susann Luetjen.

Finally and most of all, I want to thank my family. My beloved and enchanting wife, Anna, has accepted all the hours and engagement I have spent on this book, and so have our kind children, Anton, Carl, and Marianna.

Anders Åslund
Washington, DC
January 2015

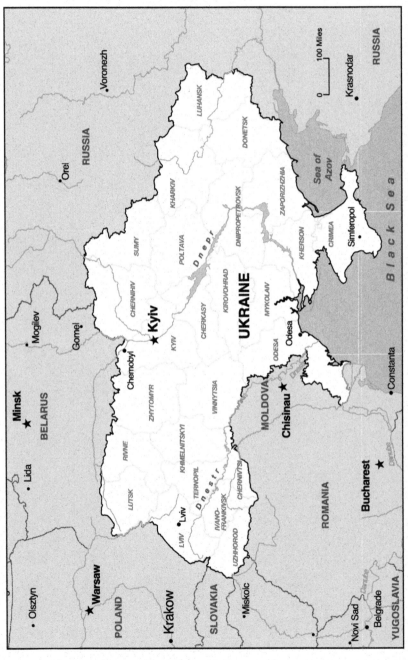

I

A STRATEGY OF RADICAL AND COMPREHENSIVE REFORM

1

Introduction: Ukraine on the Precipice

Ukraine has not yet died,
The glory and the freedom!
Still upon us, brave brothers,
Fate shall smile!
Our enemies will vanish
Like dew in the sun;
We too shall rule
In our country.

—National Anthem of Ukraine

Ukraine is facing its worst crisis since becoming independent in December 1991. The military aggression from Russia, which has annexed Crimea and invaded parts of Donbas in eastern Ukraine, threatens its existence as a nation. The intentions of Russian president Vladimir Putin have an inordinate bearing on Ukraine's future but are unknown. Military matters will certainly determine how Ukraine's future unfolds, but they are beyond the scope of this book. I focus instead on the extraordinary opportunity that the existential crisis presents for Ukraine to reform its state and economy and rid itself of the old and embrace the new. To anchor my analysis, I assume that the current ceasefire in the east holds.

At the same time the country is embroiled in an economic catastrophe left behind by former president Viktor Yanukovych. Ukraine's economic situation is spiraling out of control with a burgeoning budget deficit, rapidly rising public debt, plummeting exchange rate, and surging inflation. The country is on the verge of an inflation-depreciation cycle and international default. Roughly two-thirds of the output contraction derives from Russia's military aggression in Donbas, but the financial crisis that the current government inherited from the old regime has ravaged the economy. Ukraine needs to carry out substantial budget cuts, undertake major structural reforms, and mobilize foreign support to overcome this financial crisis.

A root cause of Ukraine's problems is pervasive corruption, which is front and center in this book. The crisis offers Ukraine's policymakers a golden chance to build a sound strategy to contain corruption and reform from the top down. Success can never be guaranteed, but failure can be assured by doing nothing. Many institutions and experts have offered laundry lists of measures that Ukraine should carry out, but not many have proposed how to do so. Drawing on lessons from reform strategies of successful postcommunist countries, this books sets out to do just that. As Poland's great reformer Leszek Balcerowicz (2014, 25) put it, "a risky policy was preferable to a hopeless one." If the democratically elected leaders fail to solve Ukraine's basic problems this time, Ukraine might cease to exist.

Ukraine's reforms had started taking place as this book went into production in December 2014. The new Ukrainian government had been appointed and its program adopted, but the government had not begun working. Events in the country are occurring at a fast and unpredictable pace. My aim in this book is to offer the policy line and not narrate the story in real time. I have focused on recommending reforms that Ukraine ought to undertake to resolve its existential crisis.

What Went Wrong?

Ukraine's postcommunist transition has been most protracted and socially costly (see box 1.1 on some basic facts about the country). The leadership's main early goal was nation building and the economy was not given due attention. The long delay in economic reforms led to hyperinflation, extreme rent seeking, and output collapse. In the mid-1990s, President Leonid Kuchma brought about financial stabilization and privatization, but not growth.

Ukraine's fundamental problem is that it did not experience any clear break from the communist system. Its tardy transition to a market economy bred pervasive corruption by giving the old elite ample opportunities to transform their power into personal wealth. They did so with great success, to the detriment of society, building a rent-seeking oligarchy that was never effectively challenged during Ukraine's 23 years of independence from the Soviet Union. Ukraine's economy has consistently underperformed because of pervasive corruption since independence.

The regime of President Yanukovych, 2010–14, was a nightmare for Ukrainians. It was a predatory regime despite the fact that Yanukovych was democratically elected. To begin with, he appeared to reestablish the oligarchy, but within a year he started concentrating power and wealth to his own family circle, upsetting not only the populace but also the big businessmen.

Ukraine's standing is best identified by comparing its performance on four parameters: GDP per capita in purchasing power parities, GDP per capita at current prices and exchange rates, economic growth, and governance.

Ukraine's economy has done far worse than any of its big neighbors. Figure 1.1 shows its GDP per capita in purchasing power parities in comparison with Poland, Russia, and Turkey. In 1990, Ukraine, Poland, and Turkey were at similar levels. Since then, Poland and Turkey have approximately doubled their GDP per capita at fixed prices, while Ukraine has declined by one-fifth, according to the World Bank (2014a).

If we instead look at GDP per capita at current prices and exchange rates in 1989 and 2013, we find that Ukraine was slightly ahead of Russia and at the

Box 1.1   Ukraine: Some basic facts

Ukraine is the largest country in Europe with an area of 604,000 square kilometers. Ukraine has a population of 45 million, including Crimea and Donbas. Ethnic Ukrainians comprise 78 percent of the population and ethnic Russians 17 percent. About half of the population speaks Ukrainian and half Russian, but almost everybody speaks both languages, which are East Slavic languages that very close to one another, and many speak a mixture of the two languages. Ukrainian dominates in the west and the center, and Russian dominates in the east and the south.

Ukraine is a unitary state with 25 regions and two cities with regional status. According to its constitution of 2004, the country has a presidential-parliamentary system. It became independent from the Soviet Union in December 1991. The nation traces its roots to Kievan Rus that was founded in 882, but it was absorbed by neighboring countries. Ukraine was independent from 1918–21.

Ukraine has had regular, competitive presidential and parliamentary elections. Its presidents have been: Leonid Kravchuk, 1991–94, Leonid Kuchma, 1994–2005, Viktor Yushchenko, 2005–10, Viktor Yanukovych, 2010–14, and Petro Poroshenko since 2014.

Ukraine enjoys a central geographical location in Europe, bordering on seven countries. It is dominated by an enormous plain with fertile black soil, making it the traditional bread basket of Europe. Ukraine's large rivers have offered both water and good river transportation. In the east, Ukraine has large assets of coal and iron ore, which led to the early development of a strong metallurgical industry, morphing into a large machine-building industry. In the 1980s, its economic structure was reminiscent of Poland's.

In 2013, services accounted for 63 percent of Ukraine's GDP, industry 27 percent, and agriculture 10 percent. Of its exports, 26 percent went to the European Union and 24 percent to Russia. Its main export goods are steel, agricultural goods, and machinery (World Bank 2014a, UN Comtrade database, 2014).

level of Poland and Turkey in 1989, while the other three countries were at a level approximately three times higher than Ukraine's in 2013 (IMF 2014e).

How could this have happened? Figure 1.2 offers an overview of real economic growth rates from 1989 to 2013, comparing Ukraine with Poland and Russia. We can distinguish five periods. In the early transition, 1991–94, Ukraine's lack of economic policy resulted in hyperinflation and massive output fall. Ukraine did far worse than Russia, which attempted serious reform even if it did not quite succeed. Poland, by contrast, did nearly everything right at the outset of its postcommunist transformation. It started growing in 1992, reaching a sound growth rate.

In 1995–99, Ukraine's GDP continued to shrink, which was also true of Russia, while Poland maintained a high growth rate. In the decade of 1989–99, Ukraine's GDP fell by a total of 61 percent, compared with 52 percent for Russia, whereas Poland's GDP rose by 22 percent (UNECE 2000, 225). Evidently,

Figure 1.1   GDP per capita (PPP), Ukraine, Poland, Russia, and Turkey, 1990 and 2012

constant 2010 international dollars

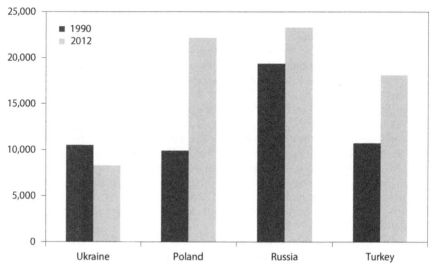

PPP = purchasing power parity
Source: World Bank (2014a).

Figure 1.2   GDP growth in Ukraine, Poland, and Russia, 1989–2013

annual percent change

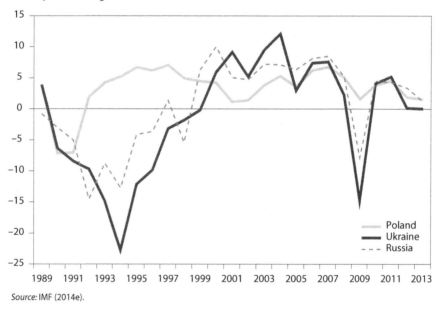

Source: IMF (2014e).

Poland surged ahead thanks to its early, radical, and comprehensive market reforms (Åslund 2013a).

In the third period, 2000–07, the roles reversed. Finally, Ukraine started growing fast at an average of 7.5 percent a year, Russia almost kept up with a growth of 7 percent a year, and Poland's economy expanded by an average of only 4.1 percent a year.

The global financial crisis of 2008–09 revealed that Ukraine's finances had been massively overheated. The country had thrived on a big financial bubble, which burst in September 2008. Its GDP plunged by 15 percent in 2009, while Russia's GDP plummeted by 7.8 percent, but Poland's GDP grew (IMF 2014e). The Russian economy was also somewhat overheated, while Poland had maintained strict monetary discipline. The aftermath of the crisis brought little relief to Ukraine. It suffered the worst crisis and has recovered the least. In 2012 and 2013, Ukraine recorded no growth at all because of Yanukovych's predatory economic policies.

To sum up, only in the eight years 2000–07 did Ukraine perform better than Russia and Poland. Countries that had similarly poor economic performance in the 1990s were Russia, Moldova, and Kazakhstan. These four countries had ended up in an underreform trap of rent seeking and oligarchy (Åslund, Boone, and Johnson 2001). Around 2000, they all broke out of it and started growing fast, but Ukraine has gotten stuck once again.

Improved governance is crucial to increase economic growth and welfare. Governance becomes more important for growth as an economy advances (Acemoglu 2008). Figure 1.3 illustrates Ukraine's standing with regard to freedom and corruption among 21 postcommunist countries. Most of these countries belong to one of two groups, which both represent stable equilibriums.

All the Central and East European countries that have become members of the European Union (EU) have advanced to full democracy and succeeded in containing corruption. They have entered a stable equilibrium, with democratic forces checking the government so it does not become too corrupt.[1] Most of the post-Soviet countries, by contrast, have ended up in a suboptimal equilibrium, where corruption thrives because predatory authoritarian regimes maintain it to their benefit.

Four former Soviet republics fall between these two equilibriums, namely Ukraine, Moldova, Georgia, and Armenia. They are freer than the other post-Soviet countries, but not fully democratic. In terms of predominantly oligarchic rule Armenia is probably most similar to Ukraine. Only Georgia is less corrupt than the most corrupt EU members, whereas Ukraine is as corrupt as the authoritarian post-Soviet countries. Interestingly, all four countries are members of the EU Eastern Partnership. At present, Georgia, Moldova, and Ukraine harbor hopes of edging closer to the EU members, having concluded Association Agreements with the European Union. Armenia, by contrast, has been pressured by Russia into joining the Eurasian Economic Union and it

---

1. Hungary could slip away from this favorable equilibrium, but that has not been recorded as yet.

Figure 1.3 Democracy and corruption, 2013

Freedom House Political Rights and Civil Liberties Rating (1=free, 7=not free)

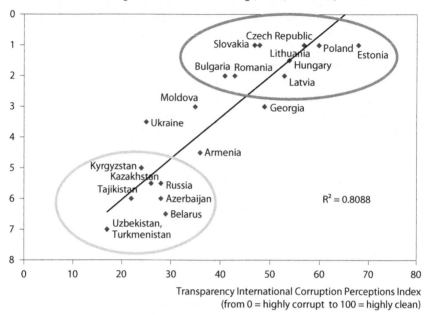

Transparency International Corruption Perceptions Index
(from 0 = highly corrupt to 100 = highly clean)

Sources: Freedom House (2014), Transparency International (2013).

seems to be sliding toward that marsh of corruption and authoritarianism. Still, these four countries face the choice between an optimal EU equilibrium and suboptimal CIS equilibrium.

A score of big businessmen have captured the state in Ukraine, more than any other postcommunist country (EBRD 1999). They dominate large sectors of the economy, notably energy, metallurgy, mining, and chemicals, letting neither foreigners nor smaller Ukrainian businessmen into these sectors. They made their fortunes through rent seeking, primarily gas trade, in the early 1990s, and by capturing the state they have managed to maintain their rents. The oligarchs have controlled the state through large representation of their own in the parliament and in the government, but they have also bought the services of all kinds of senior officials in retail (Åslund 2009).

The prominent role of the oligarchs in Ukrainian society has been for both good and bad. Competition between the big business groups has kept Ukraine quite an open society, unlike for example Russia, but these groups have also rendered society corrupt and lopsided to their benefit (Åslund 2006, Åslund and McFaul 2006).[2] President Yanukovych tried to consolidate power in the

---

2. The best book on post-Soviet oligarchs is Freeland's (2000) discussion of the Russian oligarchs in the 1990s. Frishberg (2008) has written extensively about the Ukrainian oligarchs without men-

hands of his family as in many other post-Soviet countries. In doing so, he turned against both the people and the oligarchs. An important reason for his political demise was that powerful big businessmen owned most of the television channels, which exposed his follies.

Something Happened on the Road to Vilnius

On November 21, 2013, the Ukrainian Cabinet of Ministers decided "to stop the process of preparation for the signing of the Association Agreement" between Ukraine and the European Union.[3] Prime Minister Mykola Azarov announced the decision upon returning from a bilateral meeting with Russian prime minister Dmitry Medvedev in St. Petersburg.

Ukraine had planned to sign this important agreement at the European Union (EU) Eastern Partnership summit in Vilnius on November 28–29. The Ukrainian Parliament had even scheduled the adoption of the last two laws required by the European Union, namely on the prosecutor's office and on permission for former prime minister Yulia Tymoshenko to leave prison to go abroad for back surgery. But President Yanukovych balked because these two laws were crucial for establishing European legal norms in Ukraine and they would deprive Yanukovych of his control over Ukraine's legal system. The government's official excuse was that it wanted to restore the trade it had lost with Russia because of the Kremlin's politically motivated trade sanctions.

There was a silver lining. The Association Agreement was not dead, only suspended. It could be revived but that required a change of Ukrainian leadership. Yanukovych was the evident obstacle. His economic policy had made him excessively dependent on the Kremlin, forcing him to block Ukraine's European integration, which a large majority of his people supported. In the evening of November 21, popular protests erupted against the government decision to say no to Europe on Independence Square (*Maidan Nezalezhnosti*) in Kyiv. They did not end until long after the Yanukovych regime had fallen.

On November 28–29, the European Union held its long anticipated Eastern Partnership summit in Vilnius. Yanukovych attended. On arrival, he declared that he would sign the Association Agreement. Yet, in the morning of November 29, he emerged, with German chancellor Angela Merkel and the two EU presidents José Manuel Barroso and Herman van Rompuy, empty-handed with a vacant smile on his face.

Ukrainskaya pravda summarized the situation in one headline: "Viktor Ya-

---

tioning their real names, while Puglisi (2003) and I (Åslund 2009) have named them and their companies.

3. "Azarov otkazalsya ot Soglasheniya ob assotsiatsii s ES" ["Azarov refused the Association Agreement with the EU"], *Ukrainskaya pravda*, November 21, 2013.

nukovych has departed from history."[4] The opposition cried treason and called for the ouster of the Azarov government and the impeachment of Yanukovych. Braving freezing temperatures, the protesters camped out peacefully on the Maidan. Soon they were hundreds of thousands, to the surprise of both government and protesters. Since the Orange Revolution in 2004, Ukraine's civil society had been thriving with many popular protests all over the country, but usually they were small. The conventional wisdom was that Ukrainians were so disappointed with the outcome of the Orange Revolution that they would not take to the streets en masse again, but that proved to be a faulty assumption. Gradually, the name of this event evolved from Euromaidan to the Revolution of Dignity. The rest is history encompassed in this book.

A Strategy for Economic Reform

In May 2014, my colleague Simeon Djankov and I organized a conference in Budapest on the lessons from postcommunist economic transformation a quarter century later. We mobilized top reformers from 10 postcommunist countries to write papers about their insights, including Leszek Balcerowicz from Poland, Václav Klaus from the Czech Republic, Mart Laar from Estonia, and Anatoly Chubais from Russia (Åslund and Djankov 2014).[5]

The experiences of the postcommunist countries have varied greatly. The two most obvious successes are Poland and Estonia, whose GDP has doubled after communism. Both benefited from an early return to economic growth, and they have enjoyed enduring democracy. By contrast, Hungary has had limited growth of 24 percent from 1990 to 2012 (World Bank 2014a).

For Ukraine, the most relevant reform prototypes are Poland in 1989 (Balcerowicz 2014), Czechoslovakia in 1990 (Klaus 2014), Estonia in 1992 (Laar 2014), Latvia and Lithuania in 2009 (Åslund and Dombrovskis 2011), and Georgia in 2003 (Bendukidze and Saakashvili 2014). All these countries were in severe crises at the time, which they successfully resolved through radical, comprehensive, and front-loaded reforms carried out while they enjoyed popular support.

The first part of this book presents such a strategy of radical and comprehensive reform for Ukraine. The second part summarizes what went wrong, that is, how Ukraine ended up in this difficult economic and political situation. The third contains policy proposals to resolve the main problems.

Chapter 2 answers why Ukraine can and should opt for radical reform. The country is under attack from a far stronger Russia and its economy is in shambles. As long as the war is limited, Ukraine has an opportunity for reform that it should not waste. The time to reform is ripe also because Ukraine's big businessmen, the so-called oligarchs, have been seriously weakened, rendering

---

4. Mustafa Nayem, "Viktor Yanukovych vyshel iz istorii" ["Viktor Yanukovych has departed from history"], *Ukrainskaya pravda*, November 29, 2013.

5. I have summarized my own lessons in Åslund (2013a).

them pliable to reform. The chapter also gleans lessons for Ukrainian policy-makers from reform experiences of the most relevant postcommunist economies in Central Europe, the Baltics, and Georgia.

Hardly any reform has been successfully carried out without substantial international support. Chapter 3 argues that now that the Ukrainian Parliament has ratified its Association Agreement with the European Union, Europe can function as Ukraine's anchor for modernization. It should assist Ukraine in its reforms as it did in Central and Eastern Europe, offering a legal, economic, and political model as well as a vast export market. The European Union should also consider giving more financing to Ukraine than before. A Marshall Plan for Ukraine, with the onus on Europe, is my recommendation.

The second part of the book asks what went wrong. Two chapters cover the formation of the new state and the Yanukovych regime. The third part, consisting of six chapters, is devoted to resolving Ukraine's difficulties. A profound systemic reform needs to start with politics and proceed with reform of the state from the top down. Fiscal reform is vital to resolve the rampant crisis and should be the first economic task. Energy reform is a must to contain corruption, which is one of the main causes of the country's problems. Ukraine's social sector must be made more efficient so that the citizens can receive real benefits. Social reforms, therefore, cannot wait. Since the country is in an economic crisis, these policy suggestions concern the immediate future. My intention is by no means to cover all aspects but to focus on what is important in the short term to put Ukraine on the path to long-term development. Chapter 6 sets the stage by detailing the evolution of Euromaidan, the popular protests that erupted in November 2013 and led to the ouster of President Yanukovych in February 2014. The next five chapters propose a cure to Ukraine's ailments by offering policy suggestions on key issues.

Politics Must Come First

Among postcommunist reformers, Laar (2002) and Klaus (2014) best understood the importance of politics and democracy for successful economic reform. The old political establishment wants to preserve the old ideology and structures, which should be abandoned. Therefore, a democratic breakthrough, as Ukraine experienced in February 2014, must be followed by new democratic elections.

Ukraine has already succeeded on this front. It held free and fair presidential elections on May 25, electing Petro Poroshenko with a majority of 55 percent of the votes cast. On October 26, Ukraine held early parliamentary elections, which were won by three democratic, liberal, and pro-European parties.

Chapter 7 explains why politics must come first. A systemic change—as Ukraine so desperately needs now—requires hundreds of new laws, which only a democratic parliamentary majority that supports reform can adopt, because quality legislation requires an orderly legislative process. Parliamentary committees need to clearly define laws to enhance their quality, and in the process a constituency in favor of each law arises. Without a newly elected democratic parliament little reform is possible.

Ukraine should also abolish legal immunity of parliamentarians to make them accountable. For successful parliamentary elections, three conditions are essential. Full transparency must be established of the finances both of candidates and political parties to weed out the large amounts of illegal funds that have characterized recent Ukrainian elections. Transparency can be ensured only if it is accompanied by independent auditing of financial statements. Moreover, to reduce the demand for campaign financing, strict limitations on electoral financing and advertising need also be imposed. It should no longer be possible to purchase a safe seat in parliament.

A fully proportional election system with "open party lists," that is, free choice of candidate within the party in question, appears the best system to reduce electoral corruption. Ukraine has started on this road but not completed it because members of the old parliament did not want to vote against their own interests. The new parliament is likely to take further steps.

By and large, Ukraine has maintained the extreme Soviet overcentralization more than other post-Soviet states. The essence of its constitutional reform must be to decentralize power to render Ukrainian politics more functional and democratic.

Next Comes Reform of the State

The state needs to be reformed and cleansed of corruption. There is too much continuity from the Soviet state. Ukraine needs a clear break from the old system, as Estonia and Georgia did resolutely. The new Ukrainian government needs to move fast to clean up the government from the top and render it more efficient and service oriented.

Chapter 8 recommends that the first step be to close and merge superfluous or even harmful state agencies. A large number of inspection agencies should be closed swiftly because they have no role to play in a modern free economy. It is better to close them all at once. The government has started merging agencies and reducing staff, but it needs to go much further.

Another step is lustration, that is, wholesale dismissal of judges, prosecutors, and law enforcement officials deemed to be corrupt. The most appropriate precedent is the complete change of judges in eastern Germany after the German reunification. Ukraine needs to draw on international support and attract young lawyers not susceptible to corruption. Also, law enforcement needs to be lustrated from the top down. Ukraine has adopted a lustration law, so this important cleansing has already started.

A full reform of the public administration should follow. Ministers must be made responsible and accountable. Preferably, one state agency after the other should be sorted out as was done in Estonia and Georgia. The EU twinning of state agencies is useful in this regard. A clear distinction should be made between political appointments, which should be limited, and civil service appointments, which should be based on merit rather than seniority.

Ukraine has far too many civil servants who earn too little. This is no way to attract qualified or efficient staff. Many superfluous civil servants should be laid off, and their wage funds be distributed among other civil servants. Both skills and remuneration must be raised.

The state should regulate only what really has to be regulated given that the government capacity to regulate is so limited. The World Bank Ease of Doing Business Index is an excellent tool for how to proceed. The number of procedures, their cost, and their time should be minimized, as many countries have done so successfully.

In 2000, Ukraine privatized agricultural land, distributing it to the members of collective farms and the employees of state farms, but private sales of land were not legalized. Repeatedly, the Ukrainian government has delayed the legalization of private sales of agricultural land. Such sales should finally be legalized. The main beneficiaries of the current system are large agricultural holding companies that lease the land for up to 49 years at minimal prices. Only when private sales of land become legal can Ukraine develop viable family farms on a large scale. Otherwise, farmers cannot use their land as collateral and thus cannot raise much credit.

Public Finances Must Be Fixed

Chapter 9 discusses reform of public finances to resolve the rampant financial crisis. The budget deficit is too large and expanding fast. Public debt was 41 percent of GDP in 2013, but with a rising budget deficit, collapsing output, and the sharp depreciation of the hryvnia the International Monetary Fund (IMF) expects public debt to reach 67 percent of GDP, which might be excessive for Ukraine, given its limited credibility on financial markets.

Public expenditures are far too large at 52.7 percent of GDP in 2014 (IMF 2014d, 41). The Baltic countries have public expenditures in the range of 34 to 38 percent of GDP,[6] which appears to be the right level for Ukraine as well. Its current excessive public expenditures both depress economic growth and contribute to the corrupt enrichment of the rich and powerful in Ukraine. Cuts should focus on two items that stand out as inordinately large, namely energy subsidies of 10 percent of GDP and public pension expenditures of no less than 16 percent of GDP. The energy subsidies amount to nothing but corrupt enrichment and should be eliminated instantly, and needy consumers should be compensated with cash transfers.

Strangely, state revenues have stayed quite high as a share of the official

---

6. Eurostat, "Total general government expenditure % of GDP 2013," http://epp.eurostat.ec.europa.eu/tgm/table.do?tab=table&init=1&plugin=1&language=en&pcode=tec00023 (accessed on August 1, 2014).

economy, partly because of high tax rates on labor, creating a large underground economy, and partly because of draconian tax collection. The number of taxes needs to be reduced to nine, as the government proposes, and the high payroll tax must be cut, since it is not collected in any case. The flat personal income tax should be reintroduced to render Ukraine competitive.

Tax collection needs to be simplified. The tax code of 2010 should be substantially revised to reduce corruption and injustice. The current proposed revision rightly calls for the restoration of simplified taxation for small entrepreneurs. The 2010 tax code also aggravated the already extensive transfer pricing of the large, well-connected companies, which paid neither profit taxes nor dividends to minority shareholders because all their profits were transferred to tax-free offshore havens. The value-added tax refunds for exporters should be made automatic to clean up the racket of tax officials demanding commission on these refunds. The tax police needs to be abolished to end the lawless persecution of taxpayers.

Ukraine's extremely centralized public finances need to be significantly decentralized to regions and local authorities in line with the decentralization of political power. Finally, competitive public procurement must be introduced. A law on public procurement that insists on open public tenders for both Ukrainian and foreign companies was adopted in the spring of 2014, and this time it should be implemented.

The Energy Sector: Ukraine's Cancer of Corruption

For the last two decades, the main source of enrichment in Ukraine has been to trade natural gas between minimal state-controlled prices and high market prices, first between Ukraine and Russia and since 2010 within Ukraine. Each year a few operators have made a few billion dollars on this trade. The top gas traders have regularly bought Ukraine's politics to maintain this boondoggle. According to the IMF (2014b, 87), energy subsidies amounted to 7.6 percent of GDP in 2012 and they are likely to have risen to 10 percent of GDP in 2014.

Chapter 10 calls on the new government to swiftly adjust the prices of natural gas, coal, and electricity to costs and markets, which would save the budget the cost of these large subsidies each year. Some of that amount should be given as social compensation to the poor. Each of Ukraine's nine IMF agreements has contained a condition on regular increases of gas prices, but every government has increased the gas price once to receive the first IMF tranche but then stopped, as the top gas trader has persuaded the government not to raise gas prices further. These failures show that it is time to abolish all energy subsidies instantly. The new CEO of Naftogaz, Andriy Kobolyev (2014), advocates such a reform.

The reasons for a speedy abolition of all the energy subsidies are many and strong. First of all, this is the main source of top-level corrupt revenues in Ukraine. The country can neither combat its corruption nor become a full democracy without eliminating the energy subsidies. Nor can it afford these large energy subsidies, which do nothing for the welfare of the nation. Because of its low, subsidized energy prices, Ukraine has the greatest energy intensity of production in Europe. No measure would enhance Ukraine's welfare more easily than energy saving. This is a matter of national security. Ukraine can live on its own gas and coal production if it economizes on energy, and higher prices are the only effective means of doing so. The low price cap on natural gas produced by state-owned companies amounts to severe discrimination against domestic production in favor of expensive imports from Russia. If the domestic prices were equalized with import prices, Ukrainian producers would have strong incentives to increase energy production. Most of the energy subsidies go to the rich and powerful. If the energy subsidies of 10 percent of GDP in 2014 were abolished, a limited share, 1 to 2 percent of GDP, would be sufficient as full cash compensation to the poorest half of the population. The World Bank has experience doing this in Latin America, and Ukraine started operating such a system on July 1, 2014.

All state energy companies need to be subject to proper corporate governance with effective boards of directors and external auditing, which is being made public. The energy sector should be unbundled, and the production companies should be prepared for privatization. Ukraine should establish energy markets, which are now missing.

Social Reforms Cannot Wait

Social reforms are always complex. They involve the whole population and large inert bureaucratic systems. As chapter 11 details, Ukraine has pursued minimal reforms in the social sphere. Today they can no longer be ignored. The social sector is both too important and too poorly run to be left for later.

The first question is the allocation of funding. Ukraine's pension expenditures are very large at 16 percent of GDP, which should be gradually reduced to a normal level of 8 percent of GDP. Ukraine attempted a limited pension reform in 2011, but it had little impact. Many old nomenklatura benefits are still in place and should be abolished. The retirement age needs to continue to rise, and the issuing of early pensions should be tightened. Ukraine should finally adopt a three-pillar pension system, which has been discussed for over a decade, with a minimal state pension, a second pillar of mandatory private pension savings, and a third pillar of private pension savings.

Another concern is the inefficient provision of services. In both education and health care, fewer funds should be spent on real estate than services. As the number of school children has fallen sharply, the number of schools should be reduced accordingly and the superfluous real estate sold off.

In health care, the number of hospitals should be reduced, while primary care should evolve and the consolidated hospitals should be provided far better equipment. The number and structure of staff should be adjusted to actual needs, and the salaries for skilled staff raised. Decentralization and competition on the market with private providers should increase quality and efficiency.

A Vision for Ukraine in 2020

What can Ukraine realistically achieve by 2020? The aim must be to build a free society, integrated with Europe and living in peace with steadily rising economic welfare.

With its democratic breakthrough in early 2014, Ukraine has probably already reached the level of democracy as measured by Freedom House. Its next great governance endeavor should be to match the ranking of Georgia, Latvia, and Lithuania on the Corruption Perceptions Index of Transparency International (2013), that is, to rise from the current ranking of 144 to 43 (Lithuania) or 55 (Georgia).

On the fiscal front, by 2020, Ukraine should have balanced its budget and achieved fiscal sustainability. For this, public expenditures should be cut sharply from the current level of 53 percent of GDP to 35 percent of GDP, which is the recent average of Latvia and Lithuania, the fastest growing countries in Europe. Continued high public expenditures would depress economic growth. Such a reduction of public expenditures would also allow for big tax cuts. All small nuisance taxes should be abolished and the high payroll tax slashed.

By 2020 the state apparatus would have undergone major reform, with new judges and prosecutors running an honest system of justice and law enforcement. All superfluous inspection agencies would have been abolished. Administration would be decentralized considerably and consolidated, rendering government services effective, efficient, and nonintrusive. Prices would be free and set on the market.

Similarly, supply of social services would be streamlined. Education, health care, and family allowances would receive more funding, while the cost of public pensions would be slashed. In education and health care, the government would have sold off real estate and devoted the funding to improve services.

If Ukraine reaches these goals, then it should be able to generate an average economic growth of 5 to 7 percent a year from 2015 to 2020. The growth is likely to come from four sectors: agriculture with food processing, services, high technology, and new manufacturing based on domestic and foreign direct investment oriented toward exports to the European market.

2

Why Ukraine Can and Should Opt for Radical Reforms Now

To wait means to fail.
—Mart Laar (2014), former prime minister of Estonia

Russian military aggression has plunged Ukraine into an existential crisis, necessitating urgent radical reforms for survival. It is unclear what Russian president Vladimir Putin intends to do with Ukraine. We therefore need to consider a reform strategy that holds water in various scenarios. Many have questioned whether democratic and market economic reform can be pursued during war and wonder whether Ukraine can reform in spite of Russian aggression. The answer is yes, as long as the war is limited to a small area and not a major economic distraction. A minor war on national territory could even spur the country to realize that it can no longer continue its old bad ways and has to pursue reinvigorating reform.

Many countries have fought substantial wars on their own territories and endured severe economic crises while carrying out major economic reforms. Turkey did so under Prime Minister Recep Tayyip Erdoğan (2003–14), while pursuing a bloody civil war against Kurdish insurgents. Another example is Colombia under President Álvaro Uribe Vélez (2002–10), who executed an even bloodier war against left-wing guerillas. Israel stands out as an example of a country that has maintained sound economic policies regardless of its many wars. Closer to Ukraine, the Russian-Georgian war of August 2008 spurred the Mikheil Saakashvili administration to undertake more radical reforms. The three Baltic republics rated as top reformers in the early 1990s, while harboring as many as 150,000 Russian soldiers on their territories. The last Russian soldiers departed from the Baltic states in August 1994, when Estonia and Lithuania completed their key reforms.

What kind of reform strategy should Ukraine pursue? In its current rampant crisis, Ukraine needs front-loaded, radical, and comprehensive reforms from the top down. Only such reforms have been truly successful in postcommunist countries, and the more difficult the situation, the more radical the reforms should be. The power of the oligarchs has to be broken. Ukraine is the last post-Soviet country where oligarchs remain truly powerful, but they are currently under great pressure.

The successful postcommunist countries—Poland, the Czech Republic, Slovakia, Estonia, Latvia, Lithuania, and Georgia—are the most relevant reform prototypes for Ukraine. These countries share several similarities with Ukraine, economically, politically, and socially, and show that radical reform is possible in turbulent times.

Skeptics ask whether Ukraine can succeed when it has failed so many times. The nation has not suffered a more severe existential crisis before. To survive it has to reform hard and fast or risk oblivion. In the absence of tough reforms, a financial meltdown with unpredictable but probable negative political consequences is all too likely. Few incentives to reform are stronger than that.

What Are Putin's Intentions?

On the night of February 27, 2014, so-called small green men (*zelyonye chelovechki*), Russian special forces without insignia, occupied the regional Crimean Parliament in Simferopol. They appointed a minor local politician, Sergey Aksyonov, prime minister, although his party had received only 4 percent of votes in the recent regional elections. The following night, these "small green men" occupied Crimea's two international airports, opening them to Russian military transport planes. Russian agents had thoroughly infiltrated the Ukrainian army, and the new Ukrainian military command was even more penetrated. The newly appointed commander of the Ukrainian navy defected to Russia. Within days, Russian special forces seized the whole of Crimea without killing more than one Ukrainian solider. They celebrated their success with video clips on YouTube.[1] Interestingly, they announced that they started their operation on February 22, the day Viktor Yanukovych fled. On March 18, Russia formally annexed Crimea (Putin 2014a).

By April, "small green men" were popping up in southern and eastern Ukraine. On May 2, during clashes in Odessa many of them were killed in a fire that broke out in the building they were in. Only in half of Donbas, the easternmost region in Ukraine, did the Russian insurgents find significant local support, but even there they did not appear to find a majority favoring secession from Ukraine. In September 2014, an admittedly small and imperfect poll by the Democratic Initiatives Foundation named after Ilko Kucheriv and the Kyiv International Institute of Sociology found that 42 percent of Donbas residents wanted to stay in Ukraine but with more autonomy from Kyiv and 7 percent wanted to stay in Ukraine with no changes, while 26 percent wanted

---

1. The Russian special forces televised their success on YouTube, www.youtube.com/watch?v= XUZmHUsLic4 and www.youtube.com/watch?v=FAdcV8Xg6X.

the Donetsk People's Republic or the Luhansk People's Republic to be independent and 16 percent wanted to join Russia—that is, 49 percent were for Ukraine and 42 percent for Russia.[2]

The secessionist movement did not start as a domestic rebellion but as Russian military aggression, though locals as well as Russian mercenaries were recruited. Thousands of regular Russian soldiers and hundreds of tanks and armored vehicles have been involved. Ukrainian forces had been advancing until August 22, and the Ukrainian leadership believed that they could oust the Russian forces.

But then Russia sharply increased its military engagement, losing many soldiers and armaments in Ukraine. The Ukrainian leadership realized that Ukraine could not win militarily against Russia and clear its own territory. On September 5, Presidents Petro Poroshenko and Vladimir Putin concluded a ceasefire agreement (OSCE 2014a) and added a more detailed agreement on September 19 (OSCE 2014b). Despite the ceasefire, fighting did not stop, but it was contained. According to the Office of the United Nations High Commissioner for Human Rights (OHCHR 2014, 4) from mid-April to October 31, "at least 4,042 were killed and 9,350 were wounded in the conflict-affected area of eastern Ukraine." Unofficial assessments were three times larger.

This book is not about the Russian-Ukrainian war or the Western economic sanctions imposed on Russia. But to understand how reforms in Ukraine may or may not proceed, we have to make some assumptions about Russia's aims and future behavior. The natural starting point is President Putin's statements. His most substantial statements were in his big speech to the Russian Federal Assembly on March 18 and his annual television call-in program on April 17.

Putin's novel point was to define nationality by language and ethnicity and not by statehood or passport. He also unapologetically embraced revanchism: "The USSR fell apart.... It was only when Crimea ended up as part of a different country that Russia realized that it was not simply robbed, it was plundered." His concern went far beyond Crimea: "Millions of people went to bed in one country and awoke in different ones, overnight becoming ethnic minorities in former Union republics, while the Russian nation became one of the biggest, if not the biggest ethnic group in the world to be divided by border" (Putin 2014a). In these statements, he returned to what he had said at the North Atlantic Treaty Organization (NATO) summit in Bucharest in April 2008.

The Russian president expressed sympathy for what he depicted as the poor Ukrainians: "I understand why the Ukrainian people wanted change. They have had enough of the authorities in power during the years of Ukraine's independence. Presidents, prime ministers, and parliamentarians changed, but their attitude to the country and its people remained the same. They milked

---

2. Democratic Initiatives Foundation, "Majority of Donbas Population Wants to Live in Ukraine," September 2014, http://dif.org.ua/en.

the country, fought among themselves for power, assets, and cash flows and did not care much about the ordinary people" (Putin 2014a).

At the same time, he saw the new Ukrainian rulers as illegitimate: "However, those who stood behind the latest events in Ukraine had a different agenda: They were preparing yet another government takeover; they wanted to seize power and would stop short of nothing. They resorted to terror, murder, and riots. Nationalists, neo-Nazis, Russophobes, and anti-Semites executed this coup" (Putin 2014a).

Against all this injustice, Putin offered assistance to what he claimed to be the suffering ethnic Russians living in Ukraine: "Those who opposed the coup [in Ukraine] were immediately threatened with repression. ...[T]he residents of Crimea and Sevastopol turned to Russia for help in defending their rights and lives, in preventing the events that were unfolding and are still under way in Kiev, Donetsk, Kharkov, and other Ukrainian cities. Naturally, we could not leave this plea unheeded; we could not abandon Crimea and its residents in distress. This would have been betrayal on our part" (Putin 2014a).

In the end, Putin blamed the West: "Our Western partners, led by the United States of America, prefer not to be guided by international law in their practical policies, but by the rule of the gun. They have come to believe in their exclusivity and exceptionalism, that they can decide the destinies of the world, that only they can ever be right. They act as they please: Here and there, they use force against sovereign states, building coalitions based on the principle, 'If you are not with us, you are against us'" (Putin 2014a). He failed to address the fact that by annexing Crimea Russia had violated half a dozen ratified international treaties.

Putin's version of recent history was clearly at variance with reality. In the same March 18 speech Putin (2014a) stated: "Russia's Armed Forces never entered Crimea; they were there already in line with an international agreement. True, we did enhance our forces there...." One month later, however, he effectively admitted that he lied when he denied sending in Russian troops: "Russia did not annex Crimea by force. Russia created conditions—with the help of special armed groups and the Armed Forces, I will say it straight—but only for the free expression of the will of the people living in Crimea and Sevastopol" (Putin 2014b). The Kremlin has continued to insist that it is not a party to the war in Ukraine and has persistently denied using military force in eastern Ukraine, but these denials cannot be taken seriously, since evidence of the opposite is overwhelming.

On April 17, Putin started talking about "Novorossiya"—New Russia—an old tsarist term referring to eastern and southern Ukraine coined at the time of Catherine the Great in the late 18th century. The Bolsheviks banned this term soon after the revolution because of their new regional division of the Soviet Union. By reviving this old imperialist term, Putin appeared to lay a Russian claim to eight eastern and southern regions of Ukraine. Since 2008, he has repeatedly claimed that Ukraine is not a country (Åslund 2009) and has continued to use the imperialist term of Novorossiya.

There are at least three plausible interpretations of Putin's intentions. One is that he is ready to take what he can through war, while being intentionally vague. Second, since the NATO summit in Bucharest in April 2008, the Kremlin has made clear that it does not accept Ukraine becoming a member of NATO (Åslund 2009, 227–28). Since the summer of 2013, the Kremlin has also objected to an Association Agreement between Ukraine and the European Union. A third hypothesis is that Putin does not accept any democratic breakthrough in an East Slavic country, perceiving this as dangerous precedent for Russia justifying a possible preemptive strike. Putin's vehement reaction against the Orange Revolution points in that direction. Given that the democratic breakthrough already took place in February 2014, one may presume that Putin's prime interest is that Ukraine will fail.

My preferred interpretation is that Putin wants Ukraine to collapse economically and thus politically to prove that democracy is not suitable for Eastern Slavs. This version is consistent with his interest in keeping Ukraine out of Western alliances, and it does not contradict gradual Russian territorial expansion. If Ukraine's failure is the Kremlin's objective, Putin has no obvious need for further military aggression. Nor does he have any interest in peaceful coexistence with Ukraine. Accordingly, Russia can be expected to carry out various forms of aggression against Ukraine.

From this perspective, Russia's destruction of vast parts of the Donbas infrastructure makes sense. Russian forces have bombed bridges and power stations in areas under their control in Donbas, and they have looted at least one armaments factory in Luhansk, Luhansk Electrical Factory, transferring it to Russia.[3] These actions suggest that the Kremlin is not intent on annexing the occupied territories in Donbas. Instead, its two Minsk accords with Ukraine seem to aim at imposing all the costs for providing Donbas with pensions and other social costs on Ukraine, while depriving Ukraine of all revenues from this area.

Russia's interest in further military advances could be balanced by three factors: the rising cost of Western sanctions against Russia, Ukrainian military resistance, and domestic Russian attitudes to the war with Ukraine.

The war with Russia has severely damaged the Ukrainian economy. The loss of Crimea has deprived Ukraine of 3.7 percent of its GDP. It is no longer included in official statistics, while Donbas is. To a considerable extent that means costs but no benefits. In October 2014, the occupied territories accounted for 2.6 percent of Ukraine's area, 3.3 million people (7.3 percent of the population), 10 percent of GDP, and 15 percent of industrial output (Dragon Capital 2014). In December, most forecasters predicted a decline in GDP of 7 percent in 2014. Roughly two-thirds of the decline derived from the war in Donbas, which is the old coal and steel region of Ukraine. In October,

---

3. "Lugansky elektromekhanichesky zavod perenosit proizvodstvo v Rossiyu" ["Luhansk Electrical Plant Is Transferring Its Production to Russia"], *Ostrov*, September 24, 2014, www.ostro.org/lugansk/economics/news/454963 (accessed on October 25, 2014).

Ukraine's coal production was down by 66 percent and its steel production down by one-third.

Of the region's population of 3.3 million, about 900,000 had fled by late October. According to the Ukrainian State Emergency Service, 417,410 people were internally displaced in Ukraine, while the Office of the United Nations High Commissioner for Human Rights recorded that 454,339 people had fled abroad, 387,355 of them to Russia (OHCHR 2014, 24). These numbers tally with opinion polls suggesting that preferences in the occupied territories are roughly divided between Russia and Ukraine.

The military front has not moved since September 5, although a very bloody battle took place over Donetsk Airport. Without delving further into war scenarios, I shall simply assume that the ceasefire holds in the sense that the front does not move, though plenty of blood may be spilt.

In the long term, Ukraine of course wants to regain all its territory and safeguard its national integrity. In the interim, Ukraine has three clear interests. First, it wants to maximize its security while minimizing the cost of war. Second, given that Ukraine does not receive any tax revenues or value added from the occupied parts of Donbas, Ukraine should also minimize its expenditures on this region. On November 15, President Poroshenko signed a decree that cut off all Ukrainian state funding to the occupied territories. Energy subsidies should also be withdrawn. Third, the territories held by Ukraine and the rebels should be demarcated in some way, so that people can gain elementary security. For the purposes of this book, I assume that Ukraine will succeed in these three endeavors.

Why This Time Is Different in Ukraine

Most of the time countries do not pursue reforms until they really have to. Given how formidable and multifaceted the crisis in Ukraine is, the new government has no rational option but to undertake reforms as fast as possible for multiple reasons. Muddling through is no longer an option, and the only real alternative is a financial meltdown (see section at the end of this chapter). The question is how able the government is to act rationally.

First, Ukraine is running out of money. In July 2014, the International Monetary Fund (IMF) foresaw that in a stress scenario Ukraine's public debt would surge to 134 percent of GDP in 2016 (IMF 2014d, 49). If Ukraine does not change course, it will default before that happens. In October 2014, IMF managing director Christine Lagarde stated that to "assume that the additional funding will have to come from the IMF I think is rather far-fetched."[4] Accordingly, Ukraine has to cut public expenditures sharply in 2015.

Second, radical reform is a matter of national survival. Ukraine is at war with far stronger Russia. So far, the war has been limited, but nobody knows

---

4. Ian Talley, "Ukraine Will Need More Bailout Funding, IMF's Lagarde Says," *Wall Street Journal*, October 9, 2014.

how it will evolve. Ukraine has to strengthen its military, which requires economic potency, leaving it little choice but to carry out the key reforms swiftly.

Third, Ukraine should use this crisis to break the preponderance of corruption and oligarchic rule. The oligarchs have suffered considerable damage to their assets in the war-torn areas of Ukraine, rendering them weak. The crisis offers a chance to finally break their disproportionate influence over the state for good. Yet, if the main rent-seeking mechanisms are not eliminated soon, resourceful businessmen will find new ways of making money on the state.

In today's Ukraine, the main form of rent seeking is gas arbitrage. Under Yanukovych, a couple of his oligarchs appear to have benefited from this trade. If the domestic prices are not unified at the market level soon, somebody else will pick up this business.

Fourth, the war with Russia has forced Ukrainians to come together as never before. As the great political scientist Charles Tilly (1992) put it: "War made the state and state made war." Marches with people wearing traditional Ukrainian folk shirts, *vyshyvanki*, are being held all over the country, and youngsters are painting railings in the Ukrainian national colors blue and yellow. The Orange revolutionaries did not use the Ukrainian national symbols to avoid being divisive and instead chose the neutral orange color. The blue-and-yellow Ukrainian flag is no longer controversial but unites the nation. One sees Ukrainian flags everywhere.

This national cohesion has the Ukrainian people demanding action and results. I passed by the parliament on September 16, when it discussed the draft law on lustration. Thousands of people demonstrated in support of the law. Even so, the parliament still dominated by the old elite adopted this law with a single vote. Parliament Speaker Oleksandr Turchynov caught the public mood, shouting to the parliament: "If you do not vote for lustration, there will be castration instead."[5] One parliamentarian opposing lustration was dumped in a garbage bin. Popular suspicion runs high, and many are talking about a third Maidan if the current government does not reform the state.

The public supports most reforms, obviously the elimination of red tape and cumbersome taxation. People want the rule of law through good courts and an honest police force. Ukrainians are dissatisfied with the current provision of health care and education in their country.

For all these reasons it is easier to carry out big reforms when the public is most eager and ready for reforms, even if they are unpopular. Latvia's prime minister Valdis Dombrovskis realized that it was politically easier to carry out a fiscal adjustment of 9.5 percent of GDP in the midst of the crisis in 2009 than a minor budget adjustment of 1.5 percent of GDP in 2012. He closed half the state agencies, sacked one-third of all civil servants, and cut public wages by 28 percent. Somewhat to his surprise, he found that this was popular and he was reelected twice (Åslund and Dombrovskis 2011). He concluded that he

---

5. Parliament Today, video, *Ukrainskaya pravda*, September 16, 2014.

should have front-loaded the reforms even more. People are prepared to accept a lot of suffering for a year or two, but after that they do not understand why they should continue to tighten their belts.

Also, people accept a paradigm shift much more easily than a partial change within the existing paradigm. If one minor liberalization occurs, people ask why that specific liberalization took place. If most sectors are liberalized, people instead ask why the rest have not been liberalized as well, because they have accepted the new liberal paradigm.

Reforms should ensure an early return to economic growth because people also expect to see results reasonably soon. In the 1990s, Ukraine pursued gradual and tepid reforms. As a result, it had no economic growth for a decade. Even before the current crisis, Ukraine had not recovered its output level of 2007. Similarly, after the global financial crisis, Greece undertook many relatively small fiscal adjustments, which kept the economy contracting for seven bitter years. By contrast, Estonia, Latvia, and Lithuania quickly returned to growth after only two years from similar output contractions in 2009, and these three countries have been growing fast since then because they carried out radical fiscal adjustments and combined them with structural reforms.

Ukraine's new government seems to realize the need for urgent radical reforms and has elaborated a "Strategy for Reform 2020" (Reforms in Ukraine 2014), in which it identifies eight priority reforms: tax reform, anticorruption reform and lustration, judicial reform, decentralization and state governance reform, deregulation and development of entrepreneurship, reform of the law enforcement system, reform of the national security and defense system, and healthcare system reform. The strategy contains two state programs on energy independence and global promotion of Ukraine and also lists 62 additional reforms. Ukraine requires a handful of competent and decisive managers to take charge of economic policy on the basis of a democratic parliamentary majority and swiftly push through fundamental changes. This is not the time for building consensus and certainly not with the old establishment, which is naturally opposed to losing power and wealth. Since Euromaidan and the elections, the old vested interests have been somewhat subdued, but they won't be for long. The government, therefore, needs to act before the old elite recovers and gathers strength. Fast action is the best way of convincing them that the rules of the game have changed. President Poroshenko and Prime Minister Arseniy Yatsenyuk have to prove that they are up to this Herculean task.

Thus, the arguments are overwhelmingly in favor of Ukraine undertaking key reforms as soon as possible now that the parliamentary elections are over and a new government has been formed (cf. Åslund 2013a, 41–44). But the question remains whether the new leaders are really determined and able to do so.

Most Relevant Reform Prototypes

Given the many similarities among postcommunist countries in the former Soviet bloc, the most relevant models are those where reform succeeded in the midst of severe economic crisis, notably Poland in 1989 (Balcerowicz 2014), Czechoslovakia in 1990 (Klaus 2014), Estonia in 1992 (Laar 2014), Georgia in 2003 (Bendukidze and Saakashvili 2014), and Latvia and Lithuania in 2009 (Åslund and Dombrovskis 2011).

All too often, Western economists draw on experiences of Western countries, which are at best irrelevant but often harmful. The institutional setup is so different in postcommunist countries, and the level of economic development so much lower, that few things characteristic of developed Western economies also apply to these countries (Åslund 2013a).

Poland represents classical early, comprehensive, and radical reform (Balcerowicz 1992, Sachs 1993). Poland and Estonia stand out as having more than doubled their GDP in real terms after communism. Since 2003, Georgia has been a star reformer. During the global financial crisis, Latvia and Lithuania stood out for their resolute crisis management, which led to high economic growth.

All these countries pursued reforms that were radical, comprehensive, and front-loaded. No country has failed because it attempted too fast and radical reforms, but all gradual reforms in crisis situations have failed. The list is long: Romania, Moldova, Ukraine, Belarus, Azerbaijan, Kazakhstan, Tajikistan, Turkmenistan, and Uzbekistan. Most Central and East European governments lose elections, but the radical reformers have won more often than the nonreformers and several have returned to power.[6] A politician who wants to be reelected would be well advised to firmly resolve his or her country's problems.

Economics is not a precise science, but the successful postcommunist countries share many common lessons. One is that the window of opportunity for reforms after a democratic breakthrough is brief and has to be utilized (Balcerowicz 1994). Therefore, it is important to front-load reforms so that many, comprehensive reforms are carried out as fast as possible, because, in the words of former Estonian prime minister Mart Laar (2014, 77), "to wait means to fail." Delay in implementing reforms will only allow the old rent-seeking establishment to mobilize its resistance and defeat the reformers. Laar (2002) also noted that reforms are best adopted in big chunks, because the resistance will be as great against small changes.

The problem with the Ukrainian state is that the old Soviet system remains alive and well with all its bureaucracy and centralization. Political will to

---

6. The outstanding success is Václav Klaus. The Estonian and Latvian governments were reelected after their shock cures in 2009. Mikulas Dzurinda has been Slovak prime minister thrice. Balcerowicz and Laar were both returned to power. Mikheil Saakashvili and his party were reelected.

pursue a fundamental reform has never prevailed. Even the Orange Revolution failed to make a dent in Ukraine's tenacious old structures.

Former Czech president Václav Klaus (2014, 55) taught the "necessity of a total and unconditional liquidation of the communist political and economic system." The old Soviet system has proven more stable than desired in the postcommunist countries, so its disruption should be maximum, because the danger does not lie in instability but in the persistence of the old system.

Reformers increasingly recognize that "you cannot change the behavior of people, so you have to change the people in charge instead" (Åslund and Djankov 2014, 6). Another lesson is that the "secret police has turned out to be the worst part of the old elite because it is the least transparent, but powerful, professionally competent, international, lawless, ruthless and it has strong networks. It has proven ideal as an organized crime network" (Åslund and Djankov 2014, 7). Ukraine needs a sweeping lustration to oust corrupt and criminal senior officials of the old establishment. Estonia carried out the most radical lustration, which has served the country well; it has the least corruption of all postcommunist countries according to all corruption indexes.

Georgia, widely considered a failed state in the early 2000s, reformed successfully. After the Rose Revolution in 2003, President Saakashvili turned his nation around. The key to his success lay in his pursuit of very radical reforms in one area after the other. Reforms disrupted the status quo in the selected sectors, but they were not implemented in parallel (Bendukidze and Saakashvili 2014). Ukraine should also select key sectors for reform and then proceed to others. Georgia is particularly inspiring for Ukraine because it carried out these reforms long after the end of communism when corruption was the main problem.

In both Georgia and Estonia, the reform ministers were very young, mostly in their thirties and some in their twenties, because the reform leaders wanted to draw on young talent not poisoned by the old system. Georgia attracted many nationals who had studied and worked abroad for several years, which Ukraine could also do. Young, inexperienced people make mistakes, but they dare to do what older people wrongly consider impossible. To attract Ukrainian youth living abroad, the government must raise public service salaries as an incentive for them to return and live comfortably.

Overall, Estonia offers the ideal package of early and comprehensive radical reforms. Poland, which is about the same size as Ukraine, went through more complex reforms, but the leading ideas were the same. Georgia, Slovakia, Latvia, and Lithuania have carried out great catch-up reforms.

The Power of the Oligarchs Has Declined

The ultimate argument of reform skeptics in Ukraine is that the oligarchs will not allow reforms. This argument is weak because Ukraine's oligarchs are on the wane.

"Oligarch" is an ancient concept, with an "oligarchy" defined as "government in the hands of a few."[7] In Russia and Ukraine, oligarch became a popular label for the wealthiest tycoons around 1994. An oligarch in Ukraine is a very wealthy and politically well-connected businessman, a dollar billionaire (or nearly so) who is the main owner of a conglomerate of enterprises, usually including media, and has close ties to the president.[8]

Bradford de Long (2002, 179) has suggested that a present-day billionaire would be a good proxy for a "robber baron" of 19th century America. It might be more appropriate to call them plutocrats, because their aim is to make money rather than to rule the state. Joel Hellman (1998) has coined the phrase "state capture" to characterize the relationship between big businessmen and the state in a country such as Ukraine, because these big businessmen influenced the state by multiple means.

In Newport, Rhode Island, the palaces, or "cottages," of the American robber barons have stood intact since the 1890s. They have been preserved but the original fortunes are gone. The robber barons made their wealth on coal, steel, and railways during the great commodity boom before World War I (Morris 2005). In the 1960s and 1970s, their palaces were sold for a mere 2 percent of the original real cost. Similarly, Ukraine's steel, gas, and coal barons made their fortunes in the 1990s and 2000s (Frishberg 2008). They and their mansions in Koncha-Zaspa, the elite area southwest of Kyiv, may meet a similar fate as the US robber barons and their Newport cottages.

A combination of economies of scale and state capture during the Industrial Revolution created robber barons or oligarchs. Typically, they thrived in industries with large economies of scale—transportation (railways and shipping), commodities (steel, coal, oil, and timber), and banking. Strong oligarchic groupings are common also in well-governed countries such as Canada, Finland, and Sweden. In fact, oligarchy is the normal state of corporate governance in most of the world (Morck, Wolfenzon, and Yeung 2005). Yet, it can be broken up, which is common in developed societies. Two recent examples are Finland and Canada.

The big Ukrainian fortunes in the 1990s were made on gas trade with Russia. The business model was parasitical arbitrage, in which corrupt business players purchased gas at low state-controlled prices and then reaped huge profits by selling the gas at free markets. The gas traders did not have large companies but were opportunistic dealmakers. Their practice was called "sitting on the pipe," because they benefited from price differentials between the two ends of the pipe, that is, at a state enterprise and on the free market.

Ukraine's reforms of 2000 brought about an abrupt change. The fortunes of the steel and coal barons, who produced rather than just traded, surged

---

7. As defined in the Oxford University Press Dictionary.

8. Four excellent journalistic books on the Russian oligarchs show how they evolved and operated: Brady (1999), Freeland (2000), Hoffman (2002), and Klebnikov (2000). Less has been written on the Ukrainian oligarchs; see Puglisi (2003), Grygorenko, Gorodnichenko, and Ostanin (2006), and Åslund (2006).

with the commodity boom (most of all Rinat Akhmetov, followed by Victor Pinchuk). Suddenly, the oligarchs owned concrete producing companies, and they certainly knew how to increase production and productivity fast (Grygorenko, Gorodnichenko, and Ostanin 2006). The new big businessmen were so resourceful that they succeeded in organizing production where most failed, not allowing any red tape to stop them. Oligarchic privileges persisted, but they were largely limited to tax benefits, state subsidies, transfer pricing, select state procurement, and exclusive privatizations.

Daron Acemoglu (2008) has explained that oligarchs can be quite productive, stimulating economic growth at an intermediate level of economic development by keeping taxation low and labor markets free. At a higher level of economic development, however, other factors become more important, namely a good business environment and easy entry for startups. Dominant big businessmen are not prone to supporting such endeavors. Therefore democratization is vital for successful market economic reform.

> An "oligarchic" society, where the political power is in the hands of major producers, protects their property rights but also tends to erect significant entry barriers against new entrepreneurs. Democracy, where political power is more widely diffused, imposes redistributive taxes on producers, but tends to avoid entry barriers. When taxes in democracy are high and the distortions caused by entry barriers are low, an oligarchic society achieves greater efficiency. Because comparative advantage in entrepreneurship shifts away from the incumbents, the inefficiency created by entry barriers in oligarchy deteriorates over time. The typical pattern is one of rise and decline of oligarchic societies. An oligarchic society may first become richer, but later fall behind a similar democratic society. (Acemoglu 2008, 1)

A simpler explanation is that little can be produced without a modicum of law and order. In the early post-Soviet years, lawlessness and disorganized crime ravaged Ukraine and Russia. In a first step, crime became organized and therefore less unpredictable and bloody. In a second step, producing oligarchs established their own security forces, which greatly facilitated production (Volkov 2002, Brady 1999).

Today, oligarchic privileges are falling apart under pressure from international financial institutions and civil society. Subsidies to oligarchic enterprises are difficult to defend; the State Fiscal Service is going after transfer pricing; and the public demands competitive and open public procurement and privatization auctions.

The only substantial source of old-style oligarchic revenues is the domestic trade of natural gas, which is bought at $30 per thousand cubic meters and resold at $380 per thousand cubic meters (Kobolyev 2014). If natural gas prices are swiftly adjusted to the market this business will disappear and with it the oligarchs. The main gas trader, Dmytro Firtash, is out of jail on bail in Vienna,[9]

---

9. Angelika Gruber, "Ukrainian Industrialist Firtash Released after Posting Bail," Reuters, March 21, 2014.

while Ukraine's last energy oligarch, Serhiy Kurchenko, has been sanctioned by the European Union and Canada.[10]

In most post-Soviet countries, oligarchs have lost out as political power brokers. In Russia and Kazakhstan, the rulers seized control of the big private corporations years ago, expanding their own crony empires, and independent oligarchs are merely a distant memory (Dawisha 2014). In 1992, Estonia wiped out its metal-trading gangs by liberalizing exports and commodity prices, becoming the most honest and transparent postcommunist country (Laar 2002, Transparency International 2013). Neighboring Latvia, by contrast, delayed its deregulation of oil prices and exports by one year, allowing three oligarchs to capture the political system until the crisis of 2008 exposed them. Only in 2010 and 2011 did parliamentary elections finally cut them down to size (Åslund and Dombrovskis 2011).

At present, Ukraine stands out as the last postcommunist outpost where tycoons wield substantial political power, but they are being dealt one blow after the other. The global commodity boom is over. Steel, iron ore, and coal prices have fallen and are not likely to rise any time soon. Businessmen who own commodity assets are suffering, including most of the big ones: Rinat Akhmetov, Ihor Kolomoisky, Hennadiy Boholiubov, Victor Pinchuk, Serhiy Taruta, Borys Kolesnikov, Vadim Novinsky, and Kostyantin Zhevago. Ukraine's banking sector is also reeling under the current economic crisis, which has hit many banks, notably the two main owners of PrivatBank, Ukraine's largest bank, Kolomoisky and Boholiubov. Firtash's Bank Nadra is effectively bankrupt (table 2.1).

Yanukovych tried to follow Putin's example by attempting to expropriate the fortunes of the old oligarchs. Russian economists Sergei Guriev and Konstantin Sonin (2009, 1) have modeled this drama "a weak dictator does not limit rent-seeking. A strong dictator does reduce rent-seeking but also expropriates individual oligarchs." Yanukovych followed that model, but he moved too fast, which contributed to his fall. Still, the old tycoons remain weakened, and the Yanukovych family has been banished.

The war in Donbas has caused significant damage to those with assets there, in particular Akhmetov, Firtash, Taruta, Novinsky, and Kolesnikov. Firtash also owns two big factories in Crimea. Russian trade sanctions are designed to hit pro-European businessmen, especially Poroshenko, Pinchuk, and Taruta.

Public demands for transparency are reducing the possibilities for big businessmen to buy politics and even to evade tax. Every day, the media exposes suspect deals to criticism, dissuading businessmen from conducting dubious transactions. The public demand to cut political campaign expenditure means loss of revenue for owners of television channels, namely Firtash (Inter),

---

10. *Official Journal of the European Union,* "Council Regulation (EU) No. 208/2014 of March 5, 2014, concerning restrictive measures directed against certain persons, entities and bodies in view of the situation in Ukraine," European Commission, March 6, 2014.

Table 2.1   Main oligarchs in Ukraine, 2014

Oligarch	Partners	Industries	Main companies	Forbes wealth assessment, 2014
Rinat Akhmetov	Vadim Novinsky	Steel, coal, electricity, banking	System Capital Management, DTEK, Metinvest, TV Ukraina	$10.4 billion, $1.5 billion
Victor Pinchuk		Steel pipes, television	Interpipe, ICTV, STB, Nova Ukraina	$3.0 billion
Ihor Kolomoisky	Hennadiy Boholiubov	Banking, oil, ferroalloys, airlines	PrivatBank, Ukrnafta, Ukrainian International Airlines	$1.4 billion, $1.7 billion
Dmytro Firtash	Serhiy Lyovochkin, Yuriy Boiko	Gas, chemicals, television	Ostchem, Stirol, Severodonetsk Azot, Inter	$500 million
Serhiy Taruta		Steel	Industrial Union of Donbas	Lost most
Petro Poroshenko		Chocolate, sugar, agriculture, shipbuilding	Roshen	$1.2 billion

Source: Forbes, The World's Billionaires, www.forbes.com/billionaires/#tab:overall_country:Ukraine.

Akhmetov (television channel Ukraina), Kolomoisky and Boholiubov (1+1), and Pinchuk (ICTV).

Because of the war, Russian big businessmen have lost their voice in Ukrainian politics. The Russian state banks (VTB, VEB, Sberbank, and Gazprombank), Gazprom, Lukoil, Tatneft, Alfa Bank, and mobile phone companies MTS and Vimpelcom (Kyivstar) have all played major roles in the Ukrainian economy, but now they have little say.

A couple of developments have gone in the opposite direction of buttressing the strength of some oligarchs, however. The election of Poroshenko, the seventh wealthiest businessman in Ukraine, as president is of course the most striking event. As the war started in the east, President Poroshenko tried to appoint several top businessmen as regional governors. As of November 2014, however, only one of them remains, Kolomoisky as governor of Dnipropetrovsk region. This is an important post, and Poroshenko would be well advised to limit his authority or remove him from office when the worst of the war is over. The October 2014 elections appear to have sharply reduced the share of businessmen in parliament.

Since 2000, Akhmetov has been Ukraine's richest man by a big margin. His wealth is comparatively easy to assess, since he uses normal corporate structures, and assessments of his fortune illustrate the decline of Ukraine's tycoons. In January 2013, *Forbes* ranked him the 26th richest man in the world with a fortune of $22.2 billion. In October 2014, by contrast, *Forbes* lowered its estimate of his wealth to $10.4 billion (Babenko 2014). He is continuing to bleed because about half of his business empire is located in the occupied territories of Donbas, where several of his coal mines and steelworks stand still.[11] Other major Ukrainian businessmen are likely to see a similar dwindling of fortunes.

The point is often made that the oligarchs should pay back and contribute to the resolution of Ukraine's financial crisis. On the face of it, this might sound like a good idea, but on second thought it is not. The government has two options. One is to try to defeat the oligarchs, in which case it should not expect their support but tax them as normally as possible. The alternative is to make a deal with the oligarchs, which Ukrainian politicians do all the time, but that is the fundamental problem and must be avoided. In 1994, President Leonid Kuchma chased the oligarchs of the day away—Yuhym Zviahilsky, Ihor Bakai, and Vadim Rabinovich. Zviahilsky and Rabinovich even fled from Ukraine for one to three years (Åslund 2009, 87). Kuchma's mistake was that a year later he started compromising with the oligarchs and made deals with them. Similarly, seven big Russian bankers financed Boris Yeltsin's reelection campaign in 1996. After succeeding, they wanted to be repaid far more, blocking reforms (Freeland 2000). This mistake must not be repeated, but then the Ukrainian state should not expect any voluntary contributions from the oligarchs either.

Another idea is that the new Ukrainian government should confiscate the assets of the Yanukovych family and apply them to state funding. While a sound legal idea, it is not likely to generate large state funds. Former prosecutor general Oleh Makhnitskiy claimed that the Yanukovych regime took $100 billion out of the country, but only a negligible portion is likely to be returned. To begin with, the total amount is probably exaggerated and is perhaps only half that amount. For months, the prosecutor's office failed to build any case against the supposed culprits due to a combination of a lack of relevant laws, presumed corruption among the investigators, and difficulties finding evidence (Vorozhbyt 2014).

Turkish statistics show a capital inflow of $8.5 billion from Ukraine during the critical week at the end of February when the Yanukovych regime collapsed.[12] Far more money is likely to have flown to other jurisdictions outside the reach of Western courts, such as Russia, where most of the Yanukovych clan seems to be in exile. Until the Ukrainian criminal law and criminal-procedural law were amended in the fall of 2014, the Ukrainian state could not prosecute anybody in absentia, which saved the Yanukovych refugees, who were largely,

---

11. On September 13, 2014, Maxim Timchenko, CEO of Akhmetov's power and coal company DTEK, told me that out of their 140,000 employees, 80,000 worked in rebel-held territories.

12. "Vo vremya Madana iz Ukrainy v Turtsiyu mogli vyvesti $8,5 mlrd" ["During Maidan They Could Transfer $8.5 Billion from Ukraine to Turkey"], *Ukrainskaya pravda*, October 16, 2014.

perhaps all, in Russia. According to the Ukrainian State Financial Inspection, the total assets of the Yanukovych gang that were frozen amounted to $1.42 billion in mid-November.[13] In a simultaneous statement, Prosecutor General Vitaliy Yarema claimed that more than $2 billion of assets had been frozen.[14] In general, little is collected of the loot of corrupt dictators and never more than $1 billion and it usually takes years. Because of its poor legal system Ukraine is likely to collect less than most (Vorozhbyt 2014).

Surprisingly, most Ukrainians still think their oligarchs are powerful, although they have suffered one blow after the other and lost out in other postcommunist countries. By international standards, their wealth is quite limited. The Russian war on Ukraine has devastated many of their companies located in the east, and several have been hit by Russian trade sanctions. They are mainly in old commodity industries, which are likely to face low prices for years to come. Several have had to flee Ukraine. The parliamentary elections in October 2014 clearly hit them, and the government program aims at sharply reducing their benefits. All around Ukraine, big businessmen have lost out and now claim to accept the new rules of the game. Ukrainian state and civil society have never been as strong in relation to the tycoons as they are right now. The state has an opportunity to establish legal order and a level playing field.

The Threat of Populism Is Also on the Wane

Old-style communism is dead in Ukraine. In the October 2014 parliamentary elections, the Communist Party received only 3.9 percent of the votes cast and fell below the 5 percent threshold for representation. This was the first time since the Bolshevik Revolution in 1917 that the communists were not represented in the Ukrainian Parliament. Nor did any other socialist or left-wing party enter parliament. Ukrainian analyst Oleksandr Kramar (2014) summed up the situation: "Since the Orange Revolution, the traditional left-right electoral division has been increasingly supplanted by a civilizational choice between Russia as a continuation of the USSR and Europe."

Little understanding of market economic ideas has taken hold in Ukraine. For years, populism filled this ideological vacuum. Its essence was a popular conviction that economic constraints are not binding, which is the definition of populism in European lingo. A broad opinion has favored more social expenditures than the government can afford, although ordinary Ukrainians receive very little support from the state and have endured poor governance. Among the post-Soviet countries, not even unreformed Belarus has as high public expenditures as Ukraine. In recent years, Ukraine's public expenditures

---

13. "Na schetakh Yanukovicha uzhe zablokirovali 1,42 milliarda dollravo" ["On the Accounts of Yanukovych $1.42 billion Have Been Blocked Already"], *Ekonomichna pravda*, November 18, 2014.

14. "Yarema: GPU arestovala 35 milliardov Yanukovicha i Ko" ["Yarema: The General Prosecutor of Ukraine Arrested 35 Billion Hryvnia of Yanukovych & Co."], *Ukrainskaya pravda*, November 15, 2014.

have lingered around 50 percent of GDP, while the average of the post-Soviet countries has been one-third of GDP (IMF 2014e).

Similarly, the fixing of the exchange rate has been popular, and few politicians have dared to speak in favor of a floating exchange rate, although Ukraine repeatedly has suffered from unsustainable current account deficits, being forced to drastically depreciate its currency in 2008 as well as 2014.

In spite of Ukraine's large budget deficit and burgeoning public debt, some Ukrainian economists and politicians talk about international financing for renewed economic growth. They advocate fiscal and monetary stimulus to achieve higher economic growth. In this thinking, they are greatly influenced by two Nobel Prize winning economists. Joseph Stiglitz (2002) preached that the Washington Consensus is wrong. A typical statement of his is that "the net effect of the policies set by the Washington Consensus has all too often been to benefit the few at the expense of the many, the well-off at the expense of the poor" (Stiglitz 2002, 20). The reality is very different. Poland and the other successful postcommunist countries followed the Washington Consensus policy of free markets, private enterprise, and responsible fiscal policy (Williamson 1990) and achieved high growth to the benefit of all, while Ukraine did not and achieved no growth but the enrichment of a few.

In one article after the other, *New York Times* columnist Paul Krugman has argued that austerity is always harmful, including in the successful Baltic states. He never noticed that seven EU countries have been forced into IMF financial stabilization programs since 2008, and countries such as Latvia and Greece lost a quarter of their GDP because of their severe financial crises in spite of ample IMF and EU financing. Ukraine's problem is that money is not a free utility printed by the central bank as in the United States. But international financing is neither free nor unlimited.

Estonia's president Toomas Hendrik Ilves has taken on Krugman. In 2012, when Estonia had emerged with the highest growth in Europe, he ridiculed Krugman's advocacy against its successful austerity, contending that "Krugman didn't know what he was talking about" when it came to his country. "We're just dumb & silly East Europeans," Ilves said sarcastically about Krugman. "Unenlightened. Someday we too will understand. Guess a Nobel in trade means you can pontificate on fiscal matters & declare my country a 'wasteland.'"[15]

A big blow to sound fiscal policy, alas, has been delivered by none other than the IMF. For years, the IMF helped to ensure global financial stability. Critics pay it a backhanded compliment when they say its initials stand for "It's mostly fiscal." When the IMF forgets that, it becomes part of the problem.

In October 2012, the IMF (2012) published a note in its authoritative semiannual *World Economic Outlook*, arguing that fiscal multipliers—the change in output induced by a change in the government's budget deficit—were larger

---

15. Melissa Jeltsen, "President of Estonia Slams Paul Krugman: 'Smug, Overbearing & Patronizing'," *Huffington Post*, June 6, 2012.

in current circumstances than previously thought. Tight fiscal policy, in other words, would squeeze output more than economic modelers had typically supposed. The implication was that fiscal adjustment should be delayed.

In January 2013, the IMF's chief economist, Olivier Blanchard, and his colleague Daniel Leigh (2013) explained this finding in a working paper, but it does not apply to policy on Ukraine. First, the whole paper is based on forecasts of economic growth. In the early stage of a crisis, forecasts tend to be widely off the mark. For example, in December 2008, the IMF forecast that Latvia's GDP would fall 5 percent in 2009; it plummeted 18 percent (Åslund and Dombrovskis 2011). The performance of the forecasts is just too poor to be taken seriously. Second, the argument presumes that a country has access to the capital market. But emerging economies in crisis usually lose access to private international funding—sometimes suddenly and unexpectedly, despite having little public debt. Third, in the midst of a crisis, the political economy is conducive to radical reform, as people are often ready to accept radical budget reform and severe belt-tightening. Later, it is much more difficult. A crisis is a terrible thing to waste.

Fourth, the Blanchard-Leigh paper is entirely short-term, focusing on GDP in the year after a fiscal adjustment, but what matters is long-term economic growth, and that depends on structural reforms. Ukraine faced a lost decade in the 1990s and has lost another six or seven years since 2009. Finally, Blanchard and Leigh dealt only with 27 developed European economies, which do not include Ukraine. It does not have access to international financial markets, which the authors seem to take for granted.

Wisely, Blanchard and Leigh (2013, 6) concluded, "The short-term effects of fiscal policy on economic activity are only one of the many factors that need to be considered in determining the appropriate pace of fiscal consolidation for any single country." Yet the IMF management went ahead and made fiscal forbearance its official policy, significantly damaging the serious debate about fiscal crisis resolution in emerging economies for which their arguments has no validity.

During the 2008–12 European financial crisis, the three Baltic countries carried out rapid fiscal adjustment of 8 to 10 percent of GDP in one year and returned to solid growth within two years thanks to rigorous structural reform and much lower public expenditures. Greece, by contrast, has suffered six years of persistent economic decline due to its tardy fiscal adjustment and structural reforms. In recent crises, radical and front-loaded fiscal adjustment with structural reforms have proven much better both economically and politically in economies in the euro area periphery than painful, slow reforms. The Baltic countries proved that a front-loaded fiscal adjustment leads to fast recovery of financial confidence, sound public finances, substantial and beneficial structural reforms, and early and vigorous economic growth. To top it all, the Estonian and Latvian governments were reelected (Åslund and Dombrovskis 2011). Why choose a clearly worse option in a real crisis? Oleh Lyashko, the leader of the Radical Party, stands out in this populist competition.

In his presidential campaign platform in May 2014, he called for lower taxes and even higher pension expenditures.[16] Before the October 2014 elections, he called for raising healthcare expenditures as a share of GDP to 40 percent by 2010 (Gorodnichenko et al. 2014). Former finance minister Viktor Pynzenyk, one of the few nonpopulists in Ukrainian politics, told me that in Ukrainian political parlance, "radical reform" means higher public expenditures.[17]

A group of Western-trained economists evaluated the economic programs of the political parties before the October 2014 elections. They ranked Yatsenyuk's People's Front at the top (22.1 percent of the votes cast) followed by the Poroshenko Bloc (21.8 percent). These were the two big winners of the elections, and the surge of the People's Front was a great surprise. Most populist was indeed the Radical Party, which received only 7.4 percent of the vote, followed by the Communist Party, which insists on far-reaching nationalization and redistribution but did not enter parliament (Gorodnichenko et al. 2014). The rather hopeful conclusion is that irresponsible populism is not all that popular.

In the October 2014 elections, the parties that formed the Ukrainian government won the public debate over populism. Now they need to use this political mandate while it is still valid and pursue the necessary economic reforms and public expenditure cuts.

The Alternative: Financial Meltdown

What if the government does not implement the reforms I prescribe in this book? Is there a middle way? Given how precarious Ukraine's situation was at the time of writing in December 2014, no middle way appears possible. The nation faces a stark choice between front-loaded, rigorous reform and a financial meltdown. The nature of financial meltdowns is well known (Reinhart and Rogoff 2009, Kindleberger and Aliber 2005). All indicators show that Ukraine is headed in that direction. A financial meltdown could be followed by the collapse of Ukraine as a state.

A financial meltdown in Ukraine would likely be reminiscent of the Russian financial crash of August 1998—default, high inflation, a frozen banking system, falling output, and panic. The critical factors at play are shrinking international reserves, a rising budget deficit, a falling exchange rate, rising inflation, and a collapsing banking system. These factors would kill output, which would devastate the economy and standard of living.

The crucial concern is the level of international reserves. They fell to $7.5 billion at the end of 2014, corresponding to just over one month of imports. As a consequence, the market has lost confidence in the Ukrainian hryvnia, whose value plummeted to 16 hryvnia per dollar in early November from 8 hryvnia

---

16. Radikalna Partiya Olega Lyashka (Radical Party of Oleh Lyashko), Programma (Program) 2014, http://liashko.ua/program (accessed on October 22, 2014).

17. Personal conversation on September 15, 2014.

per dollar, halving its value. As international reserves decline further, those who can are exchanging hryvnia for dollars or euros and taking the money out of the country. Ukraine has extreme currency regulations, and dollars don't seem to be available for businesses or individuals. Yet, the thinner the market becomes, the faster the currency can fall.

The critical factor in a potential financial meltdown is the banking system. The banks are suffering from currency mismatches, making huge losses on the falling hryvnia. The more the hryvnia depreciates, the greater the bank losses will be. The National Bank of Ukraine (NBU) and the Ukrainian government face a severe dilemma: Should they close or recapitalize the failing banks? If they close too many banks, credit would dry up and output contract. If they recapitalize the banks, the budget deficit would expand perilously, and the only financing available would be monetary emission or printing money. The NBU and related state banks financed by the NBU already hold 60 percent of Ukraine's public debt. The exchange rate of the hryvnia falls with every announcement of another bank recapitalization. An additional issue is that related lending is standard in large parts of the Ukrainian banking system. In fact, more than 80 percent of the lending of one particular bank has gone to enterprises belonging to the bank's main owner.

The scenario is all too clear. Ukraine has entered a depreciation-inflation cycle. As the exchange rate falls, more banks will collapse. As long as the government recapitalizes them, the budget deficit will increase, and monetary emission will rise, and so will inflation, which reached 25 percent in 2014. Inflation can surge far higher if the exchange rate collapses. Because of the extreme currency regulations, foreign payments barely work, and as this vicious cycle worsens the banking system will freeze. Output and the standard of living would then plummet.

Together three measures can prevent such a meltdown. First, Ukraine should close the truly insolvent banks rather than recapitalize them to minimize the needed public expenditures. Second, the government needs to cut its public expenditures on the order of 10 percent of GDP—as the Baltic governments did in 2009—to save the country and convince foreign creditors that it can manage the nation's finances. Third, after having proven its fiscal rigor, the government should call for sufficient international financing through a renewed IMF program, expanded EU financing, and a Marshall Plan for Ukraine as discussed in chapter 3.

Should the meltdown occur, ironically, it would force the government to undertake the same radical measures that it should have taken to prevent the meltdown to begin with. But the government would be doing so after suffering far more, almost as Ukraine did in 2000 or as Russia did after the crash of August 1998, and presumably that would be with a new government.

3

Ukraine Needs Europe as a Model and International Anchor

> *Here is the plan for reforming the country. It...is the Association Agreement between Ukraine and the European Union.*
>
> —Prime Minister Arseniy Yatsenyuk (2014a)

Hardly any country has succeeded in carrying out a fortuitous change of political, legal, economic, and social systems without international support. Countries embarking on reform usually look to one or more countries as their political, legal, and economic role models. This search is rarely random. Nations that desire modernization and development tend to turn to countries that function well, usually close to their own culture. Thus, Northern and Eastern Europe traditionally adopted German models of law, state, and education. To avoid contradictions a comprehensive model is preferable. Furthermore, foreign governments often provide assistance to a nation that adopts its model.

Role models usually tend to be wealthy countries, which have all adopted a reasonably free market economy, as embodied in the Washington Consensus, formulated by John Williamson (1990) and propagated by the international financial institutions and the European Union.

Among the postcommunist countries, Estonia most deliberately sought the ideal model. Estonian prime minister Mart Laar (2002) tried to adopt the German model as much as possible, because it was the modern version of the old Estonian model. Still, he did not do so blindly. He also selected certain elements from other countries, which he perceived as superior.

Europe as an Anchor for Modernization

The European Union played a dominant role as a reform model and supporter of the postcommunist transition of the 11 Central and East European (CEE) countries that have become EU members. Old EU members and the European Union have functioned as peer countries, helping applicant countries realize their dream of "returning to Europe." The European Union offered considerable market access early on and helped them undertake their market reforms and return to economic growth. It transferred its market economic model by setting legal and administrative standards and provided substantial technical assistance. It offers substantial financial support to its new members, which receive up to 3 percent of GDP in net EU grants. The European Union also has great education exchanges and a free market for education for citizens of its member states.

The European Union can and should be Ukraine's international anchor, providing all the different kinds of support to Ukraine that it has offered to the enlargement countries. Thanks to Ukraine's Association Agreement with the European Union, a legal basis for such mutual engagement now exists.

Legal codes are borrowed from one of four modern legal systems: the Anglo-American common law, the French or Latin civil law, the German civil law, and the Scandinavian civil law (La Porta et al. 1998). Two thousand years ago, Roman law spread around the Mediterranean. Two hundred years ago, Napoleon Bonaparte promoted his Napoleonic code in competition with British common law. Today, we live in the era of the *acquis communautaire*, the common EU body of law currently of some 250,000 pages.

All EU candidate members had to adopt the *acquis*. It consists not only of EU statutory documents, legal acts, and international conventions but also precedents from the European Court of Justice and is expanding all the time (Sushko et al. 2012, 11). With the *acquis*, the EU accession countries adopted most institutions characteristic of EU countries, which resolved many problems of their postcommunist transition. The European Union demanded democracy and assisted in its construction. It also insisted on the building of an ordinary market economy. All 28 EU members have succeeded in these endeavors; they would not have been admitted as members otherwise.

European Assistance since Independence

After Ukraine's independence, the European Union offered two kinds of assistance, agricultural credits and technical assistance. The agricultural credits were never justified given that Ukraine had been and will remain the breadbasket of Europe, and the conditions of these credits were not particularly beneficial. From 1999 to 2006, the European Union offered some €2.5 billion in grants through Technical Assistance for the CIS (TACIS) (Sushko et al. 2012, 41). However, this aid was encumbered with so many internal political EU conditions that most of this funding went to consultants of EU countries, making the aid quite inefficient.

With the introduction of the European Neighborhood Policy (ENP), the European Union ended TACIS and launched the European Neighborhood and Partnership Instrument (ENPI) in 2007, which was more focused on the needs of the recipient country and on the need to improve governance. EU support to Ukraine rose as the total ENPI assistance for Ukraine amounted to €3.2 billion in 2007–13 (Sushko et al. 2012, 42). The budget support can be either general or sectoral, and it is given on conditions akin to those of International Monetary Fund (IMF) or World Bank funding, though the amounts are much smaller.

The ENPI technical assistance aims at supporting institutional, legal, and administrative reforms as well as promoting economic and private sector development. A novelty of the ENPI technical assistance is "twinning." State agencies in various EU countries have committed themselves to reforming their Ukrainian counterparts. Civil servants from a state agency in one EU country are commissioned to their counterpart in Ukraine for a long-term project to reform it. These civil servants assist in carrying out a comprehensive reform of the Ukrainian agency, drafting new legislation, suggesting reorganization, providing new work routines, and training the staff. This method of reform has proven highly effective in the new member states in CEE and is a reason why their governance has greatly improved. By April 2014, Ukraine and the European Union had already undertaken or initiated 60 twinning projects (Center for the Adaptation of the Civil Service to the Standards of the European Union 2014).

For the EU seven-year budget period of 2014–20, the European Commission has committed loans and grants of €11 billion. This package consists of four major components. However, the money coming from the European Commission is actually less than in the previous seven-year period. EU assistance grants amount to €1.4 billion and EU macrofinancial assistance loans to €1.6 billion, adding up to €3.0 billion. In addition, the European Commission foresees up to €3 billion in financing from the European Investment Bank for long-term investment for 2014–16 and €5 billion in loans and investments from the European Bank for Reconstruction and Development (European Commission 2014a). Clearly, the amount from the European Commission will have to be raised.

The European Union is also assisting through education. More than 32,000 Ukrainians are currently studying in European universities, and their number might be substantially larger as many young Ukrainians obtain a residence permit in an EU country and study there because most EU countries have minimal tuition fees. The favorite destination of Ukrainian students is Poland, which happily accepts thousands of Ukrainian students. With the new Erasmus+ student exchange program, the European Union will offer more opportunities for Ukrainian students at EU universities. The European Commission has estimated that more than 4,000 young Ukrainians will benefit from these university exchanges. For schools, the European Union has organized eTwinning, in which 101 Ukrainian schools have engaged (European Commission 2014a).

Russia Is Not the Model for Ukraine

The question is often raised whether Russia is the best model for Ukraine. After all, its GDP per capita at current exchange rates is three times as high as Ukraine's (Poland's is higher). But Russia needs to solve its own problems first. It is no democracy and suffers from endemic corruption in the absence of real rule of law. Its trade policy is increasingly protectionist, and its market is often closed to Ukraine. In the social and health spheres, it suffers from the same problems as Ukraine with even lower life expectancy.

In no regard is Russia a useful model for Ukraine. Nor has it provided any resources for Ukraine's development. Able young Ukrainians have visited many Western countries but not Russia because it does not offer scholarships to Ukrainians. By contrast, Russia's shady gas trade has aggravated corruption in Ukraine, as elaborated in chapter 10. John Kornblum (2014) has summed up the state of affairs: "Ukrainians are fed up with Russian sponsored corruption and seek a better future in the West." Nor is Russia's penchant for armed aggression against neighbors helpful. Russia needs to cure itself before it can help any other nation.

President Vladimir Putin has promoted the Eurasian Economic Union as an alternative to the European Union, but it is a small organization of three countries, Russia, Belarus, and Kazakhstan, completely dominated by Russia. These countries are authoritarian, corrupt, and alien to the rule of law. The treaty of the Eurasian Economic Union of some 700 pages is a rudimentary trade agreement and poses no competition to the *acquis communautaire*. Contrary to its self-professed aim, this grouping is highly protectionist both toward the outside world and each another.

The Dream of Europe

After the collapse of communism, the European Union offered "a return to Europe"—that is, membership in the European Union—to Central Europe, the Baltics, and Southeastern Europe because they were widely perceived as constituent parts of "Europe." Ukrainians have been divided in their attitudes toward Europe. Predominantly Ukrainian-speaking western and central Ukraine has looked to Europe, while Russian-speaking eastern and southern Ukraine has felt greater affinity for Russia and its regional organizations.

In the early 1990s, Ukraine was left behind without much foreign policy when the CEE countries sought as close cooperation with the European Union as possible. In 1992-93, the European Union concluded so-called Europe Agreements with the Central and Southeast European countries and free trade agreements (FTAs) with the Baltic states in 1994 and Europe Agreements in 1995. The Europe Agreements were association agreements aimed at broadly integrating these countries into the European Union, by not only lowering barriers to trade but also establishing a framework for political dialogue and harmonizing legislation, although they did not promise EU membership. They provided free trade in industrial goods within ten years, but the EU agricultural market remained closed.

All the CEE countries applied for membership in the European Union as early as they were allowed. In July 1997, the pioneers—Poland, the Czech Republic, Hungary, and Estonia—were invited to negotiate terms of membership. In 1999, Latvia, Lithuania, Slovakia, Romania, and Bulgaria received such invitations. Their future EU membership dominated their outlook. The European Union was by far the most important international community. Radical trade liberalization helped the CEE countries to reorient their trade at extraordinary speed toward the European Union, which soon accounted for two-thirds of their trade (Baldwin 1994, Messerlin 2001).

The European Union had nothing to offer on national security, however. So the CEE countries also applied for membership in the North Atlantic Treaty Organization (NATO). In 1999, the first batch consisting of Poland, the Czech Republic, and Hungary became full members of NATO. In 2004, a second wave of Bulgaria, Estonia, Latvia, Lithuania, Romania, Slovakia, and Slovenia joined NATO. NATO accession was conditioned not only on military matters but also on the establishment of democracy and a market economy, reinforcing EU demands. NATO membership preceded EU membership slightly for most countries. Foreign direct investment (FDI) started flowing in large volumes into Bulgaria and Romania after they joined NATO, three years before their EU entry. Evidently, NATO membership made Western investors feel safe.

Most postcommunist countries liberalized their foreign trade considerably, but from the outset EU policy caused a rift between the EU accession countries, including the Baltic states, and the countries in the Commonwealth of Independent States (CIS). The European Union became the savior of CEE, opening its vast market to the accession countries early on, but it did not offer anything to countries farther to the east, such as Ukraine (Åslund and Warner 2004).

After Leonid Kuchma was elected president in July 1994, Ukraine started developing a foreign policy. Kuchma's idea was a "multivector" policy, developing closer and friendlier relations with both Russia and the European Union (Wolczuk 2002). In 1995, in a speech at the Council of Europe in Strasbourg he asked for the first time for Ukrainian membership in the European Union. He based his request on Article 49 of the Treaty of the European Union, which states that any European country may apply for membership. Kuchma's request was met with a deafening silence, although he repeated it numerous times.

At its council meeting in Copenhagen in 1993, the European Union had formulated its criteria for accession of postcommunist countries:

- *Political criteria*: stability of institutions guaranteeing democracy, the rule of law, human rights, and respect for and protection of minorities.

- *Economic criteria*: a functioning market economy and the capacity to cope with competition and market forces.

- *Administrative and institutional criteria*: capacity to effectively implement the *acquis* and ability to take on the obligations of membership.

Ukraine did not meet any of these conditions. In addition, the Union reserved the right to judge its capacity to absorb new members and to decide when a candidate country had met these criteria.[1]

---

1. European Commission, "Enlargement: Accession criteria," September 7, 2012, http://ec.europa. eu/enlargement/policy/glossary/terms/accession-criteria_en.htm#.

European Neighborhood Policy and Eastern Partnership

For many years, the European Union hardly paid any attention to Ukraine. In 1994, it concluded a bilateral Partnership and Cooperation Agreement with Ukraine as it did with all other CIS countries (apart from Tajikistan), but these agreements contained little substance.

In 2003, the European Union was about to complete its great eastern enlargement. It had freed up policymaking capacity and started showing new interest in Ukraine and other neighboring countries. In March 2003, the European Union launched its European Neighborhood Policy, which was designed for neighbors in both Western CIS and North Africa. It attempted to standardize the EU approach to friendly neighbors, offering them more market access and interaction. Ukraine seized this opportunity.

The Orange Revolution was accompanied by new Ukrainian enthusiasm for Europe, and it brought democracy to the country, which the European Union demanded for closer cooperation and the ENP was a convenient instrument. In February 2005, Ukraine concluded a substantial initial action plan with the European Union, committing itself to carry out many reforms, with plenty of EU assistance.

In 2008, the European Union took a step further when it presented its Eastern Partnership. It singled out six European CIS countries—Ukraine, Belarus, Moldova, Georgia, Azerbaijan, and Armenia—for such cooperation. They were no longer connected with non-European countries in North Africa or the Middle East. The European Union offered far deeper integration through Association Agreements. The first candidate was Ukraine (Sushko et al. 2012).

In May 2009, the European Union launched its Eastern Partnership with the six ENP countries, declaring: "The main goal of the Eastern Partnership is to create the necessary conditions to accelerate political association and further economic integration between the European Union and interested partner countries" (Council of the European Union 2009). In addition to deep and comprehensive free trade agreements (DCFTAs), the European Union offered broader Association Agreements, involving political and legal aspects.[2] Ukraine was given the most attention, followed by Moldova and Georgia. These DCFTAs would offer much more than greater market access, including the harmonization of rules and institutions, bringing about a potentially far-reaching integration of these six countries with the European Union.

To Ukrainians, the most immediate and most important issue is visa-free travel to the European Union. Moldova achieved this important goal starting May 1, 2014. Ukraine and the European Union have agreed on an action plan on visa liberalization. Two key EU demands are secure identification documents—that is, biometric passports—and control of illegal migration. The

---

2. Since the DCFTA forms the bulk of the Association Agreement, these terms are often used as synonyms, which is not quite correct. These two parts have been negotiated separately, and in media reports it is often unclear whether a decision concerns the political part of the Association Agreement, the DCFTA, or the whole agreement.

Ukrainian government hopes to get the right to visa-free travel in 2015, but Ukraine can hardly control illegal migration,[3] since it does not control large parts of its border with Russia in Donbas. Thus, Russia can effectively block Ukraine from getting visa-free status.

European Association Agreement

Ukraine's Association Agreement with the European Union evolved slowly, reflecting its size and importance. It is both the most extensive international agreement that Ukraine has concluded and the most extensive agreement that the European Union has completed with a third country.

The Orange government saw EU accession as its main international ambition, launching negotiations with the European Union about an Association Agreement in March 2007. The European Union required that a counterpart be a member of the World Trade Organization (WTO) to conclude a free trade agreement. The Orange government accelerated Ukraine's accession to the WTO, which it joined on May 16, 2008. Initially, the negotiations on the Association Agreement were tardy because it was a pioneering agreement for both parties. The European Union used its Association Agreement with Ukraine as a template for its later negotiations with Moldova and Georgia, which therefore went much faster.

However, the election of Viktor Yanukovych as president in February 2010 posed considerable political problems for the European Union. In February 2010, Yanukovych won with a slight margin over Prime Minister Yulia Tymoshenko in a reasonably free and fair presidential election. While he had opposed the membership action plan for NATO, Yanukovych favored the Association Agreement with the European Union and even made his first trip abroad as new president to Brussels. He continued the negotiations on an Association Agreement.

At the end of 2010, Ukrainians and others in Europe increasingly perceived Yanukovych's regime as corrupt and authoritarian. The European Union insisted that he comply with human rights and the rule of law in Ukraine, which slowed the negotiations. Yanukovych promised to fulfill all the EU conditions, but his credibility was limited as his actions went in the opposite direction. The European Union postponed the conclusion of the Association Agreement and introduced extra steps to delay the process. At a Ukraine-EU summit in Kyiv on December 19, 2011, the two parties announced that they had completed the negotiations. On March 30, 2012, the heads of the negotiating delegations initialed the text of the agreement in English (Sushko et al. 2012, 9). On July 19, 2012, Yanukovych and EU presidents initialed the Association Agreement, but they did not sign it.

---

3. "ES o vizakh: u Ukrainy uverenny progress, no otmeny viz poka ne budet" ["The EU about Visas: Ukraine Has Made Certain Progress, But No Abolition of Visas Will Take Place As Yet"], *Ukrainskaya pravda*, November 12, 2014.

In the summer of 2013, Moldova, Armenia, and Georgia caught up with Ukraine, also concluding DCFTAs with the European Union. Ukraine was the big headache for EU officials, being both important and complicated. Without Ukraine, the Eastern Partnership was no big deal, but EU officials balked at the Yanukovych government's flagrant violations of human rights and the rule of law. They continued to hope that Ukraine would make amends so that Yanukovych could sign the Association Agreement at the European Union's Eastern Partnership summit in Lithuania's capital, Vilnius, on November 28–29, 2013, but in the end he did not. After Yanukovych's ouster and the presidential election in May 2014, Petro Poroshenko signed the Association Agreement on June 27, 2014.

The Association Agreement is large and substantial (EEAS 2013). It is comprehensive, covering all areas of interest. It offers enhanced cooperation in 28 key policy areas, including political cooperation, foreign and security policy, justice, and freedom. It aims to accelerate the deepening of political and economic relations between Ukraine and the European Union and gradually integrate Ukraine into the EU internal market. The Association Agreement thus provides for significant legal, regulatory and political convergence with the European Union, for which the European Union offers considerable assistance. Yet it stops short of granting EU membership.

The Association Agreement consists of seven parts or "titles." They comprise 486 articles filling 477 pages of text and large annexes. The seven parts are:

1. general principles (two articles),
2. political dialogue and reform, political association, cooperation and convergence in the field of foreign and security policy (10 articles),
3. justice, freedom, and security (11 articles),
4. trade and trade-related matters (312 articles),
5. economic and sector cooperation (116 articles), and
6. financial cooperation with antifraud provisions (7 articles), and
7. institutional, general, and final provisions (27 articles) (EEAS 2013).

The DCFTA is part four of the Association Agreement and includes two large annexes, which fill about 2,000 pages. The fifth part is also economic, containing regulations of energy, statistics, taxation, communications, transportation, and many other matters involving Ukraine adopting EU standards. Thus, the trade and economic parts dominate the agreement.

The second article of the Association Agreement contains the objectives of this treaty in four dimensions: values, political and security, economic and trade, and legal. In practice, the European Union does not have much to do with security, but the other three components are of substance. As Poroshenko (2014) stated in his presidential inauguration speech: "For me European democracy is the best form of government invented by mankind."

Most of the Association Agreement is a long list of hundreds of legal measures that Ukraine commits to undertaking in order to adopt the legal and technical standards of the *acquis communautaire*. If it is successful in this endeavor, it will reform its Soviet-like state apparatus and install a modern, well-functioning European state administration as the CEE countries have done.

The DCFTA is a substantial FTA. Its declared aim is: "The Parties shall progressively establish a free trade area over a transitional period of a maximum of 10 years starting from the entry into force of this Agreement" (EEAS 2013, 32). It decreases or eliminates existing trade barriers between Ukraine and the European Union, leading to increased mutual trade. It abolishes mutual customs tariffs, although the current average EU tariff on manufactures is only 1.19 percent and 2.45 percent in Ukraine, so the impact will be limited. The effect will be more significant for agricultural goods, the average EU tariff on which is 7.42 percent versus 6.41 percent in Ukraine, and agricultural goods are set to account for about one-third of Ukraine's exports in 2014. The transition period is asymmetric, meaning that Ukraine obtains immediate access to the EU market, while Ukrainian producers may shield themselves behind some tariffs for up to ten years. The DCFTA also covers regulatory convergence in competition policy, state aid, property rights, and energy policy (Giucci 2013).

The main advantages for Ukraine will be better access to the vast EU market; increased inflow of foreign direct investment, which will modernize the Ukrainian economy, restructure enterprises, and create jobs; and harmonization of regulatory and institutional standards, which will improve the business environment and rule of law in Ukraine (Dabrowski and Taran 2012b, 23–24). Implementation of the Association Agreement will not only eliminate nontariff barriers but also contribute to the convergence of Ukraine's regulatory framework with the European Union, integrating Ukraine into the EU economic and legal space, in particular into the single European market.

On September 16, 2014, both the Ukrainian Parliament and the European Parliament ratified the Association Agreement with Ukraine. The Ukrainian Parliament adopted it overwhelmingly with 355 votes out of 381, with the remaining 26 not participating in the vote.[4] In the European Parliament, 535 voted in favor, 127 against, and 35 abstained,[5] with the pro-Russian extreme right and left voting against the Association Agreement.[6] On September 25 President Poroshenko declared that Ukraine intends to apply for membership

---

4. Verkhovnaya Rada Ukrainy, "Rezultaty poimennogo golosovaniya" ["Results of the Vote"], September 16, 2014, http://w1.c1.rada.gov.ua.

5. European Union at the United Nations, "European Parliament Ratifies EU-Ukraine Association Agreement," September 16, 2014, http://eu-un.europa.eu.

6. Vote Watch Europe, September 16, 2014, www.votewatch.eu//en/term8-eu-ukraine-association-agreement-with-the-exception-of-the-treatment-of-third-country-nationals-lega.html (accessed on September 16, 2014).

in the European Union in 2020.[7] The Ukrainian Parliament also adopted a declaration on "Ukraine's European Choice" with 289 votes, which declares Ukraine's desire to become a member of the European Union.[8]

Growth through Integration into the European Supply Chain

Ukraine's economy is ready to transform from old Soviet industry to a more modern economic structure. In trade, the European Union has opened its market to Ukrainian goods, while Russia imposed severe trade sanctions on Ukraine.

In the early 1990s, forecasts of East European trade were made using the gravity model, which predicts the volume of trade a country will have with other countries on the basis of GDP and proximity. The forecasts predicted a drastic reorientation of the postcommunist countries' trade toward the West, primarily to the European Union (Collins and Rodrik 1991, Hamilton and Winters 1992). Oleh Havrylyshyn and Hassan Al-Atrash (1998) found that CEE undertook such a reorientation of its commerce as early as 1992, but the CIS countries continued to trade too much with one another.

Poor trade relations with the European Union contributed to the strange evolution of CIS trade. For too long, Ukraine had little trade with the European Union because two-thirds of its exports consisted of so-called sensitive products, metals, agricultural produce, chemicals, and textiles, which were subject to severe protectionism by the European Union (Messerlin 2001, Åslund and Warner 2004). In the 2000s, this EU protectionism eased.

In 2013, Russia and the European Union each received about one-quarter of Ukraine's exports (table 3.1). Both have had a persistent large trade surplus with Ukraine, reflecting that they have been more protectionist than Ukraine in their bilateral trade. With the DCFTA, Ukraine should get far more market access in the European Union, while Russia's trade sanctions will reduce its market access there. On May 1, 2014, Ukraine achieved free market access to the European market. Ukraine's trade started developing pretty much as expected. Its exports to the European Union are set to increase in 2014 (Yatsenyuk 2014b), while its exports to Russia fell by 50 percent toward the end of the year because of Russia's trade sanctions. Ukraine's exports of agricultural goods skyrocketed.

Many institutions—mainly Polish and Ukrainian institutes and the World Bank[9]—have made quantitative assessments of the effects on the Ukrainian

---

7. "Poroshenko: Ukraina namerena podat' zayavlenie o chlenstve v ES v 2020" ["Poroshenko: Ukraine Is Intent on Applying for EU Membership in 2020"], *Ukrainskaya pravda*, September 25, 2014.

8. "Rada prinyala zayavlenie o budushchem chlenstve v ES" ["The Parliament Adopted a Declaration on Future EU Membership"], *Ukrainskaya pravda*, September 16, 2014.

9. Recent relevant studies are Dabrowski and Taran (2012a, 2012b), Giucci (2013), Maliszewska, Orlova, and Taran (2009), Movchan (2011), Movchan and Giucci (2011), Movchan, Giucci, and

Table 3.1 Ukraine's exports and imports, 2000 and 2013

| | Exports | | | |
| | 2000 | | 2013 | |
Trading partner	Billions of US dollars	Percent of total exports	Billions of US dollars	Percent of total exports
Total	14.6	100	63.3	100
EU-27	4.8	33	16.7	26
Russia	3.5	24	15.1	24
Other CIS	0.9	6	7.0	11
Asia	1.5	10	7.5	12
Other	3.8	27	17.0	27

| | Imports | | | |
| | 2000 | | 2013 | |
Trading partner	Billions of US dollars	Percent of total imports	Billions of US dollars	Percent of total imports
Total	13.9	100	77.0	100
EU-27	4.2	30	27.0	35
Russia	5.8	42	23.2	30
Other CIS	2.2	16	4.7	6
Asia	0.5	4	12.1	16
Other	1.2	8	10.0	13

CIS = Commonwealth of Independent States

Source: UN Comtrade database (accessed on September 8, 2014).

economy of Ukraine's accession to the Eurasian Customs Union (comprising Belarus, Kazakhstan, and Russia) versus implementation of the DCFTA. Using standard gravity and computable general equilibrium models, all have obtained similar results. Veronica Movchan and Ricardo Giucci (2011, 11) provide the most complete recent mainstream study of the effects on Ukraine of both the DCFTA and the Customs Union. They concluded that in the long term, the DCFTA would add 11.8 percent to Ukraine's GDP, while the Customs Union would reduce it by 3.7 percent. The DCFTA would substantially increase trade (both exports and imports), whereas the Customs Union would reduce trade. Other studies offer similar numbers. The biggest impact comes from exports. Oleksandr Shepotylo (2013, 21) estimated that the "expected long run gains in Ukrainian exports to all countries under the CU scenario are equal to 17.9 percent,... and under the EU scenario 46.1 percent." Surprisingly, the highest unrealized potential is in exports to CIS countries, notably to Russia.

Kutsenko (2010), Movchan and Shportyuk (2012), Shepotylo (2010, 2013), Tarr (2012), and von Cramon-Taubadel, Hess, and Bruemmer (2010).

A counterstudy by economists affiliated with the Eurasian Economic Union presented analysis that was not based on calculations but on scenarios and peculiar assumptions. They claimed that Ukraine's DCFTA with the European Union would result in "Ukraine [losing] up to 1.5% of its baseline GDP" (Ivanter et al. 2012, 40). Apparently, the authors include the effect of Customs Union trade sanctions against Ukraine. However, if Ukraine joined the Customs Union, then "Over the period of 2011-2030, the total cumulative effect of the creation of the SES [Single Economic Space] and Ukraine joining it on the four countries can reach $1.1 trillion in 2010 prices...." (Ivanter et al. 2012, 41). This "study" seems more like propaganda rather than research as it appears to be neither substantiated nor plausible (cf. Eurasian Development Bank 2012).

Many countries have experienced the combination of Russian trade sanctions and EU trade liberalization. The typical pattern has been that first Russia has cut off most trade in both directions. The victims have redirected their trade to the European Union. After a few years, new trade evolves, often with new companies and products, but Russia's share of the trade stays much smaller than before the trade war (Åslund and Warner 2004). In the early 1990s, all the CEE countries, especially the Baltic countries, successfully turned their trade flows away from Russia to the European Union. In 2006, Moldova and Georgia were hit by more severe Russian trade sanctions than those against Ukraine. Moldova's share of exports to Russia plummeted from 40 percent in 2005 to 16 percent in 2007, but even so its total exports actually increased primarily due to rapid expansion of its exports to Europe. Georgia was not as dependent on Russia, but the share of its exports to Russia fell from 18 percent in 2005 to 4 percent in 2007, while its total exports actually surged by 42 percent (table 3.2). The disruption of trade with Russia greatly helped the Mikheil Saakashvili government to combat corruption in Georgia.

Ukraine is slightly more dependent on Russia than Georgia was but much less so than Moldova, and it has a much more diversified economy. Moreover, Ukraine has free trade with Europe. Thus, the Ukrainian government should not be too concerned about Russian trade sanctions, although individual businessmen will be hard hit (cf. Giucci and Kirchner 2013).

A switch of markets will change the goods composition of Ukraine's exports, exactly as it did in CEE. Ukraine's exports to Russia and to the European Union differ substantially. In 2013, one-third of Ukraine's exports to Russia consisted of machinery compared with only 11.5 percent to the European Union. Steel accounted for 37 percent of Ukraine's exports to the European Union and 20 percent to Russia. The third big export industry is agriculture, accounting for 24 percent of Ukraine's exports to Europe and 9.5 percent to Russia. Ukraine's fourth traditional export commodity is chemicals, which accounted for 9 percent of its exports to Russia but hardly anything to Europe (table 3.3).

Russia has often imposed trade sanctions on Ukraine, as it has on so many other post-Soviet countries. In late 2014, Russian exports had fallen by about half from the peak in 2012. The current intensification of sanctions started in July 2013. Overall, they are hitting four industries: gas, steel, food, and ar-

Table 3.2 Exports of Moldova and Georgia, 2005–13

	2005	2006	2007	2008	2009	2010	2011	2012	2013
Destination					**Moldova**				
Total (millions of US dollars)	796	712	846	986	780	935	1,215	1,390	1,620
EU-27 (percent of total exports)	29.7	42.4	43.0	40.9	40.0	36.8	46.8	53.4	51.9
Russia (percent of total exports)	39.7	18.5	15.7	21.7	25.0	27.6	20.2	17.5	14.3
					Georgia				
Total (millions of US dollars)	865	935	1,232	1,497	990	1,286	1,701	1,614	1,855
EU-27 (percent of total exports)	25.0	24.0	21.5	22.3	21.8	20.7	23.3	17.5	23.2
Russia (percent of total exports)	17.8	8.1	3.7	1.9	2.0	2.6	1.9	1.9	7.9

Source: UN Comtrade database (accessed on September 9, 2014).

Table 3.3 Composition of Ukraine's exports to the European Union and Russia, 2013

Exports to the European Union	
Product	**Percent of total exports to the European Union**
Steel	36.6
Agriculture	23.8
Machinery	11.5
Mineral fuels, oils and their products	6.3
Wood and articles of wood	3.7
Articles of apparel and clothing	2.3

Exports to Russia	
Product	**Percent of total exports to Russia**
Machinery	33.6
Steel	19.9
Agriculture	9.5
Chemicals	8.6
Paper and paperboard	5.1
Salt, sulphur, earth, and stones	3.1

Source: UN Comtrade database (accessed on September 8, 2014).

maments. Ukraine has cut its gas imports from Russia because the latter has been demanding usury prices since April 2014. Russia has blocked imports of steel pipes from Ukraine because of antidumping claims and also imports of several food items, citing sanitary and phytosanitary problems. Ukraine has attempted to cut its supply of armaments to Russia, though some continues. Ukraine can beneficially redirect its food and steel exports, in particular to the now quite open EU market, even if many agricultural products are still subject to quotas. Modernization of Ukraine's machine-building industry is long overdue.

Considering that Ukraine's economic structure in 1989 was surprisingly similar to Poland's, one could guess that its structure will evolve as Poland's did if Ukraine's reforms and integration with Europe are successful. Initially, Poland exported more steel and chemicals, but soon these industries went into decline. Ukraine's chemical industry produces primarily fertilizers from previously cheap Russian gas and looks like a sunset industry. Ukrainian steel exports are likely to decline in the short term, but Ukraine enjoys evident comparative advantages and can presumably remain a competitive steel producer after substantial modernization. Agriculture and food processing are currently the boom industries, as Ukraine is restoring its position as the breadbasket of Europe.

Central Europe's economic development has been so successful because the countries are part of the European, primarily German, supply chain. If the Ukrainian state reduces its interference in the business of enterprises and instead makes property rights more secure, Ukraine should be able to thrive as the new link in the European supply chain. Foreign direct investment from Europe and North America will spur this development, but as elsewhere the country itself makes the most investment. Ukraine has a substantial machine-building industry, but most of its exports to Russia are parts for the Russian military-industrial complex, which is not likely to continue for mutual political reasons. Skilled engineers are a great asset for economic development, and they can presumably be mobilized for new production, as has happened in CEE, which would require Schumpeterian creative destruction. New enterprises under new management could utilize this valuable human capital. Ukraine also has a promising high-tech industry of software and information technology, which will greatly benefit from rule of law.

Curiously, Ukraine's domestic economic structure has actually transformed more than its foreign trade. In spite of limited reforms, Ukraine has adopted a market economy, which has altered the composition of its GDP. Since 1989, the Ukrainian service sector has doubled from 29 percent of GDP to 63 percent. The agricultural share of GDP has plummeted from 22.9 percent in 1989 to 10.4 percent in 2013, remaining larger than elsewhere because of unique agricultural endowment and relatively low GDP. The share of manufacturing in GDP has fallen sharply from 39 percent of GDP in 1989 to 14 percent in 2013, which is a normal share for a developed economy. Characteristically, other industries, mainly steel and chemicals, nearly doubled their share from 1989 to 2000 but fell to 13 percent of GDP in 2013 (table 3.4). The service sector is likely to continue to grow, and agriculture's share in GDP is likely to stay higher than in other modern economies, while the role of steel and chemicals is bound to decline.

Table 3.4 Structural composition of Ukraine's GDP, 1989, 2000, and 2013 (percent of GDP)

Sector	1989	2000	2013
Services	28.7	46.6	62.6
Agriculture	22.9	17.1	10.4
Manufacturing	39.3	19.2	13.7
Industry (except manufacturing)	9.1	17.1	13.2

Note: Industry comprises value added in mining, manufacturing (also reported as a separate subgroup), construction, electricity, water, and gas.

Source: World Bank (2014a).

The Russian aggression is hurting the Ukrainian economy badly, hitting the Donbas rustbelt the worst. Yet, this cloud may have some silver lining. Ukraine's foreign trade might finally be modernized as happened in the CEE countries in the early 1990s, which in turn drove the modernization of their domestic economies. The corruption in Ukraine's trade with Russia may be broken and the old Soviet industry compelled to restructure. In the long run, the Ukrainian economy will benefit as did Saakashvili's Georgia.

Will Ukraine's European Integration Proceed?

Ukraine's European integration should not be taken as a given. An Association Agreement does not necessarily lead to EU membership. Turkey concluded its Association Agreement with the European Union in 1963, but it is not even close to becoming an EU member.

Over time, the European Union has increasingly focused on the qualitative aspects of its enlargement. EU Commissioner for Enlargement Štefan Füle (2014) characterized the enlargement process as relying on three key pillars: the rule of law, economic governance, and public administration reform with the strengthening of democratic institutions.

On September 12, 2014, four days before the ratification of the Association Agreement in the Ukrainian and European Parliaments, the European Commission, Russia, and Ukraine agreed to delay the implementation of the DCFTA, the fourth part of the Association Agreement, by 16 months until January 1, 2016 (European Commission 2014b). The other parts of the Association Agreement are still supposed to be implemented from 2014. They include political dialogue, support for political reform in Ukraine, cooperation on foreign policy, justice and security, and sectoral cooperation in areas such as transportation, health, education, research, and energy.

Everything was wrong with this decision (Speck 2014, Sadowski 2014). For years, the European Union has maintained that its bilateral agreements with third parties are not subject to the approval of another state. But now it abandoned this principle because of Russia's military aggression in Ukraine, giving "Russia incentives to raise the pressure because it opens a large window of opportunity to prevent the DCFTA from entering into force. The pressure could be military, economic, or diplomatic" (Speck 2014).

Most of the economic reforms the European Union requires from Ukraine are incorporated in the DCFTA. Ideally these EU demands should have been imposed just after the formation of a new government after the October 2014 parliamentary elections, but EU pressure is now absent. The delay of the DCFTA may put a brake on reforms. Poroshenko responded that Ukraine would proceed with legal, political, economic, and social reforms on a broad front, which would make it possible for Ukraine to apply for EU membership in 2020.[10]

Instead of showing commitment to Ukraine, the European Union undermined its credibility with the Ukrainian nation. It also damaged its legitimacy by abandoning normal decision-making procedures. Germany and France appeared to put pressure on the European Commission and Ukraine in line with Russia's interests without consulting other EU members. Pro-Ukrainian EU member states protested both against how this decision was made and its content.

The European Union appeared to maintain its position that as an FTA the DCFTA cannot harm Russia's interest, and Russia already has the CIS FTA with Ukraine. Russia, however, strangely claims that EU goods will be remarked as Ukrainian and be exported to Russia without customs tariffs. Therefore, Russia threatened to revoke its FTA with Ukraine. In addition, it demanded the renegotiation of the DCFTA between Ukraine and the European Union to exclude 20 percent of Ukraine's export goods (2,376 out of 11,600 tariff lines) from the DCFTA.[11] On September 19, Russia formalized this position in a government decree, although it had committed itself to maintaining free trade with Ukraine one week earlier in the agreement with the European Union and Ukraine. The president of the European Commission, José Manuel Barroso (2014), responded in a letter to President Putin expressing "strong concerns about the recent adoption of a decree by the Russian government proposing new trade barriers between Russian and Ukraine." The Kremlin did not appear impressed.

Thus, the EU action unleashed exactly what it was supposed to avert, further Russian aggression in trade policy. Ukraine prepared countersanctions for 800 tariff lines, but smaller countries can rarely benefit from trade sanctions against bigger ones. Since Russia mainly exports oil and gas to Ukraine, the latter's sanctions hardly make a dent. According to WTO rules, a country can raise its tariffs to the average level, and Russian average tariffs are almost three times higher than Ukraine's (Panchenko 2014).

---

10. "Ukraine's Leader Sees Country Applying for EU Membership 'in Six Years' Time'," Reuters, September 25, 2014.

11. "Rossiya vydvinula Ukraine i ES svoi spisok izmenenii v assotsiatsiyu" ["Russia Presented Ukraine and the EU with Its List of Amendments to the Association"], *Ukrainskaya pravda*, September 10, 2014.

Ukraine Needs a Marshall Plan

Ravaged by war and severe economic and financial crisis, Ukraine is in profound need of foreign aid, not only credits but also substantial grants. Its emergency calls for a Marshall Plan.[12] Now as in 1947, US Secretary of State George C. Marshall's (1947) words ring true: "It is logical that the United States should do whatever it is able to do to assist in the return of normal economic health to the world, without which there can be no political stability and no assured peace." But today, the onus rests on the European Union because it has the necessary means.

The need for a Marshall Plan was raised when the Soviet Union collapsed, but then there was no war destruction, no military threat, and no particular need for a new Western alliance. For too long, Europe ignored the wars in Yugoslavia in the 1990s, which is now seen as a big mistake. Since the ouster of Yanukovych, several people have suggested that Ukraine needs and deserves a Marshall Plan.[13] In fact, a Marshall Plan is much more appropriate for Ukraine today than it was for the postcommunist countries in the early 1990s.[14]

Ukraine is in the midst of a frightful financial crisis, primarily caused by the war the Kremlin launched against Ukraine on February 27, 2014, when the first Yatsenyuk government was appointed. Russia has blown up the power stations in Donbas, stopping pumps in the coal mines, which have been flooded. On September 13, Prime Minister Arseniy Yatsenyuk assessed the war damages to physical infrastructure at $9 billion, and that amount has since risen substantially. Donbas's humanitarian crisis calls for Western humanitarian aid.

Like Europe after World War II, Ukraine needs to rebuild its state and economy. After its democratic breakthrough in February 2014, election of President Petro Poroshenko on May 25, and parliamentary elections on October 26, Ukraine appears to be ready for this Herculean task. If the European Union is serious about its recently ratified Association Agreement with Ukraine, it needs to show so now.

If the needed capital is provided as credits, Ukraine will not be financially sustainable. In April 2014, the IMF (2014a) concluded a two-year Stand-By Arrangement with a total international financial support of $33 billion for two years, of which the IMF itself would contribute $17 billion. The rest of the funding would come from the World Bank, the European Union, the European Investment Bank (EIB), the European Bank for Reconstruction and Development (EBRD), and various bilateral creditors. Almost all this "aid" consists of credits, which Ukraine will have to pay back. If Ukraine continues drawing on credits at the current speed, while output is collapsing, the country is likely

---

12. This section draws on Åslund (2014b).

13. Kyiv attorney Daniel Bilak (2014), philanthropist George Soros (2014), Deputy Prime Minister Volodymyr Groisman (2014), and French philosopher Bernard-Henri Lévy (2014).

14. The prime sources for the Marshall Plan are Hogan (1987) and Milward (1984).

to default on its international payments. In the course of 2014, Ukraine received a total of $8.2 billion of international financial support. The IMF itself disbursed $4.6 billion, but Ukraine paid back $3.6 billion in debt service, leaving a net loan of only $1 billion.

At the end of 2014, Ukraine's international reserves were as low as $7.5 billion. In December, the IMF saw a need for another $16 billion on top of its own committed balance of $12.4 billion for the remaining 16 months of its program, implying a total financial need of $28 billion.[15] In the whole of 2015–16, however, Ukraine faces a public debt service in foreign currency of $33 billion. On that basis, JPMorgan assessed Ukraine's total public international financing need at $40 billion for 2015 and 2016, assuming Ukrainian international reserves of merely $15 billion at the end of 2016,[16] while anything less than $25 billion would appear imprudent, corresponding to three months of imports. Then the financing need for anticipated debt service and buildup of reserves would be $50 billion for 2015–16. On top of that would come war damages, which Prime Minister Yatsenyuk assessed at $9 billion in September 2014.

This amounts to a total international financing need of almost $60 billion for the two years 2015–16. But Ukraine can hardly assume so much new debt, even if it attracted such financing. The IMF (2014d, 39) presumed that public debt would surge from 41 percent of GDP at the end of 2013 to 68 percent at the end of 2014, but it warned that it could get out of control and double to 134 percent of GDP in 2016 (IMF 2014d, 49). Ukraine needs a solution other than taking on more debt. One option is a truly severe austerity policy. Another is a different Western attitude to financing the country. Ukraine's current situation calls for not only credits but also grant financing. Its citizens will have to make the greatest sacrifice, but former prime minister of Lithuania Andrius Kubilius has proposed that the European Union should commit 3 percent of its €1.0 trillion budget for 2014–20, that is, €30 billion or $37 billion, in grants to Ukraine. This amounts to a Marshall Plan for Ukraine. The countries that became EU members in 2004 had their annual net EU grants capped at 3 percent of their GDPs. The actual disbursements have varied but at times they have reached 6 to 7 percent of GDP in a single year. For Ukraine, grants of €30 billion over seven years would correspond to about 3 percent a year of its 2013 GDP. The Committees on European Affairs and Foreign Affairs of the Lithuanian Parliament approved such an initiative of a new Marshall Plan for Ukraine.[17] In July 2014 the Ukrainian government formed a working group on a Marshall Plan for Ukraine, chaired by Deputy Prime Minister Volodymyr Groisman.

---

15. Peter Spiegel, "IMF Warns Ukraine Bailout at Risk of Collapse," *Financial Times*, December 9, 2014.

16. Nicolaie Alexandru-Chidesciuc, "Ukraine: Further Drop in FX Reserves; Large Financing Needs over Next Two Years," JPMorgan, December 9.

17. Lithuanian Parliament, "Seimas Committees Approved the Strategy on Lithuania's Support for Ukraine, Providing for a New Marshall Plan for Ukraine," press release, November 14, 2014.

At present, it might be difficult to imagine that the United States would contribute substantial funds to Ukraine, but that should not be the case. John Sopko, the special inspector general for Afghanistan reconstruction, has stated that to date "the United States government has provided over $104 billion for Afghanistan reconstruction... but in many ways it has gone unnoticed almost hidden in plain sight." Moreover, "it is widely believed the United States will continue to fund reconstruction at another $5 billion to $8 billion annually for years to come."[18] In Ukraine, US funding can offer real benefits and make all the difference.

The ultimate motive of the Marshall Plan was to stand up against the Soviet threat. Once again, the West faces such a situation, even though Putin's Russia is much weaker than Joseph Stalin's Soviet Union. If the West is not prepared to support Ukraine militarily, it has all the more reason to provide it with appropriate financial and political support. Europe has to counter this threat.

Finally, the West itself needs a new form of alliance. NATO is not enough and no other alliance involving both the European Union and the United States exists. For years, Putin has repeatedly pursued aggression involving gas, trade, internet, information, and military. Countries that bilaterally support Ukraine, such as the European Union, the United States, Canada, Japan, and other Western countries, should come together to stop Putin before he proceeds beyond Ukraine to Moldova, Georgia, and the Balkans.

---

18. John F. Sopko, speech at Georgetown University, Washington, September 12, 2014.

II

WHAT WENT WRONG

4

Nation Building but Little Reform, 1991–2010

Ukraine is not Russia.

—Leonid Kuchma (2003)

In a referendum on December 1, 1991, 90 percent of the Ukrainian population voted for independence.[1] Participation was high at 84 percent. In each of Ukraine's 25 regions, a majority voted for the nation's independence, with 54 percent even in Crimea. For seven decades the Communist Party of the Soviet Union and the KGB had ruled Ukraine. Now Moscow accepted its independence, but the new nation was deplorably unprepared.

Leonid Kravchuk, a moderate senior Communist Party apparatchik, was democratically elected the country's first president. During his three years in power he was preoccupied with building national symbols rather than a well-functioning state or economy. He pursued no real economic policy and did not implement any reforms. This policy vacuum led to hyperinflation and enabled a small group of clever businessmen to profit from the economic chaos. Their rent-seeking machine bred a few wealthy businessmen who became known as oligarchs.

In July 1994, Leonid Kuchma, the manager of Ukraine's largest armaments factory in Dnipropetrovsk, was elected president with the support of voters from the eastern part of the country. He introduced elementary economic order and carried out a normal macroeconomic stabilization with the assistance of the International Monetary Fund (IMF). In 1995, Ukraine implemented mass privatization, and in 2000 the country finally achieved sufficient deregulation to restart economic growth after a decade of economic decline. Kuchma improved Ukraine's poor relations with Russia to such an extent that

---

1. This chapter draws on my book Åslund (2009, chapters 2 to 6).

both countries concluded a Treaty on Friendship, Cooperation and Partnership in 1997.[2]

In late 2004, the Orange Revolution erupted as a popular protest against fraudulent presidential elections, which were rigged by Viktor Yanukovych and his supporters to bring him to power. A new election was won by the West-oriented democratic forces under the leadership of President Viktor Yushchenko and Prime Minister Yulia Tymoshenko, but the new Orange government dissolved in renewed political chaos. Rather than implementing reforms, in 2005 the Orange government fought over old privatizations. In 2008–09, a new financial crisis hit Ukraine. Meanwhile, relations with Russia soured over gas and the North Atlantic Treaty Organization (NATO).

Leonid Kravchuk: Preoccupation with Nation Building, but Political Chaos, 1991–94

Ukraine's first presidential elections were held on December 1, 1991. Leonid Kravchuk, chairman of the parliament and former second secretary of the Communist Party of Ukraine, won with 61.6 percent of the votes, followed by nationalist Vyacheslav Chornovil, who received 23.3 percent (Kuzio 2000, 194–201).

Kravchuk was a peculiar politician. I met him first at the World Economic Forum in Davos in January 1990. He struck me at first as far too simple but jovial and likable. Andrew Wilson (2002, 182) captured his character thus:

> Always a consummate opportunist, Kravchuk became Ukraine's preeminent figure in the build-up to independence by skillfully constructing a public persona that was most things to most people. As president, he sought to delay any final act of self-definition for as long as possible by maintaining the broadest possible consensus amongst elites.

Three broad forces formed Ukraine's politics throughout the 1990s: the national-democratic movement Rukh in western Ukraine with 20 to 25 percent popular support, the hard left of communists and socialists in eastern Ukraine with 40 percent support, and an amorphous center. The national democrats were the driving force, but because of their stalemate with the communist left, the opportunistic center held power throughout the 1990s. The nationalist leaders understood that they were too weak to gain power on their own and sought "a grand bargain" or "historical compromise" with the national communists (Wilson 2002, 174). This center was pragmatic and driven by self-interest. To quote Oscar Wilde, they knew "the price of everything and the value of nothing." It consisted of the old Soviet establishment that no longer cared about ideology but wanted to stay in power.

The political center held power, but it had no strategic goal, and the hard left held a blocking minority in parliament. As a consequence, minimal legisla-

---

2. As a matter of disclosure, I worked as an economic advisor to President Kuchma from 1994 until 1997.

tion was promulgated in the 1990s. A dysfunctional constitutional arrangement hindered both the president and prime minister from passing legislation, but the parliament could oust neither. The result was stalemate and frequent political crises. A positive effect, however, was the development of pluralism with strong checks and balances.

A popular caricature in 1994 showed a row of apparatchiki with the caption "Ukraine's old communist rulers." The second picture was identical, but its caption read "Ukraine's new national rulers." Ukraine's communists had their cake and ate it too. No one—not the KGB or Moscow or the Communist Party—supervised them, and they could quietly appropriate Soviet state property.

The real power struggle was not between the right and left but within the old communist elite, the state enterprise managers or "red directors." They formed two major regional and branch factions. Yuhym Zviahilsky led the managers of the coal mines and steelworks in Donetsk, whereas Leonid Kuchma spearheaded the managers of military industry in Dnipropetrovsk. On the face of it, these two rival forces were confusingly similar, but they favored different economic policies. Kuchma promoted gradual market reforms, while Zviahilsky rejected them. The missing force in Ukrainian politics was liberalism. In 1992–93, Kuchma was prime minister under Kravchuk, and then Zviahilsky replaced him in 1993–94.

The 1994 presidential elections became a major battle between two middle-aged members of the old nomenklatura, Kravchuk and Kuchma. Kravchuk presented himself as the father of the Ukrainian nation and the master of peace, a unifier and conciliator, appealing to Ukrainian nationalists, but he had no economic policy. Kuchma attacked Kravchuk's economic policies, calling the economy "a catastrophe" and Ukraine "bankrupt." He demanded change and a market economic reform. His second theme was the need for better relations with Russia. His election slogan was: "Russia and Ukraine: Less walls, more bridges."[3] He campaigned as the leader of Ukraine's Russian speakers.

In the runoff on July 10, Kuchma won with 52 percent of the votes over Kravchuk's 45 percent in an election that was considered free and fair. The election was not about ideology but partly about economics, and the country was mobilized into two regional camps: Ukrainian speakers in the west and center voted for Kravchuk whereas Russian speakers in the east and south voted for Kuchma (Kuzio 1997, 39–66).

Hyperinflation and Output Collapse, Breeding Rent Seeking and Oligarchs, 1992–94

No economy has fared as poorly in peacetime as Ukraine did from 1989 to 1999. For a decade, Ukrainian GDP plummeted by a total of 61 percent, according to official statistics (UNECE 2000, 225). The real decline was consider-

---

3. Anton Kriukov, "Ukraine-Russia: The Process Has Started," *Zerkalo nedeli*, October 15, 1994.

ably smaller, perhaps half, but still substantial. The cause of this disaster was the absence of economic policy.

The ignorance of market economics was astounding. Suspicious of both Poles and Russians, Ukrainians objected to "shock therapy." A national consensus favored gradual reforms promoting a "socially oriented market economy," which became a pretext for doing nothing. As a consequence, the old administration remained intact and the old Soviet bureaucrats held on to their posts. The Soviet economic system persisted, with its state orders, which were remnants of central planning.

Ukraine's early economic policy amounted to the issuing of massive ruble credits financing subsidies to industry and agriculture, while the government tried to restrict inflation through rationing and price controls. Huge budget deficits were monetized by the National Bank of Ukraine (NBU), which led to hyperinflation of 10,155 percent in 1993. This was qualified madness. The advice of international financial institutions got lost in the constitutional chaos, with president, prime minister, and parliament blaming one another.

By 1994, neither plan nor market governed the Ukrainian economic system. The old centrally planned economy stopped functioning, but no market economy emerged. Prices of most essential goods were controlled, although most prices were freely set, and the state strictly managed foreign trade. The government tried but largely failed to control deliveries between state enterprises. Enterprises remained predominantly state-owned. In 1993, the European Bank for Reconstruction and Development (EBRD 1994) assessed that only 15 percent of Ukraine's GDP originated in the private sector.

Output fell like a stone from 1989 to 1994 (figure 1.2). Officially, the total decline in GDP in these five years was 48 percent (UNECE 2004, 80). This drop, however, was offset considerably by the growth of the underground economy, which expanded from 12 percent of total GDP in 1989 to as much as 46 percent of actual GDP in 1995—a large share in comparison with other postcommunist countries (Kaufmann and Kaliberda 1996).

Hyperinflation, which reached 2,730 percent in 1992 and 10,155 percent in 1993 (figure 4.1), was the main cause of this output collapse. Price liberalization led to monthly inflation peaking at 91 percent in December 1993. Hyperinflation disrupted all economic life and demoralized society. It was the result of the maintenance of the ruble zone, excessive monetary expansion, and too large public expenditures (Dabrowski 1994; De Ménil 1997, 2000). The NBU was new and weak, and it was subordinate to the parliament, which often decided to issue huge credits. The NBU pursued no interest rate policy, offering most credits at a subsidized rate of 20 percent per annum, rendering any loan from the NBU a state subsidy.

Ukraine started off with a colossal budget deficit with no constraint on public expenditures. The Ministry of Finance was very weak in the Soviet system, being the state accountant rather than a policymaking unit. The parliament freely decided on large new expenditures. State finances were in shambles. The 1992 budget prescribed a deficit of 2 percent of GDP, but the

Figure 4.1   Annual inflation in Ukraine, 1992–2004

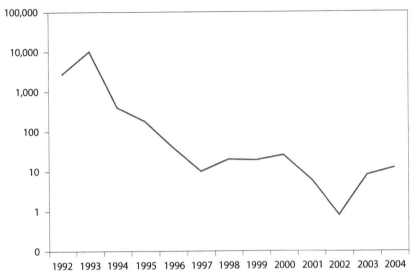

log of rate of inflation

Sources: EBRD (1997, 1999, 2002, 2003, 2004, 2005).

parliament expanded it to an untenable 29 percent of GDP (figure 4.2), which was financed through the hyperinflationary issuance of money. The budget for 1994 was officially balanced with revenues and expenditures reaching 86 percent of GDP! When the illusive revenues stopped at half of the planned share of 86 percent of GDP, which was their usual level, sequestering started, making wage and pension arrears the bane of the 1990s (Dabrowski, Luczyński, and Markiewicz 2000; Banaian 1999).

Contrary to wide expectations, Ukraine's state revenues did not collapse with the Soviet system and hyperinflation but stayed nearly constant at slightly over 40 percent of official GDP because state enterprises paid most of the taxes in advance, and state banks deducted these taxes directly from their bank accounts. The government further increased tax rates. In 1994, the progressive income tax peaked at 90 percent for as modest an income as $100 a month, but nobody paid such taxes. Ukraine's tax system was formally confiscatory, but tax evasion was rampant.

The small communist elite who remained in power designed the postcommunist transition to make money on economic distortions (Åslund 1995, Hellman 1998, Shleifer and Vishny 1998). To maximize their rents, they needed a slow transition. On September 22, 1993, Kravchuk appointed Zviahilsky acting prime minister. Zviahilsky managed Ukraine's largest coal mine in Donetsk in eastern Ukraine. Together Kravchuk and Zviahilsky tried to rebuild a command economy, but their aims were very different. Kravchuk, who knew nothing of economics, although he had a Soviet doctorate in economics, now

Figure 4.2   Consolidated state budget deficit in Ukraine, 1992–2004

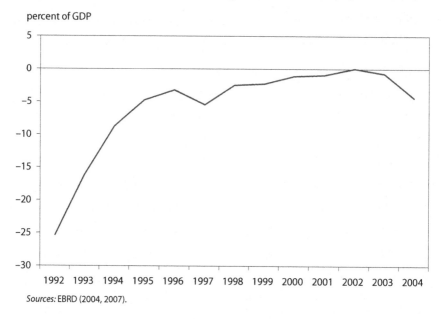

percent of GDP

Sources: EBRD (2004, 2007).

opposed a market economy, while the clever Zviahilsky realized that regulations bred rents to the privileged few, that is, to him and his friends. He regulated prices and foreign trade, allowing state subsidies to cover differentials between controlled prices (Kravchuk 2002, 56–58).

Only Zviahilsky and his business partners reaped benefits from this policy reversal. They controlled foreign trade licensing and made money on arbitrage between low domestic prices of energy, metals, and chemicals and much higher world market prices, keeping these rents in their narrow circle (Wilson 2005, 9). He has thrived as one of the leading businessmen in "old Donetsk" and been a steady member of Ukraine's parliament, being one of the powerbrokers in the Regions party of Ukraine. At 81, he was even reelected in October 2014 and became the dean of the new parliament. His large coal mine Zasiadko is infamous for many fatal mining disasters, in particular the 2007 blast that killed 101 miners.[4]

Several rent-seeking methods evolved in Ukraine. One was to buy metals and chemicals in Ukraine, which were kept cheap domestically because of price regulation, and sell them abroad at the world market price. This required access to metals and export permits. In 1992 commodities accounted for about 40 percent of Ukraine's exports (IMF 1993, 113), and their average domestic price was about 10 percent of the world market price. Hence, rents from exports totaled some $4.1 billion, or 20 percent of the country's GDP, in 1992.

---

4. "Ukraine's mine death toll rises," BBC News, November 20, 2007.

The beneficiaries were managers of state metallurgical companies, commodity traders, foreign trade officials, and some politicians.

The second trick was to import natural gas from Russia at a low subsidized exchange rate and resell it at a higher domestic price. If the government paid for the deliveries because of state guarantees for gas imports, it was even more profitable. The beneficiaries were a small number of gas importers and their government partners, who shared the profits with their Russian partners in Gazprom. Each year, a few Russian officials and a few Ukrainian businessmen shared a few billion dollars. To protect their rents, they elevated the gas trade to a Russian-Ukrainian national conflict.[5]

The third way was subsidized credits. In 1993, when Ukraine experienced 10,155 percent inflation, huge state credits were issued at an interest of 20 percent a year. State credits were therefore sheer gifts, given to a privileged few. Net credit issued to enterprises was no less than 65 percent of GDP in 1992 and 47 percent of GDP in 1993 (calculated from IMF 1993, 109; IMF 1995, 73, 105).

The fourth form of rent seeking was straightforward budget subsidies, which amounted to 8.1 percent of GDP in 1992 and 10.8 percent of GDP in 1993 (IMF 1995, 94). They were concentrated on agriculture and energy, that is, gas and coal. The struggle to receive these subsidies criminalized the energy sector (IMF 1995, 94).

In this way, a small group of privileged insiders usurped a substantial share of GDP in the early years of transition. They accumulated their riches in tax havens abroad, which amounted to capital flight. In 1994, the concept of oligarch was already established in Ukraine. All the main oligarchs traded gas with Russia, as Ihor Bakai, Ukraine's foremost gas trader, stated: "All rich people in Ukraine made their money on Russian gas" (Timoshenko 1998). The essence of enrichment was to buy gas at a low state-regulated price and sell it at a high market price shielded by monopoly.

The social consequences were becoming acute, and the very cohesion of Ukraine was in danger, as it was approaching state bankruptcy. In 1994 the US Central Intelligence Agency (CIA) issued a National Intelligence Estimate entitled "Ukraine: A Nation at Risk," postulating that Ukraine might fail as a state and that it might cease to exist in 5 to 10 years (Pifer 2004).

In July 1994, when Kuchma became president, his five priorities were financial stabilization, privatization, integrity of Ukraine, adoption of a new constitution, and improved relations with Russia and the United States. Within two years he had accomplished these five goals.

In October 1994, Ukraine concluded its first stabilization agreement with the IMF. In the summer of 1996, Ukraine had no inflation, and in September 1996 it introduced the national currency, the hryvnia. In 1995, the government carried out a much-delayed voucher privatization largely based on the Russian

---

5. Good sources are Balmaceda (1998, 2004, 2013), Lovei (1998), Von Hirschhausen (1999), and Global Witness (2006).

Figure 4.3   EBRD Transition Index, Ukraine versus Poland and Russia, 1994–2007

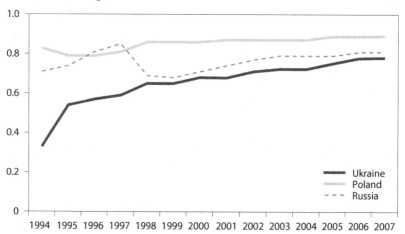

index (0 = low, 1 = high)

EBRD = European Bank for Reconstruction and Development

Note: The formula of this index is 0.3 times EBRD's index for price liberalization and competition policy, 0.3 times EBRD's index for trade and foreign exchange liberalization, and 0.4 times EBRD's index for large-scale privatization, small-scale privatization, and banking reform. Thus this index represents liberalization to 73 percent, while the rest is privatization.

Sources: De Melo and Tenev (1997); Havrylyshyn and Wolf (2001); author's calculations from EBRD (1998, 1999, 2006, 2007).

model. Because of the long delay the quality of the privatization was lower than that in Russia, but most Ukrainian enterprises were privatized, which was a precondition for economic growth. Separatism in Crimea, which had been aggravated by the economic crisis, was peacefully averted in 1995. In June 1996 Ukraine finally adopted the new constitution with a large parliamentary majority and without major political crisis.

After 1996, however, Kuchma lost momentum. The Russian financial crash of August 1998 threw Ukraine into another financial crisis. Still, in the fall of 1999 he was reelected president for a second term. He appointed a reform government that delivered a second dose of reform in 2000, focusing on deregulation.

Initially, Ukraine was far behind both Poland and Russia in market economic reforms as measured by the EBRD transition index (figure 4.3). In 1995, its macroeconomic performance had improved, which this index did not reflect. Despite its gradual progress over the years, it never reached even Russia's rather unsatisfactory level and stayed far behind Poland's reform successes. Yet, the reforms of 2000 were sufficient to kickstart the Ukrainian economy. During the eight years from 2000 to 2007, Ukraine finally started catching up with an average annual growth of 7.5 percent.

Kuchma did not opt for radical reforms. He was satisfied with financial stabilization, privatization, and fast economic growth. Rather than breaking up the post-Soviet system, he managed it through divide and rule, playing the oligarchs as well as the law enforcement agencies against each other in a fashion reminiscent of Boris Yeltsin's rule in Russia. He coped with rather than clamping down on corruption.

Complicated Relationship with Russia

After independence, Russia was Ukraine's most important foreign partner. The two countries had two main outstanding political issues: the division of the Black Sea Fleet and the status of its headquarters, the Sevastopol naval base on Crimea. After his reelection in July 1996 Russian President Yeltsin had sufficient political and physical strength to pursue his long-desired settlement with Ukraine.

On May 28, 1997, the Ukrainian and Russian prime ministers signed three intergovernmental agreements on the division, basing, and cost of the Black Sea Fleet. Ukraine leased the port facilities in Sevastopol to Russia for 20 years (until 2017) for $98 million a year. The lease could be extended for five more years by mutual consent, allowing Sevastopol to remain the headquarters of the Russian Black Sea Fleet (Wolczuk 2002, 29–32, 36–38). Yet Crimea, Sevastopol, and the Black Sea Fleet remained rallying cries for Russian nationalists.

As a follow-up, on May 31, 1997, Russia finally recognized Ukraine's borders by signing the Treaty on Friendship, Cooperation and Partnership with Ukraine. It clarified the two countries' mutual respect for each other's territorial integrity and the inviolability of their borders. Russia also abolished the many trade barriers it had raised against Ukraine. These Russian-Ukrainian agreements were Kuchma's great achievements and the high point of their relationship. By and large, Russia had accepted Ukraine's demands and reconfirmed its recognition of Ukraine's sovereignty of Crimea and Sevastopol.

Trade policy was never the Kremlin's strong suit and was always confused within the former Soviet Union. Trade among the former Soviet republics was not liberalized for the first three years of their independence, 1992–94. It became a preserve for old-style state planners and state trade prevailed (Michalopoulos and Drebentsov 1997, Michalopoulos and Tarr 1996).

In April 1994, all countries in the Commonwealth of Independent States (CIS) except Turkmenistan signed a multilateral free trade agreement (FTA), but it was of low quality and never came into force because Russia did not ratify it. Instead most CIS countries concluded similar bilateral FTAs with one another. Russia and Ukraine did so in 1993, and it has been the legal basis for their trade. Yet, whenever any powerful constituency so desired, both countries frequently resorted to protectionist measures, such as imposing sudden quotas, tariffs, or outright prohibitions, which often disrupted Russian-Ukrainian trade. Since neither was a member of the World Trade Organization (WTO), they had no recourse to any rules-based dispute settlement mechanisms.

In 2003, Russian president Vladimir Putin turned toward Ukraine because of the upcoming presidential elections there in late 2004. He wanted to tie Ukraine closer to Russia and its closest partners, Belarus and Kazakhstan. He presented a new scheme, the Common Economic Space (CES), designed to be acceptable to Ukraine. It was multilateral, excluded the Central Asian countries, and was exclusively economic.

On February 23, 2003, the CES was launched with great fanfare in Moscow, with a common declaration by the four presidents of Russia, Ukraine, Kazakhstan, and Belarus. The CES was designed to be a customs union as well as a currency union, coordinating the four countries' entry into the WTO. In September 2003, they concluded an agreement that was ratified by all four parliaments. President Kuchma accepted the CES with hesitation, as did his prime minister, Yanukovych, but three prominent ministers resigned in protest against the CES. After the Orange Revolution, the scheme died (Åslund 2009, 170–71).

The Orange Revolution: Political Chaos Again, 2004–10

The Orange Revolution was Ukraine's epic moment. For one month from November 22 until December 26, Ukraine dominated global news. People who had never heard of Ukraine learned that this was a brave, well-organized, peaceful, and democratic nation. The three political leaders Viktor Yushchenko, Yulia Tymoshenko, and Viktor Yanukovych became known globally in spite of their difficult names. Everything worked out peacefully and democratically. It was a moment of national euphoria and pride. Ukraine seemed as if it could do no wrong.[6]

Seldom has a major political event been so filled with drama and hope. For years, the presidential election had been scheduled for the end of October 2004, coinciding with the end of President Kuchma's second term, because the 1996 constitution did not allow a president more than two consecutive terms. Moreover, Kuchma's popularity was in the doldrums, making his reelection implausible. The old regime seemed tired, divided, and increasingly authoritarian, while the booming economy was taken as a given.

Ukrainians faced a clear-cut choice. For the foreseeable future, the presidential elections represented their only chance to gain greater freedom and more rule of law. Russia clarified that the other option was Putin-style authoritarianism. Askold Krushelnycky (2006, 1) summarized the situation: "Ukrainians recognized they were at a historic crossroads: these were the most important elections ever held in their country and the vote would determine whether Ukraine chartered a path westwards towards democracy, or whether it would be subsumed in a putative new authoritarian Russian empire."

When I visited Kyiv in July 2004, people said that Yushchenko would win the real presidential election but that Yanukovych would fraudulently steal it.

---

6. This section draws on Åslund and McFaul (2006), Wilson (2005), and Karatnycky (2005). Stanisławski (2005) offers a useful summary of facts.

Then, protesters would take to the streets and repeat the Georgian Rose Revolution of November 2003. The decisive issue was whether sufficiently many people would take to the streets fast enough to mount a popular revolution, or if the protests would dissipate. This scenario played out exactly as predicted, so both sides were well prepared (Åslund 2009, 175–76).

The Orange Revolution erupted because Kuchma's candidate, Prime Minister Yanukovych, lost, but he stole the runoff between him and Yushchenko. Kyiv saw several cold winter days of tense standoffs between hundreds of thousands of protesters and thousands of riot police. The president refused to order the riot police to shoot at the demonstrators because he was intent on retiring in peace and freedom in his country.

A roundtable was held with Kuchma, Yanukovych, Yushchenko, and EU mediators Javier Solana, high representative for foreign affairs, and Polish president Alexander Kwaśniewski. On December 8, 2004, all parties agreed on a rerun of the runoff on December 26 and the adoption of substantial amendments to the 1996 constitution. The political system was transformed from a purely presidential to a parliamentary-presidential system, giving more power to the parliament. On December 26, Yushchenko won a free and fair election with 52 percent versus 44 percent for Yanukovych.[7]

Yet the aftermath of the Orange Revolution was an anticlimax. Yushchenko turned out to be irresponsible and incapable. Five years of political chaos ensued with four governments, two parliamentary elections, and two major gas conflicts with Russia. In addition to Yushchenko's incompetence, the chaos was caused by the absence of a governing coalition in parliament and a new, imperfect constitution. Captive, competing courts aggravated disputes. Little was done to reform the state or rein in corruption.

On New Year's Day 2005, the newly elected president took a holiday for ten days in the Carpathian mountains. He had appointed a working group of eight Orange leaders, who were supposed to agree on the composition of the new government, but Yushchenko had given them no instructions and refused to take phone calls. Since all its members wanted to become prime minister, the working group agreed on nothing.

On January 23, Yushchenko was inaugurated and he appointed Yulia Tymoshenko prime minister. After appointing his administration, Yushchenko went on a world tour to celebrate his victory. When he finally started paying attention to Ukraine, his appointees had fallen out in vicious infighting without accomplishing much on policy. In early September 2005, he sacked them all. The Orange coalition government had fallen victim to revolutionary hubris.

Yushchenko, Tymoshenko, and Yanukovych dominated Ukrainian politics from 2005 to 2010. All three appeared center-right and favored European integration. Yushchenko and Tymoshenko were heroes of the Orange Revolution with support in western Ukraine. Yushchenko represented a broad center-right coalition, in which he was the moderator rather than leader. Tymoshenko

---

7. Central Election Commission of Ukraine, www.cvk.gov.ua (accessed on July 18, 2008).

commanded her own strictly disciplined bloc, which was more focused on her than on ideology. As former governor of Donetsk oblast, Yanukovych represented Donbas and the Russian speakers in eastern and southern Ukraine, but most of all he represented the big businessmen in Donetsk, especially Rinat Akhmetov.

Ironically, all three came from the east, Yushchenko from Sumy oblast, Tymoshenko from Dnipropetrovsk, and Yanukovych from Donetsk. Only Yushchenko was an original Ukrainian speaker. The three had clearly different views on one issue: the North Atlantic Treaty Organization (NATO). Yushchenko favored membership, while Yanukovych just wanted to cooperate with NATO, and Tymoshenko avoided saying anything. Each was supported by specific big businessmen.

The next five years witnessed a parlor game with these three players. Each of them led a big party in parliament, and no government could be formed without two of them, but they never concluded a tenable agreement. Tymoshenko was prime minister from February to September 2005 and again from December 2007 to February 2010. Yanukovych was prime minister from August 2006 to December 2007. Yushchenko loyalist Yuriy Yekhanurov served as prime minister from September 2005 to August 2006. Only Yekhanurov's government worked well, not least because Yushchenko did not oppose him. During Yanukovych's term and Tymoshenko's second term, Yushchenko vetoed most of their decisions.

The parliament was a circus with many factions and numerous independent members. The Orange Revolution had transformed public opinion, and many parliamentarians defected from the old establishment parties to be with any incumbent government, but they kept floating. The Orange parliamentary support peaked at 377 votes out of 450 when Tymoshenko was confirmed as prime minister, but soon the parliament had no operative majority. The government had to solicit support in parliament for each vote.

No early elections were held, and politicians focused on the parliamentary elections scheduled in March 2006, pursuing populist policies to maximize their votes. The March 2006 elections punished Yushchenko's Our Ukraine party, which got only 81 seats. The Yulia Tymoshenko Bloc gained strength, receiving 129 seats. The winner was Yanukovych's Regions party with 186 seats. Socialists and communists held the balance with 33 and 21 seats, respectively.[8] Seemingly endless negotiations over a new government ensued. In August, more than four months after the elections, Yanukovych persuaded the communists and socialists to form a coalition government. His government harbored the same main ministers as his cabinet from 2002 to 2005. The old Kuchma oligarchy seemed to have been restored. In hindsight, Yushchenko should have dissolved the parliament and called new elections immediately after his inauguration in January 2005, as newly elected president Petro Poroshenko did in August 2014.

---

8. Central Election Commission of Ukraine, www.cvk.gov.ua (accessed on September 31, 2007).

The December 2004 constitution came into force in January 2006. Rather than clarifying the situation it muddled the waters. Yushchenko and Yanukovych fought tooth and nail over their respective powers, and in April 2007 Yushchenko dissolved the parliament against Yanukovych's protests. Eventually, Yushchenko and Yanukovych reached a compromise on early parliamentary elections in September 2007. This time, Yulia Tymoshenko Bloc was the main victor with 156 seats. Together with Our Ukraine's 72 seats, these two parties had a slight majority of 228, that is, only two seats.[9] Yushchenko and Tymoshenko concluded a substantial coalition agreement, and on December 18 Tymoshenko was confirmed as prime minister.

Strangely, from that moment onward Yushchenko did whatever he could to block Tymoshenko's every step, using his veto indiscriminately as he had done against Prime Minister Yanukovych. In practice, the government did not have a parliamentary majority and could pass only vital legislation.

Yushchenko had effectively switched sides. In the presidential elections in early 2010 and the parliamentary elections in October 2012, he was perceived as a "technical" candidate for Yanukovych, adopting a new extreme nationalist position to embarrass and discredit Tymoshenko. He even testified against Tymoshenko in the political court case Yanukovych instigated to imprison her. He and his family stayed in the official presidential residence at considerable public expense until February 2014.[10]

Behind each political leader stood major businesspeople. Yanukovych had the strongest and most steady support from three big businessmen: Rinat Akhmetov, the steel and mining king from Donetsk, the gas trader Dmytro Firtash, and the Donetsk businessman Andriy Kliuev. Yushchenko's Our Ukraine benefited from the support of four big businessmen: the chocolate king Petro Poroshenko, the two nuclear power partners David Zhvania and Mykola Martynenko, and the trucker Yevhen Chervonenko. The Industrial Union of Donbas, a competitor of Akhmetov in Donetsk, supported the Yulia Tymoshenko Bloc. Privat Group, the biggest business group after Akhmetov's, kept arm's-length distance from the parties, switching between Yushchenko and Tymoshenko. Several businesspeople who had been politically important under President Kuchma reduced their political roles: His son-in-law Victor Pinchuk left parliament, where he had previously had a party faction of 40 deputies (Åslund 2009).

Several big businessmen sat in parliament with large subfactions of their own. The common view was that two-thirds of the deputies were dollar millionaires. Not only the parliament but also the government and the presidential administration were captured. Poroshenko became national defense and security advisor, while both Zhvania and Chervonenko became ministers.

---

9. Ibid.

10. "Yushchenko s`ekhal s gosdachi" ["Yushchenko Moved out of the State Dacha"], LB.ua, March 21, 2014.

Yushchenko took a gas trader, Oleksandr Tretyakov, as his first assistant. No attempt was made to handle conflicts of interest, which on the contrary were allowed to thrive.

Although the three leading political parties were officially center-right, calling for liberalization and privatization, they were primarily guided by business interests. Each government adopted a formal program but it was abandoned, leaving the government without a common ideology or program. Yushchenko's secretariat was a wonder of disorganization not seen since Kravchuk's days.

Stalemate over Reprivatization, 2005

In February 2005, the Orange government came to power with Ukrainians earnestly hoping for earth-shattering reforms. At long last corruption would be purged and the state administration would start functioning. Several organizations had formulated concrete reform programs with a broad consensus.[11] Alas, no comprehensive reforms were launched. Instead, the Orange coalition plunged into internecine strife.

The all-consuming issue for the new government became reprivatization, that is, the renationalization and renewed sale of state enterprises that had been privatized at low prices to favored insiders. During the presidential election campaign, Yushchenko campaigned for one repeat privatization, the steelworks Kryvorizhstal, but now he went further. On February 10, 2005, he stated: "We will revoke every privatization case that was conducted in breach of law."[12] Prime Minister Tymoshenko took the lead. She called for the reconsideration of 3,000 privatizations, whereas Yushchenko tried to limit the number to 20 or 30.

The reprivatization discussion was highly personalized. Tymoshenko focused on enterprises belonging to Pinchuk and Akhmetov, the two beneficiaries of the Kryvorizhstal privatization. Their two competitors, Privat Group and the Industrial Union of Donbas, which were closer to the Orange government, welcomed reprivatization, hoping to seize assets from Pinchuk and Akhmetov. The other big businessmen who had financed the Yushchenko campaign reckoned it was payback time. The courts revoked the June 2004 sale of Kryvorizhstal for $800 million, and a new sale, or reprivatization, for $4.8 billion was successfully organized. As a result, the government gained 2 percent of GDP but lost three to four times more in economic growth in 2005. Far more important, it lost the opportunity to fight corruption and pursue successful market economic reform.

At a lower level, reprivatization became reminiscent of corporate raiding, the illegal seizure of private enterprises, which is the scourge of Ukrainian capi-

---

11. For example, Blue Ribbon Commission for Ukraine (2005), which I co-chaired. Other programs were presented by EBA (2004) and OECD (2004).

12. Dragon Capital, *Dragon Daily*, February 11, 2005.

talism. By March 2, the prosecutor general announced that criminal cases had been initiated against some 2,000 people because they had violated the law during privatization.[13] One opinion poll showed that 71 percent of Ukrainians supported a revision of privatization of the biggest state enterprises, and only 11 percent preferred to leave everything as it was.[14] However, throughout the postcommunist world, privatization of large enterprises has been unpopular after the fact, although it is vital for the success of both democracy and market economy (Åslund 2013a). That reprivatization is a popular idea does not mean that it should be undertaken. The Orange Revolution had originally aimed at introducing the rule of law, but the government penalized some oligarchs and favored others. The protracted public debate over reprivatization undermined property rights and business confidence, and the increased tax pressure aggravated the burden.

Soon, Ukrainian society woke up from the euphoria of the Orange Revolution. In late March, the leading intellectual weekly *Zerkalo nedeli* complained about "revolutionary populism."[15] In mid-May 2005, Yushchenko changed his own position on reprivatization and started scolding his prime minister for her relentless campaign for it, forgetting his own statements: "From the first day, I said that neither I nor my team aim at the nationalization or re-privatization of any object of property."[16]

Tymoshenko's populist economic policy resulted in economic growth falling from 12 percent in 2004 to –1.6 percent in August 2005, by about one percentage point each month. Because of the government chaos few laws were enacted. Tymoshenko's defenders praised the adoption of several WTO laws and the elimination of 3,600 unnecessary regulations, but the business community hardly noticed any improvement. After her departure, economic growth was quickly restored, while reforms remained stalled.

Resolution of a Severe Financial Crisis, 2008–09

Like many other emerging economies, Ukraine enjoyed magnificent growth averaging 7.5 percent for eight straight years during the global credit and commodity boom, 2000–07. European economic convergence appeared a realistic option.

---

13. "Genprokuratura obvinyaet 2 tysyach chelovek v hezakonnoi privatizatsii" ["The General Prosecutor Accuses 2,000 People of Illegal Privatization"], *Ukrainskaya pravda*, March 2, 2005.

14. "Bolshinstvo ukraintsev podderzhivaet ideyu peresmotra itogov privatizatsii" ["A Majority of Ukrainians Supports the Idea of a Revision of the Results of Privatization"], *Ukrainskaya pravda*, May 14, 2005.

15. Nataliya Yatsenko, "Revolyutsionnaya byudzhetnaya tselesoobraznost" ["Revolutionary Budgetary Expediency"], *Zerkalo nedeli*, March 26, 2005.

16. "Yushchenko ne otdast Krivorizhstal gosudarstvu, no eshche dolzhen podumat" ["Yushchenko Does Not Give Kryvorizhstal to the State, But He Needs to Think More"], *Ukrainskaya pravda*, May 13, 2005.

On paper, the government had been fiscally conservative, with a budget close to balance in 2005–07. The public debt shrank to 12 percent of GDP in 2007. With international currency reserves of $37 billion, Ukraine seemed in good financial shape (IMF 2014e). Furthermore, foreign direct investment largely financed the moderate current account deficit.

But the Ukrainian economy was highly cyclical, with steel dominating its exports. In 2008 the Ukrainian economy was seriously overheated with annualized inflation peaking at 31 percent in May. The problem did not lie in the state budget but in too rapid credit expansion spurred by large capital inflows. In particular, West European banks were buying private Ukrainian banks. The yields on Ukraine's eurobonds had shot up to 20 percent a year, a level characteristic of countries in external default.

The Lehman Brothers bankruptcy on September 15, 2008, delivered a hard blow to Ukraine, as access to international financing suddenly stopped. An eerie gloom engulfed Kyiv in early October 2008. Many large construction projects came to an abrupt halt. Until then, office space had been impossible to find at any price. Now it was abundantly available at a fraction of the previous rent.

From July to October 2008, global prices of many commodities, notably steel, fell by half. The Ukrainian steel companies cut production drastically, and laid off workers. Falling steel exports aggravated Ukraine's trade deficit. Production in key industries, such as steel, mining, and construction, plunged by 50 percent in two months. In October 2008, the government had no choice but to turn to the IMF for emergency funding. On November 5, the Executive Board of the IMF approved a two-year Stand-By Arrangement program of $16.4 billion for Ukraine.

The IMF had learned its lesson from the East Asian crisis in 1997–98, when it was criticized for escalating its demands for fiscal discipline and structural reform to counter crony capitalism. Now it retreated to the more rudimentary old Washington Consensus, as formulated by John Williamson (1990), focusing on three basic IMF requirements: a fully financed budget, a realistic exchange rate, and recapitalization of the banking system. The drawback, however, was that Ukraine was not forced to undertake significant structural reforms, which it needed badly.

GDP fell by 14.8 percent in 2009. Ukraine let its exchange rate depreciate, which almost eliminated the current account deficit of 7 percent of GDP in 2008. The budget deficit grew with falling output, but as elsewhere the IMF accepted a large deficit and contributed to its financing. The budget deficit reached 10.8 percent of GDP in 2009, including bank recapitalization. Ukraine never had any serious problem with its international reserves, which bottomed out at $24 billion, more than one-fifth of GDP, at the beginning of 2010. Unemployment peaked at 9 percent of the labor force, as Ukrainians accepted large wage cuts without protest. Virtually every household had a private agricultural plot, which helped the poor through subsistence agriculture.

By the summer of 2009, Ukraine had received three tranches of almost

$11 billion from the IMF, and the acute crisis was over.[17] In the fall of 2009, the IMF withheld the remaining tranches. The main reason was that the parliamentary opposition passed a law on social standards that would have boosted public expenditures by 2.5 to 7 percent of GDP in 2010 and thus have busted the budget. Yanukovych's Regions party and President Yushchenko spearheaded this law.

By the end of 2009, economic growth returned to Ukraine. Public expenditures had risen from a high level of 44 percent of GDP in 2005–07 to 49 percent of GDP in 2009 and 2010. The budget deficit was only reduced to 8.1 percent of GDP in spite of an IMF program (IMF 2014e). Ukraine had gone through a severe financial crisis but failed to undertake any of the badly needed structural reforms. The Tymoshenko government had no chance of doing so in the face of united opposition from Yanukovych and Yushchenko.

Conflicts with Russia over Gas and NATO

Ukraine's relationship with Russia has always been fraught with conflict. Since independence, Ukraine had major problems with its gas trade with Russia, which dominated Russian-Ukrainian trade because Ukraine imported large volumes and transited even bigger volumes to European countries.[18]

This gas trade remained in a time warp from the early postcommunist transition. The natural gas originated from the state-dominated Russian giant corporation Gazprom, and it was sold to Ukraine through dubious private gas traders. The prices Russia charged Ukraine for gas were below international prices, consistently $42 per 1,000 cubic meters (mcm) from 1996 to 2003 (Balmaceda 2013, 124). Ukraine did not pay in cash but offered transit services in return and was always in arrears. In Ukraine, most of the Russian gas was sold to industry at much higher prices. Much of the gas was traded with Turkmenistan rather than Russia (Global Witness 2006).

A few gas traders in Russia and Ukraine made fortunes. Often Ukrainian gas traders did not pay for the gas, passing on their debt to Russia to the Ukrainian state through formal or informal state guarantees. Gazprom did not mind large arrears, hoping to use them to acquire Ukrainian gas pipelines and other assets, as it did in several other postcommunist countries, such as Belarus and Moldova. Gazprom's founder, Russia's Prime Minister Viktor Chernomyrdin, controlled Gazprom, while President Kuchma functioned as an arbiter between Ukrainian gas traders (Balmaceda 2013).

At the time of the Orange Revolution, these obsolete nonmarket arrangements were breaking down for several reasons. In 2001, President Putin took control of Gazprom. From that time until 2008, European gas prices rose steadily. Putin pushed aggressively for higher prices, wanting either more cash

---

17. "IMF Completes Second Review Under Stand-By Arrangement with Ukraine and Approves US$3.3 Billion Disbursement," IMF Press Release No. 09/271, July 28, 2009.

18. This section largely draws on Balmaceda (2013, 93–153).

or Ukrainian gas assets. The Orange revolutionaries criticized the murky gas trade, since it was a key source of enrichment of the country's oligarchs. They called for transparency, for cash payments instead of barter, and for Gazprom to pay higher transit fees to Ukraine.

In the fall of 2005, the latent Russian-Ukrainian gas conflict became acute. Russia wanted to raise the gas price for Ukraine from $50 per mcm first to $95, then $150, and finally $230. When no agreement was reached, on January 1, 2006, Gazprom stopped its gas deliveries to Ukraine for three days. Then, it suddenly accepted a gas price of $95 per mcm, although Germany was paying $296 per mcm at the time. However, a new intermediary took over this trade, the offshore trading company RosUkrEnergo. Gazprom owned half of the company and it later became public that 45 percent belonged to the then unknown Ukrainian gas trader Dmytro Firtash.

This agreement had serious drawbacks. Instead of achieving transparency, it brought in a dubious new intermediary. The gas price rose haphazardly. In 2007, it surged to $135 per mcm and in 2008 to $180 per mcm, and nobody could tell why. RosUkrEnergo was given control not only over the gas trade between Russia and Ukraine but also over a substantial part of the highly profitable sales of gas to industry in Ukraine, squeezing out state-owned Naftogaz Ukrainy, which was left with lossmaking sales to the population at low prices. Yushchenko controlled the gas trade at the time so this was his deal (Balmaceda 2013, 123–29).

In January 2009, in the midst of its frightful financial crisis, Ukraine experienced an even worse gas crisis with Russia. At the time, Prime Minister Tymoshenko was competing with President Yushchenko over control of the Ukrainian gas sector. Russia was pushing hard for a higher gas price, seemingly intent on exploiting Ukraine's political division and economic weakness. Tymoshenko was calling for transparency, a European price formula, and the exclusion of all intermediaries, notably RosUkrEnergo, while Yushchenko wanted to keep the old arrangement with RosUkrEnergo.

On January 1, in the midst of another cold winter, Russia cut off gas supplies to Ukraine and after a week its gas transit through Ukraine to various European countries. Much of Europe was deprived of gas for two weeks. On the night of January 18–19, Russian prime minister Putin, who had stepped down as president in 2008, settled a deal with Tymoshenko in Moscow, making evident the political nature of the gas conflict.

The January 2009 Russian-Ukrainian gas agreement changed this trade substantially. The main agreement was published, finally bringing some transparency to this trade. Tymoshenko managed to eliminate RosUkrEnergo and Firtash. The agreement contained a price formula based on the European pricing principle, but the "European" base price was far too high, though Tymoshenko achieved a substantial discount for the first year. Ukraine committed itself to purchasing much more gas than it needed, and the agreement contained a strict "take-or-pay" clause, obliging Ukraine to pay for the whole volume whether it took the gas or not. The contract guaranteed a minimum

Russian gas transit through Ukraine of 110 billion cubic meters per year, which Gazprom never took seriously, while it fixed a low transit fee for ten years. Gazprom was awarded the right to sell one-quarter of the imported gas directly to industrial users in Ukraine (Balmaceda 2013, 134).

This agreement was a victory for Tymoshenko over Yushchenko, but most of all a triumph for Putin over a divided Ukraine. But, by cutting off gas for two weeks to Europe, Gazprom had tarnished its reputation as a reliable supplier, leading to a lasting decline in its sales to Europe, which started developing alternative sources of supply and larger storage capacities. Formally this was a ten-year agreement, but only conditions unfavorable to Ukraine were fixed for ten years. The unfavorable nature of the agreement raised suspicions over Tymoshenko's motives, and in 2011 Yanukovych had her prosecuted and sentenced to jail for seven years for "abuse of power," which was not proven during the farcical court proceeding.

Another major bone of contention between Putin and Ukraine was NATO. President Yushchenko aspired to Ukraine's full integration into the Euro-Atlantic community, including NATO. In January 2008, Yushchenko asked NATO for a membership action plan (MAP) to be granted to Ukraine at its summit in Bucharest in April 2008, which unleashed Moscow's wrath. US president George W. Bush supported Ukraine's MAP, and so did several new eastern NATO members, but most old European NATO members opposed it because of limited domestic Ukrainian support for NATO and staunch Russian opposition.

NATO did not offer Ukraine a MAP at its summit in Bucharest in April 2008, although its communiqué stated boldly: "NATO welcomes Ukraine's and Georgia's Euro-Atlantic aspirations for membership in NATO. We agreed today that these countries will become members of NATO.... MAP is the next step for Ukraine and Georgia on their direct way to membership. Today we make clear that we support these countries' applications for MAP."[19]

President Putin was also allowed to attend the NATO summit. In a closed meeting on April 4, 2008, he intimidated Ukraine, effectively threatening to end its existence:

- "As for Ukraine, one third of the population are ethnic Russians. According to official census statistics, there are 17 million ethnic Russians there, out of a population of 45 million... Southern Ukraine is entirely populated with ethnic Russians."

- "Ukraine, in its current form, came to be in Soviet-era days.... From Russia the country obtained vast territories in what is now eastern and southern Ukraine...."

- "Crimea was simply given to Ukraine by a CPSU Politburo's decision,

---

19. Bucharest Summit Declaration issued by the Heads of State and Government participating in the meeting of the North Atlantic Council in Bucharest on April 3, 2008, www.nato.int.

which was not even supported with appropriate government procedures that are normally applicable to territory transfers."

- "If the NATO issue is added there, along with other problems, this may bring Ukraine to the verge of existence as a sovereign state."[20]

In a sharp reversal of the policy of his predecessor Boris Yeltsin, Putin challenged Ukraine's legitimacy as a sovereign state and its territorial integrity. He claimed that its composition was artificial, its borders arbitrary, and the 1954 transfer of Crimea to Ukraine illegal. He ignored that Russia had guaranteed all these rights to Ukraine in half a dozen ratified international treaties. The NATO summit in Bucharest closed the road to NATO membership for Ukraine.

***

The Orange Revolution left Ukrainians with a bitter aftertaste. A popular conclusion was that there was little difference between Ukrainian politicians regardless of political color. They were all equally corrupt. Neither state nor economy had been modernized. The economic system had not changed. Corruption and oligarchs continued to rule the country. The only difference was that some oligarchs had risen at the cost of other oligarchs. People perceived two clear differences. The Orange camp was more incompetent and more pro-European than Yanukovych, who favored somewhat closer relations with Russia. Yet, Ukraine had become a free and full democracy, according to Freedom House, which people did not appreciate much. Partly they took democracy as a given, and partly they reacted against the obvious dysfunction of the Ukrainian state.

---

20. "What Precisely Vladimir Putin Said at Bucharest," *Zerkalo nedeli*, April 19, 2008.

5

The Yanukovych Regime: The Ultimate Predation, 2010–14

Whatever Tymoshenko did, I will do the opposite.

—Former president Viktor Yanukovych[1]

In hindsight, it is difficult to understand how Viktor Yanukovych could have won the presidential elections in February 2010. As the Ukrainian political scientist Serhiy Kudelia (2014, 20) put it: "In the wake of the Orange Revolution, Yanukovych seemed done. His failed attempt to steal the bitterly contested 2004 presidential election, coupled with humiliating revelations about his criminal record (as a young man he spent several years behind bars for robbery and assault), should have put to rest any further political hopes."

"Yanukovych was born to a poor family in the industrial Donets Basin, and his brushes with the law in his late teens and early twenties resulted in a pair of jail terms."[2] In the 1990s, he made his political career in Ukraine's easternmost region of Donetsk, which attracted attention for high-level murders in the mid-1990s.[3] Yanukovych had surged as the top politician of Rinat Akhmetov, Donetsk's king of metallurgy and mining. Akhmetov had risen to prominence after a head of his business clan, Akhat Bragin, was killed in 1995. Akhmetov replaced Bragin as the chairman of the Shakhtyar soccer club,[4] and since his formation of his holding company System Capital Management in 2000, he has been ranked as the richest man in Ukraine. Yanukovych advanced to regional governor from 1997 to 2002. In 2002–05 and again 2006–07, he was prime minister of Ukraine. In 2004 as well as 2010, he was the presidential candidate of Ukraine's foremost oligarchs.

---

1. Interview with *Korrespondent* magazine, October 1, 2009.

2. "Viktor Yanukovych," *Encyclopaedia Britannica*, www.britannica.com/EBchecked/topic/1010118/Viktor-Yanukovych (accessed on January 14, 2015).

3. "Akhat Bragin," *Kyiv Post*, December 10, 2008; Åslund (2009, 113).

4. "Akhat Bragin," *Kyiv Post*.

Yanukovych won mainly because the Orange rule had discredited itself, seeming to be as corrupt as the Donetsk group but more incompetent. Yanukovych was perceived as an effective executive. Many thought that unlike Viktor Yushchenko he could get things done. But he did not have a reputation for honesty. After his ouster, people entered his palace outside Kyiv and marveled at the obvious embezzlement of state treasures. People even talked about making it a "museum of corruption."[5] On January 12, 2015, Interpol declared him wanted on charges of "Misappropriation, embezzlement or conversion of property by malversation, if committed in respect of an especially gross amount, or by an organized group."[6]

He was the candidate of two constituencies. One was the Russian-speaking south and east, which accounted for almost half the country, giving him a captive vote of nearly 40 percent of Ukraine. His other constituency was the rich and powerful, who trusted he would safeguard and reinforce their wealth. He sounded more liberal than Yushchenko, advocating deregulation, lower taxes, and European integration.

Initially, as expected, Yanukovych restored the oligarchy. Then for half a year he attempted economic reform. Soon, however, corruption at the top level reached a new apogee, when Yanukovych developed "capitalism in one family." The economic outcome was, not surprisingly, stagnation. The key bone of contention both with Russia and domestically was the European Association Agreement.

Oligarchy Restored

On February 7, 2010, Yanukovych won the presidential elections in a runoff with 49 percent against Yulia Tymoshenko's 45.5 percent, with the balance voting against both candidates. As usual, participation was impressive at 69 percent, although people claimed to be tired of politics. The elections were orderly and democratic.

Eighteen candidates participated in the first round on January 17, but the real choice was between the eastern candidate Yanukovych and the western candidate Tymoshenko with her signature blond braid. Both of them had been prime minister twice, and incumbent Prime Minister Tymoshenko had held that post since December 2007. As expected, Yanukovych received 35 percent of the votes in the first round and Tymoshenko 25 percent, because the east was politically more consolidated than the west. In the second round, Tymoshenko caught up but not fully (Åslund 2010a).

To outside observers, the outcome of these elections was extraordinary. Yanukovych represented top oligarchs of ill repute. Why would anybody vote for a man who was perceived to have stolen the 2004 elections through mas-

---

5. Andrew Higgins, "Ukraine Palace Is Still Emblem of Dysfunction," *New York Times*, September 8, 2014.

6. "Ukraine ex-leader Yanukovych wanted by Interpol." BBC, January 12, 2015.

sive fraud and significant repression? How could he win a reasonably free and fair election?

There were at least five explanations. First, regional loyalties trumped politics. Every Ukrainian election has been a vote of the west and the center against the east and the south. As the east and the west are similar in size, each side tends to win every second time, since they mobilize against one another. It was eastern Ukraine's turn to win, and Yanukovych was its candidate.

Second, the Yushchenko administration had been spectacularly chaotic and unable to rule. Hardly any reforms were adopted during the five years of Yushchenko's presidency (Havrylyshyn 2014), and corruption seemed as bad as before (Transparency International 2013). Since Tymoshenko had been prime minister for half that period, Yushchenko's failures were also blamed on her. Many educated Ukrainians opposed both candidates, whom they saw as members of the political old guard.

Third, Ukraine had endured a horrendous financial crisis in 2008–09 and the standard of living had plummeted. Even though economic growth returned at the end of 2009, the economic failure weighed upon the Orange rulers.

Fourth, Yushchenko acted as a "technical" spoiler candidate on the extreme nationalist right against Tymoshenko in the 2010 elections. He tried to attract nationalist votes from her and force her further in the direction of Ukrainian nationalism to scare off centrist voters from her toward Yanukovych.

Finally, Yanukovych was the candidate of most of the oligarchs, notably Akhmetov, Dmytro Firtash, and Andriy Kliuev. As a consequence, he had far more financing and television advertisements than Tymoshenko. In this situation, it was actually impressive that Tymoshenko lost by only 3.5 percent, which demonstrated her campaign skills and the division of the country. Ukraine's liberal and democratic voters were devastated.

On March 11, Yanukovych formed his new government. It was a coalition with a majority of 239 out of 450 parliamentarians. The coalition partners were Yanukovych's Regions party (172 deputies), the communists (27 deputies), the Lytvyn Bloc (named for Speaker Volodymyr Lytvyn; 20 deputies), and 20 deputies who had abandoned the opposition parties, the Yulia Tymoshenko Bloc and Yushchenko's Our Ukraine. In essence, this was a Regions government, with a composition strikingly similar to Yanukovych's two governments from 2002–05 and 2006–07. It can also be described as a coalition of nine oligarchic groups, and the cabinet consisted of several big Donetsk businessmen.

The main clans were Prime Minister Mykola Azarov's subfaction of old Donetsk comprising Russophile eastern Ukrainian officials. The Donetsk top businessmen Akhmetov and Kliuev each led one oligarchic clan. The gas trader Firtash headed a third oligarchic group, which controlled the energy portfolios. Kliuev became first deputy prime minister and Akhmetov's business partner Borys Kolesnikov became deputy prime minister for Euro 2012 and soon for infrastructure. The apparent purpose of this government was to restore oligarchy and facilitate the enrichment of the oligarchic factions close to Yanukovych. The government was stuffed with big businessmen and abounded with conflicts of interest.

Yanukovych quickly consolidated power. He controlled the presidential administration, the government, the parliament, and also the courts. Swiftly after the presidential elections, he made hundreds of political appointments. Yanukovych steamrolled one law after the other through an obedient parliament, replacing Yushchenko's gridlock. Kuchma's style of ruling had been quite different, balancing various constituencies against one another, law enforcement agencies as well as big businessmen and regions.

No Ukrainian president had enjoyed such vast powers, but Yanukovych was not satisfied. On October 1, the Constitutional Court, which he controlled, abolished the parliamentary-presidential constitution of 2004 and restored the presidential constitution of 1996, giving the president greater power. The local elections in October 2010 were rated by objective outside observers as the dirtiest elections since independence. Freedom House (2011) downgraded Ukraine to only partially free and Reporters without Borders relegated it to 131st out of 178 countries in terms of press freedom.[7]

In August 2011, Tymoshenko was arrested and sentenced to seven years in prison for abuse of power in a blatantly flawed court proceeding.

Brief Economic Reform in 2010

Yanukovych presented himself as a committed market economic reformer. He soon visited Brussels, Moscow, and Washington in that order. He adopted an extensive coalition program called "Stability and Reform." It did not mention the European Union, but otherwise it was a decent market economic reform program. He set up a Reform Committee with himself as chairman.[8] He established a score of working groups headed by top officials and with broad participation. Yet Yanukovych used the need for economic reforms as an argument for his reining in democratic freedoms. Politically, his reign was certainly dynamic, with febrile legislative activity.

Yanukovych's first big task was to reduce the price of gas from Russia by 30 percent. On April 21, he achieved a lower Russian gas price by extending the Russian lease on the Sevastopol naval base for 25 years until 2042. He adopted a realistic budget for 2010, with an official budget deficit at 5.3 percent of GDP, below the 6 percent of GDP demanded by the International Monetary Fund (IMF). In June, Yanukovych presented an ambitious market economic

---

7. Reporters without Borders, 2010 World Press Freedom Index, http://en.rsf.org/press-freedom-index-2010,1034.html.

8. "Yanukovych nashel sebe novuyu dolzhnost" ["Yanukovych Found Himself in a New Position"], *Ukrainskaya pravda*, March 17, 2010.

reform program for his five years in power.[9] In July, he concluded a two-and-a-half-year Stand-By Arrangement program with the IMF backed by $15 billion in credits.[10] Ukraine swiftly carried out the prior actions required by the IMF, such as tightening the state budget and raising gas prices for consumers.

The "reforms" that followed these striking steps, however, benefited only a few big businessmen. Yanukovych favored privatizations, but they were neither transparent nor competitive and generated surprisingly small revenues. Ukraine's national telecommunications company, Ukrtelecom, was sold to the single buyer who was allowed to bid, an Austrian private equity fund, at the minimum price, while the ultimate buyer remained unknown for some time.[11] Many such privileged sales followed, especially of public utilities and mines.

The IMF had compelled Yanukovych to promulgate a new law on state procurement requiring open competition, but initially major infrastructure projects connected with the Euro 2012 soccer championship were excluded from competition and soon the parliament excluded virtually everything. Notwithstanding the boom in agriculture, Yanukovych halted its development through a temporary embargo on grain exports, reserving export quotas for certain associates.

The tax code adopted in November 2010 was supposed to be the key reform law, but it marked the end of reforms. Its main objective was to cut taxes on dividends of big corporations to merely 5 percent and to facilitate transfer pricing, while it increased the tax burden on small entrepreneurs. This disparity mobilized one million small entrepreneurs in protest all over Ukraine.[12] In an apparent charade, the all-powerful Yanukovych vetoed the tax code, eliminating its worst statutes, but the big international auditing companies assessed that the tax system had deteriorated, and many small businesses closed down.

Ever Worse Economic Policies Leading to Stagnation

Like most former Soviet states, Ukraine was subject to predatory rule. Yanukovych had two predominant objectives: to maintain power and to enrich his closest circle. A common idea in political economy is that a firmly entrenched ruler has an interest in the nation's economic growth, even if he happens to be

9. "Prosperous Society, Competitive Economy, Effective State: Program of Economic Reform for 2010–2014," Committee of Economic Reform of the President of Ukraine, www.president.gov.ua/docs/Programa_reform_FINAL_2.pdf.

10. IMF, "IMF Executive Board Approves US$15.15 Billion Stand-By Arrangement for Ukraine," Press Release no. 10/305, July 28, 2010.

11. "Ukrtelecom sale closed, tender casts doubt on privatization transparency," Kyiv Post, March 12, 2011.

12. "Thousands Protest in Ukraine over Tax Reform," Kyiv Post, November 16, 2010.

corrupt, while a ruler uncertain of his continued power is more interested in gaining as large a share as possible of the existing wealth. The late economist Mancur Olson (2000) called the former a stationary bandit and the latter a roving bandit.

Initially, Yanukovych appeared to be like a stationary bandit, with an apparent interest in boosting economic growth. Soon, however, he revealed himself to be a roving bandit, wanting to concentrate as large a share as possible of the existing wealth to his family as fast as possible, caring little about his nation's future, though he also nurtured a populist streak.

After November 2010, reforms fizzled out. In February 2011, an IMF mission and the government agreed on three key conditions: reduction of the budget deficit, gas price hike, and pension reform.[13] Belatedly, the government carried out a pension reform in July 2011,[14] but it never fulfilled the other two IMF demands. Therefore, after its first two quarterly disbursements in 2010 the IMF stopped disbursing funds to the Yanukovych government.

The July 2011 pension reform was badly needed, because Ukraine spent no less than 18 percent of its GDP on public pensions, more than twice as much as the European average. Pensions were moderated, and a gradual increase in the retirement age was legislated (see chapter 11). In May 2012 President Yanukovych sharply increased the minimum living standard, causing an extraordinary increase in pensions, which unfortunately eliminated the positive financial effect of the pension reform (Tkachenko 2013).

The most important IMF condition was that the government hiked domestic gas prices to reduce Naftogaz's losses of 2 percent of GDP each year, which were ultimately financed by the state budget, that is, the taxpayers. Naftogaz sold gas to consumers and utilities at prices far below the price it pays Gazprom. After raising gas prices once, Yanukovych refused to again raise the very low gas prices and aborted the reform of the gas sector. He insisted on low regulated gas prices. His official justification was that the population would suffer from higher gas and utility prices, but a more likely reason was that the Yanukovych family benefited from arbitrage between low fixed prices and high market prices.

The second IMF condition was to reduce the budget deficit. Instead, the government increased it from 5 percent of GDP in 2011 (including the Naftogaz deficit) to 6.7 percent of GDP in 2013 (figure 5.1). Yanukovych sought as large a budget deficit as he could possibly finance to transfer public wealth to his family but also fund populist public expenditures. In 2013, Ukraine's public expenditures were 48 percent of GDP, which was far too high for a country at Ukraine's level of economic development (figure 5.2).

From 2011 onward, Yanukovych no longer made any pretense of pursuing

---

13. IMF, Statement by the IMF Mission to Ukraine, press release 11/43, February 15, 2011.

14. "Zakon Ukrainy Pro zakhodi shchodo zakonodavchogo zabezpechennya reformuvannya pensiynoi sistimy" ["Law of Ukraine on Reform of the Pension System"], July 8, 2011, http://zakon4.rada.gov.ua/laws/show/3668-17/page (accessed on January 14, 2015).

Figure 5.1　Ukraine's budget balance, 2000–2014

percent of GDP

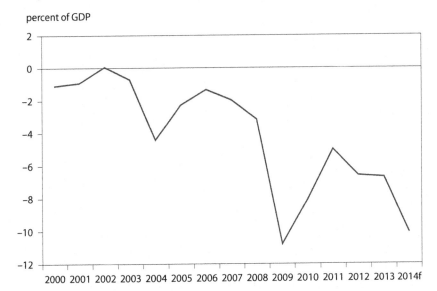

f = forecast

Note: I use JPMorgan statistics for 2009–13 because the IMF's *World Economic Outlook* statistics do not include the Naftogaz deficit. 2014 IMF forecast includes the Naftogaz deficit.

Source: 2000–2008: IMF (2014e); 2014 forecast: IMF (2014d); 2009–13: JPMorgan, Europe, Middle East, and Africa, *Emerging Markets Report*, July 8, 2014.

economic reforms to raise credits from the IMF but pursued predatory economic policies. Rising international bond yields were of little concern to him as long as Ukraine had access to international financing.

Still, Ukraine's public debt was only 41 percent of GDP at the end of 2013 (figure 5.3). Since international interest rates were abnormally low, investors chased high yields in emerging markets, which benefited Ukraine. The Ukrainian government could ignore IMF demands because it retained international market access through 2012 and borrowed on the international eurobond market at 10-year yields of 7.5 to 9.5 percent. In 2013, however, this window of market access closed.

The IMF demanded that Ukraine introduce a more flexible exchange rate, which is a codeword for depreciation. But the National Bank of Ukraine kept the exchange rate of the hryvnia pegged at too high a level, 8 hryvnia per US dollar, from 2009 to November 2013. As a consequence, Ukraine's current account deficit peaked at 9 percent of GDP in 2013 (a deficit of more than 4 to 5 percent of GDP is usually considered worrisome) (figure 5.4). To defend the excessively high exchange rate, the National Bank of Ukraine rendered currency regulations ever more severe and hiked interest rates to a very high level. In 2012, I spotted billboards with the picture of the French actor and friend of Putin Gérard Depardieu promising 19.5 percent interest on one-year time

Figure 5.2   Public expenditures in Ukraine, 2000–2014

percent of GDP

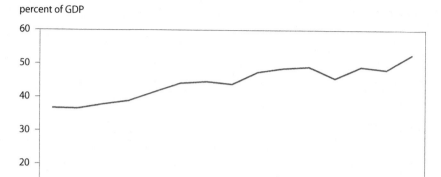

F = forecast
Note: 2014 IMF forecast includes Naftogaz deficit.
Source: IMF (2014e).

Figure 5.3   Public debt in Ukraine, 2000–2013

percent of GDP

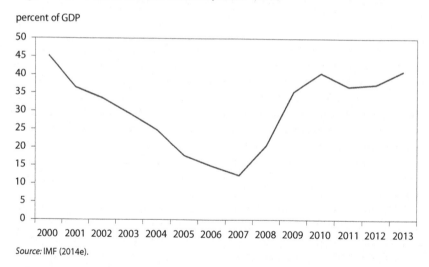

Source: IMF (2014e).

deposits in a Ukrainian savings bank. The high interest rates kept inflation at zero in 2013, but they also killed investment and thus economic growth.

Conversely, Ukraine's international reserves dwindled. In September 2011, they peaked at $38 billion. Then, they steadily shrunk to a low of $12.4 billion in April 2014 (figure 5.5), corresponding to only 2.4 months of imports. The

Figure 5.4   Ukraine's current account balance, 2000–2013

percent of GDP

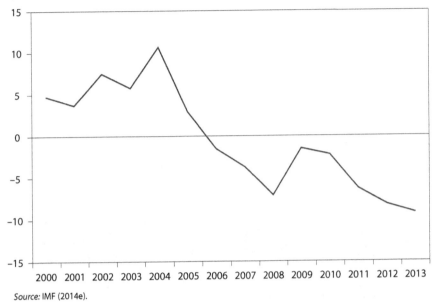

Source: IMF (2014e).

market expected a sizeable depreciation of the hryvnia. By end-2013, it was obvious that Ukraine could not manage its foreign finances without an IMF program.

It is difficult to imagine a worse economic policy. The IMF mission that visited Ukraine in October 2013 issued a press release that shocked those accustomed to the Fund's usual diplomatic bromides. It stated that the Fund continued to insist on a more flexible exchange rate, "ambitious fiscal consolidation," and reform of the markedly inefficient energy sector. The only positive note in the statement involved some minor improvements in the business environment, such as simplified procedures for construction registration of real estate ownership rights. "Much remains to be done, however," the communiqué noted.[15] International financial institutions could not understand Yanukovych's policies and distanced themselves from what they increasingly viewed as the practices of a kleptocrat.

Before Yanukovych's presidency, Ukraine's output had plunged by 15 percent during the global financial crisis in 2009. The economy recovered in 2010 and 2011, but only by 5 percent a year, and Yanukovych's economic policy brought output to a standstill in 2012 and 2013. From mid-2012 until the last quarter of 2013, it fell for five quarters.

---

15. IMF, Statement by IMF Mission to Ukraine, press release no. 13/419, October 31, 2013.

Figure 5.5   Ukraine's total international reserves, January 2010 to May 2014

billions of current dollars

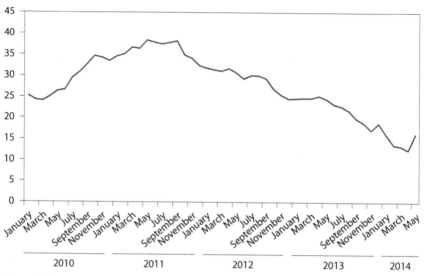

Source: IMF, *International Financial Statistics*, 2014.

The situation was growing untenable. Ukraine needed to devalue to improve its current account balance. It had to cut public expenditures sharply to reduce its budget deficit, and it had no choice but to seek IMF help to replenish its quickly shrinking foreign reserves. All this was obvious, but the young Yanukovych family ministers merely lobbied the IMF, hiring ever more expensive Washington lobbyists. They could not believe that the IMF meant what it said in its many public statements and identical private statements. On the contrary, used to their business model, they wondered whom to bribe and how much.

Capitalism in One Family

In Romania in the 1980s, people talked about "socialism in one family," since President Nicolae Ceaușescu had concentrated all power and wealth to his own family. Under Yanukovych, a similar development occurred in Ukraine, though it was crony "capitalism in one family."

In a first major cabinet change on December 9, 2010, Yanukovych reduced the number of ministries from 20 to 16. He frequently changed his government in a clear pattern: Yanukovych was concentrating power in the hands of his family. Increasingly, he appointed family loyalists from Donetsk to many national and regional posts, especially friends of his son Oleksandr, who were called "the family." By December 2010, he had gained full personal control over all the power ministries—what Vladimir Putin accomplished in April 2001 in Russia.[16] The number of oligarchic groups in the government was steadily reduced from nine in spring 2010 to only two—the Firtash and Akhmetov groups—in 2013.

On October 28, 2012, Ukraine held ordinary parliamentary elections. Numerous opposition leaders, notably former prime minister Tymoshenko and former interior minister Yuri Lutsenko, were sentenced to prison on purely political grounds. Yanukovych was unlikely to win in proportional elections; accordingly the electoral law was amended so that only half the parliamentarians were elected proportionately. The other half was elected in single-mandate constituencies with a simple majority, offering more opportunities for manipulation and great advantages to a big party.

Regions lost the proportional part of the elections, obtaining only 30 percent of the votes, while the three opposition parties together gathered a total of 50 percent: Fatherland (*Batkivshchyna*) of Tymoshenko and former speaker Arseniy Yatsenyuk received 25.5 percent, world champion heavyweight boxer Vitaliy Klitschko's party "Punch" (UDAR) 14 percent, and the nationalist Freedom party (*Svoboda*) 10.4 percent. The Communist Party, which sided with Yanukovych, got 13 percent.[17]

The government used its control over the majority of the Central Election Commission to falsify the results in tight single-mandate elections. Zhanna Usenko-Chornaya, deputy chair of the commission, passed the judgment: "the dirtiest elections in Ukraine's history."[18] The European Parliament, the European Commission, the Organization for Security and Cooperation in Europe (OSCE), the Parliamentary Assembly of the Council of Europe, and the NATO Parliamentary Assembly concurred. The OSCE concluded: "The 28 October parliamentary elections were characterized by the lack of a level playing field, caused primarily by the abuse of administrative resources, lack of transparency of campaign and party financing, and lack of balanced media coverage."[19]

Even so, according to the final official count, Regions got only 185 of 445 seats against 178 for the opposition (Fatherland 101 seats, Punch 40, and Freedom 37). The balance went to the Communist Party (32 seats) and independents (50 seats). It was widely reported that eventually the Regions party bribed and intimidated the communists and most independents to join them,

16. "Yanukovych uvolil 15 ministrov, no chast'perenaznachil" ["Yanukovych Dismissed 15 Ministers but Reappointed Some"], UNIAN, December 10, 2010, www.unian.net/politics/435775-yanukovich-uvolil-15-ministrov-no-chast-perenaznachil.html.

17. Central Election Committee, "Elections 2012," www.cvk.gov.ua/pls/vnd2012/wp300?PT001F01=900.

18. "Deputy Head of the Central Election Committee: The Dirtiest Elections in History," *Ukrainskaya pravda*, November 1, 2012.

19. Organization for Security and Cooperation in Europe, International Election Observation, Ukraine—Parliamentary Elections, October 28, 2012, Statement of Preliminary Findings and Conclusions, Kyiv, October 29, 2012, www.osce.org/odihr/elections/96675?download=true.

while also purchasing some opposition deputies. By November 2013, only 168 deputies remained with the opposition, but that number was sufficient to deprive Yanukovych of a two-thirds constitutional majority.

I visited Kyiv just after the elections. Representatives of the opposition and nongovernmental organizations rejoiced. Against all odds, they had stood up against the pervasively corrupt regime and won a popular majority. The three opposition parties decided to take their seats in parliament but declared jointly: "These parliamentary elections are an important step towards the overthrow of the criminal regime of Yanukovych. They will give the Ukrainian public confidence in their own ability to influence the government and change it."[20]

On Christmas Eve 2012, Yanukovych appointed a new government. Rather than reaching out, he further narrowed his slim power base. Now he gave all the economic portfolios to his family loyalists. The Yanukovych clan's share of cabinet posts increased significantly from five to nine out of a total of 21, and Akhmetov's share rose from two to six ministers. Everyone else was marginalized.[21]

Young friends of Oleksandr Yanukovych took over the economic bloc of the government. Their leader was Serhiy Arbuzov, 36, who had been governor of the central bank, the National Bank of Ukraine. He became first deputy prime minister. His friends, Finance Minister Yuriy Kolobov and Agriculture Minister Mykola Prysyazhniuk, retained their jobs, while former minister of ecology Eduard Stavytsky advanced to minister of energy and Oleksandr Klymenko became minister of revenues and duties. Thus Yanukovych kept his control over security, finance, and agriculture, while expanding into energy.

This government composition was not what one would expect from someone seeking to hold on to power. With its narrow base and limited competence, it was likely to weaken the president's standing in the parliament and Ukrainian politics at large. It did not bode well for the president. The government faced three big tasks: to govern, to break Ukraine's foreign isolation, and to salvage the country from a vulnerable financial situation. There was little reason to believe that it would be able to perform any of these tasks. Yanukovych seemed to have overplayed his hand. How would the big businessmen who had been eliminated from his government react? Yanukovych's popularity rating had fallen to 15 percent, according to the pollster Rating Group,[22] but he seemed remarkably indifferent.

---

20. "The Opposition Does Not Recognize the Elections, But Will Not Give Up Their Seats," *Zerkalo nedeli*, November 12, 2014, http://zn.ua/VYBORY-2012/oppozitsiya_ne_priznaet_vybory,_no_ot_deputatskih_mandatov_ne_otkazhetsya.html.

21. "Yanukovych Appointed a New Cabinet of Ministers: Korolevska Got a Seat," *Ukrainskaya pravda*, December 24, 2012.

22. "Reitingi Politikiv" ["The Politicians' Ratings"], www.ratinggroup.com.ua/cardiogram/politicians (accessed on January 14, 2015).

Corruption at the Top Level Reaches New Apogee

Many countries are corrupt, but in Ukraine corruption is pervasive (Kaufmann 1995, 1997). It commonly manifests as state capture, meaning that the top policymakers have captured the state for their own financial gain (EBRD 1999).[23] Currently, Transparency International (2013) ranks it 144 out of 177 countries on its Corruption Perceptions Index. While corruption has declined in Poland, it has stayed constantly high in Ukraine (figure 5.6).

Yet the nature of corruption has changed. It has become more concentrated at the highest level of government, as fewer share the spoils. Russia's late finance minister Alexander Livshits once famously stated: "You need to share!"[24] Everybody understood that he referred to revenues earned through corruption. In 2010, when Yanukovych became president and restored the oligarchy he seemed to have absorbed this wisdom, but soon he started concentrating political power and corrupt revenues to his family. This wealth was conspicuous in the luxurious (and distasteful) residences of his cronies.[25]

In February 2014, Prime Minister Arseniy Yatsenyuk accused the Yanukovych regime of stealing $70 billion from the state during its four years in power. That corresponds to one-fifth of Ukraine's GDP in 2013. He said: "During the last three years, a total amount of approximately 70 billion US dollars was taken out of Ukraine's financial system and transferred to off-shore accounts. Now it is clear that these means were taken as credits with state guarantee and were robbed by representatives of the former government." He continued: "Public debt has now reached $75 billion. In 2010, when Viktor Yanukovych became president, this debt was half as large. The country's foreign exchange reserves, which amounted to $37 billion three years ago, fell to $15 billion. Actually more than $20 billion in international reserves were squandered, while we received $37 billion of loans that have disappeared in an unknown direction."[26]

The Yanukovych family accumulated large and evident wealth. In a single year, Serhiy Kurchenko, a 27-year-old manager, amassed a business empire in energy trade, oil refining, media, and banking worth some $3 billion.[27] The Kurchenko empire has since collapsed and his two banks have been closed.

---

23. I have elaborated on this topic in Åslund (2014a).

24. "Ex-Minister Livshits Is Buried in Moscow," *Moscow Times*, April 30, 2013.

25. For example, Andrew Higgins, "Ukraine Palace Is Still Emblem of Dysfunction," *New York Times*, September 8, 2014.

26. Transcript in Ukrainian available at http://portal.rada.gov.ua/meeting/stenogr/show/5179. html. "Yatsenyuk: The Former Government Transferred 70 Billion Dollars Off-shore," *Ukrainskaya pravda*, February 27, 2014.

27. *Korrespondent* magazine, which was purchased by Kurchenko, estimated his wealth at $2.4 billion in November 2013, which was probably an understatement. "Reiting samykh bogatykh ukraintsev, Sergey Kurchenko" ["Rating the Richest Ukrainians, Sergey Kurchenko"], *Korrespondent*, November 2013.

Figure 5.6 Corruption Perceptions Index, Ukraine versus Poland, 2000–2013

index (0 = highly corrupt, 10 = highly clean)

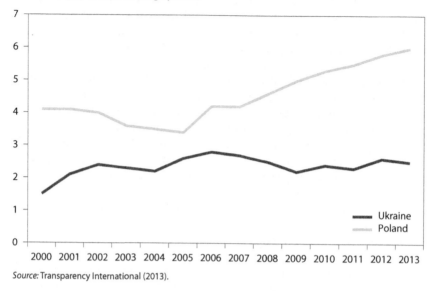

Source: Transparency International (2013).

The Yanukovych family allegedly enriched itself during its four-year reign through energy subsidies, discretionary public procurement, embezzlement from the state, privileged privatization, fraudulent refunds of value-added tax to exporters, extortion, and corporate raiding (i.e., forcing a businessman to sell his enterprise involuntarily at a low price). Thanks to Ukraine's excellent independent media, especially the websites *Ukrainska pravda* and *Dzerkalo tyzhnia,* we have a picture of how much money has been embezzled and who has benefited.[28]

Gas trade has remained a major source of unjust enrichment. Since 2010 arbitrage seems to have become mainly domestic. Each year the state oil and gas company Naftogaz bought 17 billion cubic meters of natural gas domestically produced by partially state-owned companies at the fixed low price of $53 per 1,000 cubic meters (mcm) (Radeke, Gucci, and Naumenko 2012, 3). The price was kept so low allegedly to provide consumers with cheap gas, but these gas flows were not properly recorded. Much was leaked to the commercial sector, where gas prices were based on the Russian price of $410 per mcm. According to Deputy Prime Minister Volodymyr Groisman, 40 percent of a total volume of 17 billion cubic meters of gas—worth $2.5 billion—was spir-

---

28. Since my Russian is better than my Ukrainian, I use their Russian names *Ukrainskaya pravda* and *Zerkalo nedeli* in my references.

ited away in that fashion.[29] Evidence strongly suggests that somebody close to Yanukovych made a fortune out of reselling this gas to industrial customers. Perhaps this is why Yanukovych opposed any gas price hike so adamantly. Rent seeking in the coal and nuclear energy sectors was similar but smaller in scale through a combination of state subsidies and arbitrage between controlled and free prices. The IMF (2014b, 87) assessed that 7.6 percent of GDP was being spent on energy subsidies.

Yanukovych distributed large infrastructure projects, notably those connected with the Euro 2012 soccer championship but soon almost everything, at his discretion. The World Bank (2014b) found that "only 35 percent of public procurement by value used competitive methods in 2013." In general, the government is perceived to have paid twice as much as needed for such projects. They should generate a few billion dollars a year in corrupt revenues. The examples reported below as well as anecdotal evidence suggest that a kickback of 50 percent through overpricing was considered standard.

One example is the construction of the stadium in Lviv for Euro 2012. In August 2008, the Lviv city administration announced a tender for the construction of the new stadium. The Austrian company Alpine submitted a proposal to build the stadium for $191 million, but Ukrainian authorities were willing to pay only $116 million, which Alpine rejected.[30] The Lviv city administration quickly found an alternative company, Azovintex Ltd., which was close to Ukrainian businessman Serhiy Taruta.[31] After the presidential elections in 2010, newly appointed Deputy Prime Minister Kolesnikov changed the contractor for the Lviv stadium to the Donetsk-based Altkom company, registered in Belize, considered to be closely connected to Kolesnikov.[32] The European Investment Bank had intended to contribute to the financing of the stadium, but withdrew in protest against this process. In the end, the total cost of construction rose to $370 million,[33] almost twice as much as initially offered by Alpine, which had successfully built or reconstructed all arenas in Austria for the 2008 European soccer championship.

Another example is Naftogaz's purchases of oil rigs. In 2011–12, Yanukovych's minister of energy, Yuriy Boyko, ordered Naftogaz's subsidiary Chornomornaftogaz to buy two rigs for offshore drilling in the Black Sea.[34] It did

---

29. *Ekonomichna pravda*, September 11, 2014.

30. Alpine, "Press Release: Alpine backs out of Lemberg Stadium project," Vienna, October 10, 2008, www.alpine.at/wp-content/uploads/lemberg_en.pdf.

31. Mark Rachkevych, "Runaway Costs," *Kyiv Post*, March 11, 2011.

32. Serhiy Shcherbyna, "Khto zarobliaye na Euro-2012? Lviv mil'iardy" ["Who earns at Euro 2012? Lviv billions"], *Ukrainskaya pravda*, May 14, 2012.

33. Cabinet of Ministers Resolution "On approval of the State Program for preparation and holding in Ukraine Euro 2012 Football Championship," No. 357, April 14, 2010, with further amendments, http://zakon1.rada.gov.ua/laws/show/357-2010-%D0%BF/print1392527685799749.

34. In March 2011, the first rig was purchased in an "open" tender, in which two interconnected

so for $800 million from a company registered in the United Kingdom, belonging to Boyko. However, Boyko's trading company had bought them for only $470 million, handsomely rewarding him with a profit of $330 million.[35] These two deals were televised by the independent channel TVi with invoices and all relevant documentation.[36] Boyko remained a minister until the fall of Yanukovych. In June 2014, the prosecutor's office started investigating this case, but Boyko was merely called a "witness."[37] In the October 2014 elections, he was elected a member of parliament and is a leader of the Opposition Bloc, the remnant of Yanukovych's Regions party.

Another source of corruption was outright theft from the government. In Ukraine a special, admittedly Russian, word is used for "stealing from the state budget" (verb: *deribanit'*, noun: *deriban*). The Yanukovych family mastered this art. The new government is trying to assess how much was embezzled from each ministry, and the numbers are large, a few billion dollars a year.

The Battle over the European Association Agreement

In one regard Yanukovych diverted from his otherwise quite consistent predatory policies. He favored an Association Agreement with the European Union, while he opposed Ukrainian membership in the Russian-led Customs Union with Belarus and Kazakhstan.[38] This was a dangerous game: By taking this step, Yanukovych aroused great popular hopes in Ukraine, while antagonizing Moscow.

In favoring European integration, he followed the international economic policy initiated by President Leonid Kuchma. After his election victory, Yanukovych continued negotiations with the European Union on the deep and

---

companies participated: Highway Investment Processing (based in Great Britain) and Falcona Systems Limited (New Zealand). The Singapore-based company Keppel produced the rig, first purchased by Seadrill, which resold it to an "undisclosed buyer incorporated in the UK" for $248.5 million. That company later sold the rig to Ukraine for $400 million. See Yuriy Nikolov and Oleksiy Shalaisky, "Vyshka dlia Boyka" ["Rigs for Boyko"], *Zerkalo nedeli*, May 27, 2011. In October 2011, the second tender was one by a Latvian company, but the trading mechanism was the same. With a couple of intermediaries in Norway and United Kingdom, the price was increased from $220 million to $400 million, ultimately paid by Chornomornaftogaz. See "Ukraina maizhe vdvichi pereplatyla za druhu vyshku Boyka" ["Ukraine paid almost two times more for the second Boyko's tower"], *Ukrainskaya pravda*, April 23, 2011.

35. "More Questions as New Details Emerge over Naftogaz Rig Purchase," *Business News Europe*, September 2, 2013.

36. Natalia Sedletsk, "Drilling Rig for Yuriy Boyko. Who Pocketed $150 Million?" YouTube, June 22, 2011, www.youtube.com/watch?v=By2Kbz-ctRU (accessed on August 25, 2014); "Where the Money for the Boyko's Rig Went to?" (sic) YouTube, January 29, 2012, www.youtube.com/watch?v=AygJgn__6U0 (accessed on August 25, 2014).

37. "Genprokuratura nachala rassledovanie po "vyshkam Boyko" ["Prosecutor General's Office Opened an Investigation into the 'Boyko Towers'], LB.ua, June 18, 2014.

38. I have discussed this in Åslund (2013c).

comprehensive free trade agreement (DCFTA), successfully concluded in November 2011, and the Association Agreement in March 2012. Yet, the European Union held up the signing because of new concerns about violations of human rights and rule of law in Ukraine, and at the time the Association Agreement was the only reform Yanukovych was pursuing, which lent him little credibility. On July 19, 2012, the DCFTA was initialed, but not signed.

Yanukovych had strong reasons to sign the Association Agreement. A large majority of Ukrainians persistently polled as pro-European, and the president's advisors considered that his reelection in March 2015 would be difficult if the agreement was not signed. All the leading Ukrainian businessmen favored the agreement. The European market was ten times larger than the Russian market and the obvious area for future expansion, although Russia and the European Union each accounted for one-quarter of Ukraine's exports in 2012. All too often Russia imposed protectionist measures, interrupting their exports. They also wanted to defend their properties from the president's predators.

The Kremlin, however, took the opposite view. All along, Russia's president Vladimir Putin had expressed nostalgia about the Soviet Union, and in April 2005 after the Orange Revolution he stated: "the collapse of the Soviet Union was the biggest geopolitical disaster of the century" (Putin 2005). To him, the key element of a minimal restoration of the Russian empire has been the inclusion of Ukraine.

In June 2009, Prime Minister Putin surprised everybody by stating that Russia, Belarus, and Kazakhstan would enter the World Trade Organization (WTO) as a Customs Union. The three countries agreed to unify their customs tariffs, essentially at Russia's high level. In 2010, the Customs Union came into existence, with the implementation of a common customs tariff and joint customs code. In January 2012, border controls were abolished. A joint secretariat, the Eurasian Economic Commission, was set up in Moscow with a staff of more than 1,000 people. The Eurasian Development Bank in Almaty, Kazakhstan, and an arbitration court in Minsk were also established (Movchan and Giucci 2011).

Putin's aim was to transform the Customs Union into a Eurasian Economic Union by 2015—a political counterpart to the European Union—although Belarus and Kazakhstan resisted closer political integration. Yet the three countries did sign a substantial agreement founding the Eurasian Economic Union in May 2014 after the Kazakhs carefully eliminated all political content. The difference is best understood thus: "The ostensible purpose of [the Eurasian Union] is economic. Its primary objectives, however, are geopolitical, and these are to be achieved in large part by economic means" (Adomeit 2012). Russia tried to pressure all former Soviet republics to join. In 2013, Armenia and Kyrgyzstan signed a letter of intent and Tajikistan may do so as well, but Putin's real goal was to integrate Ukraine.

Although the Customs Union was Russia's dominant priority, the countries in the Commonwealth of Independent States (CIS) concluded a multilateral FTA in October 2011. Only eight countries signed it. Russia, Belarus, and

Ukraine ratified it so that it came into force and became the basis for trade between Russia and Ukraine, replacing their bilateral FTA of 1993. It introduced two major novelties, namely that WTO rules and procedures should apply to CIS members belonging to the WTO and that a customs union could be a party to the FTA. The agreement exempts almost all goods from customs tariffs. However, Russia's export taxes on commodities, such as gas and oil, still apply to Ukraine, and Russia imposes quotas for certain sensitive products such as steel pipes. Russia also continues to block imports of agricultural products, dairy, and meats on alleged sanitary grounds (Giucci 2013). Thus, in a trade conflict between Russia and Ukraine, the WTO should take precedence, but the role of the Customs Union is confusing, since neither Belarus nor Kazakhstan belongs to the WTO.

The only way to make sense of the Kremlin's trade policy is to see it as politics mixed with old Soviet economic thinking. Sergey Glazyev, a former minister for external economic relations, became Putin's personal advisor on Eurasian integration in July 2012. He is the main advocate of the Eurasian Economic Union and embraces state capitalism and protectionism (Åslund 2013c). Glazyev wants to reduce competition so that countries lagging technologically, such as Russia and Ukraine, can produce and export more without technological advancement. He favors import substitution over competition and open markets. For the Kremlin trade policy is primarily a foreign policy weapon.

Yanukovych, for his part, firmly opposed accession to Putin's Customs Union, which would have reduced both his power and economic growth in Ukraine. Yet, for a long time the Kremlin did not pay much attention to Ukraine's dealings with the European Union, presumably thinking that the European Union could not possibly accept Yanukovych's shenanigans. Suddenly, in July 2013, Moscow woke up. It wanted Ukraine to reject the European bid and join its Customs Union with Belarus and Kazakhstan. Glazyev put it candidly: "We are preparing to tighten customs procedures if Ukraine makes the suicidal step to sign the association agreement with the EU."[39]

Without warning or negotiations, Russia started a trade war with Ukraine, blocking exports to the Russian market of steel pipes, chocolates, and various agricultural goods, products produced by pro-European Ukrainian businessmen. In August, Russia blocked most Ukrainian exports for 10 days by complicating customs procedures at the border. These trade sanctions were accompanied by multiple sharp warnings about major trade sanctions, presented by Glazyev:

> By signing an association agreement with the European Union, Ukraine would be depriving itself of its sovereign right on all issues of trade policy

---

39. Filipp Sterkin, Maksim Tovkailo, and Maksim Glikin, "Prichina tomozhennoi voiny s Ukrainoi–bol'shaya politika" ["The Reason for the Customs War with Ukraine–Big Politics"], *Vedomosti*, August 19, 2013.

that we have handed over to the Customs Union. For us, Ukraine would stop being a strategic partner, because it would be disappearing as an international partner, as an entity under international law, because it will have to agree all its actions on trade with the European Union.[40]

On August 22, Putin warned that if Ukraine concluded the Association Agreement with the European Union, "the Customs Union countries must think about safeguards."[41] Russia's first deputy prime minister Igor Shuvalov told Ukraine's prime minister Mykola Azarov that if Ukraine opened its border to the European Union, Russia would be forced to limit its imports from Ukraine to defend its domestic production.[42]

At the end of August, Yanukovych changed his tune to the benefit of the European Union. He not only said that he wanted to sign the Association Agreement but claimed that he accepted all the EU conditions lock, stock, and barrel, and jumpstarted a legislative process to have them all adopted before the Eastern Partnership summit in Vilnius. A score of important laws went through the parliament, the last being the new electoral law. Yet the two bills that did not pass were the ones that mattered the most: a law to release Tymoshenko for medical treatment in the West and a vital judicial law on transforming the prosecutor's office. Without the latter all the planned law enforcement reforms become toothless. It is possible that Yanukovych did not want the Association Agreement but only wanted to appear as if he did.

40. BBC Monitoring, "Kremlin aide warns Ukraine over EU integration," Rossiya 24 TV, August 27, 2013.

41. Vladimir Putin, "Soveshchanie o sotsial'no-ekonomicheskom razvitii Rostovskoi oblasti" ["Meeting on Socioeconomic Developments in the Rostov Region"], August 22, 2013, www.kremlin.ru (accessed on August 29, 2013).

42. Maksim Tovkailo and Sergey Titov, "Moskva predlozhila Kievu sdelat' vybor mezhdu Evropeiskim i Tamozhenym soiuzami" ["Moscow Proposed that Kiev Make Its Choice between the European Union and the Customs Union"], Vedomosti, August 27, 2013.

III

HOW TO FIX IT

6

Euromaidan and the Demise of the Yanukovych Regime, November 2013 to February 2014

If this is a revolution, it must be one of the most common-sense revolutions in history.
—Timothy Snyder (2013), Yale University

In its last year, the Yanukovych regime grew increasingly surreal. The president concentrated power and wealth to an ever smaller group of family and friends, while doing nothing to satisfy his population. Ukraine's already fragile institutions were further undermined.

The population grew alienated. When I visited Crimea in September 2011, I talked to a couple of middle-aged women from Sevastopol. They had voted for Yanukovych, but now they complained that he had abolished the "Sevastopol Salute," their city's annual festivity, for no apparent reason. He ignored the wishes of his people, who had had enough.

Yanukovych's equivocation over his policy on the European Association Agreement was his ultimate mistake. His initial interest in advancing European integration ran counter to his other blatantly predatory policies, offering the Ukrainian nation hope. In the fall of 2013 he allowed the Europe issue to crowd out everything else from Ukrainian political discourse.

On November 6, Yanukovych stated: "By choosing to get closer to the European Union, we are making a pragmatic choice for optimal and rational modernization."[1] He promised repeatedly that he would sign the Association Agreement, and Ukrainians started believing him. Yet, on November 21, his government announced that it would not sign the agreement. Ukrainians were greatly disappointed because this was their single hope. Yanukovych's about-face instigated the Euromaidan demonstrations, with protesters draped in European and Ukrainian flags.

---

1. James M. Gomez and Kateryna Choursina, "Yanukovych Defends Ukraine EU Trade Pact as Competitiveness Lags," Bloomberg, November 6, 2013; "EC—eto pragmatichno, no prekrashchat' sotrudnichestvo s drugimi nel'zya," ["The EU—That Is Pragmatic, But We Cannot Stop Cooperation with Others"], *Ukrainskaya pravda*, November 6, 2013.

Yanukovych continued making increasingly bad mistakes until the Ukrainian Parliament finally ousted him on February 22. The parliament quickly restored the 2004 constitution with stronger parliamentary powers and appointed a new government, which adopted a very different government program: Ukraine reversed course toward democracy, market economic reform, and European integration.

Violence Erupts on the Maidan

In the early hours of November 30, 2013, the situation on the Maidan took a sharp turn for the worse. Riot police cleared out 300 demonstrators legally holding the fort on Independence Square. Thirty-five were injured and 31 detained, although no demonstrator was accused of resisting. The official reason for the cleansing of the square was to raise a Christmas tree. Yanukovych lamented the violence, without blaming the police, while the minister of interior apologized for using excessive force. For the first time, the Ukrainian authorities used serious violence against the population; the Orange Revolution had been nearly bloodless.

Three developments occurred simultaneously. First, the opposition called for massive peaceful demonstrations. Hundreds of thousands of people came out in the street on Sunday, December 1, and reoccupied the Maidan. The main slogans were: "The boar [Yanukovych] to the [Christmas] tree!" "Down with the gang!" "Ukraine is Europe," "Christmas without Yanukovych," "We do not forgive!" and "Revolution!"[2] The EU ambassador and nine ambassadors from EU countries joined the demonstration. The United States, the European Union, and various EU countries condemned the authorities' violence against peaceful and legal demonstrators. Demonstrations spread to almost all the big cities in Ukraine. Nobody loved the European Union more than the Ukrainians.

Second, defections started in Yanukovych's inner circle. His chief of staff, Serhiy Lyovochkin, resigned, but Yanukovych refused to accept his resignation. A stream of Regions parliamentarians, including several former ministers, began crossing the aisle to the opposition. The Regions had only 207 seats out of the actual 442 seats in parliament, but usually 31 communists and 35 nonaffiliated parliamentarians supported it, whereas the three opposition parties had 168 seats.[3] Yanukovych risked losing control over the parliament, as many parliamentarians adjusted to the wind. The special forces of the Ministry of Interior in Lviv in western Ukraine refused to obey orders to clear out demonstrators,[4] and they were soon followed by others in the western regions.

---

2. Serhiy Rakhmanin, "Sed'moi Maidan" ["The Seventh Day of Maidan"], *Zerkalo nedeli*, December 6, 2013.

3. Official results of voting in the Verkhovna Rada, November 21, 2013, http://w1.c1.rada.gov.ua/pls/radan_gs09/ns_golos?g_id=3371.

4. "L'vovskii 'Berkut' otkazalsya vypolnyat' prikazy Kieva" ["'Berkut' in Lvov Refused to Carry Out Orders from Kyiv"], *Ukrainskaya pravda*, November 30, 2013.

Third, the authorities brought in a large number of paid hooligans, so-called *titushki*—young men in sportswear and many with masks—to attack both the riot police and peaceful demonstrators in staged provocations. The combination of thousands of violent hooligans and riot police fighting for the regime made the Euromaidan quite different from the Orange Revolution. The Euromaidan became a warlike operation with ragtag uniforms, barricades, and check points, while the Orange Revolution had been a peaceful dance. All along, people feared that Yanukovych would declare a state of emergency. As during the Orange Revolution, protesters camped out in tents on the Maidan, but this time several public buildings in the neighborhood were occupied.

At the outset, five evident leaders of the opposition took the stage together on the Maidan. They included the three party leaders, heavyweight boxer Vitaliy Klitschko of UDAR (Punch), the experienced politician and technocrat Arseniy Yatsenyuk, who led Yulia Tymoshenko's party *Batkivshchyna* (Fatherland), and Oleh Tyahnybok, the leader of the nationalist party *Svoboda* (Freedom). Former minister of interior Yuriy Lutsenko, who was one of the leaders of the Orange Revolution, was the most revolutionary leader. Petro Poroshenko, Ukraine's chocolate king and former minister, seemed the most resourceful organizer. His television Channel 5 covered the Euromaidan as it had broadcast the Orange Revolution.

These politicians were highly experienced. At 39, Yatsenyuk had already held many high government posts. Poroshenko and Lutsenko had been leaders of the Orange Revolution as well as ministers. Missing were former president Viktor Yushchenko, who was widely considered to have betrayed the Orange Revolution, and former prime minister Tymoshenko, who was serving a seven-year prison sentence on politically motivated charges that she abused her power. Yet, her picture hung on the big Christmas tree on the Maidan.

The old opposition leaders, however, did not enjoy much authority, and the protestors were greatly dissatisfied with their perceived passivity. Some new leaders had emerged. Andriy Parubiy, a Fatherland parliamentarian, rose to prominence as the commander of the Maidan. Moscow complained about the rise of the hard right on the Maidan, in particular the so-called Right Sector led by Dmytro Yarosh, but they were only a few hundred strong; the Maidan gathered hundreds of thousands on peak days. The Maidan took on a life of its own with its defenders organized in groups called *sotni* (hundreds) of different political inclinations. A large number of civil activists came to the fore. On stage, entertainers and speakers followed each other.

Media exposure had improved considerably since the Orange Revolution. Then mobile phones, the independent internet news service *Ukrainskaya pravda*, and Poroshenko's television Channel 5 had been key (Prytula 2006), while the official and private television channels had been more or less hostile to the protesters. Now, the television channels owned by big businessmen tended to be rather objective, notably Ihor Kolomoisky's 1+1 and Victor Pinchuk's ICTV. Poroshenko's Channel 5 was still there and supported the opposition, as did the reinforced *Ukrainskaya pravda*. The respected independent *Weekly Mirror* had established a similar internet news service. Facebook, Twitter, and other social media were important novelties, capturing the mood of Maidan virtually.

As Serhiy Leshchenko (2014, 52) put it: "It all began with a simple Facebook post." On November 21, *Ukrainskaya pravda* journalist Mustafa Nayem invited fellow Ukrainians who shared his disaffection with Yanukovych's policy reversal to join him for a protest on the Maidan.[5] Soon afterward, Nayem started a popular online television channel, HromadskeTV. Online news coverage was better and more objective than ever. It was very popular, and its role cannot be overestimated. Millions of people watched the live broadcast of the events.

A stalemate evolved between the two camps. The protests continued and the democratic opposition seemed ready to take over, while Yanukovych's camp appeared reluctant to apply harsh methods to suppress the protests, but nor did it give up. The regime maintained the power of government, but it did not control the country and it enjoyed no popular majority.

Yanukovych's Deal with Putin

In the fall of 2013, Putin and Yanukovych held several private meetings in Russia. Finally, on December 17 the two presidents met in Moscow to conclude a series of agreements, which changed the Ukrainian situation.

In the midst of political and economic chaos, Ukraine was quickly running out of international reserves because of a fixed exchange rate that it could not possibly defend. Yanukovych needed to change economic policy and mobilize substantial international financing. To save Yanukovych and insert himself onto the center stage of the Ukrainian drama, Putin offered Yanukovych a credit of $15 billion, which was sufficient external financing until the presidential elections scheduled for March 2015. Russia let its sovereign wealth fund buy $15 billion of Ukrainian bonds and it swiftly purchased two-year Ukrainian eurobonds denominated in dollars for $3 billion with a yield of 5 percent.

Putin also cut the price of Russia's gas exports to Ukraine for the first quarter of 2014 by one-third to $268.50 per 1,000 cubic meters, providing considerable cost savings to Ukraine's energy-dependent producers and consumers, but this price was just below the approximate market price in the region. In addition, Russia eased some but not all trade sanctions against Ukrainian exports to Russia. The two countries also concluded a few agreements on production cooperation, essentially in the armaments industry, involving large Antonov military transportation airplanes, shipbuilding, and construction of space rockets. One agreement concerned the building of a bridge over or tunnel under the disputed Kerch Strait at the Azov Sea, which seemed to potentially undermine Ukraine's claim to Crimea.[6]

---

5. Mustafa Nayem, "Uprising in Ukraine: How It All Began," *Open Society Voices*, April 4, 2014, www.opensocietyfoundations.org/voices/uprising-ukraine-how-it-all-began.

6. Agata Wierzbowska-Miazga and Arkadiusz Sarna, "The Moscow Deals: Russia Offers Yanu-

Both sides maintained great secrecy about the negotiations and the details of most of the agreements, leaving the Ukrainian opposition to fear that their president had given up some sovereignty to Russia. This was a victory for both Putin and Yanukovych, but it resolved none of Ukraine's economic or political problems as was obvious to the Ukrainian opposition.

It was as if Putin had pulled a rabbit out of a hat, magically solving a series of problems in one set of agreements. He tied troubled Ukraine financially to the Kremlin, while luring it away from the European Union. It was also a victory of authoritarianism over democracy and of corruption over European legal reforms. Nor did it cost Putin anything. The risk but also the yields on some of Russia's reserves increased, and the lower gas prices secured the important Ukrainian gas market for Russia.

This deal was also a personal victory for Yanukovych. The European Union had tried to persuade him to opt for the rule of law and democracy. By pretending to be serious about negotiating accession, Yanukovych had convinced Moscow to provide the international financing he needed to sustain Ukraine's debts until the presidential elections, and the Russians did not ask him to pursue any pesky reforms. Now, he and his family could indulge in authoritarian rule and personal enrichment, although it was difficult to see how he could survive the presidential elections with such a policy.

The Ukrainian nation was the main loser. A significant majority of Ukrainians wanted Yanukovych to sign the European Association Agreement, expecting to gain from access to its markets, job opportunities, and presumably visa-free travel. They hoped that democracy and the rule of law would be reinforced in Ukraine. But their president had let them down. Short of violent revolution, the opposition's only feasible road to victory was to attract more defectors from Yanukovych's faction in parliament to oust the government. On December 19, the parliamentary opposition had tentatively grown from 168 in November to 217 deputies, but they needed nine more defectors to reach a majority.

After Yanukovych's agreement with Putin, Ukraine's financial crisis ebbed and the political crisis entered a lull. The stalemate was reinforced. Neither side could win without resorting to substantial violence. People continued to work while the Maidan protests persisted.

On January 16, 2014, Yanukovych ended this standoff by unexpectedly compelling the parliament to adopt nine dictatorial laws. "A series of laws passed hastily and without following normal procedure did away with freedom of speech and assembly, and removed the few remaining checks on executive authority. This was intended to turn Ukraine into a dictatorship and to make all participants in the Maidan, by then probably numbering in the low millions, into criminals" (Snyder 2014c).

kovych Conditional Support," Centre for Eastern Studies, December 18, 2013, www.osw.waw.pl/en/publikacje/analyses/2013-12-18/moscow-deals-russia-offers-yanukovych-conditional-support.

These measures were reminiscent of the authoritarian laws Putin had promulgated in Russia in 2005 in response to Ukraine's Orange Revolution.[7] Many Ukrainians presumed that the writer of the laws was Putin's aide Vladislav Surkov, the author of Putin's "sovereign democracy," who had been transferred to deal with Ukrainian politics in the Kremlin. A government crackdown threatened all opposition activists with imprisonment, giving them little choice but to stand firm. Yanukovych had crossed the Rubicon, transforming the power struggle to a winner-takes-all battle. But, as Timothy Snyder, professor of history at Yale University, who chronicled the Maidan, wrote, "Ukraine is not Russia. Too many Ukrainians have tasted too much freedom for too long. The people resisted this sudden attempt at tyranny. Mr. Yanukovych lost control over local institutions of power" (Snyder 2014a). The protests turned violent, and three protesters were killed in Kyiv.

During the weekend of January 25–26, Yanukovych lost territorial control over the country, as the opposition occupied the regional administrative headquarters in the western half of the country. The unrest spread throughout Ukraine except Crimea and Luhansk in the east, the two most Russia-oriented regions. In parliament, Yanukovych's remaining support was shaky, and opinion polls suggested that only one-quarter of the population was with him. He had to rely on the Berkut riot police and hired thugs. The president had lost administrative and political control over the country.

In spite of growing protests from the nationalist right, the opposition leaders still found it worthwhile to negotiate with Yanukovych. On January 28, in an attempt to salvage the situation, the now ambivalent parliament revoked the repressive laws of January 16. Prime Minister Azarov and his Cabinet of Ministers resigned, which did not resolve anything.[8]

The next day Yanukovych committed yet another political mistake. He forced the parliament to vote for his version of an "amnesty" bill for political prisoners. Amnesty would be granted only if the protesters first vacated the buildings they had occupied and ended their protests. The opposition, having lost all faith in Yanukovych, found his gambit unacceptable. He went to parliament himself and threatened recent defectors. Even so, he managed to mobilize a slim majority of 232 votes (226 were needed).[9] This turned out to be a Pyrrhic victory.

Yanukovych had effectively united the opposition around one demand: his resignation. They also called for early parliamentary and presidential elections as well as the reinstitution of the parliamentary-presidential constitution of 2004, which the Constitutional Court had obediently abolished in October

---

7. Will Englund, "Ukraine Enacts Harsh Laws against Protests," *Washington Post*, January 17, 2014.

8. Richard Balmforth and Pavel Polityuk, "Ukraine PM resigns amid unrest, parliament revokes anti-protest laws," Reuters, January 28, 2014.

9. "Rada progolosovala za amnitsiu po stsenariu vlasti" ["Rada Voted for the Government's Version of amnesty"], *Ukrainskaya pravda*, January 29, 2014.

2010 upon Yanukovych's command. The only topic that the opposition was willing to discuss with Yanukovych was the conditions for his resignation.

Ouster of Yanukovych and Restoration of the 2004 Constitution

On February 18, 2014, the authorities tried to break the impasse by escalating violence. Police shot 18 people dead in the center of Kyiv. Two days later, snipers reportedly belonging to the Ukrainian Ministry of Interior killed a large number of people. The opposition named the victims the "Heavenly Hundred," who were recognized as martyrs.

Yanukovych had gone too far. After three months of public protests, turmoil, and violence, the opposition finally achieved a major breakthrough on Friday, February 21. Two developments occurred in parallel: an EU mediation and a shift in the majority in parliament. Most accounts emphasize the EU mediation, but the change in parliamentary majority was far more important.

Thanks to mass defections from the Regions party protesting the massacres of February 18–20, the opposition at long last won a majority in parliament. Late at night on February 20, 236 out of 450 deputies voted for a resolution calling on all armed forces to stop shooting on protesters and to return to their barracks.[10] Sixty-eight parliamentarians had defected from the Yanukovych camp. They were largely big businessmen and their representatives in parliament. Akhmetov and Firtash, the last two oligarchs in the Yanukovych camp, were seen as their leaders. Many of Yanukovych's most loyal lawmakers started fleeing the country, predominantly to Russia. His power base was quickly disintegrating. The shift of power in parliament made all the other changes possible.

Also on February 20, the EU Foreign Affairs Council, comprising foreign ministers from all EU countries, decided to impose visa and financial sanctions on a score of top Ukrainian officials responsible for the violence.[11] While the bottom was dropping out from under the Ukrainian president, three EU foreign ministers—from Germany, France, and Poland—spent hours negotiating with him.

In the midst of the negotiations on February 21, Yanukovych stated that he had to take a phone call from President Putin, after which he suddenly made substantial concessions in negotiations with the three opposition party leaders mediated by the three EU ministers. A Russian representative was also present but did not sign the agreement. At the same time, the security guards around the presidential administration and the Cabinet of Ministers withdrew

---

10. "Deputaty progolosovali za prekrashchenie ognia" ["Parliamentarians Voted to Stop Fighting"], *Ukrainskaya pravda*, February 20, 2014.

11. Council of the European Union, "Ukraine: EU agrees on targeted sanctions," February 21, 2014, www.consilium.europa.eu/homepage/showfocus?focusName=ukraine-eu-agrees-on-targeted-sanctions&lang=en.

in trucks. The European negotiators got the impression that Putin had told Yanukovych to pack up and leave. The agreement consisted of six points.

First, the parliament was to restore the presidential-parliamentary constitution of 2004, which the Constitutional Court illegally abolished on October 2010 to grant Yanukovych sweeping powers. The parliament did so later in the day with 386 votes, far more than the required two-thirds constitutional majority of 300 votes.[12] Yanukovych's defeat was so complete that he ordered his own deputies to vote in favor. As occurred the previous evening, the parliamentarians stood up and sang the national anthem after their vote. The signatories also declared their intention to create a coalition and form a national unity government within 10 days.

Second, the agreement called for the adoption of substantial improvements to the 2004 constitution in September 2014. Third, early presidential elections would be held no later than December 2014. Also, new electoral laws would be passed and a new Central Election Commission would be formed on the basis of proportionality. Fourth, the recent acts of violence would be investigated jointly by the authorities, the opposition, and the Council of Europe, Europe's primary human rights organization. Fifth, the president guaranteed not to impose a state of emergency, and both sides committed themselves to abstaining from acts of violence. Finally, the parliament was requested to adopt a new law of amnesty for protesters.

After the three opposition leaders—Vitaliy Klitschko, Yatsenyuk, and Oleh Tyahnybok—had signed the agreement with Yanukovych, they went down to the Maidan. The protesters were unhappy and complained that the accord did not contain anything about the resignation of Yanukovych, the dissolution of the parliament, or the arrest of Minister of Interior Vitaliy Zakharchenko. In the end, the protesters' ruling body, the Maidan Council, approved the agreement 34 votes to 2.[13]

The next day Yanukovych departed for Kharkiv in the east, and a week later he surfaced in Russia as did several of his top loyalists. Many things happened in parallel in the parliament. Immediately after Yanukovych's escape, his outlandish residence Mezhyhiria was opened to the public, which flocked to it in large numbers. It struck the visitors as both luxurious and in very bad taste, looking more like Disneyland with a pirate ship and a zoo than a palace. It appeared like the dream of a poor street boy who had got all he ever wanted but did not know how to indulge in luxury. The grand villas of other prominent members of the Yanukovych family were also opened, and they too displayed great wealth but no taste. Plenty of documents on Yanukovych's corrupt transactions were found at Mezhyhiria.[14]

---

12. "Konstitutsia 2004 goda vernulas" ["The Constitution of 2004 Has Returned"], *Ukrainskaya pravda*, February 21, 2014.

13. "Sikorski: This Agreement God Himself Blessed," *Ukrainskaya pravda*, February 21, 2014.

14. Jurij Kultschynski, Jürgen Schrader, and Bernhard Riedmann, "360-Grad Ansichten: Janukowitschs Gold Villa" ["360-Degrees Views: Yanukovych's Gold Villa"], *Der Spiegel*, February 2014.

On February 21, the parliament, with a majority of 372 votes, legislated against any prosecution of arrested protesters.[15] It also voted to oust Zakharchenko. With 322 votes, it decided to free former prime minister Tymoshenko.[16] The parliament had the two-thirds majority, with which it could overrule a presidential veto.

On February 22, the parliament voted to oust Yanukovych with a majority of 328 votes and decided to hold early presidential elections on May 25 (Snyder 2014b). Tymoshenko was released from prison, and her right-hand man Oleksandr Turchynov was elected speaker of parliament and then acting president.

As during the Orange Revolution in 2004, the European Union provided the critical mediation services, while both Russia and the United States stayed on the sidelines. President Putin's aggressive gamble to draw Ukraine into Russia's sphere of influence had suffered a serious setback. Yanukovych's downfall was hardly surprising. He had made every conceivable political mistake, confusing ruthless steamrolling with political strength.

The New Government and Its Program

The last days of February were ripe with revolutionary fervor. On February 27, the opposition formed a new government. It consisted of three parties, Fatherland, *Svoboda*, and Euromaidan activists; Klitschko and his UDAR party chose not to join the government. In effect, Fatherland came to dominate with one-third of the portfolios. Its leader, Arseniy Yatsenyuk, became prime minister. Half a dozen of the ministers were Maidan activists, mainly liberal intellectuals. *Svoboda* received three portfolios.

The new government was criticized on two fronts: One that it contained too many inexperienced activists "who had only stood on the Maidan," and the other that it contained too many old faces. In fact, only four of the 23 ministers had been ministers before, but they did include the prime minister, the finance minister, and the energy minister. Yatsenyuk presented his government as a "kamikaze" government, which was supposed to carry out heroic reforms in the next three months, presuming that a new government would be formed in June after the presidential elections.

On the day of its appointment, the Ukrainian government issued its action program.[17] It was brief with six pages, but it offered a clear sense of direction. Of all the government programs that have been issued since Ukraine became independent, none has been so coherent and sensible. It contained 23 priorities. The top 10 in abridged form were:

---

15. "Rada osvobodila ot presledovaniy vsekh aktivistov Maidana" ["Rada freed all Maidan activists from prosecution"], *Ukrainskaya pravda*, February 21, 2014.

16. "Rada osvobodila Tymoshenko. Ona vot-vot vyidet iz kolonii" ["Rada released Tymoshenko. She is about to leave the prison"], *Ukrainskaya pravda*, February 22, 2014.

17. Programma Deyatel'nosti kabineta ministrov Yatseniuka [Action Program of the Cabinet of Ministers of Yatensiuk], *Ukrainskaya pravda*, February 27, 2014.

1. Safeguard the sovereignty and territorial integrity of Ukraine.

2. Sign the European Association Agreement.

3. Develop good neighborly relations with the Russian Federation.

4. Conclude a new stabilization program with the International Monetary Fund (IMF) and attract financial support from the IMF and the European Union.

5. Stabilize the financial situation.

6. Secure the rule of law through judicial reform.

7. Reform law enforcement.

8. Punish the culprits for violence against the Euromaidan protesters.

9. Form a new governance system on the basis of rule of law, openness, and transparency of the government.

10. Carry out lustration of law enforcement and judges.

Other major objectives were: impose strict control over the budget, hike energy tariffs and provide social compensation, reform the political system and electoral legislation, hold honest and transparent presidential elections in 2014, and demonopolize the economy.

These priorities were followed by a long list of legislation to be enacted. All this seemed impossible to do within three months. Since Ukraine had not enacted sensible laws for so long, many draft laws had been collected on the shelves of the parliament; they could quickly be dusted off and promulgated. Some of them were not of sufficiently good quality, and the speed of the legislative process did not allow for much improvement, but in three months the new government probably adopted more laws of significance than the Orange government did in five years.

Three months later, the Euromaidan public relations initiative issued a document enumerating no fewer than 60 achievements of the new government (Euromaidan Press 2014). The list was quite impressive. It covered almost all the fields—politics, economics, and justice. I discuss the details of the new laws in following chapters.

Ukrainians were most concerned about justice, and the immediate concerns had been satisfied. The constitution of 2004 had already been reinstated. The government abolished 158 acts of the Azarov government and adopted a law on free access to public information and on lustration. It fired 24,000 government officials and the privatization of state dachas in Koncha-Zaspa began. Mezhyhiria and other mansions of government officials built with stolen funds were confiscated. All political prisoners were freed and the riot police eliminated.

Economic policy was dominated by the conclusion of a new two-year Stand-By Arrangement with the IMF (2014a) with $17 billion of financing. In return, Ukraine adopted a law on open and competitive public procurement. Substantial cuts in public expenditures were undertaken. The government increased gas prices for the population by 56 percent, and the exchange rate was allowed to float.

Ukraine signed the EU Association Agreement on June 27 and ratified it on September 16. Gas deliveries from Europe were organized through Slovakia, Poland, and Hungary, making it possible to cut excessively expensive gas purchases from Russia. The European Union opened its borders for Ukrainian goods, admitting 98 percent of Ukrainian imports free of customs taxes. The necessary laws for a visa-free regime with the European Union were enacted, and the Ukrainian government hoped it would come into force in 2015. Meanwhile, Ukraine announced that it would exit the Commonwealth of Independent States.

By July, however, most reform legislation was halted. Some blamed the government for not being sufficiently interested in reforms, but the defectors from Yanukovych's Regions party had never favored reform. After a few months of the new regime, they started voting in line with their old special interests.

Another problem lay in the system of appointing officials. A group of "gray cardinals" appointed ministers down to the local officials on the basis of a party quota system. The gray cardinals were responsible for the illegal financing of the political parties and did not play any prominent political role, but they handled appointments according to the old rules of clientele. Competence or other merits were not necessarily taken into account. A minister could not appoint his or her deputies, who naturally did not obey him or her. One consequence was that Ukraine got a minister of defense who did not issue any order until Crimea was lost. Another consequence was that the country got prosecutors who let the whole Yanukovych family off the hook without prosecution.

Ukraine needed new parliamentary elections and a reform of the state to rid itself of the old political system.

Avoiding the Mistakes of the Orange Revolution

As President Yanukovych departed from Ukraine, questions arose whether a new democratic government could avoid the mistakes and disorder that prevailed after the Orange Revolution. The situation was quite different, but the policy lessons from the mistakes of the Orange Revolution remain poignant.

The mood after Euromaidan could not be more different from the atmosphere after the Orange Revolution. Then, the victors were high on euphoria. Now, the Maidan was tainted with blood and Ukraine was subject to severe Russian military aggression, with Russia having annexed Crimea and devastated large parts of Donbas. Corruption and government dysfunction were no longer issues of inefficiency but matters of national security and sovereignty. The challenge of the democratic government was to save the nation.

Ukraine has not been blessed with strong leaders. The risk that the country would pick another president so incompetent or detrimental seemed small, but will he have the required strength?

Not only the leaders but also the Ukrainian people were euphoric in early 2005. This time, however, the public mood is heavy with suspicion. Ukrainians are aware that the democratic opposition is also deeply corrupt. Civic society has grown much stronger. It is not prepared to give authorities the benefit of the doubt. The new worry is that they will be so suspicious that they will block everything.

In 2004, the economy grew by 12 percent, limiting economic concerns. Democracy appeared secure, and no Russian threat was apparent. Now the situation is much more sinister. In 2013, the economy stagnated and is forecast to further decline in 2014. Ukraine had large twin deficits in 2013, which had to be cured. The current threat is financial meltdown, and the question is whether enough people understand the magnitude of this danger.

A decade ago, European integration was a pipe dream. Now with the signing of the substantial EU Association Agreement, Ukraine has made a civilizational choice. The agreement contains a blueprint for reform of the Ukrainian state on European lines, and the European Union has committed substantial technical assistance to achieve this goal.

Three big lessons stand out from the Orange Revolution. First that it did not provide a break from the corrupt political and judicial system. The best way of cleaning out a pervasively corrupt parliament is early parliamentary elections. To cleanse the state and judicial system from corruption, a far-reaching turnover of staff is required.

The second lesson is that incentives must be realigned to reduce the inclination of officials toward corruption. Gradual change on this front is not an option because it would only allow the old system to corrupt the new rulers, who would then abandon reform in favor of rent seeking. The classical corruption traps must be eliminated as soon as possible from the top down.

Finally, "reprivatization," the renationalization and renewed privatization of enterprises, must be avoided. The idea was to reduce the wealth of the oligarchs, who had grown rich from privatized enterprises, but the debate became highly destructive and undermined property rights. The government should simply confiscate property embezzled by the Yanukovych family. President Poroshenko has taken a firm stand against reprivatization.[18]

---

18. "Poroshenko protiv reprivatizatsii" ["Poroshenko is against reprivatization"], *Ekonomichna pravda*, October 14, 2014.

7

Political Reform
Must Come First

Elections are the best means of lustration.
—President Petro Poroshenko (2014)

Politics does not have to wait in the midst of an economic crisis. In fact, it is key to achieving the reforms necessary to resolve the crisis. Throughout the world, young reformers have usually started as economic technocrats (Williamson 1994). Many budding reformers thought politics was too dirty for them. Only later did they realize that politics is crucial. Euromaidan activists thought the same, but as the parliamentary elections approached a couple dozen entered the ballot on several different party lists.

Among the East European reformers, two leaders understood politics early on. Czechoslovakia's Václav Klaus, a professor of economics, was an exceptional politician. Every Saturday he went out to talk to ordinary people, preaching his reform messages over and over again as well as learning how to sell his message. Estonia's prime minister Mart Laar (2002, 2014), who was a doctor of history, best understood the importance of democracy for economic reform. Reformers had to take care of politics first because successful reforms could be carried out only through a parliamentary majority.

Ukraine has the chance and must take it now. The old political establishment is an obsolete structure and cannot be reformed. The best way of doing away with it is through democratic elections. Ukraine achieved a democratic breakthrough in February 2014, which was followed by democratic elections at all levels of government. A major systemic reform requires the promulgation of hundreds of new laws, which is possible only with a reformist parliamentary majority.

Arguably, the 2014 democratic breakthrough was more profound than the previous ones in 1991 and 2004. A big difference was that Ukrainians finally took down the hundreds of Lenin monuments. Former Lithuanian prime minister Andrius Kubilius has set this as the litmus test of the real end of communism. The next steps are that the democratic activists march into parliament through free and fair elections and then take over the government. By necessity this will be a messy process as some revolutionaries learn statecraft while others fail.

A popular argument is that reformers must seek consensus, but Laar (2002) argued the opposite. In a severe crisis, when the solution depends on a clear break from the old system, no consensus is possible or even desirable, whereas a simple majority in parliament is vital for reform (cf. Sachs 1994). Only after a reform has succeeded does a consensus arise around it, as has been the case in Poland and the Baltic states.

Even more important is that Ukraine's elections be transparent. The finances of political parties as well as candidates need to be fully disclosed to the public. At the same time, campaign financing and television appearances need to be regulated to limit the costs and level the playing field. The electoral system also needs to be fixed. Ukraine's semiproportional system was designed to maximize the power of wealthy businessmen. A fully proportional system is preferable.

Ukraine is about to amend its current 2004 constitution decentralizing considerable powers to the regions. Although not on the current political agenda, Ukraine should consider moving to a fully parliamentary system. All postcommunist democracies have parliamentary systems, while all authoritarian postcommunist states have presidential systems.

Early Presidential and Parliamentary Elections Were Key

After the ouster of Yanukovych, it was vital that Ukraine held early presidential elections to get a legitimate president. On May 25, 2014, Petro Poroshenko won a convincing victory with 55 percent of the votes cast in the first round of Ukraine's free and fair presidential elections.[1] This was the first time in the country's postcommunist history that a candidate won outright without a runoff.

Early parliamentary elections were also vital. It was not long before the old parliament turned against the new government. On July 4, Ukraine's prime minister, Arseniy Yatsenyuk, told parliament that his patience had run out because it had not supported two dozen draft laws the Cabinet of Ministers had submitted. Instead the parliament passed eight populist laws with no funding. Yatsenyuk exclaimed: "This is a show of unlimited populism and a lie to people. There is no such money." He continued: "As the Head of the Ukrainian Government, I believe that it is very hard for the Government and Parliament to work in such a fashion, and even harder for Ukraine and Ukrainians."[2]

The parliament was defective and it had become politically obsolete after Euromaidan. Earlier in the year, on February 20, the democratic opposition

---

1. Central Election Commission, www.cvk.gov.ua/info/protokol_cvk_25052014.pdf.

2. "Yatsenyuk prigrozil Rade posledstviyami provala sotrudnichestva s Kabminom" ["Yatsenyuk Threatened the Parliament with the Consequences of Collapse of Cooperation with the Cabinet of Ministers"], *Ukrainskaya pravda*, July 4, 2014.

formed a new democratic government majority with the help of defectors from Yanukovych's Regions party. These defectors were no idealists but largely businessmen who entered parliament to nurture their business interests. Rinat Akhmetov and Dmytro Firtash controlled the two biggest factions of defectors. They had abandoned Yanukovych when he was no longer politically viable, but after the revolutionary fervor abated they stopped supporting reforms, once again focusing on their commercial interests. After June 2014, the parliament enacted hardly any sensible economic laws, making early parliamentary elections vital.

On July 24, Yatsenyuk announced his government's resignation after two of the three coalition partners, the UDAR Party of Vitaliy Klitschko, the mayor of Kyiv, and the nationalist *Svoboda*, withdrew from the ruling coalition.[3] The real reason for his resignation was to facilitate early parliamentary elections. Ukraine's Constitution allows such elections when the parliament does not form a governing coalition within 30 days.

Acting fast so the nation would not be left with an unrepresentative parliament opposed to reform, on August 25, President Poroshenko (2014) dissolved the parliament and called for early parliamentary elections on October 26, since the parliament had failed "to form within one month a coalition of parliamentary factions," in accordance with Article 90 of the constitution. Article 77 states that a special election of the parliament should be held within 60 days from the publication of the decision on the preterm dissolution of the parliament.[4] Yatsenyuk stayed on as the leader of a caretaker government.

A new parliament was needed to reflect Ukraine's changed mood after the February 2014 democratic breakthrough. Numerous politicians had discredited themselves and even fled the country, while new political stars had been born. Both needed to be reflected in the new parliament. The incumbent parliament was elected in October 2012. It was widely perceived as Ukraine's least free and fair election since the end of communism in 1991 (see chapter 5).

The old parliament was perceived as pervasively corrupt. Oleh Rybachuk, the chief of staff of President Viktor Yushchenko, realizing the depth of corruption one year after the Orange Revolution, resigned and started a nongovernmental organization called *Chesno* (Honestly). *Chesno* examined the apparent expenditures and legally declared incomes of all the 450 members of the previous Ukrainian parliament (2007–12) and found that 282 were involved in corruption. One hundred parliamentarians met the condition of their declared incomes conforming to their lifestyle, but when *Chesno* added five other financial criteria of honesty only four parliamentarians met them.[5]

Most of the members of parliament were widely seen as there to make

---

3. "Yatsenyuk Resigns as Parliament Elections Likely to Be Held in the Fall," *Kyiv Post*, July 25, 2014.

4. Constitution of Ukraine, February 22, 2014, http://zakon4.rada.gov.ua/laws/show/254%D0% BA/96-%D0%B2%D1%80/print1397506758591654.

5. Chesno website, http://2012.chesno.org/deputies.

money rather than to pursue their political convictions. Any effort to weed out corruption had to start with the legislature. Even the Regions' parliamentary faction leader, Oleksandr Yefremov, suggested: "Every people's deputy is guilty of what happened and is happening in our country. Thus it would be logical to start with ourselves. Therefore, all those who were elected from 1990 to 2014 should have no right to be elected to the new parliament. I think that would be honest and would amount to lustration and a complete reset of the government."[6]

One major reason for the political chaos in Ukraine from 1991 to 1994 was that the country had not dissolved its predemocratic parliament of 1990 but allowed it to linger until 1994, greatly damaging the nation. Similarly, after the Orange Revolution of late 2004, the Orange leaders did not dissolve the parliament and immediately hold fresh parliamentary elections but focused on the elections scheduled for March 2006.

The earlier the post-Soviet countries held their first parliamentary elections, the more democratic they would become. Estonia, the reform star, held its elections in September 1992, Latvia in September 1993, Lithuania in October–November 1993, Russia in December 1993, Moldova in February 1994, Ukraine in March 1994, and Armenia in July 1995 (Åslund 2002, 379). Only the first three are full democracies today.

At least one major political institution in a country, either the parliament or president, should be reasonably legitimate. Therefore, simultaneous elections are unwise. Until the May 2014 presidential elections, the Ukrainian parliament was the most legitimate, but after the democratic presidential elections in May the president was the most legitimate institution. The aftermath of the Arab Spring uprisings in Egypt and Libya show how dangerous a vacuum of legitimate institutions can be. Authoritarian rule tends to return under the pretext of defending the country against chaos and anarchy.

Ukraine did the right thing by first holding presidential elections, then quickly dissolving the parliament and holding early parliamentary elections while the reformers were still empowered from Euromaidan. The next step planned for 2015 is regional and local elections.

Successful Parliamentary Elections: The Foundation for Reform

On October 26, 2014, Ukraine held the parliamentary elections President Poroshenko had called for in late August. These elections were fully constitutional, and everybody seemed to realize that Ukraine needed early elections for a more representative parliament. The elections were well administered, with thousands of international observers assessing them as free and fair.

The Ukrainian Parliament is supposed to have 450 seats, half of which are

---

6. "Yefremov predlagayet zapretit' ballotirovat'sya tem, kto uzhe byl v Rade" ["Yefremov proposes to ban running for those who have already been in Rada"], *Ukrainskaya pravda*, July 21, 2014.

Table 7.1   Results of the parliamentary elections, October 26, 2014

Party	Share of proportional vote (percent of total votes cast)	Number of seats
People's Front	22.1	81
Petro Poroshenko's Bloc	21.8	148
Self-Help	11.0	32
Opposition Bloc	9.4	40
Radical Party	7.4	22
Fatherland	5.7	19
Independents and small parties	22.6	81
Total	100.0	423

Sources: Central Election Commission, 2014, www.cvk.gov.ua; Verkhovna Rada, Deputy Factions and Groups of VIII Convocation, 2014, http://gapp.rada.gov.ua/radatransl/Home/Factions/en.

distributed through a proportional election with a threshold of 5 percent and the remaining half through majority vote in one-mandate constituencies. But Russian occupation of Crimea and parts of Donetsk and Luhansk oblasts left 27 seats vacant: 12 single seats in Crimea and 15 of the 32 seats in Donbas. Thus, the parliament now has only 423 seats.[7]

The elections were a great victory for the pro-Western, reformist, center-right forces. The three winners were the like-minded People's Front of Prime Minister Yatsenyuk (22.1 percent and 81 seats), President Poroshenko's Bloc (21.8 percent but 148 seats), and the new civil activist party Self-Help of Lviv Mayor Andriy Sadoviy (11.0 percent and 32 seats). These three parties were evident coalition partners. Together they had a solid parliamentary majority of 261 seats (table 7.1). They formed a coalition with the 19 deputies of Yulia Tymoshenko's Fatherland party, the new populist Radical Party of Oleh Lyashko, which had been riding high in the opinion polls but fell back to 7.4 percent (22 seats), to reach a constitutional majority of 302 votes. One more party entered parliament, the Opposition Bloc, the remnant of Yanukovych's Regions party, which received surprisingly many votes at 9.4 percent (40 seats), leaving a balance of 81 representatives of independents or small parties.

The Ukrainian party system had been completely transformed. Of these

---

7. "Pro-Western Parties Win Parliamentary Elections," *Dragon Capital: Political Update*, October 27, 2014. Verkhovna Rada of Ukraine, "Deputy Factions and Groups of VIII Convocation," 2014, http://gapp.rada.gov.ua/radatransl/Home/Factions/en (accessed on January 26, 2015). The exact size of the factions changes frequently. Nineteen independent deputies formed the faction People's Will and another 19 deputies Economic Development, both of which may be described as oligarchic, while 39 stayed outside of all factions.

six parties, only Fatherland had existed before. The Opposition Bloc was a clear successor of the Regions party, but its vote share had fallen by two-thirds. Of the 423 deputies, a majority of 236 or 56 percent had never been parliamentarians before.[8] The elections were disastrous for the extreme right and left. President Poroshenko commented that for the first time in 96 years the Communist Party was not represented in the Ukrainian parliament, receiving only 3.9 percent of the votes. Nor did any other leftwing extremists enter parliament. On the nationalist right, Freedom (*Svoboda*) received only 4.7 percent of the vote, winning merely six single-mandate seats. The Right Sector, which Russian propaganda had created, gathered only 1.8 percent.[9]

Participation dropped to 52 percent from close to 70 percent in previous parliamentary elections. It was much higher in the western and central parts of the country than in the eastern and southern regions, reflecting both the war and apparent alienation of the eastern voters.

This result seemed like a vote for reform and against populism and extremism. The three most reformist parties won. The unexpected strong support for Yatsenyuk's National Front was a vote of confidence in him as prime minister. Self-Help, with its novel civil activists, could offer the necessary transparency within the government. The parliament is reasonably consolidated but represents all the relevant interests, and numerous civil activists have entered parliament. The *Financial Times* concluded in an editorial: "Ukraine's parliamentary elections...confirm the pro-western direction of its politics, producing for the first time a legislature clearly dominated by those favouring closer ties with the EU."[10]

Formation of a New Reform Government

After the elections, the five pro-European parties pursued long negotiations. They agreed to form a coalition government and adopted a 73-page coalition agreement, which was a list of legislative measures to be undertaken with a deadline for each measure. This was a broad coalition with 302 seats out of 423, an almost two-thirds majority. The agreement lacked clear strategic goals or a rationale for all these measures, and the rampant financial crisis was simply left out.

President Poroshenko reappointed Yatsenyuk as prime minister and on November 27 he was approved with nearly full support of the coalition. On December 2, Yatsenyuk appointed his new government. The five coalition partners each appointed their quota of ministers, with an emphasis on competence and youth. This was a highly technocratic government. In stark

---

8. "Ukraintsy obnovili Radu na 56%" ["Ukrainians Renewed the Parliament to 56%"], *Ukrainskaya pravda*, October 31, 2014.

9. Central Election Committee, "Parliamentary Elections 2014," www.cvk.gov.ua.

10. "Ukraine Sets Its Face toward the West," *Financial Times*, October 29, 2014.

contrast to previous Ukrainian governments, the new government consisted of young professionals, the cream of Kyiv's financial professionals, with an average age of 43. Only five of the 20 ministers had been ministers before, as members of Yatsenyuk's previous government since February. Apart from the prime minister, they were the ministers of interior, defense, foreign affairs, and education.

Three ministers are foreign nationals, who were awarded Ukrainian citizenship the same day they became ministers. Natalie Jaresko, a US citizen from the Ukrainian diaspora, became finance minister, Lithuanian Aivaras Abromavičius economy minister, and Aleksandre Kvitashvili of Georgia minister of healthcare. The government selected foreign nationals partly to ensure that they were not involved in corrupt Ukrainian schemes. A sign of the government's competence is that all but two of the 20 ministers speak English, while only two ministers spoke English in President Yanukovych's last government. A few ministers, however, had evident links to discredited big businessmen.[11]

Yatsenyuk focused on developing a more operative government program, which he presented to the government on December 9 and two days later to the parliament. He offered nearly everything a reformer could have asked for, and he backed it up with a strong narrative to appeal to Ukrainians (Yatsenyuk 2014b). He saw Europe as the anchor, aim, and means of Ukraine's reforms: "Our basic course is a European course.... Our final aim is Ukraine's membership of the European Union. But to achieve that goal it is necessary to go through a serious test, to carry out radical changes and to make Ukraine European." He pointed to the external threat to Ukraine's sovereignty and the "internal aggression" from corruption to justify his radical approach. To meet the security threat in 2015, Ukraine would raise its military expenditures to up to 5 percent of GDP.

Yatsenyuk's key slogans were "decentralization, deregulation, and debureaucratization." The old Soviet technical standards were to be abandoned for European standards in line with the Association Agreement with the European Union. The state administration had been cut by 10 percent in 2014 and would be reduced by another 10 percent in 2015. Anticorruption policy was a major emphasis. Ukraine was to establish a public register of owners of all property and enterprises in Ukraine. The entire law enforcement system was to be reformed, and all judges scrutinized. All these changes were supposed to take place in the course of two years, 2015–16. How much was to be done each year is mostly not specified.

On economic policy, three points stand out as a litmus test of Ukraine's intentions. First, public expenditures need to be cut by 10 percent of GDP. Second, energy prices should be raised to the market level, which would finally eliminate the corruption that has been taking place via arbitrage. "We will raise all energy prices and tariffs to the market level at the same time as we

11. Milan Lelich and Yuliya Samsonova, "Chto my znaem o novykh ministrakh" ["What We Know about the New Ministers"], *Focus*, December 4, 2014.

offer benefits and subsidies to those who should receive them, that is, all poor people in Ukraine" (Yatsenyuk 2014b). Third, a law on the agricultural land market needed to be adopted, though not immediately because of the lack of a cadaster.

Yatsenyuk's speech contained dozens of other reform proposals. The number of enterprises excluded from privatization would be reduced from 1,500 to 300. The others would be sold off as the market allowed. All state corporations would be subject to international audit. The labor market would be liberalized. All medicines certified in Western countries would be allowed in Ukraine without the current cumbersome certifications, as had been done in Georgia. Comprehensive healthcare insurance would be introduced and education financing would be based on achievements. Wherever possible, EU assistance would be requested and EU standards adopted.

Yatsenyuk put the government program to a vote and it was adopted with 269 votes, as almost all the members of the coalition supported it. Yet, the program encountered substantial criticism from the coalition, especially from members of the Poroshenko Bloc. Yatsenyuk's speech was only eight pages long, and he presented the government program in 13 PowerPoint slides.[12] Critics complained that it was too short and did not reflect everything in the coalition program, while the government's aim was to explain the purpose of the reforms, offer a policy focus, and focus on the acute financial crisis. Civil activists complained that they had not been involved and that the process had not been transparent. They also worried that the cut in the public administration was too limited and that the reform of law enforcement was not clear. They suspected that the president and prime minister were not committed to reform and to combating corruption but wanted to maintain the old system. In a populist vein, they avoided mentioning the government's proposals on three critical issues: sharp public expenditure cuts, unification of energy prices, and legalization of private sales of agricultural land.

In sum, key political changes had been carried out. Democratic elections of both president and parliament had been held. The next step would be local elections in 2015 after a law on decentralization was passed. A parliamentary coalition supporting a pro-European course and market reform had been established. A reform government had been formed. The government had presented an operative reform program with a clear reform narrative. A large parliamentary majority had approved the government's reform program. The next steps would be to convince the population that these reforms were the right ones, to legislate major reforms, and to attract sufficient international funding to keep Ukraine afloat financially.

---

12. Programma Deyatel'nosti kabineta ministrov Ukrainya [Action Program of the Cabinet of Ministers of Ukraine], Ukraine's government portal, December 9, 2014.

Increase Transparency and Control Campaign Funding

Corruption is the essence of Ukrainian politics. Like the US Senate in the Gilded Age, the Ukrainian Parliament is a club of dollar millionaires in an otherwise poor country. Political corruption has many interlocking features.[13]

Ukrainian election campaigns are among the most expensive in the world. The 2010 presidential campaign and the 2012 parliamentary campaign each cost about $1 billion or 0.5 percent of GDP. In relation to GDP, that is 1,000 times more than a US election campaign. Before Yanukovych's political demise, he was rumored to have amassed a war chest of $3 billion for the presidential election planned for March 2015. Private assessments by insiders suggest that the 2014 parliamentary elections were much cheaper, probably $250 million to $300 million.[14] Many billboards went unused during the campaign. Needless to say, all these expenditures are unofficial and illegal, but in Ukraine nobody would be elected without sizeable and expensive television advertisements.

To contest elections, Ukrainian political parties need considerable campaign financing, almost always illegally acquired. Each party has a gray cardinal in charge of the party's *obshchak*—Russian word for an organized crime group's communal fund of illegally accumulated money. The gray cardinal (they are all men) is usually a parliamentarian, sometimes even a faction leader, and a prominent businessman.

Yanukovych's Regions party could fill its *obshchak* through extortion. The other parties had to sell goods and services. Any party could buy a "safe" seat in parliament for up to $5 million. The ruling party or coalition sold lucrative jobs (*khlebnye mesta*), such as state enterprise CEO jobs, state committee chairmanships, and governorships (Åslund 2009, 2014a). Posts of judges were also traded. In a coalition government, gray cardinals of coalition partners agreed on who would be allowed to sell what job. Thus a minister was not permitted to appoint his or her deputies, because they would obviously not listen to "their" minister. Economy Minister Pavlo Sheremeta resigned in August 2014 because he was not allowed to appoint his deputies.[15]

After buying their offices, parliamentarians and senior officials needed to finance their purchases and turn a profit. They did so through corruption: *deriban*, kickbacks from public procurement, extortion, and corporate raiding. Thus, many of them were committed to corruption. Certain industries, such as nuclear energy, tend to be controlled by the same businessmen regardless of the government in power. In other privileged industries, such as gas, key

---

13. This section draws on Åslund (2014a).

14. Interviews with financial and political experts in Kyiv, September 11–17, 2014, and January 19–22, 2015.

15. "Sheremeta nazval prichinu svoei otstavki" ["Sheremeta Named the Reason for His Resignation"], *Ukrainskaya pravda*, August 21, 2014.

businessmen often change with elections. Many businessmen switch political affiliations, always wanting to be on the right side of the ruling government (Åslund 2014a).

Most big businessmen wanted to become parliamentarians to influence regulations and budget allocations. In addition, they enjoy parliamentary immunity, which Euromaidan activists have strongly demanded be abolished.[16] Maidan activists, who are now members of parliament, may shame the other deputies into giving up their immunity, which President Poroshenko has demanded as well.[17] Membership in parliament is then likely to become less attractive to dubious businessmen.

The fundamental insight is that not only the Ukrainian economy but also Ukrainian politics are pervasively corrupt. The old system hardly allowed anybody to come to power unless they were prepared to play the corruption game. Cynical Ukrainians do not ask whether corruption will decline but who will benefit under the new rule. In September 2014, the popular view was that the post-Yanukovych regime was as corrupt as the Yanukovych regime. It is vital to oust corrupt politicians, but the whole political system needs to be reformed to prevent corruption.

Corruption is not inevitable. It is a choice. Among the postcommunist countries, Estonia is the least corrupt, thanks to early, comprehensive, and radical political and market economic reforms. Georgia has drastically reduced corruption since 2003 thanks to even more radical reforms (Bendukidze and Saakashvili 2014).

The most effective tool for fighting corruption is transparency (Rose-Ackerman 1999). In 1766, Sweden adopted the first Freedom of Information Act in the world. At the time, Sweden was an aristocratic or oligarchic society politically not too different from Ukraine today. The French and Russian ambassadors competed in bribing top officials. When one aristocratic party gained power in parliament, it wanted to expose the corruption of its predecessors. It did so by adopting a truly radical law that declared that all documents be made available to the public, except national security or personal medical records (Carlsson and Rosen 1961, 145–46). Since then, all declarations of income and wealth in Sweden have been available to the public. Every year, newspapers publish the names and incomes of the richest in each town in Sweden, making it difficult to hide illicit revenues or fortunes.

Five years later, Denmark adopted a similar law, also to expose the misdeeds of the aristocracy. These laws stuck and were shared by the then dependent nations of Norway, Iceland, and Finland. Many countries have freedom of information acts, but none as far-reaching as the ones in the five Nordic

---

16. At the Yalta European Strategy conference in Kyiv, September 11–14, 2014, one of the strongest demands from the floor was the abolition of parliamentary immunity.

17. "Porshenko mechtaet ob otmene neprikosnovennosti deputatov" ["Poroshenko Is Dreaming of the Abolition of the Immunity of Deputies"], *Ukrainskaya pravda*, October 3, 2014.

countries. Corruption in these countries has continuously been far less than in other countries (Transparency International 2013).[18]

In communist countries, secrecy was even more sacrosanct than openness is in democracies, rendering transparency all the more effective in breaking the old communist way of ruling. In 2010, Ukraine finally adopted its first freedom of information act, but it seems to have had no impact. In the spring of 2014, the country promulgated a new freedom of information act. Whether it will have real teeth remains to be seen.

To be truly transparent, Ukraine needs to do several things. To begin with, it needs to publish all legal acts, which it has done, but many more public documents should be available on the web. Thanks to a law from the Orange period, all court decisions are published on the web.[19] Public exposure discourages judges from passing clearly illegal verdicts in exchange for bribes, although in Ukraine it has proven difficult to shame corrupt judges into obeying the law. At the end of July 2014, no fewer than 38,787,313 court verdicts were available on the web.[20]

Similarly, all public financial information, such as budgets at all levels, should be put on the web, not only public procurement documents but also the whole bidding process should be carried out through e-government. Ukraine's lively and impressively accurate independent media and civil society will undoubtedly expose all the corruption they can find through their online publications, which is bound to drive down corruption if people exposed are prosecuted.

The government itself should also investigate state institutions. In Western Europe, public auditing chambers have existed for hundreds of years. After the collapse of communism Ukraine established its Auditing Chamber (*Rakhunkova Palata*), which is subordinate to the parliament so that it is independent from the government, but it has not functioned well because it has been highly politicized, complaining about privatization taking place rather than how it was carried out. The Auditing Chamber should be an apolitical expert body with access to the necessary information and resources to hire qualified people.

Private finances of parliamentarians must be made transparent. At present, the publicly available personal financial statements show ludicrously low numbers. These declarations should be subject to independent auditing. Candidates and political parties should both be scrutinized in independent audits.

One of the biggest expenditures of political parties is on election campaigns, notably television ads. They are well monitored by Ukrainian nongov-

---

18. Another important principle is prohibition of conflicts of interests, which is discussed in the next chapter.

19. Law of Ukraine "On Access to Court Decisions," December 22, 2005, http://zakon4.rada.gov.ua/laws/show/3262-15.

20. Unified State Register of Court Decisions, www.reyestr.court.gov.ua.

ernmental organizations, and the prices are set transparently on the market, allowing fairly accurate assessments of these costs. The inordinately high election campaign costs must be reduced, and the government should legislate to limit television advertising, or even prohibit it. Instead, candidates could engage in official televised debates. Like many European governments, Ukraine should regulate television coverage of election campaigns.

Today, the gray cardinal in each party in Ukraine handles large illegal private party financing, which should be prohibited. Campaign financing should be strictly limited to two sources: public funds and party membership fees. Similar restrictions are standard in many European countries, such as Germany. To effectively prohibit private funding is particularly important because large corrupt Russian funds are bound to flood the country in all future elections unless rigorous transparency rules are imposed.

The government's anticorruption strategy for 2014–17 instructs the parliament to promulgate a law on budget financing of political parties in Ukraine, as is the case in most countries.[21] If Ukraine can cut the cost of an election from $1 billion to a more normal amount below $50 million, then many other reforms will be feasible. The two elections in 2014 were clearly much cheaper than previous elections but much bigger cuts in costs are needed, which many Ukrainians are aware of. Victor Pinchuk, one of Ukraine's wealthiest businessmen, wrote: "We must prevent in Ukraine that money gives access to political power and that political power gives access to money."[22]

Move to Fully Proportional Elections

Ukraine's politicians are not for sale; they are only for rent. Thus goes a popular adage in Ukraine. Since 1990, Ukraine has held eight parliamentary elections. All have been competitive, but how free and fair they were has varied.

Ukraine has experimented with three electoral systems. It started off with a first-past-the-post voting system in single-mandate districts, followed by a semiproportional system, leading to fully proportional elections in 2006 and 2007, but it regressed to a semiproportional system in 2012. The incumbent business interests refused to change this system for the elections in October 2014, because they recognized that it facilitated their reelection. The new parliament can and should revert to fully proportional elections.

A review of the evolution of the Ukrainian electoral system, the election outcomes, and their shortcomings reveals great fragmentation and weak political parties, rendering coalitions unwieldy and unstable. The elite, which was dominated by state officials, has been taken over by businessmen, but its power has never been threatened (Åslund 2009).

The problems with Ukrainian elections have varied over time. In the first

---

21. "Politicheskie partii teper' budut finansirovat'sya iz budzheta" ["Now the Political Parties Will Be Financed from the Budget"], *Ukrainskaya pravda*, October 16, 2014.

22. Victor Pinchuk, "God Est" ["One Year"], *Ukrainskaya pravda*, March 26, 2014.

two parliamentary elections in 1990 and 1994, which followed the first-past-the-post system in single-mandate constituencies, most candidates were barely known and the outcomes seemed rather accidental, benefiting old state officials and communists.

In the elections of 1998 and 2002, half the deputies were elected proportionally and half in single-mandate constituencies. These elections favored new wealthy businessmen, who came to dominate the political system. After both elections, the parliament was badly fragmented with 13 to 14 party factions, most of which were characterized as "oligarchic."

Big businessmen also held sway in the fully proportional elections in 2006 and 2007, but these were the only elections that were truly free and fair. The proportional elections did away with the fragmentation of parties, consolidating them into five major parties. Admittedly, these parties found it difficult to form coalitions, but more because of the personalities involved than the nature of the electoral system.

In the 2012 elections, Ukraine reverted to a semiproportional system, because Yanukovych knew that he could win more seats in the one-member constituencies and also pressure independent businessmen who won such seats. This system inflated campaign expenditures and led to less free and fair elections. Also in 2014, the single-mandate districts allowed some of the most odious politicians to be reelected. Civil activists found that of the deputies who had voted for Yanukovych's dictatorial laws on January 16, 2014, 64 were reelected, 54 in one-member constituencies and 10 on the party list of the Opposition Bloc.[23] The dozen or so representatives of the hard nationalist right who entered parliament were all elected in one-member constituencies.

This brief review of Ukraine's parliamentary elections suggests that a purely proportional system—as in the parliamentary elections of 2006 and 2007, the country's most democratic—works best for the country. Single-mandate constituencies do not work well in Ukraine because many have been bought by businessmen, who rule their districts like feudal lords and use their vote in parliament to promote their own commercial interests. One-member constituencies breed corruption, keeping political parties weak without ideology and party discipline. In established democracies, by contrast, political parties are consolidated and have some ideology and party discipline. If done repeatedly, switching parties is almost considered shameful behavior.

A hurdle for representation is needed, at least 3 percent and not more than 5 percent, though the exact level is not too important. Given the great political fragmentation in many European countries and previously in Ukraine, a high threshold of 5 percent might seem preferable, but the need for new political parties could justify a lower threshold. One nightmare that must be avoided is the October 1991 elections in Poland, which resulted in 29 parties entering parliament because of the absence of a threshold.

---

23. "Ukraintsy obnovili Radu na 56%" ["Ukrainians Renewed the Parliament to 56%"], *Ukrainskaya pravda*, October 31, 2014.

A major concern in Ukraine is the buying and selling of parliamentary seats for big sums. After winning a seat in parliament, an independent candidate often trades his or her vote to the highest bidder. One countermeasure is so-called open party lists, allowing a citizen to vote both for a party and a specific candidate, which prevents a candidate from buying a "safe" seat from a party. Germany and Finland have such systems, where people vote for both party and person.

Nongovernmental organizations and Euromaidan activists overwhelmingly favor proportional elections and open lists.[24] These were even part of the new government program in February 2014, but the old parliament refused to adopt the relevant legislation. Such an electoral system would decrease the power of the party leaders, which explains their opposition. The counterargument is that political parties in Ukraine remain weak, and defections are common. Unless a party can use the whip and oust parliamentarians who defect, party discipline is bound to be low.

Curiously, political extremism is not much of a concern. The Communist Party and other extreme leftwing parties lost significance with the Orange Revolution, when Yanukovych's Regions party absorbed most of their votes. They have withered and are unlikely to become politically significant again. Nor have hard nationalist parties had much luck in Ukraine, as was evident in the two 2014 elections. Few European countries have recorded as few extremist voters as Ukraine.

Decentralize Power

President Poroshenko has made the amendment of Ukraine's Constitution one of his top priorities, and a broad consensus prevails about several necessary changes. The concept of decentralization has been elaborated by a working group headed by Deputy Prime Minister Volodymyr Groisman, former mayor of Poroshenko's home town Vinnytsia, where he pioneered municipal reforms. They included transparency, swift provision of government services, and one-stop shop for services. Groisman aims at a substantial decentralization of power, giving the regional and local administrations more political and economic power.

Ukraine has essentially retained the extreme Soviet overcentralization of power. It has far too many state institutions with too many employees but few relevant powers at too many administrative levels. Ukraine needs to carry out far-reaching decentralization, as virtually all other postcommunist countries in Europe have done. The Yatsenyuk government approved a Concept of the Reform of Local Self-Government and Territorial Organization, which can serve as a basis for such a reform (Cabinet of Ministers 2014a). Poland stands out as a particularly successful model of regional reform.

The planned decentralization is supposed to improve administration on

---

24. For a full civil activist argument, see Ostap Kuchma (2014).

four fronts. First, the Ukrainian state administration would function better when decisions about execution and financing of state policy are made at a lower administrative level. Second, decentralization would increase democratization, since democratically elected representatives should make most decisions at each administrative level instead of the current centrally appointed governors.

Third, the Ukrainian government administration contains too many entities and administrative levels, badly requiring consolidation. The two lowest levels of the administrative hierarchy (communities and districts) need to be merged and their number sharply reduced for viability. The establishment of an effective system of local governance requires joint reform of local self-government and the state administrative-territorial system. The goal should be to create a clear three-tier system of territorial units, which could serve as a territorial base for local and regional self-governance: communities, districts (*raiony*), and regions (*oblasti*) (Center for Political and Legal Reforms 2014). When determining the powers of each level of authority, the EU subsidiarity principle should be the guide: All administrative tasks should be carried out at as low a level as is practical.

Finally, government finances, both taxation and expenditures, need to be decentralized as well, as discussed in chapter 9. Ideally, public services should be decentralized to the lowest feasible level. Each level of government should receive its revenues primarily from taxes that it controls and collects itself. Authorities would then stop harassing local businessmen, and their interest in imposing nuisance taxes would ebb, as such practices would hinder local development and thus the tax base and tax revenues. Meanwhile, local and regional elections of both councils and executives will lead to transparency and democratic control with checks and balances.

In the new scheme, the community would be the basic unit of the administrative-territorial structure. They need to be merged around economically viable locations to function satisfactorily. The community's head and council should be elected by direct vote. Local self-governments should possess sufficient property and financial resources to be able to fulfill their mandates. Local tasks should include police, firefighting, and provision of most administrative services.

Also, districts (*raiony*), the second level of self-governance, require major consolidation. They should be responsible only for public tasks that cannot be successfully performed at the community level. They should have their own executive committees, which would require an amendment of the constitution. Provision of in-patient medical care is a natural task of district-level self-governance.

The 24 oblasts or regions should be the territorial basis for regional self-governance. Their main tasks should be to ensure the region's social and economic development, promote investment, develop regional transportation infrastructure, advance culture, sports, and tourism, protect the environment, preserve a region's ethnic and cultural uniqueness, and operate specialized healthcare and educational institutions. The region's residents should elect their regional councils directly, and their executive bodies should work as regional self-governments.

The executive branch at the local level needs to build more effective relations with both the Cabinet of Ministers and local self-government. In order to ensure political neutrality and professionalism, the heads of local public administration should be career civil service officials. Tasks should be clearly divided between the local public administration and the local self-government. A territorial-administrative reform was prepared in 2014 and could be implemented in 2015. One guideline is the European Charter of Local Self-Government, which Ukraine has ratified.[25]

The Kremlin's demand for "federalization" is a red herring. It does not refer to real federalization but is an attempt to undermine Ukraine's national sovereignty and territorial integrity because Moscow insists that Ukrainian regions should be entitled to pursue their own foreign and defense policy as well as hold referendums on secession from Ukraine.

A Parliamentary System Is Preferable

Originally, many postcommunist countries were mixed presidential-parliamentary systems, but most of these nations have evolved. Today, the Central and Eastern European democracies have developed parliamentary systems, while the authoritarian post-Soviet countries have reinforced presidential rule. The relatively free post-Soviet countries—Armenia, Georgia, Kyrgyzstan, Moldova, and Ukraine—have been moving toward parliamentary systems. Empirically, the positive correlation between democracy and parliamentary system is evident in this region. The causality is also apparent (Åslund 2013a).

The reinstituted Ukrainian Constitution of December 2004 is one of the few parliamentary-presidential constitutions in the region. From the point of view of democracy, it was an improvement on the 1996 presidential constitution, but a normal European parliamentary system would be far better. Ukraine is not likely to adopt a parliamentary system now when the president is amending the constitution, but it should be done whenever politically feasible.

Political scientists have debated the relative merits of presidential and parliamentary rule for long. Prominent political scientist Juan Linz (1990) has formulated the dominant judgment that in general parliamentary systems are preferable. A parliamentary system is all the more important in postcommunist countries. Better than a presidential system it can seize control over the state apparatus and rebuild it.

The former communist countries were left with a contradictory constitutional inheritance. They had written constitutions that had been promulgated but never applied, coming to life only after communism. To a surprising ex-

---

25. *Pravitel'stvenny portal*, September 2, 2014, www.kmu.gov.ua.

tent, constitutions and politics were seen as national prerogatives, and most countries tried to draw on precommunist national history, however miserable it had been, and international experience was ignored. The impact of Western models was much more limited than in the economic sphere.

The USSR Supreme Soviet was a rubberstamp parliament that convened twice a year to adopt a couple of laws each time. Many of its members were token representatives of various social strata, such as picturesque milkmaids, rather than powerbrokers. According to the USSR Constitution of 1977 and its Ukrainian sequel of 1978, however, the parliament was powerful and sovereign. In the free world, Montesquieu's (1748/1977) principle of the division of power had prevailed since the late 18th century. The communists, however, had never accepted that principle, which they considered circumscribed the power of the Communist Party. After communism, public understanding of the benefit of a clear division of power was missing. On the basis of the written Soviet republican constitutions, post-Soviet parliamentarians demanded substantial executive powers. These constitutional problems were aggravated by the lack of party structures and the not fully democratic parliamentary elections in 1990.

Immediately after communism, the presidency was given strong powers in most postcommunist countries to offer firm leadership and strengthen newly born states, but inspired by Western Europe and influenced by EU institutions, the powers of presidents in Central and Eastern Europe have been increasingly reduced. Legislation became the concern of parliament, the government was accountable to parliament, and the president focused on constitutional and international issues.

In the former Soviet Union, presidential powers have persistently been much stronger than in Central and Eastern Europe, but parliaments have challenged them, leading to virulent conflicts. Presidents reacted to irresponsible parliaments by demanding more power, but the parliaments usually refused, pointing to the corruption of the government. The most dramatic strife occurred in Russia in September–October 1993, ending with bloodshed after the president had dissolved the predemocratic and unrepresentative parliament, which launched an armed uprising. Similar conflicts occurred in Armenia, Belarus, Kazakhstan, Kyrgyzstan, Moldova, and Ukraine, but they were resolved without bloodshed.

Over time, some clarity has evolved. The less democratic a country is, the stronger its presidential powers. Georgia, Moldova, Ukraine, Armenia, and Kyrgyzstan have moved toward stronger parliamentary systems, whereas all the other post-Soviet countries have reinforced presidential powers, which has coincided with the strengthening of authoritarian rule (Åslund 2013a).

The empirical evidence is clear: All Central and East European countries have parliamentary systems, and they are all democratic with comparatively good governance. All the authoritarian countries in the former Soviet Union have presidential systems. In between, five former Soviet republics, namely Ukraine, Moldova, Georgia, Armenia, and Kyrgyzstan, have a mixture of parliamentary and presidential systems that is frequently changing (Freedom House 2014). They are not full democracies but are relatively free. Georgia has made a clear break with corruption, and Moldova has taken distinct steps, while Ukraine, Armenia, and Kyrgyzstan remain pervasively corrupt (Transparency International 2013). The essence of democracy is institutions that effectively represent the public interest, and elections are the main vehicle in their construction. The timely creation of political institutions is vital, and timely means early.

A parliamentary system has many advantages over a presidential system. First of all, it offers much more transparency. Parliamentarians can demand plenty of information from the government, which cannot refuse it. Usually, a parliamentary government based on proportional elections is a coalition government, which means that the coalition partners are checking and controlling one another, further increasing transparency (EBRD 1999).

A second great advantage of a parliamentary system is that it reinforces the capacity to legislate. Any serious reform involves the adoption of hundreds of laws, and only a real legislature can seriously undertake such a legislative endeavor. Ample attempts to rush through legislation as presidential decrees have failed to be effective. The quality of presidential decrees tends to be poor, since they are not properly vetted. Nor are they based on a significant political base, and they can easily be contradicted by new presidential decrees promoted by other lobbying groups (Remington, Smith, and Haspel 1998).

A third argument for a parliamentary system is that it contains stronger checks and balances over the Cabinet of Ministers than over the presidential administration, which has patently been above the law with its own budgets and assets. With its many hearings and public debates a parliament offers much stronger checks and balances over the government.

Finally and perhaps most importantly, the presidential system has regenerated old communist institutions. The Central Committee of the Communist Party was transformed into the presidential administration, and the regional party committees into regional administrations, which continued to interfere at will. The old communist telephone rule persists. Ukraine's presidential administration has varied in size, but it has consistently been large—559 people in 2013.[26] These bureaucracies became centers of rampant corruption because of their large assets, freedom to intervene, and absence of accountability.

The drawback is that parliamentary systems tend to be unwieldy and slow. Ukraine must not return to its long coalition negotiations of the Orange period, notably in the summer of 2006. Nor should it opt for too broad a coalition. Slovakia offers a telling example. In 1998, the united opposition against the populist Prime Minister Vladimír Mečiar won the elections, but nine parties with very different outlooks formed a coalition government, and desired reforms were stalled. In 2002, four like-minded center-right parties won the elections and formed a coalition government, which finally drove through

---

26. Presidential Administration website, www.president.gov.ua/content/limit_pa.html.

the necessary reforms (Miklos 2014). Similarly, Estonian prime minister Laar (2002) pushed through his radical reforms in 1992–94 with a majority of only one seat in parliament, though Estonia has far stronger party discipline than Ukraine. The December 2014 Ukrainian five-party collation seems too broad and too disjointed to function.

Ukraine should endeavor to establish a fully parliamentary system to improve the quality of its governance and root out the bad inheritance from its communist past.

Recommendations

1. Adopt a fully proportional electoral system with open party lists and a threshold for representation of 3 to 5 percent of the votes.

2. Subject all finances of political candidates and political parties to independent audits.

3. Firmly restrict private campaign financing.

4. Abolish parliamentary immunity.

5. Decentralize more political and economic power to local and regional levels, while reducing the number of administrative levels to three: communities, districts, and regions and consolidate communities and districts to viable sizes.

6. Depoliticize and increase the role of the Auditing Chamber, which should become an apolitical expert body.

7. Move toward a fully parliamentary system.

8

Next Comes Reform
of Ukraine's State

Deregulation, reducing power and corresponding decrease of corruption.
This is our agenda today.
—Prime Minister Arseniy Yatsenyuk (2014c)

Nothing is more difficult to reform than the state. Enterprises are simple: Their all-dominant goal is to make money, and the state can privatize them and leave them alone to make their profits. The state has many goals and is the residue of functions that cannot be privatized. Its primary aim is to guarantee the citizens national security and law and order, but it also performs all kinds of regulatory and social functions, and the citizens want good and efficient service. The market cannot function without supervision, which the state needs to provide (Tanzi 2011).

The state works in a completely different way from an enterprise. While business enterprises are theoretically disciplined by the market, the state has a monopoly on law enforcement and courts, which can engage in legally sanctioned violence. The ultimate protection against the state's abuse of its powers is democratic rule. Transparency and auditing are vital instruments, but the prime engine in successful bureaucracies is an esprit de corps in a highly qualified, well-paid, and proud civil service (Weber 1922). In practice, that means that a good state is a small state. Oliver Williamson (1975) introduced the helpful distinction between markets and hierarchies: A state is inevitably a hierarchy, which means that it can only be reformed from above.

By all measures, including public financing and share of employment, Ukraine's state is too large. Its mandate is far too extensive with all kinds of functions, most of which should not be controlled by the state. It functions poorly, because it is pervasively corrupt. The state needs to be reformed from the top down and cleansed of corruption. The new Ukrainian government favors democracy and the rule of law, and the European Association Agreement offers a blueprint for reform of the state as well as technical assistance. But the question is how to carry out these reforms. With a newly elected president and parliament, the new government needs to move fast to clean up the government from the top to render it more efficient and service oriented.

The first problem is that there are too many state agencies, often superfluous or even harmful. Their number needs to be reduced and redundant agencies closed or merged. To begin with, numerous inspection agencies with no role to play in a modern free economy should be closed.

The second step should be lustration or the purge primarily of courts of justice and law enforcement.

A third issue is public administration reform. The current administration is neither competent nor efficient. Frequently, civil servants do not know their own rules and are thus unable to obey them. The skills and integrity of civil servants need to be raised, as well as their salaries.

A fourth concern is that the state tries to control far too many things. Often, large substandard administrations regulate actions that need not be checked, while ignoring vital regulations. The number of rules and regulations needs to be cut. State regulation should be limited to what is really necessary given the pervasive corruption.

Finally, in 2000 Ukraine privatized agricultural land, distributing it to the members of collective farms and the employees of state farms, but private sales of land were not legalized. Time and again, the Ukrainian government has delayed the legalization of private sales of agricultural land, but such sales should be legalized as soon as possible.

Selecting State Agencies to Close or Merge

Ukraine has a huge public sector employing 4.42 million in 2012, which amounts to 26.7 percent of Ukraine's total workforce.[1] As of January 1, 2014, the total number of public employees in the state administration was 433,269: 335,270 civil servants (state level) and 97,999 local government officials.[2]

The number of state agencies needs to be reduced through closures and mergers. Ukraine has already closed or merged several state agencies, but a large number of superfluous and harmful agencies persist. Most of all, the state attempts to regulate what should not be checked. Another argument for mergers is to strengthen agencies that regulate, for example, energy and finance against strong vested interests. Furthermore, many administrative tasks should be decentralized to regional or local authorities. Most of Ukraine's state agencies are officially subordinate to the Cabinet of Ministers. In addition, many state

---

1. International Labor Organization, ILOSTAT Database, www.ilo.org (accessed on August 8, 2014).

2. "Derzhavna sluzhba v tsyfrakh" ["Public Service in Numbers 2014"], Center for Adaptation of the Civil Service, www.center.gov.ua/en (accessed on August 8, 2014).

agencies exist under the president, notably the presidential administration, the national defense and security council, and security services.[3]

The Ukrainian government is in flux, and several of the changes suggested here are under way. In August 2014, President Petro Poroshenko stated that out of 83 state inspections only 19 would remain.[4] On September 15, the Cabinet of Ministers decided to cut the number of inspection agencies from 56 to 27 (using another count), mainly through mergers but also by eliminating control functions. This scaling down can be done quickly and it is better to do it all at once.

As of fall 2014 Ukraine had 16 ministries, a little more than the 12 to 15 in Western countries. Most of the ministries are needed: agriculture, culture, defense, environment, economy, education and science, energy, finance, foreign affairs, health care, internal affairs, justice, and social policy. But three appear superfluous. The Ministry of Revenues and Charges had already been transformed into the State Fiscal Service. It is subordinate directly to the Cabinet of Ministers, but the Ministry of Finance should have control not only over expenditures but also over revenues.[5] The Ministry of Infrastructure should be merged with the Ministry of Economic Development and Trade. The Ministry of Youth and Sports could be merged with the Ministry of Culture, as is often the case. The Ministry of Regional Development, Construction, and Communal Services reflects overcentralization and should be abolished with the ongoing major decentralization and its tasks devolved to the regions. In December 2014, a new Ministry of Information was formed. Such a ministry should not exist in a democratic country.

Five national commissions form a second administrative level. These are quite important, dealing with the regulation of communal services, energy, the stock market, finance, and information.[6] Information should not be regulated in a free state, so the national commission on information abolished. Finance and energy sectors require sophisticated and strong regulatory bodies with great integrity. To improve their efficacy, the government has merged the national commissions for energy and communal services. Similarly, the two national commissions for securities and the stock market and financial services should be merged into one national commission on financial regulation because Ukraine's financial markets are tiny, and the financial regulation service should be strong enough to impart confidence to market actors. The

---

3. "Tsentral'nye organy ispolnitel'noy vlasti" ["Central Executive Authorities"], *Pravitel'stvenny portal*, September 10, 2014.

4. "Poroshenko obeshchaet sokrashchenie organov kontrolia" ["Poroshenko promises reduction of control bodies"], *Ekonomicheskaya pravda*, August 7, 2014.

5. Resolution of the Cabinet Ministers of Ukraine "On the State Fiscal Service of Ukraine," No. 236, May 21, 2014, http://zakon4.rada.gov.ua/laws/show/236-2014-%D0%BF.

6. "Natsional'nye Komisii" ["National Commissions"], *Pravitel'stvenny portal*, www.kmu.gov.ua/control/ru/publish/officialcategory?cat_id=246402952 (accessed on July 31, 2014).

National Bank of Ukraine (NBU) regulates the banks and has its hands full, as half the banks were close to bankruptcy in the fall of 2014.

The third bureaucratic level comprises no fewer than 25 national services, of which 21 seem to have dubious value as independent agencies. The remaining four, which should rightly be independent entities, deal with archives, aviation, intellectual property rights, and statistics. The state service regulating the development of entrepreneurship and the state service defending personal data are unnecessary and should be closed. The other 19 national services seem justified but not as independent agencies. They should be merged with the existing ministries to avoid turf battles: The Ministry of Health Care should handle AIDS and pharmaceuticals; the Ministry of Justice prisons and registrations; the Ministry of Interior emergency situations and drugs; the Ministry of Economic Development and Trade should deal with geology and export control; the Ministry of Finance with the treasury and tax collection; and the Ministry of Agriculture should handle sanitary and phytosanitary regulations. Each of these national services has its own bureaucracy with legal, human resources, accounting, and international departments and merging them would substantially reduce the number of people working there. But if EU regulations require more independent agencies, Ukraine would have to concede.

Digging deeper into the Ukrainian bureaucracy we find a fourth level of 14 state agencies. Three should be abolished. The state agency on energy efficiency is clearly redundant when the country has ministries of environment and energy. The state reserve agency is a Soviet remnant, which interferes in commodity markets and imposes unnecessary costs and corruption through embezzlement of Ukraine's resources. Similarly, the state agency for investment and national projects is dysfunctional and infamous for corruption and should be closed. Four state agencies deal with natural resources (water, forests, land, and fish). They could be brought under the Ministry of Agriculture or Ministry of Ecology and Natural Resources. Each of the remaining state agencies has distinct interest groups that are likely to fight for them, rendering it politically sensitive to challenge their independent existence. They deal with science, innovation, and informatics; movies; tourism; Chernobyl; and space. They appear unnecessary, but politics might dictate their survival.

The lower we go, the more inefficient the state administration becomes. A fifth administrative level contains 11 state inspection agencies. They are the most harmful state bodies. Considering the current Ukrainian business climate several should be abolished to the benefit of Ukraine, its population, and its entrepreneurship. Yet six of them seem necessary: the inspection agencies for architectural-construction issues, consumer protection, environment, labor, sea and river transportation, and nuclear security.

Inspection of agriculture, technology, and road transportation do not seem justified. The agricultural inspection agency, which employs 5,000 people, has no useful function but is known to engage in widespread extortion of bribes from farmers. That Ukraine still has a state price control inspection agency is outrageous. It should be abolished instantly. The very large financial inspection agency with 6,400 posts is the old control and audit directorate (*kontrolno-revizionnoe upravlenie*), an old Soviet-style body.[7] It should be replaced with an independent auditing organ under the parliament, or the parliament's current auditing chamber could carry out this function. Inspection of education should be a key function of the Ministry of Education and Science, requiring no independent inspectorate.

Many inspection organs are hidden in many other places, often subordinate to ministries. A representative of the Ukrainian tax agency is quoted as saying that the "government has 70 different bodies with licensing authority, including 40 with the power to shut down a business" (Stecklow, Piper, and Akymenko 2014). Similarly, Deputy Prime Minister Volodymyr Groisman stated that Ukraine has "80 different inspectorates, controlling organs, and control departments in ministries." He argued that at least 60 should be closed and a maximum of 20 should remain.[8] He should go further and cut 70, leaving only 10.

Toward the bottom of the Ukrainian state administration, there are five "central executive bodies with special status," usually called state committees. Three of them make sense in principle, namely the antimonopoly committee, the state property fund, and the national agency for the state service. The other two—the state television and radio broadcasting committee and state service on special communications and information protection—seem unnecessary. The former should be abolished as an unwanted agency for censorship of the media, while the latter pertains to the security services.

So far, the antimonopoly committee has functioned as a price control organ. In a Ukrainian restaurant, every single page of the menu has the signatures of the restaurant's manager, deputy manager, and accountant as well as the restaurant's official stamp. The "antimonopoly committee" has ordered restaurants to do this. It focuses on controlling prices rather than encouraging competition. The government should abolish the entire antimonopoly committee and establish a new agency rather than trying to reform this price-controlling behemoth.

I have identified 79 independent state agencies at six different levels.[9] Of these, 45 state agencies do not seem justified, leaving only 34 independent state agencies. This number might sound sparse, but I have not included many state agencies subordinate to ministries, the president, and the parliament. It would also be preferable to reduce the levels of state agencies from six to three.

---

7. Resolution of the Cabinet of Ministers of Ukraine, "Some questions on the maximum staff size of the central government institutions and their regional offices, and other public bodies," No. 85, April 5, 2014, http://zakon4.rada.gov.ua/laws/show/85-2014-%D0%BF/print1390875974587141.

8. "Iz 80 inspektsii i kontrol'nykh organov dolzhno ostat'sya maksim 20—Vladimir Groisman" ["Of the 80 Inspections and Regulatory Authorities, a Maximum of 20 Should Remain—Vladimir Groisman"], *Pravitel'stvenny portal*, July 30, 2014.

9. According to the Decree of the Cabinet of Ministers "On some questions regarding the staff number limits at executive power agencies and their regional divisions," No. 85, April 5, 2014, http://zakon4.rada.gov.ua/laws/show/85-2014-%D0%BF/print1390875974587141.

Most important is to rid the state administration of agencies that do not pertain to a modern democratic state. Ukraine has 11 such agencies. Two are remnants of the Soviet economy, the state price control inspection and the state reserve agency, as are the three inspection agencies for agriculture, technology, and road transport. Three reflect a misperception about how to build a market economy, namely the state agencies for the development of entrepreneurship, energy efficiency, and investment and national projects and the state. Three seem to interfere with personal and democratic freedom, that is, the state agencies for information, defense of personal data, and the state and radio committee.

This brief survey of Ukraine's state institutions lays bare undemocratic interference and objectionable bureaucratic excess. In many cases, the state institutions and their employees have remained even after their roles have become defunct. The Pension Fund of Ukraine is the most striking example. Its main task used to be to collect the payroll tax; in 2013 the State Fiscal Service took over this function, but the Pension Fund still exists, with 35,564 employees, for no apparent reason.[10]

It is not enough to just abolish these state agencies. Their superfluous functions inscribed in a large body of Soviet legal acts and post-Soviet decrees and laws should be eliminated and their staff laid off. If Soviet-style inspectors are transferred to new agencies, they will recreate their old inspection regimes with or without law.

The Need for Lustration

Ukrainians and people from other postcommunist countries understand the importance of lustration—the purging of government officials (from the Latin word *lustratio*, which means religious purification)—as the main means of fighting corruption (Åslund and Djankov 2014). Westerners, on the contrary, are usually unable to fathom the need for lustration.

Lustration is a major bone of contention between Westerners and people from postcommunist countries. The naïve Western view is that collective justice must not be allowed and that only individual justice is permissible. That idea builds upon the presumption that individual justice exists and that ordinary courts can handle crimes, but that is not true of Ukraine at present because courts and prosecutors are pervasively corrupt. Maidan activist Yegor Sobolev complained that "in the judicial system, only 20–25 percent of the judges are actually judges. All the others are businessmen."[11] Therefore, individual justice cannot be established unless the whole lot is ousted, which requires lustration. The actual choice is between collective justice and no justice, which explains why Ukraine needs lustration.

---

10. Ibid.

11. "Yegor Sobolev: Zakon o liustratii vypolnyat'sya ne budet" ["Yegor Sobolev: The Law on Lustration Will Not Be Fulfilled"], *Focus*, October 22, 2014.

Euromaidan raised twin concerns, lustration and corruption. A state committee was supposed to be set up for each task. Chairs were also named, Sobolev and Tetiana Chornovol, respectively, but neither of these two committees was formed. Lustration captured the public's imagination and led to a lively popular debate with the drafting of several laws. People demonstrated for a law on lustration, and on September 16 the parliament adopted such a law, with a slight majority of 231 deputies. Needless to say, the old establishment was less than enthusiastic but voted for the law because of popular pressure. On October 9, President Poroshenko signed the bill into law after evident hesitation because of strong resistance from the old establishment supposed to be lustrated.[12]

After the fall of communism, lustration emerged as a major political concern and almost all of the Central and East European countries carried out some lustration, while none in the Commonwealth of Independent States has done so (Staats 2011, Horne 2012). Much of the discussion of lustration occurred in Germany, where parallels were drawn with the insufficient denazification after World War II. The dominant German conclusion was that the nation must not be too soft once again. Another conclusion was that public access to secret police acts was vital and that the rule of law had to be maintained (Staats 2012). The aim of lustration depends on the problems. In the current Ukrainian situation, corruption, lawlessness, and national security are the key concerns. An additional focus is professional competence (cf. Stan 2009).

East Germany, the Czech Republic, Estonia, Latvia, and Lithuania carried out the most far-reaching and consistent lustrations early on. In a study of Central and East European lustrations Cynthia Horne (2012) concluded that "lustration does have a positive and beneficial effect on the trustworthiness of public institutions" (p. 422). "Transitional justice measures do contribute to trust building. More comprehensive and expeditious transitional justice measures, including lustration, trials, and file access, did positively and significantly improve trust in targeted public institutions" (p. 423).

Lustration can be carried out in various ways. One option is to sack all officials within a certain group—for example, Ukraine's judges and prosecutors—and prohibit them from ever pursuing the same profession. After World War II, East Germany pursued denazification in that manner (unless someone became a communist or secret police informer). An alternative is to sack all government officials but allow them to reapply for their old jobs. Estonia used this approach, which worked well. The state administration improved greatly, and dismissed officials could return without feeling ashamed. A third option is to screen everyone and reappoint those who pass the new test. East Germany did so quite rigorously. Out of 1,780 judges at the end of communism, 38 percent were reappointed, and out of 1,238 prosecutors only 32 percent. The

---

12. "Poroshenko podpisal 'Liustratiy'" ["Poroshenko Signed 'Lustration'"], *Ukrainskaya pravda*, October 9, 2014.

reappointed officials were generally younger and better educated (Staats 2011, 98). Finally, lustration can be limited to the prosecution of obvious criminals in ordinary court proceedings.

Who should carry out lustration? Scrutinizing every individual is labor intensive, and lustration is primarily a legal endeavor. Should corrupt judges assess whether other judges are corrupt? There are three reasonable options. One is the Estonian and Georgian approach of sacking all and rehiring after careful screening. The second option is to set up lustration committees, drawing on the Anglo-American jury tradition. East Germany partially adopted such a solution with some lawyers and politicians on its lustration committees. Because of the large workload, these committees had to be decentralized to the regional level, which resulted in practices that varied greatly by region. The third option is to engage foreigners, which East Germany did with West German retired judges (Staats 2011). For Ukraine, the Estonian and Georgian approach of sacking all appears the obvious preference.

The final question is who will replace the lustrated. The East German example offers three answers: young professionals as yet untainted by the old regime, foreign professionals, and reeducated professionals. Ukraine has a large number of young academics both at home and abroad who could fill these posts. In addition, the Ukrainian diaspora consists of several million who still speak Ukrainian. Many of them are lawyers and could assist.

The September 2014 Ukrainian law on lustration targets senior officials who worked for at least one year during Viktor Yanukovych's reign as president. They could be banned from public service for five to ten years. Because many members of parliament would have been subject to lustration, some concessions have been made after extensive negotiations: Elected officials are not subject to lustration. The prime targets are political appointees, such as ministers, chairs of state committees, and regional governors. The law also goes after officials in the highly corrupt law enforcement bodies, including members of the Central Election Commission and the High Council of Justice and directors of state-owned military-industrial enterprises.

Other targets are law enforcement officers who participated in the arrests or persecution of protesters during Euromaidan and Soviet Union officials, including people who worked in senior positions in the Communist Party of the Soviet Union, senior youth communist leaders, and employees or agents of Soviet intelligence. The repressors of Maidan and KGB agents are presumably the most numerous. This is more dangerous. After Maidan, the new government abolished the infamous Berkut riot police of some 15,000 men. Many of them joined the rebellion in Donbas, which is reminiscent of what happened in Iraq when the United States dissolved the Iraqi army.

The law clearly states the process of lustration. All implicated officials must submit a statement that they agree to be screened. If they refuse, they can be dismissed. The Ministry of Justice is supposed to set up a special public council for lustration, which would consist of activists and journalists. After judgment has been passed, the Ministry of Justice is obliged to create a public register of people who can no longer hold government positions.

As it reads, the law on lustration would scrutinize only a small number of top-level officials in the judicial system and the prosecutor's office. This group is too narrow to cleanse the judicial system because judges and prosecutors cannot be easily dismissed. The law should have targeted a far larger number of judges and prosecutors. Moreover, top officials may simply bribe to continue their public careers. If lustration does not proceed further, Ukraine's judicial system is likely to remain profoundly corrupt.

Estonia's radical reformer, former prime minister Mart Laar (2002, 315), complained that its court reform was so "influenced by European liberalism that the state completely lost control over the activities of the judges and public opinion came to view the courts as distanced not only from law but also from justice." International organizations favor anticorruption legislation, which they have forced Ukraine to adopt (see below), while showing little appreciation for lustration. Ukrainian civil society has driven demands for lustration.

The main European body for the maintenance of legal standards is the Council of Europe in Strasbourg. It is an all-European institution, not related to the European Union. Ukraine and other non-EU countries are full members. Each year, its court, the European Court of Human Rights, faults Ukraine in hundreds of cases. Fortunately, the Council of Europe (1996) changed its policy in 1996, but it remains critical of lustration and is an impediment. The Venice Commission of the Council of Europe has reviewed Ukraine's lustration; it has accepted the principal need for lustration but objects to certain aspects of the law on lustration. The most important objection is that the Ministry of Justice is carrying out the lustration and not a body independent from the executive. The Ukrainian government has promised to amend the law in line with the recommendations of the Venice Commission (Sidorenko 2014). Meanwhile lustration has been stalled.

Once the Council of Europe gives its approval, the risk remains that its European Court of Human Rights will judge some aspect of lustration out of order (Semak 2014). In that vein, the United Nations High Commissioner for Human Rights (OHCHR 2014, 35) opined: "The vetting grounds are overly broad in scope and establish a principle of collective responsibility, which is contrary to international human right law and Recommendation 7568 of the Council of Europe." As could be expected, Ukrainian judges are fighting tooth and nail against their own lustration and they can do so quite effectively through their own verdicts.

The dominant public concern, on the contrary, is that lustration will not be sufficiently implemented. As analyst Taras Kuzio wrote: "The inability of the courts and the prosecutor's office to indict senior politicians for abuse of office, and the frequency with which they have been able to bribe judges or flee abroad, is encouraging the public to take direct action."[13] Nor does the lustra-

---

13. Taras Kuzio, "Ukraine's New Parliament Will Be More Pro-European But Will It Be More Reformist?" *Financial Times*, October 20, 2014.

tion law go deep enough into the judicial system, the prosecutor's office, and law enforcement.

Initially, the government claimed that no fewer than one million people would be subject to lustration, which appears more than the law could possibly cover.[14] Later, Minister of Justice Pavlo Petrenko reduced the number to 200,000 to 300,000.[15] When launching the lustration process, Petrenko presented Poland and East Germany as sound examples: In Poland, 300,000 officials had been vetted, and 45,000 sacked with no recourse to renewed state employment, while he claimed that 1.5 million officials in East Germany had been vetted.[16] Civil society activists were greatly concerned that Ukraine's lustration would not be sufficient. They pointed to the bloated law enforcement with some 400,000 people.

Indeed, in the first wave of lustration, only 357 senior officials were ousted.[17] In the prosecutor's office and the Ministry of Interior, 132 and 91 top officials, respectively, were lustrated.[18] The Ministry of Justice set up a public register of the lustrated to name and shame them. Those registered were prohibited from public service for 10 years.[19] The minister of justice defended himself by saying that the second wave of lustration started on November 11 and that others would follow,[20] but the Venice Commission stalled lustration.

Ordinary staff cuts have been more effective. Some ministries appeared to compete with each other to cut staff. The biggest purge occurred in the State Fiscal Service, where 6,500 officials were laid off, including 85 percent of

---

14. Fred Weir, "Ukraine Purge: Communists, Cronies, and Crooks Face the Axe," *Christian Science Monitor*, October 16, 2014.

15. "Pod pervuyu volnu lyustratsii 'avtomaticheski' podpali 357 chelovek—Petrenko" ["Under the First Wave of Lustration 357 people fell automatically—Petrenko"], *Ukrainskaya pravda*, December 5, 2014.

16. "Vstupitel'naya chast' zasedaniya Kabinet ministrov Ukrainay ot 10 oktyabrya 2014 goda" ["The Introductory Part of the meeting of the Cabinet of Ministers of Ukraine, October 10, 2014"], *Pravitel'stvenny portal*, October 10, 2014.

17. "Pod pervuyu volnu lyustratsii 'avtomaticheski' podpali 357 chelovek—Petrenko ["Under the First Wave of Lustration 357 people fell automatically—Petrenko"], *Ukrainskaya pravda*, December 5, 2014.

18. "U Yaremy lyustrirovalia 132 prokurorov" ["At Yarema's 132 Prosecutors Were Lustrated"], *Ukrainskaya pravda*, November 15, 2014.

19. "Ediny gosudarstvenny liiustratsionny reyestr naschitivaet 354 cheloveka" ["The Unified State Lustration Register Contains 354 People"], *Pravitel'stvenny portal*, November 10, 2014.

20. "Pod pervuyu volnu lyustratsii 'avtomaticheski' podpali 357 chelovek—Petrenko" ["Under the First Wave of Lustration 357 people fell automatically—Petrenko"], *Ukrainskaya pravda*, December 5, 2014.

the top managers.[21] The security service sacked 2,500 employees.[22] A minister from the Poroshenko Bloc publicly charged that as many as 70 percent of the 30,000 State Security Service (SBU) employees were Russian agents.[23] A more common view is that one-tenth of all senior Ukrainian officials are old KGB informants and now work for the Russian Security Service (FSB).

To be effective, lustration needs to be fast, extensive, and accompanied by a swift reorganization of the government as outlined above. Civil service and political positions should be clearly differentiated. Salaries need to be multiplied so that civil servants under deputy ministers can enjoy a decent standard of living on their official salaries.

Anticorruption Policy

On October 14, the Ukrainian Parliament adopted a package of anticorruption laws. The fundamental law was "on the principles of state anti-corruption policy in Ukraine, anticorruption strategy, 2014-17." These laws aimed at more clearly defining corruption, increasing transparency, and creating an independent investigating organ, the Anti-Corruption Bureau, as well as a National Anti-Corruption Commission. At the same time, Ukraine tightened its legislation against money laundering.

The various laws were adopted by substantial majorities of 243 to 284 deputies. Poroshenko and Yatsenyuk both advocated them forcefully. The international community, notably the European Union, the International Monetary Fund, and the World Bank, pushed hard for these laws and made their adoption preconditions for further assistance. Ukrainian reformers emphasized deregulation and lustration but were apprehensive about new control organs, suspecting that the Anti-Corruption Bureau would be neither independent nor honest but just another center of extortion.

The targets of transparency are enterprises, real estate, and senior officials. In Ukraine offshore companies own most big companies. Traditionally, they have been located on Cyprus because of the favorable double taxation agreement since Soviet times, which allows Ukrainian companies to move their profits to their Cypriot trading company through transfer pricing. As a consequence, they do not have to pay taxes anywhere. Nor do they pay any dividends to minority shareholders, leaving the Ukrainian stock market in shambles.

Ownership of Ukrainian companies is usually shrouded in mystery. Company documents do not reveal the true owners and changes are not necessarily announced. "Privat Group, which has not been formalized as a legal entity, is one

---

21. "Pod liustratsiyu popali 6,5 tysyach nalogovikov" ["6,500 Taxmen Were Lustrated"], *Ukrainskaya pravda*, November 5, 2014.

22. "SBU nachala vtoroi etap liustratsii" ["SBU Started the Second Stage of Lustration"], *Ukrainskaya pravda*, November 18, 2014.

23. "Stets': 70 protsentov, chto v SBU—'zaslannye' ili skrytye agenty Kremlya" ["Stets: 70 Percent of the SBU Are Kremlin Agents"], *Ukrainskaya pravda*, November 23, 2014.

of Ukraine's largest business groups and incorporates Ukraine's No. 1 Privat-Bank, as well as oil, ferrous metal, food, agriculture, and transport assets."[24] Yet, its supposed main owners, Ihor Kolomoisky and Henadiy Boholiubov, show up regularly on *Forbes*'s richest people list and are identified as such.[25]

One of the new anticorruption laws requires all companies that are registered in Ukraine to disclose their ultimate beneficiaries. Yatsenyuk explained the aim: "Today companies are registered in offshore havens and the real owners of the companies can be state officials, members of the government, officials of the Presidential Administration and to find that out is impossible."[26] Real estate owners also have to declare all the property they own.

The law on prevention of corruption has also facilitated the establishment of an electronic repository of all Ukrainian public officials' income declarations, ownership of business, additional employment, and joint activities with family members and other related people.[27] All these registers are supposed to be electronic and freely available to the public. If enforced, it would enormously advance transparency in Ukraine.

Two control organs are being set up to ensure implementation. The most important is the National Anti-Corruption Bureau with 700 employees, which is supposed to open corruption cases against senior state officials, who have traditionally enjoyed immunity. The National Commission for the Struggle against Corruption is supposed to check the income declarations of state officials against their actual spending and lifestyle. Both these institutions are supposed to be independent and well paid, but it remains to be seen if that will really be the case.[28]

On paper, the anticorruption laws are a big step forward, but the Ukrainian public is highly doubtful that these laws will be implemented.

Reform of Prosecution and the Judicial System

Ukraine's judicial system, including the prosecutor's office, is in dire need of reform. Since the fall of Yanukovych, the malfunctioning of the prosecutor's office has been nothing but baffling. No action has been taken on the many

---

24. "Kolomoisky appointed head of Dnipropetrovsk Oblast Administration," Interfax-Ukraine, *Kyiv Post*, March 2, 2014.

25. *Forbes* assessed Kolomoisky at $1.4 billion and Boholiubov at $1.7 billion; see *Forbes*, November 13, 2014, www.forbes.com/profile/ihor-kolomoyskyy and www.forbes.com/profile/henadiy-boholiubov.

26. "Arseniy Yatsenyuk obratilsya k Parlamenty prinyat' paket antikorruptsionnykh zakonoproektov" ["Arseniy Yatsenyuk Turned to the Parliament to Adopt a Package of Anti-Corruption Laws"], Ukraine government portal, October 6, 2014, www.kmu.gov.ua.

27. Oleksii Khmara, "New Anti-Corruption Laws Were Castrated before Final Approval," *Kyiv Post*, October 16, 2014.

28. Ibid.

billion-dollar embezzlement cases that have been exposed in the media. The worst offenders have fled to Russia. The popular explanation is that they have paid prosecutors to close their cases, which appears all too plausible.[29] Only on January 12, 2015, were former president Yanukovych and a score of his top accomplices finally declared wanted for organized crime by Interpol.[30]

Prosecutors and judges are both excessively lenient, raising questions about whom they may be protecting. At present, Ukraine has 10,279 judges[31] and 20,367 prosecutors.[32] The almost unanimous popular view is that they are all corrupt.

An example illustrates the corruption in the system: In 2007 a constitutional court judge was caught red-handed accepting a bribe of $12 million (officially a "consultancy fee" to her retired mother). President Viktor Yushchenko sacked her, but Prime Minister Viktor Yanukovych reinstated her, claiming that the president had exceeded his legal authority.[33]

Ukraine has an independent High Council of Justice that appoints judges, but several institutions that appoint its members are considered pervasively corrupt, such as those representing judges, lawyers, and legal scholars, which each appoint three of its 20 members.[34] Corrupt lawyers and judges should not be allowed to reappoint one another. Institutions that appoint members of the High Council of Justice should be either purged or prevented from appointing judges.

On October 14, the parliament adopted a new law on prosecution, which was an important first step and one of the EU conditions that Yanukovych refused to fulfill. It sought to reduce the power of the prosecutors to the norm in developed societies. It took away the prosecutors' general oversight function, which was a Soviet inheritance that rendered them superior to judges. It eliminated their right to interfere in the lives of Ukrainian citizens and businesses. Prosecutors can no longer conduct pretrial investigations, which are now supposed to be handled by a state investigation bureau yet to be created. The qualifications to become a prosecutor are supposed to become rigorous,

29. Taras Kuzio, "Ukraine's New Parliament Will Be More Pro-European But Will It Be More Reformist?" *Financial Times*, October 20, 2014.

30. "Interpol ob'yavil v rozysk Yanukovicha, Azarova i drugikh" ["Interpol Declared as Wanted Yanukovych, Azarov and Others"], *Ukrainskaya pravda*, January 12, 2015.

31. Author's calculations based on State Court Administration orders, data from Constitution and Law of Ukraine "On judiciary and status of judges," no. 2453, July 7, 2010, http://zakon4.rada. gov.ua/laws/show/2453-17/print1390875974587141.

32. Law of Ukraine "On Prosecutor's office," no. 1789, November 5, 1991, http://zakon4.rada.gov. ua/laws/show/1789-12/print1390875974587141.

33. Pavel Korduban, "Can Ukraine's Constitutional Court Be Unbiased?" *Eurasian Daily Monitor*, Jamestown Foundation, April 17, 2007.

34. Oleksandr Bilous, "Kak sud'i roiut sebe mogilu" ["How Judges Dig Their Own Graves"], *Ukrainskaya pravda*, June 25, 2014.

and recruitment transparent. This law amended no fewer than 51 laws and 10 legal codes.[35]

In the preceding week, the parliament adopted amendments to the Criminal Code and the Criminal Procedural Code to bring to justice the nation's former leaders, who have fled the country, and to confiscate their property.[36] In a next step, Poroshenko signed a decree to form a council for judicial reform.[37]

To accomplish these goals, Ukraine needs assistance, which the European Union, the Council of Europe, Canada, or the United States should consider providing. Initially, the High Council of Justice could be made up exclusively of qualified Ukrainian-speaking lawyers, judges, and legal scholars from abroad, for example, Canada, the United States, and Europe. They should appoint new judges from the top down, drawing on young Ukrainian lawyers. After the corps of judges has been built, the High Council of Justice could be composed anew on the lines of the current constitution.

Reforming Public Administration

The reform of the communist state has turned out to be the most daunting challenge of transition. No serious policymaker argues that the state just has to get out of the way, and many argue that it should be smaller than at present and regulate less.

A rising insight is that you cannot change the behavior of people, so you have to exchange the top people instead. Former Czech president Václav Klaus (2014, 55) has stated that there had to be "an unconditional liquidation of the communist political and economic system." Far more than elsewhere, as great a disruption as possible was desirable because the communist system was strong and harmful. The old elite was corrupted by its hypocrisy claiming obedience to an ideology, in which nobody actually believed. Senior officials had to be members of the Communist Party, muddling the distinction between politicians and civil servants. Many were preoccupied with intricacies of a command economy, without relevant knowledge of a market economy. Officials were promoted by seniority rather than merit. These officials represented negative human capital, and they had to be laid off. Depoliticization, rejuvenation, and professionalization were crucial.

While it has depoliticized state administration, Ukraine has yet to rejuvenate and professionalize it. The main problem is corruption, which is linked

---

35. Oleksii Khmara, "New Anti-Corruption Laws Were Castrated before Final Approval," *Kyiv Post*, October 16, 2014; "Rada pozvolila konfiskyvat' imushchestvo Yanukovicha i sponsorov terrorizma" ["The Parliament Allowed the Confiscation of the Property of Yanukovych and Sponsors of Terrorism"], *Ukrainskaya pravda*, October 7, 2014.

36. Ibid.

37. "Prezident Ukrainy podpisal Ukaz o sozdanii Soveta po voprosam sudebnoi reform" ["Ukraine's President Signed a Decree on the Creation of a Council on Judicial Reform"], Press Service of the President of Ukraine, October 16, 2014.

with the continuity of the Soviet state administration. The Ukrainian state administration has changed less than in any other post-Soviet country.

Minister of the Cabinet of Ministers Ostap Semerak, the boss of the state administration, offered a colorful description of the "enemies of reform in Ukraine," especially "corrupt officials who do not want change but try to maintain old schemes." He continued: "It is the post-Soviet bureaucracy, which brakes all procedures and is used to imitate activity. It is incomplete, often obsolete, and unprofessional legislation."[38]

Ukrainians are fully aware and have minimal confidence in their public "servants." An opinion poll from September 2014 revealed Ukrainians' disdain especially for law enforcement and parliamentarians: 77 percent did not trust the police, 72 percent the political parties, 69 percent the judges, 67.8 percent the prosecutors, 65 percent the parliament, 61 percent the banks, and 53 percent the government, while "only" 35 percent distrusted the president.[39]

Ukrainian independence was based on a political compromise between nationalists and the old communist elite. The nationalists got an independent Ukraine, on the condition that the old communist elite would continue ruling it. The nationalists were predominantly statists having inherited a view of the state from the 1930s, seeing a large and omnipotent state as a strong state. They favored a big state apparatus, ignoring its quality (Havrylyshyn 2014).

This lingering Soviet administration needs to be undone from the top down. The fundamental problem is the large Cabinet of Ministers apparatus. In effect, the prime minister and the minister of the Cabinet of Ministers micromanage the whole government. As of August 2014, this apparatus employed 664 people.[40] It contains departments that control each ministry, and every ministry decision usually has to be cleared with that department and the relevant deputy prime minister. This excessive centralization slows decision making and worsens the quality of decisions. The State Fiscal Service is not subordinate to the Ministry of Finance, as is usually the case in Western countries, but to the Cabinet of Ministers, so the ministry does not control the state finances. The Cabinet of Ministers should be slimmed down substantially rather than duplicating the work of the ministries, and the ministries should be given more responsibility and made more accountable. The Yatsenyuk government has cut the staff of the central and local administration of 250,000 by 10 percent, or 25,000 people, and it has ordered the sacking of an additional

38. "Ostap Semerak nazval vragov ukrainskikh reform" ["Ostap Semerak Named the Enemies of Ukrainian Reforms"], *Pravitel'stvenny portal*, July 19, 2014.

39. "Bol'she vsego ukraintsy ne doveryayut militsii i politpartiyam" ["Most of All Ukrainians Do Not Trust the Police and Political Parties"], *Ukrainskaya pravda*, September 18, 2014.

40. "Ostap Semerak: Antikorruptsionnye reform—osnovnaya zadacha" ["Ostap Semerak: Our Main Task Is Anticorruption Reforms"], *Pravitel'stvenny portal*, August 15, 2014.

30 percent of the staff of the Cabinet of Ministers secretariat.[41] Perks such as official cars and charter travel have also been cut.

Similarly, the presidential administration has duplicated the work of the Cabinet of Ministers apparatus. Characteristically, it is housed in the building of the former Central Committee of the Communist Party of Ukraine, and most of the time it has continued with the old Soviet telephone rule. After the change of government in February 2014, the executive economic powers seem to have moved to the Cabinet of Ministers, where they belong. Accordingly, the presidential administration has announced that its staff will be cut by 27 percent from 579 to 423.[42]

Chair of the National Bank of Ukraine (NBU) Valeriya Hontareva made a radical proposal to cut NBU staff by 80 percent. At present, the NBU has 11,000 employees, whereas 2,000 would be appropriate for a country of Ukraine's size and economic development. The NBU still has 25 regional branches of no relevance in the modern world of electronic money.[43] Hontareva wants to trim them to five in a first round and end the NBU petty tutelage of commercial banks. The NBU requires new, more qualified staff.[44]

An even more insidious Soviet practice is the *vizirovanie*, the initialing of all government decisions, whether decree or draft law. They all require 20 to 30 signatures from all kinds of officials in the different ministries and the Cabinet of Ministers apparatus. Without these signatures the government can make no decision. This long-standing practice slows all decision making and means that nobody is individually responsible for government decisions. One would think that these multiple signatures would impede corruption, but that's not the case: Senior officials often force unsuspecting subordinates to sign dubious decisions, thus making them accomplices. They are often blackmailed, continuing the vicious circle of corruption. Young professionals are aware of this harmful practice, which is one reason why so few of them want to work for the government. The practice needs to be abolished immediately.[45]

Many working in Ukraine's state administration have little reason to welcome changes, because they have perverse incentives and the wrong skills. In the communist administration, officials tended to be engineers rather than lawyers, economists, or political scientists. They did not know how to work in

41. "Ostap Semerak: Antikorruptsionnye reform—osnovnaya zadacha" ["Ostap Semerak: Our Main Task Is Anticorruption Reforms"], *Pravitel'stvenny portal*, August 15, 2014, www.kmu.gov.ua.

42. "Shtat Administratsii Poroshenko sokratili pochti na 30%" ["The Staff of Poroshenko's Administration Was Cut by Almost 30%"], *Ukrainskaya pravda*, November 11, 2014.

43. Interview with NBU chair Valeriya Hontareva on September 17, 2014.

44. "Shtat Natsbanka mogut sokratit' na 80%" ["They Can Cut the Staff of the National Bank by 80%"], *Ukrainskaya Pravda*, August 8, 2014; "NBU poluchit novuyu strukturu po obraztsu mirovykh tsentrobankov" ["NBU will have a new structure based on the model of the world central banks"], *Zerkalo nedeli*, July 23, 2014.

45. I owe these ideas to Daniel Bilak, who has preached them since 1998.

a modern, democratic administration. Their greatest asset was their personal network (Hay and Shleifer 1998). Defeating these enemies from within has been one of the most difficult tasks of the transition. Andrei Shleifer and Robert Vishny (1998, p. 12) concluded that "deregulation and liberalization are far more important for fighting corruption than the improvement of incentives and personnel selection inside the bureaucracy."

Reform needs to start from the top with the most difficult institutions of greatest power, notably the court system and law enforcement, moving to institutions where large amounts of money are made by corrupt operators and lost by the state, such as the tax administration, the treasury, and energy regulation. A clear distinction should be made between political appointees and civil servants, and the number of political appointees should be very limited. Civil servants should be offered good salaries but also be subject to strict and clear rules against corruption, which would form the basis for personal integrity. Staff should be hired on the basis of merit, not seniority. Preference should be given to well-educated, young people. Ukraine needs to attract many of the tens of thousands of young citizens who have received university degrees from European and North American universities. The "Professional Government" initiative launched by alumni of Western universities[46] has CVs from over 1,500 alumni who are offering their help to state agencies. From a technocratic point of view, it would be ideal to sack the whole government and build a new one on modern foundations. The complication is that public services are needed all the time, and in many cases only the government can deliver them. In Russia, President Boris Yeltsin and his advisors were painfully aware that the abolition of the tsarist foreign service by the liberal Russian government in early 1917 had led to chaos, and concluded that it was necessary to work with the old administration (Åslund 1995).

Estonia and Georgia are the only two post-Soviet countries where reform has succeeded. In 1992–93, the young and radical Estonian government under Prime Minister Mart Laar (2002) opted for the maximum disruption to stop communist telephone rule and corruption. It drew up a completely new government structure with a clear distinction between political and civil service positions. It laid off all civil servants, allowed everybody to apply for the new government jobs, and their applications were judged on merit. As a consequence, Estonia boasts of the least corruption of all postcommunist countries. One caveat is that Estonia is the smallest of all transition countries, rendering its reforms easier to implement. The military in all three Baltic countries is generally considered noncorrupt and effective because they have been built up from the bottom with Western help and without old Soviet cadres.

Georgia was one of the most corrupt post-Soviet countries at the time of the Rose Revolution in 2003, when it ranked 124 out of 133 countries on the Corruption Perceptions Index of Transparency International. By 2013, it had become the least corrupt post-Soviet country, ranking 55 out of 177 coun-

---

46. "Profeciyny uryad" ["Professional Government"], http://proukrgov.info/.

tries (Transparency International 2013). Georgia's progress shows that corruption can be controlled within a reasonably short period. Georgia carried out a similar state reform as Estonia, but with a population of 5 million rather than the 1.6 million of Estonia. The government cleansed one institution after the other, for example, sacking 6,000 traffic police officers, which left the country without traffic police for a few months with no damage until a new, much smaller and better-paid corps had been built (Bendukidze and Saakashvili 2014). Ukraine should also try as far as possible to adopt the radical Georgian approach to public administration reform.

All eleven new EU members in Central and Eastern Europe have been highly successful in combating corruption through far-reaching civil service reform. The European Union has been the main engine is this endeavor, using both carrots and sticks. When a country signs an Association Agreement with the European Union, as Ukraine did on June 27, 2014, the reform process takes off. The Association Agreement contains a Ukrainian commitment to adopt hundreds of laws that are part of the EU body of common laws, the *acquis communautaire*. Their adoption amounts to a large-scale reform of the Ukrainian state apparatus. In order to facilitate this process, the European Union has geared some 60 state agencies in various EU member countries to assist their counterparts in Ukraine to adopt relevant new laws and regulations, change organizational structure, and hire new staff.

Postcommunist EU members are less corrupt than post-Soviet countries, with the remarkable exception of Georgia (figure 8.1). The European Union is most effective before a country becomes a member, because its demands are taken very seriously. But it is much more difficult for the European Union to sanction a member country. Thus, it is often argued that the European Union was too lenient with Bulgaria and Romania and let them in before they had achieved satisfactory legal standards, but these two countries are hardly more corrupt than the old EU members Italy and Greece (Transparency International 2013).

Thus, there is no reason to think that Ukraine cannot carry out a successful civil service reform to improve the quality of public administration and sharply reduce corruption. If Georgia could do so, Ukraine certainly can, and it should be easier with the solid support of the European Union.

Deregulate: Use the World Bank's Ease of Doing Business Index

The most surprising thing about deregulation is that it is intellectually so easy. Therefore most intellectuals do not think much about it. All too often, we are left with simple slogans, such as references to Adam Smith's "invisible hand" that will put everything right if the market economy takes hold.

Increasingly, the World Bank's Ease of Doing Business Index is gaining influence. It is produced by the International Finance Corporation, the private-sector arm of the World Bank, originally by Simeon Djankov. Its prime

Figure 8.1   Corruption Perceptions Index, 2013

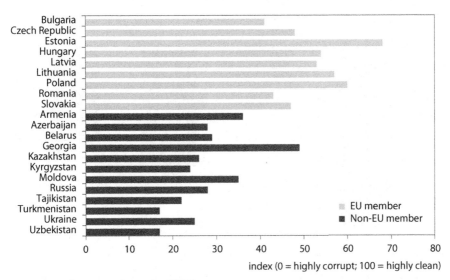

Source: Transparency International (2013).

advantage is that it is concrete. The new government should look to the Ease of Doing Business Index to see how it can advance through specific reforms. The index measures a country's progress or regress on ten concrete enterprise actions in three regards: How many procedures are needed? How many days do they take? How much do they cost in relation to income per capita in the country in question? It measures the following 11 actions: starting a business, dealing with construction permits, getting electricity, registering property, getting credit, protecting investors, paying taxes, trading across borders, enforcing contracts, resolving insolvency, and employing workers. This index not only measures performance but also offers a manual to each country on how it can improve.

Many governments have been encouraged to reform and have advanced on this index. The one drawback of the index is that it is quite narrow. Often countries deregulate substantially according to the Ease of Doing Business index but remain quite corrupt by broader measures. Georgia has been the star, advancing from 112 in 2006 to 8 in 2014 (Bendukidze and Saakashvili 2014). Other countries have not been so successful. For example, Kazakhstan rose to 50 on the Ease of Doing Business Index in 2013, while corruption persisted, pulling it down to 140 on the Corruption Perceptions Index.

Somewhat surprisingly, Ukraine advanced substantially on the Ease of Doing Business Index under the Yanukovych government, from 145 in 2011 to 96 out of 189 in 2014, but the actual enterprise environment seems to have deteriorated. Compared with its significant neighbors, Ukraine lags behind, though not very much (figure 8.2). Poland ranks 32, Turkey 55, and Russia 62.

Figure 8.2   Ease of Doing Business rankings, Ukraine, Poland, Russia, and Turkey, 2014

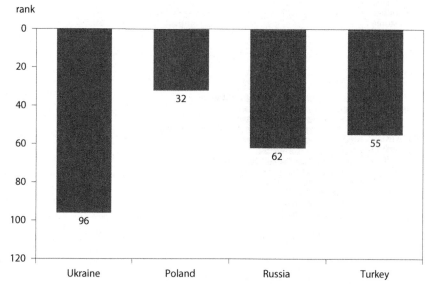

rank

Note: Ranks are out of 183 countries. Lower rank indicates greater ease of doing business.
Source: World Bank, *Doing Business Report 2015: Going Beyond Efficiency,* 2014, www.doingbusiness.org (accessed on November 3, 2014).

Five problems pose the biggest difficulties for doing business in Ukraine: getting electricity (ranking 185), trading across borders (154), resolving insolvency (142), protecting minority investors (109), and paying taxes (108). They are followed by starting a business (76), dealing with construction permits (70), and registering property (59). Enforcing contracts is not so difficult (43), nor is getting credit (17), presumably because of private banks (figure 8.3). Most of these problems can be resolved through direct administrative intervention by the central authorities, while other issues require broader reforms. For example, introducing electronic payment methods, as part of a tax system overhaul, could easily resolve problems associated with tax payments.

Ukraine has already surged 49 places on the index since 2011. It should set an ambitious target of rising by 100 places to at least 45 by 2016, repeating the Georgian achievement.

Legalize Private Sales of Agricultural Land

Ukraine was late in undertaking land reform and agriculture declined in a limbo of unclear ownership in the 1990s. Formally, the workers on state and collective farms received an equal share of their farms of on average 4 hectares. They obtained land certificates, but these were not assigned any specific area. The breakthrough came with a presidential decree in December 1999, which

Figure 8.3 Ease of doing business in Ukraine, by activity, 2014

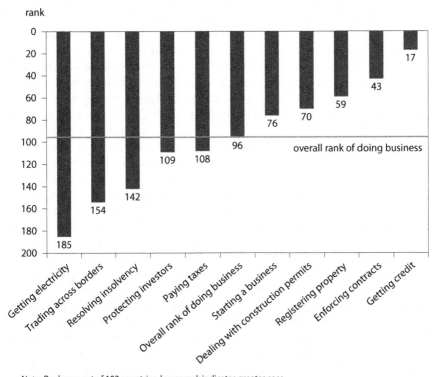

Note: Ranks are out of 183 countries; lower rank indicates greater ease.

Source: World Bank, *Doing Business Report 2015: Going Beyond Efficiency*, 2014, www.doingbusiness.org (accessed on November 3, 2014).

gave specific plots to 7 million rural dwellers within a few months. The land reform of 2000 revived Ukraine's agriculture. In October 2001, Ukraine finally adopted a Land Code that lay out the legal framework for land ownership and officially guaranteed land titles. Yet, this law was accompanied with a temporary moratorium on sales and purchases of agricultural land. The reason was that it would take time for people to receive their land certificates and for the state to organize a land registry. This moratorium has been repeatedly extended, currently until January 1, 2016.

Until the reforms, a large share of the agricultural land lay fallow. Many rural dwellers had aged and no longer wanted to till their land. They started leasing their land on a massive scale. Often, whole collective farms of usually 5,000 hectares were leased to one agro-holding. Leases are typically for a few years. Family farms also developed. Agriculture took off in a big way, particularly the production of new modern export grains, such as corn, wheat, and soy. Ukraine has regained its position as one of the largest grain exporters in the world.

However dynamic this development has been, it has not been without complications. Ukraine's fertile land of 40 million hectares has become dominated by large agro-holdings, many sized 200,000 to 500,000 hectares. These agro-holdings have expanded fast to account for half the farmland (Sarna 2014, 3). Some of them are foreign-owned, but 82 percent of the 100 biggest Ukrainian farms are domestically owned (Plank 2013).

These enormous farms are too vast to be efficiently managed. One side effect of the land reforms has been the centralization of the control of both remaining state land and leaseholds to a State Agency for Land Resources, which controls a land bank of the remaining state land. To obtain a lease on agricultural land, one has to travel to the oblast capital or Kyiv. The leases are cheap and do not keep up with Ukraine's high inflation. But the average bribe to officials in the state land administration to secure a lease is considered to be $500 a hectare, which may equal the lease (Bilenko 2014). Thus, agricultural officials and agro-holdings are the main beneficiaries of the moratorium on private sales of agricultural land, while the many small holders are the losers.

International experts and government specialists have persistently pushed for the legalization of trade in agricultural land, possibly with some restrictions with regard to size. Political parties tend to favor liberalization when they are in power and oppose it when they are out of power, breeding the popular suspicion that government officials seek to enrich themselves through this moratorium. The Yanukovych administration repeatedly promised to legalize private sales of land but never did. It was widely presumed that the Yanukovych "family" would seize the large state land reserve cheaply and perhaps even the land of people who had not properly registered their ownership (Sarna 2014). The family built up a large land bank of state land presumably for its own benefit.

Many Ukrainians fear that oligarchs will concentrate land ownership among themselves, although most experts argue that the current lease system favors big businesses. Therefore, popular sentiment is opposed to trade in agricultural land. An opinion poll in early September 2014 showed that 53 percent of the population opposed private ownership of land in Ukraine, while only 22 percent approved.[47] Many proponents of land reform are focusing on decentralization of the control of leaseholds to local authorities rather than privatization (Bilenko 2014). In the short term, the new government has limited its ambition to extend the usually very short leases. Three limitations on private ownership of land are being discussed. One is that no one should be allowed to own more than a certain area of land, another that foreigners should not be allowed to own land, and it is questioned whether legal subjects should be permitted (Plank 2013). Land prices are expected to rise but not all that much (Stubenhoff 2011).

Before legalizing private sales of land, the government has to accomplish a few tasks. In May 2014, the new government abolished the land bank at the prodding of the World Bank. The government also needs to reassure the origi-

---

47. "Bol'she vsego ukraintsy ne doveryayut militsii i politpartiyam" ["Most of All Ukrainians Do Not Trust the Police and Political Parties"], *Ukrainskaya pravda*, September 18, 2014.

nal owners of agricultural plots that their ownership is secure and transparent. The only good way to do this is to establish a public electronic database of all land holdings in the country, which the government is doing. Finally, any public land that is being privatized must be sold only through auctions, which is the new government policy.[48]

Ukraine needs to end the moratorium on private land sales to reduce corruption in the distribution of leases, more securely rewarding small land owners. The establishment of a real land market would lead to more efficient allocation of land and facilitate the entry of new farmers. Farmers would be able to use land as collateral, which would make more credit available to agriculture and thus stimulate investment. Real property rights, rather than a limited lease, would also encourage investment. A more level playing field would enable family farms to compete with agro-holdings. It is rare that a reform does it all: ensures more equality, fights corruption, and generates more economic growth. But the legalization of sales of agricultural land would be such a reform. Therefore, it should be done as soon as possible. Then, Ukraine can fully develop its extraordinary agricultural potential.

Recommendations

1. Halve the number of independent state agencies, currently 79.

2. Reduce the number of inspection agencies from 83 to no more than 20.

3. Substantially decrease state regulatory functions and abolish obsolete Soviet mandates.

4. Carry out lustration of all courts and law enforcement by sacking all judges and attracting young well-educated lawyers.

5. Pursue a public administration reform, abolishing Soviet-type functions and laying off superfluous staff.

6. Clearly distinguish political appointees and civil servants, while raising the qualifications of civil servants as well as their salaries.

7. Undertake substantial deregulation following the World Bank's Ease of Doing Business Index.

8. Legalize private sales of agricultural land.

---

48. "Zemel'ny kadastr budet publichnym, a uchastki budut prodavat'sya iskliuchitel'no cherez auktsiony—Vladimir Groisman" ["The Land Registry Will Be Public, and Plots Will Be Sold Exclusively through Auctions—Vladimir Groisman"], *Pravitel'stvenny portal*, www.kmu.gov.ua.

9

Achieving Financial Stability and Sustainability

One of the main objectives of the tax reform is to eliminate the shadow economy.
—Ihor Bilous, head of the State Fiscal Service[1]

Ukraine's fiscal policy is the nexus of everything that is wrong with the Ukrainian state and economy. The government collects too much money from the economy, but it spends far more. It uses the funds not only inefficiently but corruptly, redistributing incomes to the criminal and powerful, while depressing economic growth. The tax administration is a major cause of corruption and poor business climate. Ukraine's fiscal system does not fulfill any of its basic aims and needs thorough reform.

In 2014, Ukraine was in a rampant financial crisis of falling output, causing a rising budget deficit, leading to a fast depreciation of the currency, which in turn boosted inflation. As a consequence, half the banking system was collapsing and public debt rose ruthlessly. The underlying reason was years of financial mismanagement, but since April Russian military aggression has caused most of the output fall, rendering the financial crisis acute. It has to be dealt with swiftly and firmly.

Ukraine's public expenditures have persistently been much too high by any standard, depressing economic growth. A large share of the public expenditures consists of subsidies to the wealthiest or outright corrupt. The excessive expenditures cannot be financed, resulting in steady budget deficits and a substantial public debt. The public expenditures must be cut significantly. In the next few years the budget needs to be brought to balance if Ukraine is to be financially sustainable, and the public debt should gradually be reduced through small budget surpluses in the medium term.

The total tax revenues are surprisingly stable and have persistently been

---

1. "Ihor Bilous: Ne mogu skazat', chto sokrashchu vdvoye kolichestvo nalogovikov" ["Ihor Bilous: I cannot say that I will cut the number of taxmen by half"], *Zerkalo nedeli*, August 29, 2014.

high. The tax burden and the number of taxes should be reduced as expenditures are slashed. Taxes on labor, especially the payroll tax, are far too high and should be cut to reduce the shadow economy. Tax rates should be low and flat. The Ukrainian tax administration is not only cumbersome but also lawless. The tax system should be simplified, the tax police abolished, and taxation decriminalized. As political and state powers are being decentralized, so should the management of both revenues and expenditures. The banking system is in shambles and the front of the financial crisis. Many failing banks should be closed down because the government can no longer afford much recapitalization.

In the current crisis, Ukraine can hardly avoid default. The public debt is not very large by international comparisons, but it is skyrocketing. The best approach seems to be an agreed prolongation of the existing debt in the framework of a new International Monetary Fund (IMF) program.

The fiscal reforms should aim not only at resolving the current economic crisis but also at building the institutional foundation for sustainable long-term growth. This involves a major rethinking of the role of the state in the economy and the appropriate form and degree of state regulation.

Rampant Financial Crisis

By the summer of 2014 Ukraine had fallen victim to a serious financial crisis. According to the IMF, the 2014 budget deficit was set to reach 10.1 percent of GDP, which was based on the assumption that output would decline by 6.5 percent (IMF 2014d, 39).[2]

The main driver of the financial crisis was the contraction of output, which largely depended on the intensity of the warfare. In the first quarter of 2014, before Russian aggression hit the economy, Ukrainian GDP contracted by only 1.1 percent. In the second quarter, as Russian military aggression started in the south and east, GDP fell by 4.6 percent. In the third quarter, GDP declined by 5.1 percent year over year,[3] and in the fourth by 15.2 percent.

These numbers reflect two contradictory trends. Ukraine's annualized industrial production plunged because of fighting in Donbas—at most in August by 21.4 percent and 10.7 percent for 2014 as a whole. The war damages seem to have peaked in the third quarter, and the fourth quarter saw some recovery. The decline was driven by the fall in coal production by as much as 66 percent in October in annualized terms and steel production by one-third. At the same time, Ukraine's agriculture was growing, compensating somewhat for the industrial decline.

The second driver was the depreciation of the exchange rate. The hryvnia lost half its dollar value in a year, falling from 8 hryvnia per US dollar in November 2013, when Euromaidan started, to 16 hryvnia per dollar in mid-November 2014. In early 2014, the National Bank of Ukraine (NBU) had no choice

2. "Ukraine Needs More Financial Help, IIF Says," Reuters, September 23, 2014.

3. UniCredit Bank, "Banking Flash," Kyiv, November 3, 2014.

but to let the exchange rate float. In September–October, the NBU maintained an actual peg of 12.95 hryvnia per dollar. In early November that peg collapsed as international reserves fell below the critical level of $12.6 billion. At the end of 2014, reserves had shrunk to $7.5 billion. In spite of severe currency regulations, the economy appeared to have entered a devaluation-inflation cycle, as year-end inflation reached 25 percent. Inflation could easily rise to triple digits within a year as happened in Belarus in 2011. An advantage of the sharp depreciation of the hryvnia is that Ukraine's sizable current account deficit turned into a surplus in 2014, as imports fell far more than exports.

Banks have incurred large losses because of the depreciation of the hryvnia. The government has been caught in a hopeless conundrum. Only the Ukrainian government can bail out the banks. Ukraine has been shut out of the international debt market for two years. Since the government had no financing, it had no choice but to sell bonds to the NBU and related state banks financed by the NBU, which together hold 60 percent of Ukraine's public debt. Any announcement of recapitalization of the banks leads to new depreciation.

After the fall of Yanukovych, the new Yatsenyuk government quickly appealed to the IMF, and as early as March 2014 the IMF concluded a two-year Stand-By Arrangement with total international financial support of $33 billion for two years, of which the IMF itself would contribute $17 billion. The rest of the funding would come from the World Bank, the European Union, the European Investment Bank (EIB), the European Bank for Reconstruction and Development (EBRD), and various bilateral creditors. The program was based on benign assumptions of no further Russian military aggression but rightly emphasized the geopolitical risks.

With increased war damage, preconditions changed substantially, and the program had become unrealistic by April 2014. All indicators turned out far worse than the IMF expected. Former IMF official Susan Schadler (2014, 7) noted with understatement that the "report gives the impression that IMF staff and management find the program scenario as skewed toward optimism as markets do." This IMF program was not credible and had to be redone.

In December 2014, Ukraine's financial situation was desperate but not hopeless. Without a substantial change in the country's economic policies, a financial meltdown within three months or so appeared imminent (see chapter 2). A government had been formed and it had adopted a radical program for fiscal adjustment and structural reform. Even so, Ukraine needed substantial new financing, not only credits to replenish its international reserves but also grants to cover the substantial war damage, as argued in chapter 3.

Cut Public Expenditures

In the 1950s and 1960s, the dominant Western view was that the level of public expenditures did not matter as long as a country had its budget deficit under control. The United States had a marginal income tax exceeding 90 percent (Tanzi 2011). Even today, the IMF tends to be neutral on this issue. Axiomatically, the European Union considers the EU average ideal, without considering its economic effects.

Yet, multiple econometric studies show that low public expenditures are better than large, but of course they must be properly financed so that the public deficit does not become excessive (Barro and Sala-i-Martín 2004). The post-communist country that has persisted with high public expenditures, large budget deficits, and big public debt is Hungary—and Ukraine comes close to it. Both have public expenditures over 50 percent of GDP. While Estonia more than doubled its GDP from 1990 to 2012 in real terms, Hungary's grew by a miserable 24 percent (World Bank 2014a). The cause in Hungary as in Ukraine was that politicians refused to heed the insights of sensible economists who warned about its "premature social welfare society" (Kornai 1992, Bokros 2014). Ukraine is doing even worse, with lower GDP today than in 1990, according to the World Bank (2014a). Moreover, the less developed and the more corrupt the state is, the less public redistribution of revenue is morally justified, because it is likely to be done more inefficiently than in an honest and well-developed state (Milanovic 1998).

Ukraine's public expenditures are deeply problematic in three regards. They are far too large, misallocated, and inefficient. All along, Ukraine has had excessively large public expenditures—both budgeted and executed. In 2013 the IMF (2014b, 34) assessed Ukraine's public expenditure at 51.2 percent of GDP (table 9.1), which is high by any standard. The current average of the far more developed European Union is 49 percent of GDP.[4] By July 2014, the IMF (2014d, 41) had raised Ukraine's forecast expenditures for 2014 to 52.7 percent of GDP.

Lack of data and public awareness are major concerns. The Ukrainian government does not publish the composite state budget. The best source is the IMF, which is not focused on public education. As a consequence, hardly any Ukrainians know the size of the country's public expenditures or the budget deficit. The numbers used by the government are only the central state budget, excluding the vast pension fund and regional and local budgets as well as Naftogaz subsidization and bank recapitalizations. The government needs to come clean with the population and publish elementary budget data.

According to Wagner's law, public expenditures rise with GDP, but Ukraine remains quite a poor country, so by that token it should have low public expenditures. Moreover, high public expenditures are neither inevitable nor beneficial, and depress economic growth (Tanzi and Schuknecht 2000). The three fast-growing Baltic countries have public expenditure ratios of 34 to 38 percent of GDP. Lithuania, Europe's fastest growing country, appears a suitable standard for Ukraine. Its public expenditures are only 34 percent of GDP, and its social indicators are much better than Ukraine's (Eurostat 2014).

---

4. Eurostat, Total Government Expenditures, Percent of GDP, http://epp.eurostat.ec.europa.eu/tgm/table.do?tab=table&init=1&plugin=1&language=en&pcode=tec00023 (accessed on August 8, 2014).

Table 9.1   General government expenditure in Ukraine, 2010–14
(percent of GDP)

Component	2010	2011	2012	2013[a]	2014[a]
Total expenditure	49.0	45.6	49.0	51.2	52.7[b]
Current	46.0	42.2	45.7	48.1	48.7
Compensation of employees	11.4	10.4	11.2	11.7	11.7
Goods and services	7.3	6.8	7.4	8.0	7.9
Interest	1.6	2.0	1.9	2.3	3.3
Subsidies to corporations and enterprises	2.4	1.9	3.1	2.3	2.2
Social benefits	23.2	21.2	22.0	23.8	23.6
Social programs (on budget)	3.4	3.2	3.9	4.0	3.7
Pensions	17.9	16.2	16.6	17.8	17.9
Unemployment, disability, and accident insurance	1.9	1.8	1.6	2.0	2.0
Other current expenditures	0.0	0.0	0.0	0.0	0.0
Capital	2.8	3.0	3.1	1.7	1.7
Net lending	0.1	0.4	0.3	0.1	0.1
Naftogaz deficit	1.7	1.6	1.1	2.0	2.0

a. IMF Staff projections.
b. Includes Naftogaz balance from Ukraine's September 2014 IMF Stand-By Arrangement.
Source: IMF (2014b, 34).

Ideally Ukraine should aim at cutting its public expenditures by 18 percent of GDP over the next few years for sustainable growth and financial development.

Usually, the best way to make big fiscal adjustments is to eliminate the categories of public expenditures that cause direct harm. Cutting expenditures across the board makes people unhappy and does not propel structural reforms (Balcerowicz 1992). Three kinds of public expenditures stand out in Ukraine, namely energy and other enterprise subsidies, excessive pensions, and unwarranted expenditures on public administration.

First, the government should abolish enterprise subsidies. According to the IMF (2014b, 87), the Ukrainian government spent 7.6 percent of GDP on energy subsidies to gas, electricity, and coal in 2012. Of these only 1.3 percent of GDP was recorded in the budget, with the rest being either below-the-line operations, such as recapitalization bonds for Naftogaz, or off-the-budget writeoffs of arrears. Other enterprise subsidies in the budget accounted for 0.9 percent of GDP, bringing total enterprise subsidies to 8.5 percent of GDP. By July 2014, the IMF (2014d, 21) had raised Naftogaz's need for financial support from the state in 2014 from 4 to 7.6 percent of GDP. This increase would raise total energy subsidies to 10 percent of GDP in 2014. A country in crisis should not be doling out subsidies of such magnitude. They should be eliminated instantly (see chapter 10). Table 9.2 offers a different division of

Table 9.2 Outlays by function of Ukraine's government, 2010–12 (percent of GDP)

Function	2010	2011	2012
Total outlays	48.4	45.3	48.3
General public services	4.3	11.4	12.7
Public debt transactions	1.6	2.0	1.9
Defense	1.0	1.0	1.0
Public order and safety	2.7	2.5	2.6
Economic affairs	4.1	4.4	4.4
Agriculture, forestry, fishing, and hunting	0.7	0.6	0.5
Fuel and energy	1.1	0.8	1.2
Transport	1.3	1.3	1.1
Communication	0.0	0.0	0.0
Environmental protection	0.3	0.3	0.4
Housing and community amenities	0.5	0.7	1.4
Health	4.3	3.8	4.3
Recreation, culture, and religion	1.1	0.8	1.0
Education	7.4	6.6	7.2
Social protection	22.8	13.6	13.3

Source: IMF, Government Finance Statistics, 2013.

public expenditures from table 9.1.[5] For 2012, it shows "economic affairs" (4.4 percent of GDP) and "housing and community services" (1.4 percent) as subsidies to be eliminated. Even if the government gave 2 percent of GDP in cash compensation to the poorest half of the population, it could save 8 percent of GDP on energy and enterprise subsidies.

The most outlandish public expenditures are pensions. The IMF (2014d, 41) assessed their cost at 16.3 percent of GDP in 2014, whereas 8 percent of GDP is a reasonable level internationally. Ukraine carried out a pension reform in 2011, which did not make even a dent in pension expenditures. The country has maintained a large number of old Soviet nomenklatura benefits, largely paid from the pension fund. Many of them are labeled "special pensions," which have amounted to almost 4 percent of GDP (Betliy and Giucci 2011). The government has started cutting nomenklatura benefits, but much remains to be done.[6] The very low retirement age needs to be raised faster, and

---

5. The lower total public expenditures are explained by the exclusion of the Naftogaz deficit in this table.

6. "Poroshenko otmenil l'goty Yushchenko, Litvina, Azarova i drugikh" ["Poroshenko canceled benefits of Yushchenko, Lytvyn, Azarov and others"], *Ukrainskaya pravda*, August 4, 2014; "President lishyl l'got generalov v otstavke" ["President deprived benefits of retired generals"], *Ukrainskaya pravda*, August 4, 2014.

the loose standards for early retirement and disability pensions need to be tightened. The country needs to carry out a full-fledged pension reform with mandatory private pension savings (see chapter 11). Ukraine should aim at cutting pension expenditures by 4 percent of GDP in one year.

The Ukrainian public sector has far too many institutions, functions, and employees. As a consequence, too many public employees are not very competent because they earn too little. The obvious solution that the Yatsenyuk government has started is to cut the number of public employees sharply, while keeping the wage funds for the remaining workers. It would make sense to cut the public labor force by half and double the salaries for the rest as discussed in chapter 8. At least 1 percent of GDP can be economized on such cuts. Ukraine spends 2.6 percent of GDP on maintaining public order and safety, which is too high, and should reduce it by 1 percent of GDP (table 9.2).

At the same time public expenditure should be made more efficient, especially state procurement, which must be competitive. The Ukrainian government's total purchases of goods and services on the budget account for 8 percent of GDP; adding 1.7 percent of GDP in public capital expenditures takes the amount to almost 10 percent of GDP (IMF 2014b, 34). Under Yanukovych, kickbacks of 50 percent were considered normal from major infrastructure projects (see examples in chapter 5). One of the new government officials claimed that the total amount embezzled through procurements amounted to only one-fifth.[7] Even so, 2 percent of GDP could be saved through better procurement.

In the spring of 2014, Ukraine adopted a new law on state procurement once again to satisfy an IMF precondition.[8] Alas, within four months of the adoption of the law, deputies lobbying various business interests submitted more than 50 draft laws for exceptions (Blinov 2014). For procurement to be open and competitive, just reducing looting would yield a gain of 2 percent of GDP. The government suggests that 20 percent of total procurement could be saved through the introduction of electronic state procurement.[9]

Summing up the proposed cuts yields a reduction in public expenditures of 20 percent of GDP: elimination of enterprise subsidies (8 percent of GDP), reduction in pension expenditures (8 percent), downsizing staff (1 percent),

---

7. "Pervy zamministr kabmina Parakuda: Na goszakupkakh vorovalas' kazhdaya pyataya grivna" ["First Deputy Minister of the Cabinet of Ministers Parakuda: In State Procurement Every Fifth Hryvnia Was Stolen"], *Focus*, October 20, 2014.

8. IMF, "IMF Executive Board Approves 2-Year US$17.01 Billion Stand-By Arrangement for Ukraine, US$3.19 Billion for Immediate Disbursement," press release no. 14/189, April 30, 2014, www.imf.org/external/np/sec/pr/2014/pr14189.htm; Law of Ukraine, "Pro zdiysnennya derzhavnykh zakupivel'" ["On Public Procurement"], No. 1197-VII, April 10, 2014, http://zakon3.rada.gov.ua/laws/show/1197-18/print1383857428710001.

9. "Perekhod no elektronnye goszakupki pozvolit sekonomit' do 40 milliardov" ["Transition to Electronic State Procurement Allows the Economizing of up to 40 billion [hryvnia]"], *Ekonomichna pravda*, October 16, 2014.

cuts in law enforcement spending (1 percent), and normalization of public procurement (2 percent). While pension cuts will not be instant, these proposed changes would free up funds to spend on important, more desirable items, including social compensation.

Although Ukraine's overall public expenditures are too large, spending on some items is quite small. Most strikingly, defense expenditure of 1 percent of GDP was minuscule and needs to be increased in view of Russian military aggression. The government's goal is to raise it from 1.6 percent of GDP in 2014 to 5 percent of GDP in 2015. But a Ministry of Defense representative complained that about 90 percent of the defense budget is spent on "food, utilities and the salary of military personnel."[10] The defense sector should also lay off superfluous staff and sell unnecessary real estate. Family and unemployment benefits, which are too low, should be raised.

Some Ukrainian government representatives use the need for more military expenditures as an excuse for not cutting public expenditures in general and instead call for "financial mobilization." This makes no sense. The desired increase in defense expenditure is merely 3.4 percent of GDP, while the preferred cut in public expenditures is 20 percent of GDP. Moreover, an expansion of one kind of public expenditures is a reason to economize on other expenditures. Furthermore, Ukrainians are not likely to be more appreciative of a parasitic and corrupt state because of the war.

Slashing public expenditures urgently is all the more crucial because Ukraine is in the midst of a major financial crisis. Else, the crisis could become as ferocious as the Russian financial crash of August 1998. At the time the Russian government could not obtain any financing and had no choice but to cut its public expenditures by 14 percent of GDP from 1997 to 2000, which led to a steady economic growth of 7 percent a year for a decade. The cuts in enterprise subsidies of 16 percent of GDP leveled the playing field, opening up the marketplace for new entrepreneurs (Åslund 2007). When Moldova faced a financial crisis combined with devaluation, it also sharply cut public expenditure by 15 percent of GDP from 1997 to 1999 (Åslund 2002, 226), which led to sustained economic growth. If high public expenditures render a country financially unsustainable, sharp cuts in those expenditures do not harm the economy but instead imbue confidence and kickstart economic growth.

Similarly, in the two crisis years 2009–10, Latvia carried out a fiscal adjustment of 13.6 percent of GDP (Åslund and Dombrovskis 2011, 107). Two years of strict fiscal policy led Latvia to enjoy the highest economic growth in Europe in 2011 and Prime Minister Valdis Dombrovskis was reelected twice. Estonia and Lithuania had similar experiences in 2009–10.

All these countries carried out major fiscal adjustments by primarily cutting public expenditures fast, which cleansed the market of subsidies and

---

10. Oleksandr Lashchenko, "2012 roku finansuvannia ukrainskoi armii bude rekordno nyz'kym" ["In 2012, the financing of Ukrainian army will be at the record low level"], *Radio Liberty*, May 19, 2011, www.radiosvoboda.org/content/article/24179169.html.

barriers and spurred beneficial structural reforms, leading to rapid economic growth. Unlike Russia and Moldova, the Baltic countries did not carry out devaluation, but even so they achieved impressive growth spurts. A large budget deficit in the midst of a financial crisis does not stimulate growth but impedes it, as the Ukrainian and Russian experiences of the 1990s show (Åslund, Boone, and Johnson 2001), not to mention Greece in 2008–13. These examples run contrary to the Blanchard and Leigh (2013) argument for developed European economies that fiscal multipliers are big and positive, which are short term for one year and clearly do not apply to emerging economies.

Unlike the IMF program for Latvia in 2008, the March 2014 IMF Stand-By Arrangement for Ukraine was amazingly relaxed. It did not foresee a reduction of very large public expenditures of more than 2 percent of GDP in 2014, and "a gradual expenditure-oriented fiscal adjustment—proceeding at a pace commensurate with the economy's speed of recovery—aiming at reducing the structural fiscal deficit by around 2 percent of GDP by 2016." It anticipated enterprise subsidies—a major source of corruption—to shrink by a marginal 0.1 percent of GDP (IMF 2014a, 19, 62–63). This program was far too cautious and not commensurate with the severity of Ukraine's fiscal crisis. It is difficult to see how it could have salvaged Ukraine from default. Even after it cut Ukraine's GDP forecast for 2014 from a contraction of 5 to 6.5 percent, the IMF (2014d, 41) demanded an additional fiscal tightening of only 1 percent of GDP to a total of 3 percent of GDP. Seldom has an IMF program been so inadequate. It did not offer Ukraine any chance of economic success.[11]

In a relaxed fashion, the IMF stated that "a schedule should be adopted to raise [gas] tariffs to the cost recovery level over the next three years through semiannual increases of 20 percent until mid-2016" (IMF 2014a, 89). This pace was far too slow, giving one big and powerful businessman enough time to capture the gas arbitrage and buy Ukraine's politics. Public expenditures must be cut much faster, and the prices of natural gas and other forms of energy should be increased to the market level immediately, while those affected by high energy prices should be compensated with cash transfers.

The IMF designed such an unsustainable program for Ukraine presumably because Western governments wanted to finance Ukraine but not from their own budgets. They treat the IMF as their international reserve fund, caring little about the organization's conditionality and even less about a client country's financial sustainability.

Lower Taxes and Close Loopholes

Ukraine's state revenues are large and remarkably stable at about 45 percent of official GDP. The main concerns about Ukraine's tax system are instead a vast underground economy created by massive tax evasion, cumbersome taxation practices, and outright criminalization of the tax administration.

---

11. Dabrowski (2014) expresses similar views.

Table 9.3 Ukraine's general government revenue, 2010–14
(percent of GDP)

Tax	2010	2011	2012	2013[a]	2014[a]
Total revenue	43.3	42.9	44.5	45.5	45.3
Tax revenue	37.5	38.4	38.9	39.8	39.7
Tax on income, profits, and capital gains	8.4	8.9	8.8	9.2	8.8
Personal income tax	4.7	4.6	4.8	5.2	5.2
Corporate profit tax	3.7	4.2	4.0	4.0	3.6
Payroll tax	11.6	12.4	13.0	13.9	14.0
Property tax	0.9	0.8	0.9	0.9	0.9
Tax on goods and services	13.3	13.5	13.5	13.0	13.0
Value-added tax	9.5	10.0	9.9	9.3	9.3
Excise	2.6	2.6	2.7	2.8	2.8
Other	1.1	0.9	0.9	0.9	0.9
Tax on international trade	0.8	0.9	0.9	0.9	0.9
Other tax	2.5	1.9	1.8	1.9	2.0
Nontax revenue	5.7	4.5	5.6	5.6	5.6

a. IMF Staff projections.

Source: IMF (2014b, 34).

If Ukraine would cut its public expenditures to Lithuania's level of 34 percent of GDP in the medium term, state revenues should decline to 36 percent of GDP to allow for an annual budget surplus of 2 percent of GDP to reduce the public debt. That offers a lot of room for tax cuts, 9 percent of GDP, but public expenditures must be slashed before taxes are reduced.

Two taxes dominate Ukraine's state revenues, the payroll tax and the value-added tax (VAT). The "unified social security contribution" or payroll tax of 41 percent contributes 13 percent of GDP. In the European Union, the corresponding average rate is 36 percent of the payroll, and in the United States 15 percent. The VAT together with excise taxes yield 13 percent of GDP. The nearly flat personal income tax yields 5 percent of GDP, and the corporate profit tax 4 percent of GDP. Foreign trade taxes contribute barely 1 percent of GDP. Nontax revenues, mainly dividends from state companies and privatization revenues, add 5.5 percent of GDP (table 9.3) (IMF 2014b, 34; Yatsenyuk 2014a).

In July 2014, the Yatsenyuk government presented a Concept for Reform of the Tax System (Cabinet of Ministers 2014b). In mid-September, the government submitted its tax proposals to parliament, which refused to consider them before the elections. The reform plan focused on three problems: the shadow economy, the budget deficit, and the public debt. The government assessed the shadow economy at 34 percent of the official GDP, which seems low. Out of Ukraine's total labor force of 27 million, only 17 million are acknowledged as members of the active workforce, and many of them reveal only half of their real incomes to secure a minimum pension.[12]

The concept's first objective was to create beneficial conditions for economic growth and to bring the shadow economy into the official economy. Its second aim was transparency. The third was to develop mutual trust between taxpayers and state. The fourth objective was to reduce the time and costs of tax administration. The goal of maintaining sufficiently large state revenues came toward the end. An additional aim was decentralization (Cabinet of Ministers 2014b). Tax revenues have always been high in Ukraine regardless of the economy's performance, indicating that consecutive governments had focused on state revenues rather than economic growth. When state revenues fell short, the state tax administration unlawfully raided companies or demanded advance payments of taxes.

A large number of small nuisance taxes have characterized Ukraine's tax system. The Tax Code of 2010 reduced the number of state taxes from 29 to 18 and the local taxes from 14 to 5 (Shevchenko and Otten 2014, 2). Prime Minister Arseniy Yatsenyuk (2014a) wanted to cut the number of taxes from 22 to 9, which is the average number in Western countries. The 13 taxes Yatsenyuk wanted to abolish are sectoral taxes yielding only 2 percent of budget revenues. They cost more to administer than they yield in revenue, and they distort competition, benefiting only their collectors. These taxes are typically minor fees (Cabinet of Ministers 2014b).

The remaining taxes are sensible: personal income tax, unified social contribution, corporate profit tax, value added tax, excise tax, agricultural tax, real estate tax, import tariffs, and natural resource taxes. Ukraine has no wealth tax and no inheritance tax on residents. Capital gains are essentially taxed as income (Deloitte 2014). The proposed tax reform would give Ukraine the right tax structure by international standards.

Big corporations should be dissuaded from indulging in transfer pricing and be compelled to disclose their profits in Ukraine for taxation. Loopholes for the rich and powerful should be closed. Most importantly, all enterprises must reveal their real owners to stay registered in Ukraine and should be prevented from importing goods without paying VAT and obtaining VAT refunds when exporting.

The general trend in taxation is to move it from production, that is, labor and capital, to consumption (Tanzi and Schuknecht 2000). A VAT of 20 percent and high excise taxes on tobacco, alcohol, and some luxury products make sense, and these indirect taxes yield large revenues. Yanukovych legislated to reduce the VAT to 17 percent starting in 2015, and the IMF (2014a, 30) rightly insisted on keeping it at 20 percent. The VAT and excise taxes should be kept at their current high level.

VAT has always been controversial in Ukraine because it is riddled with

---

12. "AP: okolo poloviny ukraintsev rabotayut nelegal'no" ["Presidential Administration: About Half of the Ukrainians Work Illegally"], *Ukrainskaya pravda*, October 17, 2014.

massive evasion and fraud. Prime Minister Yatsenyuk has stated: "The most corrupt tax in the country is the value-added tax."[13] Many problems plague VAT, but they mainly concern VAT refunds for exporters. On the one hand, VAT fraud is common, with people obtaining refunds for goods not exported but sold inside Ukraine. Yatsenyuk claimed that the losses from such fraudulent VAT refund demands amounted to 20 billion hryvnia per year (Dovgan 2014). The State Fiscal Service claims that one of Yanukyvoch's loyalists arranged a scheme to smuggle petrol into Ukraine without paying VAT or custom tariffs, adding 7.6 billion hryvnia to the state revenues in six months in 2014.[14]

On the other hand, many exporters do not receive their legitimate refunds for exports, which means that their exports are subject to an informal penalty tax of 20 percent. Foreign investors in Ukraine have persistently complained about this problem. The tax authorities charge "commissions" on VAT refunds for exporters, usually 20 to 30 percent of the refund. These informal commissions peaked at 40 to 50 percent after Yanukovych became president in 2010 (Stecklow, Piper, and Akymenko 2014; Vyshynsky 2014b). In September 2014, a financial investigation of the State Fiscal Service reportedly revealed that a group of former tax inspectors had embezzled VAT refunds of 2.2 billion hryvnia.[15]

Many Ukrainians favor replacing VAT with a general sales tax, but the government's revenues from VAT are substantial. While the EU average revenues from VAT are 7 percent of GDP, Ukraine obtains 10 percent of GDP. Within the European Union, only Denmark collects as large VAT revenues. Therefore there is no realistic alternative to VAT. A sales tax could hardly be higher than 10 percent because of the distortions it causes by not taxing the whole production chain but only retail sales, and it would generate far smaller revenues (Betliy, Giucci, and Kirchner 2013). The tax authorities explain that VAT revenue is large because much of it is collected through customs. Another reason is that the government does not budget for all legitimate VAT refunds, which are thus not paid. The Ukrainian government recognizes this shortcoming and is focusing on improving the administration of VAT amid calls from the opposition parties to replace it with a sales tax. A great advantage of VAT is that even politically influential enterprises are forced to pay it.

Ukraine introduced a real estate tax of up to 1 percent of the assessed value in January 2013. Its level corresponds to Western standards, and it makes

---

13. "Arseniy Yatsenyuk rasskazal o pravitel'svennykh initsiativakh stimulirovania i detenizatsii ekonomiki" ["Arseniy Yatsenyuk Told about Government Initiatives to Stimulate the Economy and Reduce the Shadow Economy"], *Pravitel'stvenny portal*, July 31, 2014.

14. "Byudzhet Ukrainy poluchil 7,6 milliarda ot detenizatsii vvoza nefteproduktov" ["Ukraine's Budget Received 7.6 Billion from De-Shadowing of Imports of Oil Products"], *Ekonomichna pravda*, September 9, 2014.

15. "Moshenniki vmeste s eks-nalogovkiama obokrali gosudarstvo na 2,2 milliarda" ["Fraudsters Together with Former Taxmen Stole 2.2 Billion from the State"], *Ekonomichna pravda*, September 16, 2014.

perfect sense. It offers owners an incentive to utilize land and property. Yet, actual real estate taxes remain minimal and should be hiked.

The most problematic Ukrainian tax is the "unified social contribution," which is a payroll tax for pension, health care, and unemployment benefits. It is unsustainably high at 41 percent of the payroll and is a major cause of the small official labor force and the sizable shadow economy. Many workers hide in the informal economy, which deprives them of social benefits deriving from the payroll tax. The collection of the payroll tax was traditionally ineffective because it was carried out by various social funds, but since October 2013 the Ministry of Revenues and Charges (Shevchenko and Otten 2014, 2)—renamed the State Fiscal Service—has been collecting it.

Yatsenyuk's (2014a, 2014b) main idea was to keep the payroll tax at the current 41 percent for two minimum incomes and decrease it to 15 percent for higher incomes. It might appear strange to have a regressive payroll tax, but it must be seen in the light of incentives and taxation practices. The two main objectives of the unified social tax are to generate revenues and bring labor from the shadow economy into the official economy. "In the private sector, many Ukrainian businesses pay their employees partly in cash—known as 'black' salaries—to avoid social-security contributions.... Tax authorities estimate that cash payments for salaries total about $17 billion a year, resulting in at least two million workers not appearing on tax rolls" (Stecklow, Piper, and Akymenko 2014).

Most workers want payroll tax to be paid on the minimum wage so they are entitled to public pension, but neither employees nor employers have any incentive to pay more social taxes, which do not result in significantly higher pensions. Therefore, additional earnings have been paid in cash, but cash is expensive. The State Fiscal Service assessed that cash payments cost 15 percent of the turnover. To begin with, it costs about 10 percent of the payroll to generate the cash through VAT fraud and then some 5 percent of the payroll to transport and handle the cash. Knowing this, the State Fiscal Service proposed a payroll tax of 15 percent for higher incomes, which would be equal to the cost of black cash.[16] The same principle determined the level of the flat income tax in Russia in 2001 at 13 percent.

The proposed cut in payroll tax would improve both VAT and payroll tax collection. The State Fiscal Service does not think that it will have any significant impact on overall tax revenues, given the current massive tax evasion. If Ukraine carried out a pension reform with personal savings accounts, or at least tied pensions to contributions, the incentives to pay would improve dramatically.

With his 2010 tax code, Yanukovych had abandoned Ukraine's previous flat personal income tax of 15 percent for a higher rate of 17 percent, which made no sense. Yatsenyuk (2014a) proposed the reintroduction of a progressive personal income tax with three rates: 15, 20, and 25 percent. But if the government cannot collect a payroll tax of more than 15 percent, it definitely

---

16. Interview with Ihor Bilous, head of the State Fiscal Service, in Kyiv, September 17, 2014.

cannot collect an income tax of more than 15 percent, which offers no tangible benefit to the taxpayer. Moreover, most countries in this region have low, flat personal income taxes, for example, 10 percent in Bulgaria, 13 percent in Russia, 15 percent in Lithuania, and 16 percent in Romania. Being significantly poorer than these neighboring countries, Ukraine needs to have competitive taxation with a low, flat personal income tax. Reverting to the rate of 15 percent appears the natural choice.

About half of the postcommunist countries have flat personal income taxes, and as one of the more corrupt countries Ukraine needs such a tax until it has successfully reduced corruption. In Russia, the introduction of a flat income tax in 2001 led to a sharp increase in those tax revenues, as has generally been the case. Yuriy Gorodnichenko, Jorge Martinez-Vazquez, and Klara Sabirianova Peter (2009) concluded their econometric assessment that in connection with Russia's flat tax reform "large and significant changes in tax evasion" were "associated with changes in voluntary compliance." The IMF opposes flat taxes for ideological rather than economic reasons. Even so it acknowledged that "there is evidence for Russia that compliance did improve; the distributional effects of the flat taxes are not unambiguously regressive, and in some cases they may have increased progressivity, including through the impact of compliance" (Keen, Kim, and Varsano 2006; cf. Ivanova, Keen, and Klemm 2005).

Since 2009, Georgia has gone even further. It has abolished its payroll tax, introducing a single flat income tax of 20 percent (Bendukidze and Saakashvili 2014). Ukraine should follow Georgia's lead in due course.

The Tax Code of 2010 legislated a gradual reduction of the tax rate on corporate profits from 25 to 16 percent, with a rate of 18 percent in 2014 (Shevchenko and Otten 2014, 3). Few countries collect as large a share of GDP in corporate profit taxes as Ukraine, 4 percent of GDP in 2013, while the EU countries get barely 3 percent of GDP in corporate profit taxes (table 9.3, Eurostat 2014). The largest private Ukrainian companies have minimized profit taxes through transfer pricing to lower profits in Ukraine and accumulate profits in offshore tax havens. The profit taxes are therefore most burdensome for medium-sized companies, which have borne the brunt of Ukraine's severe tax collection practices. The corporate profit tax should be reduced further and all loopholes should be eliminated. Many countries in the neighborhood have adopted for equally low personal income taxes and corporate profit taxes, because small entrepreneurs can easily transform one form of income into the other. Ukraine should opt for a flat income tax of 15 percent for both individuals and corporations, as Lithuania has done; in Bulgaria it is 10 percent and Romania 16 percent.

Yatsenyuk also proposed to simplify taxation of small entrepreneurs. From 1998 to 2010, single entrepreneurs in Ukraine enjoyed a favorable simplified tax. They paid either a small lump-sum tax or a low turnover tax. This sector of microenterprises expanded rapidly to millions of people (Thiessen 2001). In 2010, the Yanukovych tax code sharply restricted this simplified tax, forcing many to close down and driving many into the underground economy. Unfortunately, official statistics of the microenterprise sector are too contradictory to allow any clear assessment of the consequences. It will be several years before Ukraine successfully manages a reasonable tax system for millions of taxpayers. Until then small entrepreneurs need a simplified tax as a shield against government arbitrariness. Fortunately, the draft tax law proposes a substantial expansion of lump-sum taxation of small entrepreneurs with limited turnover and up to 10 employees and a turnover tax of only 4 percent without VAT obligations for small entrepreneurs with a maximum of 20 employees. Moreover, small enterprises with a turnover of less than 20 million hryvnia a year, about $1.2 million, will not be subject to inspections for two years.[17]

Ukraine's agricultural sector benefits from very mild taxation, which has rightly aroused considerable controversy at the IMF. All agricultural enterprises regardless of size have been subject to a land tax of up to 1 percent of the assessed value of the land, but usually this tax has been minimal. For Ukraine's millions of poor agricultural producers this tax makes sense because they have small family plots, which enable them to survive during hard times through subsistence farming. But Ukraine's many large agroholdings of up to 500,000 hectares are in a different league. These holdings are often large integrated companies with nonagricultural enterprises as well, but they pay the very low agricultural tax for all their activities, and are also exempt from VAT. These entities should be subject to regular taxation with full bookkeeping. Conversely, the current government proposal is that such taxation should apply to agricultural companies with sales of more than 20 million hryvnia, about $1.2 million.[18]

Privatization can yield substantial additional revenues for Ukraine. Although most state-owned enterprises have been sold, 3,300 remain in state hands. The Yatsenyuk government proposes to privatize 1,251 enterprises,[19] although they may not fetch a meaningful price in the midst of the rampant financial crisis. If done through open tenders, privatization of enterprises should contribute a few percent of GDP each year for the next few years. An even larger source of income could be the sale of unused or underutilized public real estate, which could bring at least 2 percent of GDP a year.

17. "Vlast' khochet zapretit' proverki biznesa s oborotom do 20 millionov" ["The Government Wants to Prohibit Inspections of Businesses with a Turnover up to 20 Million [hryvnia]"], *Ekonomichna pravda*, September 9, 2014.

18. "Arseniy Yatsenyuk pro uriadovu reformu podatkovoi systemy v Ukraini" ["Arseniy Yatsenyuk on Government's Reform of the Tax System in Ukraine"], *Uriadovyi portal*, August 6, 2014.

19. "Pravitel'stvo obrashchaetsya k Parlamentu bezotlagatel'no prinyat's zakon o privatizatsii" ["The Government Turns to the Parliament and Demands that it Adopts a Law on privatization"], *Pravitel'stvenny portal*, September 3, 2014.

Simplify and Decriminalize Tax Administration

The Ukrainian tax administration is fraught with corruption, extortion, red tape, arbitrary police actions, and other illegalities. Collecting revenues is the least of the problems; the main concern is protecting the business community from lawless tax inspectors. Tax officials extort bribes from taxpayers, part of which is passed on to superiors in the tax administration. Under Yanukovych, the extorted funds seem to have been concentrated at the top level of the government.

Tax inspectors have also indiscriminately imposed penalties. The Tax Code of 2010 stipulates that the maximum tax penalty should not exceed 50 percent of the withheld amount (Shevchenko and Otten 2014, 2). But tax officials have routinely charged penalties that were five times larger than the amount of income being penalized, in accordance with a temporary presidential decree of June 1995. Ukraine's Supreme Court has ignored the tax code on this matter (Koval 2014).

The government's new Concept of Reform of the Tax System emphasizes building "a partner relationship between the tax authorities and the taxpayers." The rights and duties of both parties are to be strictly regulated in law. Mediation is expected to replace an administrative procedure (Cabinet of Ministers 2014b). The government should go one step further and decriminalize taxation. Competing tax collection agencies extract money from the same companies, causing what Andrei Shleifer and Daniel Treisman (2000) have called "overgrazing." These agencies do not care about the survival of the taxpayers, only how much their agency can extract.

In his tax reform speech on August 6, 2014, Prime Minister Yatsenyuk attacked the three "monsters" that pursue criminal tax inspections: two departments of the State Fiscal Service, two departments of the Ministry of Interior, and the State Security Service. He proposed abolishing all these police functions in these institutions and instead creating a Service of Financial Investigation. "On average, only officially, these three monsters carry out 61,000 inspections; 61,000 criminal cases are opened each year. Every hour 30 enterprises are investigated and subjected to criminal cases. They have no time to work. They only deal with prosecutors, policemen and investigators" (Yatsenyuk 2014a). Yatsenyuk prohibited inspections of enterprises until December 31, 2015, through amendments to the Budget Law, passed by parliament on July 31, 2014.[20] But the inspections have continued. This step was inspired by President Mikheil Saakashvili's reforms in Georgia.

The old tax administration is rotten. In the 1990s, Mykola Azarov built it from scratch. He was one of Yanukovych's closest collaborators. His overt concern was collecting sufficient taxes, not how it was done. He developed a vast tax administration with 70,000 inspectors, who became extortionists running

---

20. Law of Ukraine "On Amending the Law of Ukraine "On State Budget of Ukraine for 2014," No. 1622-VII, July 31, 2014, http://zakon4.rada.gov.ua/laws/show/1622-18/paran32#n32.

a repressive tax regime. In the early 2000s, Azarov's state racket competed with the Ministry of Interior and the State Security Service in extortion (Åslund 2009). The new head of the State Fiscal Service, Ihor Bilous, started with more than 60,000 employees, first laying off 10 percent, and then another 7 percent.[21] If taxation is decriminalized and automated, more could be cut.

Ukraine has 6,000 tax policemen,[22] who are the greatest scourge to enterprise. As policemen they are entitled to enter any firm at will and even stop its activities without showing any proof of grounded suspicion of wrongdoing. The government proposes to transform the tax police into a new Service of Financial Investigation, but that would just preserve the problem. The tax police should instead be abolished, and taxation should be decriminalized. No tax inspector should have the right to visit an enterprise without a court order. Contacts between taxpayers and the tax authority should be minimized

The long-running problems with VAT refunds for exporters should be resolved by making VAT refunds automatic, as demanded by the IMF. The new government has promised to do so by changing the whole VAT administration beginning in January 2015, claiming to make it transparent (Dovgan 2014). Businessmen remain skeptical, fearing that the government just tries to keep their funds longer in special VAT accounts.

Decentralize the Fiscal System

Ukraine maintains an excessive Soviet centralization of public finance, with both revenues and expenditures going through the central treasury in Kyiv. This overcentralization makes it impossible for state agencies to obey formal rules and breeds corruption. Fiscal decentralization should enhance the transparency and efficiency of public finance and improve incentives at all levels of government.

All state authorities are compelled to deliver virtually all revenues to the central treasury, which discourages them from collecting revenues. In effect, they are subject to confiscatory marginal taxation. Often, local authorities can retain funds collected through penalties and fines, which has led to the proliferation of such highly inefficient—and corrupt—forms of taxation (Kravchuk 1999). The natural reaction has been that each institution has established a black or gray account for additional revenues so that they control some funds themselves.

The same overcentralization applies to public expenditures. Until the recent adoption of a new law on reform of higher education, a local university had to not only seek the central treasury's permission to buy pencils but also

---

21. "Bilous: Umen'shenie chisla nalogov ne povlechet za soboi znachitel'nogo sokrashcheniya nalognikov" ["Bilous: A Reduction of the Number of Taxes Does Not Lead to a Substantial Cut in the Number of Taxmen"], *Ekonomichna pravda*, August 30, 2014.

22. Information from Bilous, September 17, 2014.

follow its stipulation on the kind of pencils to purchase and at what prices. In 2012–13, the State Treasury blocked local authorities' accounts, arguing their paperwork was not done properly, when it was clear to many that someone higher up wanted to seize these funds. Even though local authorities had money in their accounts they could not spend it.

Decentralization of political power is being widely discussed in Ukraine and is the focus of the constitutional amendments proposed by Deputy Prime Minister Volodymyr Groisman (see chapter 7). Political decentralization needs to be accompanied by fiscal decentralization. The constitution should explicitly state that both regional and local authorities are entitled to their own independent budgets formed by those authorities within the framework of Ukrainian laws.

Ideally, revenues from different taxes should be divided between central, regional, and local authorities depending on their nature. Expenditure mandates should also be divided between the central and local government. The clearer and more transparent these divisions are the better the incentives are for government at all levels to economize on public resources.

In international practice, foreign trade taxes, VAT, social taxes, and natural resource taxes go to the central government because VAT and foreign trade taxes are by necessity national. Social taxes finance social benefits, regardless of where the beneficiary lives in the country. Natural resource royalties can be huge, and they are usually national, not regional, assets. Otherwise some regions would reap windfall gains. Land, property, and small enterprise taxes, on the contrary, are naturally local. Such revenues motivate local authorities to nurture their entrepreneurs and take care of their region. Accordingly, the Yatsenyuk government's tax reform concept argued for land and property taxes to be kept with the local authorities. Corporate profit taxes and personal income taxes can be shared among the central, state, regional, and local authorities (Shleifer and Treisman 2000, 118–20).

The central government is typically responsible for expenditures on foreign policy and defense, pensions, unemployment benefits, higher education, and national infrastructure, while regional and local authorities cover local infrastructure and primary and secondary education. The financing of health care varies. In addition, the central government usually transfers funds to poor regions, and since it is difficult not to make them distortive, they should be kept relatively small.

Improve the Budget Process

Budgeting in Ukraine has traditionally been disorderly. The budget has often been adopted long after the budget year has started. The Ministry of Finance has played only a limited role in the creation of the budget, which has been formed through horse trading in the parliament's budget committee. Often revenues have fallen short after the adoption of a budget, necessitating sequestration, as occurred in 2014. Usually sequestration has meant not only cuts but also a redistribution of state funding, typically from social programs to enterprise subsidies and state administration (Åslund 2009).

The Western countries that suffered financial crises around 1990, notably New Zealand, Australia, Sweden, and Finland, established more orderly budget processes, giving their ministries of finance greater authority (Honkapohja 2009, Iwulska 2012, Kirchner 2013).[23] These reforms involved many steps.

To begin with, the budget process had to be strictly controlled by the Ministry of Finance, in a timely, transparent, and orderly fashion. The Ministry of Finance managed the budget process centrally, which strengthened it in relation to other "demanding" ministries and made it easier to pursue national financial objectives, such as a balanced budget and limited public debt. The discretionary powers of the parliament's budget committee and the parliament in general were curtailed. A rising view is that the parliament should receive the budget only to vote it up or down. All these measures aim at minimizing opportunities for lobbyism and corruption.

The Ukrainian Parliament is notorious for its impulsive lobbyism. Businessmen-parliamentarians suddenly propose legal amendments to divert budget funds to their favored interests, and before anyone figures out what is going on, they have already had the funds legally allocated. Legislative initiative by the Ukrainian Parliament needs to be limited. Former finance minister Viktor Pynzenyk has proposed that the parliament not accept legislative proposals with fewer than 50 signatures of parliamentarians.[24] The time needed to allocate additional budget funds should also be regulated.

Ukraine can considerably improve the quality of the budget process by allowing more time for budget planning. Policymakers would then concentrate on the outcomes of budget spending and make economic policies more result-oriented. This aim can be achieved by implementing a medium-term expenditure framework. Such a multiyear budgetary approach links policy objectives, expenditure policies, and tax policy in the medium term. It allows policymakers to balance short-term policy achievements against long-term needs for the country's development and increase the efficiency of the allocated public funds. The Ukrainian government could prepare a medium-term expenditure framework for 2015–17 after the crisis has faded.

The European Union has budgetary rules that Ukraine should consider adopting. In its Maastricht Treaty on the formation of the Economic and Monetary Union (EMU), the European Union adopted the "Maastricht criteria," which stipulate that the budget deficit must not exceed 3 percent of GDP and the public debt not more than 60 percent of GDP. Several EU countries, notably Germany and Poland, have adopted such public debt limitations in their constitutions. Also, supplementary budgets for unexpected expenses, such as for wars and disasters, have been restricted. A standard demand is "pay as you

---

23. Needless to say, the United States does not belong on this list.

24. Interview with Viktor Pynzenyk in Kyiv, September 15, 2014.

go," that is, any additional expenditures should be covered by additional revenues or compensated for with cuts in other public expenses.

Keep Banking Clean and Simple

Ukraine has a rudimentary financial system, with little but banking. Its banking system looked promising before the global financial crisis in 2008, being sophisticated, large, and diversified with many reputable foreign banks, but it has fallen deep into disrepair. The stock market never took off, and it is doubtful that it ever will, given that it is so backward. Ukrainian companies prefer to go abroad to sell their stocks mainly on the Warsaw Stock Exchange.

In September 2014, the National Bank of Ukraine (NBU) estimated that about half the country's banks are in such a dire state that they need to be closed. In October, it carried out a stress test of the 15 biggest banks and found that ten of them needed recapitalization, but who would do so after repeated, failed recapitalizations?[25] The main cause of the banks' losses is the big devaluation, which is ongoing, but embezzlement by owners is a major concern.

The Ukrainian banking system has been persistently convulsing for the last decade. In 2006–08, Ukrainian banks rapidly expanded lending and made extraordinary profits. Commercial banks with access to funding from the euro market could borrow short-term funds at low interest rates, while issuing consumer loans in hryvnia at interest rates of up to 50 percent a year. The artificial peg of the hryvnia to the US dollar caused this large interest gap, and the credit boom unleashed a real estate boom. The Ukrainian owners boosted the banks' assets by issuing overly large and risky loans just before they sold their shares. Many Ukrainian businessmen sold their banks because banking requires a lot of capital, which they did not have.

The overheating was extreme. West European banks purchased Ukrainian banks at crazy prices of up to five times the book value, when multiples of one or two are normal. By July 2008, 17 West European banks' share of Ukrainian banking assets peaked at 40 percent. In October, the banking system collapsed, as Ukraine experienced a sudden stop in international funding in the wake of the Lehman Brothers bankruptcy on September 15. The Ukrainian banks faced a severe currency mismatch, having taken large short-term loans in euros, dollars, or Swiss francs, while issuing loans in hryvnia, which were sharply devalued during the crisis. About one-third of the 30 biggest Ukrainian banks, all owned by Ukrainians, collapsed because of currency mismatches. Foreigners recapitalized their banks at great losses.

The IMF praised the Ukrainian authorities for their work to clean up the banking system, and all the Western banks stuck it out, until Yanukovych came

---

25. The five banks that had sufficient capital were the two big privately owned banks, PrivatBank (Kolomoisky and Boholyubov) and PUMB (Akhmetov), Austrian-owned Raiffeisen Bank Aval, and the two Russian banks, Alfa Bank and Sberbank (*Komsomolskaya Pravda v Ukraine*, September 26, 2014).

to power. Foreign and unrelated private banks could no longer work profitably in Ukraine.

Four trends became evident in Ukrainian bank ownership. First, most West European banks withdrew. Only two of Ukraine's ten biggest banks, Raiffeisen Bank Aval and Ukrsotsbank, are still owned by West European banks, Raiffeisen and Unicredit, respectively. Two or three other smaller Western-owned banks may survive, but most of the Western owners have decided to sell and leave. Second, the two traditional state banks, Ukreximbank and Oshchadbank (Savings Bank), sharply raised their share of banking assets during the crisis. The government used these banks to buy state bonds for indirect state financing and let the NBU refinance them. The number of state banks increased as private banks collapsed and were taken over by the state. Third, Russian state banks had increased their share of banking assets to 16 percent by September 2014. Fourth, businessmen close to President Yanukovych greatly advanced in the banking sector, in particular, by imposing restrictive business practices on banks owned by West Europeans.

The Yanukovych administration's hostility toward foreign presence and rigorous banking standards profoundly weakened the country's banking system. Hopefully, the biggest and seemingly best run West European banks, Raiffeisen Bank Aval and Ukrsotsbank, will survive. By contrast, in the 10 new eastern members of the European Union, West European banks remain dominant and their share of banking assets shrank only marginally during the crisis.[26]

In 2014, the Ukrainian banks were hit with a double whammy. The new Yanukovych bank owners either did not know how to run banks or did not even try; they either wanted to simply steal banking assets or were truly ignorant. In at least one big bank, more than 80 percent of the lending went to the owner.

With depreciation, Ukrainian banks incurred ever greater losses because of currency mismatches. When the government announced that it would recapitalize the banks by issuing more bonds, which the NBU would buy either directly or indirectly by providing financing to the big state banks, the market rightly identified this as monetary emission, sending the exchange rate down.[27] Intermittently, Ukraine has seen both bank runs and currency runs, in response to which the NBU has reinforced the already very strict currency regulations. The situation is so bad that Ukraine is best advised to keep its banking sector small, clean, and simple.

The government should close the many obviously corrupt banks, which might account for most of the banking system, and demand recapitalization of the banks deemed viable—presumably the two traditional state banks, Os-

---

26. The two exceptions are Slovenia, where substandard state banks remain dominant, and Hungary, where the Viktor Orban government is trying to tax foreign banks out of existence.

27. Dragon Capital, "NBU Plans to Recapitalize State-Owned Oschadbank, Ukreximbank and Ukrgazbank," *Dragon Daily*, September 22, 2014.

hchadbank and Ukreximbank, the Western banks, and the Russian banks. In 2014, the NBU closed 32 banks, but the remaining 150 are still excessive. The government must not recapitalize corrupt and dysfunctional banks but close them. Fortunately, the NBU has limited the number of systemic banks that need to be recapitalized to only eight, which seems like the right number. Credit is expected to be tight in 2015 and 2016 in any case.

Can and Should Ukraine Avoid Default?

If the Ukrainian government does not undertake a major financial tightening and mobilize new international financing in early 2015, default is likely. Yet it would offer little relief, because the public debt that can be subject to a haircut is rather small. For Ukraine, it is more important to establish a sensible economic policy and maintain good relations with its Western donors, but some debt restructuring appears more or less inevitable.

At the end of 2013, Ukraine's public debt was merely 41 percent of GDP, but it is skyrocketing. In its July 2014 public debt sustainability analysis, the IMF (2014d, 48–50) presented rather ominous numbers. Its baseline scenario was that "debt will reach 67.6 percent of GDP at end-2014, a jump of over 26 percentage points from 2013, driven by large financing needs under past unsustainable policies as well as significant exchange rate depreciation. This ratio is about 10 percent of GDP higher than at the time" of the Stand-By Arrangement. But that was an unrealistically optimistic prospect.

The IMF offered two worse scenarios (IMF 2014d, 49). "Under a growth shock, entailing a cumulative growth decline of over 9 percent in 2015–16 in addition to the projected 2014 decline of 6.5 percent, the debt-to-GDP ratio reaches 99 percent in 2016." In a "combined macro-fiscal shock" the IMF foresaw public debt going to 134 percent of GDP in 2016. Ukraine would default long before.

Public debt is not only a fiscal cost. It also reduces growth. An empirical IMF paper found that "on average, a 10 percentage point increase in the initial debt-to-GDP ratio is associated with a slowdown in annual real per capita GDP growth of around 0.2 percentage points per year, with the impact being somewhat smaller in advanced economies" (Kumar and Woo 2010). Already in its Stand-By Arrangement of March 2014, the IMF (2014b, 34) projected that Ukraine's interest payments would rise from 3.3 percent of GDP in 2014 to 4.8 percent of GDP in 2018, but it is set to rise far higher much earlier. The IMF (2014d, 41) foresaw an interest cost of 4.6 percent of GDP in 2015.

Ukraine's financial situation does not look sustainable. In December 2014, the consensus prediction is a 2014 output decline of 7 percent, more than what the IMF stress scenario projected, because of Russian aggression. Furthermore, the NBU is pursuing straightforward monetary financing, which boosts inflation and depresses the exchange rate. The falling exchange rate undermines the banks, which inevitably suffer from currency mismatches. Ukraine's public expenditures and budget deficit are far too large and rising fast.

Ukraine's public debt consists of three large chunks (table 9.4). Half of the debt is domestic, virtually all held by the NBU and state banks. The NBU holds an additional 10 percent of the debt through international bonds. In September 2014, the NBU and state banks with NBU financing held 60 percent of the country's public debt. Eurobonds account for just $16.3 billion, one-fifth of the total public debt, of which Russia holds $3 billion.[28] In addition to the data in this table, Gazprom has filed a lawsuit with the Stockholm arbitration court insisting that Ukraine repay gas arrears of $1.4 billion ($2.2 billion including penalties). Ukraine has countered with a demand for $6 billion in alleged overpayments for gas since 2010. At present, Ukraine is increasing its share of loans from international financial institutions, mainly the IMF and the World Bank.

Of these debt obligations, only the eurobonds and the debt to Russia could be partially written off. Even a substantial haircut would do little to ease Ukraine's desperate financial situation. The benefits from a debt writeoff are quite small (see chapter 3).

If Ukraine is successful in fending off Russian aggression, it should demand substantial compensation and reparations from Russia for assets taken from Ukraine, such as Crimea, gas reserves of 2 billion cubic meters held in storage in Crimea, the oil and gas company Chornomornaftogaz, companies in Crimea, monetary holdings in Crimea, and reparations for war damage, but this depends on the settlement of the war. Russia's claims on Ukraine may be put into question.

My Peterson Institute colleague Anna Gelpern (2014, 1) has argued that Ukraine should repudiate part of Russia's claims on Ukraine. This bond issue is subject to British law, which is not supposed to be used for international suppression:

> A single measure can free up $3 billion for Ukraine and send a powerful message to Russia: The United Kingdom can refuse to enforce English-law contracts for the money Russia lent former Ukrainian president Viktor Yanukovych in a failed attempt to keep him in power late last year. Ukraine would then have the option to walk away from this debt without the usual legal and market consequences of repudiation.

Given the financial situation of December 2014, the natural trajectory is default caused by a depreciation-inflation cycle. Then the government would be well advised to opt for an orderly debt reprofiling or prolongation of debt maturities in the framework of a new IMF program. A better option would be for the government to drastically cut public expenditures, link the reductions to major structural reforms, and ask for Western assistance. To cover the cost of war damages Ukraine should request humanitarian assistance from friendly

---

28. Vadim Khramov, "Ukraine: Ten Reasons Why We Think that Sovereign Debt Restructuring Is Unlikely," Morgan Stanley, September 24, 2014.

Table 9.4 Ukraine's public debt structure, 2010–13

Component	2010 Millions of US dollars	2010 Percent of GDP	2011 Millions of US dollars	2011 Percent of GDP	2012 Millions of US dollars	2012 Percent of GDP	2013 Millions of US dollars	2013 Percent of GDP
Total debt	54,300	39.80	59,220	36.24	64,500	36.52	73,110	40.47
State direct debt	40,630	29.78	44,720	27.36	49,950	28.28	60,080	33.26
Domestic debt	17,790	13.04	20,210	12.37	23,810	13.48	32,150	17.80
Obligations under treasury bills	17,381	12.74	19,811	12.12	23,436	13.27	31,796	17.60
Obligations to the National Bank of Ukraine	409	0.30	399	0.24	374	0.21	354	0.20
External debt	22,936	16.81	24,507.1	15.00	26,137.7	14.80	27,931.8	15.46
IFO loans	10,432.3	7.65	10,556.5	6.46	10,020.9	5.67	7,744.7	4.29
European Bank for Reconstruction and Development	331.3	0.24	444.7	0.27	533.8	0.30	596.3	0.33
European Investment Bank	196.5	0.14	257.8	0.16	400.8	0.23	535.9	0.30
International Monetary Fund	6,860.9	5.03	6,839.6	4.19	6,054.5	3.43	3,542.4	1.96
World Bank	3,043.6	2.23	3,014.4	1.84	3,031.8	1.72	3,070.1	1.70
Bilateral borrowings	1,415.7	1.04	1,341.8	0.82	1,138.4	0.64	910.7	0.50
Russia	996.9	0.73	899.1	0.55	801.4	0.45	703.6	0.39
Other bilaterals	418.8	0.31	442.7	0.27	337.1	0.19	207.1	0.11
Loans from foreign banks	2,000.1	1.47	2,000.1	1.22	0.1	0.00	0.1	0.00
Other external debt	1,891.2	1.39	1,885.3	1.15	1,887.3	1.07	1,897.5	1.05
SDR allocations received to the state budget	1,891.2	1.39	1,885.3	1.15	1,887.3	1.07	1,897.5	1.05
State external bonds, 2003-13	7097	5.20	8,723	5.34	13091	7.41	17379	9.62

State-guaranteed debt	13,670	10.02	14,500	8.87	14,550	8.24	13,030	7.21
Domestic debt	1,750	1.28	1,530	0.94	2,030	1.15	3,390	1.88
External debt	11,923.5	8.74	12,967.5	7.93	12,521.1	7.09	9,636.2	5.33
IFO loans	7,740.6	5.67	7,701.5	4.71	5,074.2	2.87	2,030.0	1.12
European Atomic Energy Community	65.3	0.05	55.5	0.03	47.5	0.03	39.8	0.02
European Bank for Reconstruction and Development	148.6	0.11	126.4	0.08	113.1	0.06	97.9	0.05
International Monetary Fund	7,384.5	5.41	7,361.6	4.50	4,727.9	2.68	1,648.6	0.91
World Bank	142.3	0.10	158.1	0.10	185.6	0.11	243.7	0.13
Bilateral borrowings	190.6	0.14	190.6	0.12	247.8	0.14	247.8	0.14
Loans from foreign banks	1,001.1	0.73	1,580.6	0.97	3,224.9	1.83	3,454.9	1.91
Other external debt	2,991.2	2.19	3,494.9	2.14	3,974.1	2.25	3,903.5	2.16
Total public external debt	34,759.5	25.48	37,474.5	22.93	38,658.8	21.89	37,568.0	20.80
Total public domestic debt	19,540.5	14.32	21,745.5	13.31	25,841.2	14.63	35,542.0	19.67

IFO = international financial organization; SDR = special drawing rights

Source: Ministry of Finance of Ukraine, Ukraine Bond Prospectus, February 17, 2014.

states. It is universally provided as grants, unlike financial stabilization support, which primarily consists of credits.

A common view among international financial experts is that excessive public debt should be written off early on, but what is excessive varies greatly and is a matter of opinion and policy (Reinhart and Rogoff 2009). Bulgaria and Poland reached agreements with their official creditors on substantial and conditional reductions of their foreign public debt. The first postcommunist Polish government sensibly claimed that its inherited public debt was too large and asked for a writeoff of 50 percent. After long negotiations, its creditors agreed to write off the debt in two rounds, in 1991 and 1994. In return Poland was required to pursue a strict fiscal and monetary policy and far-reaching structural reforms so that it could service the rest of the debt (Das, Papaioannou, and Trebesch 2012; Pirian 2003).

Russia defaulted on its domestic public debt in 1998. Its main regret was that default did not take place earlier and in a more orderly fashion. Hungary, by contrast, never restructured its large public debt. It has managed to service its public debt, with the intermittent assistance of the IMF, but it has not succeeded in breaking out of the fiscal trap of excessive public expenditures and public debt, forcing it to maintain higher taxes than all other countries in the region and leaving it with the lowest growth in the whole region since 2000 (Åslund and Djankov 2014).

If Ukraine desires a general debt restructuring, it should do so early, before it runs out of reserves and becomes overly burdened with IMF credits, because IMF and World Bank credits cannot be written off, as Argentina has experienced so bitterly. At the end of 2014, its international reserves were as low as $7.5 billion, which might be a reason to call for a voluntary standstill in its foreign debt service.

For long, the Ukrainian government denied the need for debt restructuring, but all governments do so until they actually do it. While visiting the United States in late September 2014, Prime Minister Yatsenyuk stated: "We strongly believe and we are confident that Ukraine will not default." But he also said Ukraine's current program with the IMF may need to be "readjusted."[29] On January 21, 2015, Finance Minister Natalie Jaresko publicly raised the need for some debt restructuring: "We'll reach out to our sovereign creditors and talk to them about their vision, our vision, how we can work together to improve the debt sustainability in the medium-term."[30]

At the same time, IMF Managing director Christine Lagarde issued this statement: "President Poroshenko informed me today that the Ukrainian authorities have requested a multi-year arrangement with the Fund, supported by the Extended Fund Facility, to replace the existing Stand-By Arrangement.

---

29. Dragon Capital, "Government Officials Rule Out Debt Restructuring," *Dragon Daily*, September 25, 2014.

30. Olga Tanas, Andrew Mayeda, and Stefan Riecher, "Ukraine to Consult Bondholders on Debt Terms After IMF Loan," Bloomberg, January 22, 2015.

The new arrangement would support immediate macroeconomic stabilization measures as well as broad and deep economic reforms over several years to ensure economic and financial stability and restore sustainable growth."[31]

The IMF had decided to redesign its program with Ukraine demanding more structural reform and a debt restructuring was presumed.

Recommendations

1. Publish the consolidated state budget in a comprehensible form on the web.

2. Cut public expenditures from 53 to 34 percent of GDP over the next few years with a first-year cut on the order of one-tenth of GDP.

3. Abolish all enterprise subsidies instantly, first and foremost energy subsidies, but offer social cash compensation.

4. Reduce spending on public pensions gradually from 16 to 8 percent of GDP.

5. Cut half of the civil servants and double the salaries for those who remain.

6. Implement transparent and competitive procurement procedures.

7. Cut tax revenues by 9 percent of GDP after public expenditures have been slashed.

8. Demand disclosure of final beneficiaries of any firm registered in Ukraine.

9. Combat transfer pricing and minimize multiple tax loopholes.

10. Decrease the number of taxes from 22 to 9.

11. Keep the VAT and excise taxes at their current levels.

12. Reduce the unified social contribution to 15 percent for incomes more than double the minimum wage.

13. Adopt a flat income tax of 15 percent for individuals and corporations.

14. Expand the simplified taxation system for individual entrepreneurs.

15. Impose ordinary taxation (corporate profit tax and VAT) on large agro-holdings.

16. Decriminalize taxation by abolishing all forms of tax police. Tax inspectors should have no right to enter an enterprise or visit an individual without a court order.

17. Simplify tax administration and further develop electronic taxation.

18. Decentralize the extremely centralized fiscal system with regard to both revenues and expenditures.

19. Divide revenues from different taxes between central versus regional and local levels.

20. Adopt a medium-range budgeting process for three years.

---

31. IMF, Statement by IMF Managing Director Christine Lagarde on Ukraine, press release no. 15/11, January 21, 2015.

10

Cleaning Up the Energy Sector

Victory is when we won't buy any Russian gas.

—Prime Minister Arseniy Yatsenyuk[1]

Ukraine's energy sector is well endowed but extremely mismanaged. Since Ukraine's independence, it has been the main source of top-level corruption, and its prime beneficiaries have bought the state. This long-lasting policy has undermined national security, caused unsustainable public costs, jeopardized the country's balance of payments, led to massive waste of energy, and capped domestic production of energy. It is difficult to imagine a worse policy. Instead, conditions should be created so that Ukraine can develop its substantial energy potential and become self-sufficient in coal and natural gas.[2]

The solution to these problems is no mystery and it has been elaborated in a large literature for the last two decades. To check corruption energy prices need to be unified. That means raising key prices four to five times, which will eliminate the large energy subsidies and stimulate energy saving, while also stimulating domestic production of all kinds of energy. To make this politically possible, social compensation should be offered to the poorest half of the population.

The energy sector suffers from many shortcomings, and most of these need to be dealt with swiftly. Otherwise, new rent-seeking interests will evolve, and soon they will become entrenched and once again impossible to defeat. The new government has a brief window of opportunity to address the most important issues.

---

1. "Ukraina osvoboditsya ot 'gazovoi zavisimosti' ot RF cherez 5 let–Yatsenyuk" ["Yatsenyuk: Ukraine Will Free Itself from Gas Dependence on Russia in 5 Years"], *Ekonomichna pravda*, September 8, 2014.

2. In writing this chapter I have greatly benefited from the wisdom of Ed Chow and Mikhailo Honchar.

To sort out these problems, this chapter first scrutinizes the energy sector in general and then the gas and coal sectors. Their essence is the corrupt enrichment of a few. Next, it proposes a large-scale reform of the Ukrainian energy sector. Specifically, it discusses how private energy production can be promoted and questions whether Ukraine really ought to pursue gas trade with Russia.

What Is Wrong with the Ukrainian Energy Sector?

To understand Ukrainian energy policy, we need to examine its potential, shortcomings, and the causes of the persistent failures to reform this flawed policy. All along, the natural gas sector has harbored the worst mismanagement. Its basic problem is Ukraine's persistently very low domestic gas price for state-owned producers, households, and utilities. Ukraine has the lowest gas prices for households in Europe (IEA 2012). According to the International Monetary Fund (IMF 2014a, 20), "The retail gas and heating tariffs remain the lowest in Europe, only 11–25 percent of the levels in other gas-importing countries in the region and significantly below even the levels in Russia."

The worst concern is the extraordinary corruption in the gas sector (Balmaceda 2013, Global Witness 2006). The fundamental problem is that the Ukrainian energy sector has never been liberalized. The state continues to control both prices and allocation, and this state power has continuously been usurped for private benefit. Many energy prices are far below the market level, while others are market-oriented and up to 12 times higher as of September 2014.

Most large Ukrainian fortunes have been built on arbitrage between low energy prices fixed by the state and market prices that are several times higher. Initially this arbitrage took place between Russia and Ukraine but today it is primarily within Ukraine. The government has financed this boondoggle of the rich and powerful with price and enterprise subsidies, provided state guarantees, and forgiven nonpayments. Inefficient state energy corporations governed poorly and not subject to public audits aggravate the corruption.

In 1998, all state-controlled oil and gas companies were integrated into an unwieldy state holding company, Naftogaz Ukrainy. It is the largest company in Ukraine with 175,000 employees producing 8 percent of GDP, but Naftogaz has never functioned well. The state budget finances its large losses. Restrictive regulation, poor property rights, and ample red tape make it impossible for all but a few well-connected operators to produce energy. Reputable foreign companies have barely played any role in the Ukrainian energy sector.

With their energy policy, successive Ukrainian governments have favored corruption through arbitrage while penalizing domestic production through price discrimination. Ukraine has a sizeable gas industry, currently contributing 40 percent of its consumption. Each year Naftogaz buys 17 billion cubic meters (bcm) of natural gas domestically produced by partially state-owned companies at an extremely low price. In September 2014, the Ukrainian government paid only $30 per 1,000 cubic meters (mcm) of natural gas produced by the state-owned producer Ukrgazvydobuvannia (Ukrgazdobycha in Russian), while the domestic market price for industry was around $380 per mcm. Ukraine could produce far more gas, both conventional and shale gas, with a normal gas price (Kobolyev 2014). The state budget covers the losses of state-owned Ukrgazvydobuvannia.

The alleged reason for keeping the production price so low is to provide consumers with cheap gas. Deputy Prime Minister Volodymyr Groisman assessed that 40 percent of the 17 bcm was resold to the commercial sector, where gas prices are based on the Russian gas price of $380 per mcm. In that fashion, somebody close to Yanukovych made a fortune of some $2.5 billion a year.[3]

In the spring of 2014, the Yatsenyuk government appointed a 34-year-old investment banker, Andriy Kobolyev, CEO of Naftogaz. Since then, Kobolyev has been the driving public voice in favor of gas reform, demanding an early unification of the gas prices. Kobolyev (2014) characterized the old policy thus: "We give you gas for 100 hryvnia [$7], and you ignore that we steal $100."

Ukrgazvydobuvannia has a large number of gas fields, but much of the Ukrainian gas is located deep down, requiring drilling of 5,000 meters or more. Such wells are expensive to drill, and the company has currently only 42 such wells. Production at such wells typically costs $200 per mcm, which Ukrgazvydobuvannia cannot afford. It would be highly profitable for a private company that can sell gas to industry for the market price of around $380 per mcm, but few are allowed to drill. In order to limit its losses, Ukrgazvydobuvannia sells unprofitable wells for close to nothing to private gas producers, which belong to half a dozen big Ukrainian businessmen (Kobolyev 2014).

Nor is the subsidization of households through low gas prices socially just. Only 5 million households, one-third of the total, enjoy these gas subsidies. The poorest part of the population lives in the countryside, buying gas tubes that are not subsidized and spending five to six times more on gas per unit than privileged urban households (Kobolyev 2014).

The Ukrainian budget cost for direct and indirect energy subsidies is intolerably high, no less than 7.6 percent of GDP in 2012, according to the IMF (2014b, 87), and it has risen considerably with the depreciation of the hryvnia in 2014. The domestic energy prices are regulated in hryvnia, while the import cost is set in dollars. Domestic consumer prices for gas were hiked 56 percent on May 1, 2014, but the depreciation of the hryvnia has been far greater, which has increased the total energy subsidies.

Every year, Naftogaz is recapitalized with $3 billion to $5 billion from the government budget to cover its debts. In August 2014, the government decided to recapitalize Naftogaz with 63 billion hryvnia, at the time $5.1 billion.[4] The

---

3. *Ekonomichna pravda*, September 11, 2014.

4. "Pravitel'stvo dokapiziziruet 'Naftogaz' na 63 milliarda" ["The Government Recapitalizes Naftogaz with 63 billion"], *Ekonomichna pravda*, August 5, 2014.

IMF (2014d) forecasts that the recapitalization of Naftogaz will amount to 7.6 percent of GDP in 2014, suggesting that Ukraine's total energy subsidies in 2014 will amount to some 10 percent of GDP. These budgetary expenditures breed corruption and should be eliminated.

Nonpayments are chronic in the energy sector and poorly collected in spite of the low prices. One reason is that those who want to divert gas to private trade have successfully opposed the installation of gas meters, which Western donors tend to discuss as a technical problem. Similarly, Naftogaz has persistently refused to subject itself to public audit, which would undoubtedly reveal plenty of fraud and embezzlement. The new management hired EY in 2014 to audit Naftogaz, and the results have not been published yet.

The large corrupt revenues have been concentrated to a few beneficiaries who have bought Ukraine's political power and law enforcement, impeding the country's democratic, legal, and economic development. Ukraine cannot afford this robbery if it is to survive as an independent country. The leading gas traders have varied, but since 2006 Dmytro Firtash has dominated. In March 2014, at the request of the FBI, he was arrested in Vienna suspected of money laundering and released on bail of $172 million, but not allowed to leave Austria.[5]

The murky gas trade between Ukraine and Russia has undermined Ukraine's national security, making the country greatly dependent on Russia, which has insisted on nontransparent trading arrangements with private intermediaries, nonmarket prices, and barter. Although state-dominated Gazprom has a monopoly on exports of natural gas and on export pipelines in Russia, and state-owned Naftogaz has a monopoly on the pipelines and controls the imports and distribution in Ukraine, dubious private intermediaries controlled this trade on both sides until 2009 (Balmaceda 2013). The only and obvious explanation of this strange arrangement was the mutual interest in corrupt dealings, as has been well documented (Dawisha 2014, 239–40).

Until 2009, Russia charged a price below a normal market level, but even so the private Ukrainian importers did not pay Gazprom, passing on the bill to the Ukrainian state, which was in the end forced by Russia to pay whether it had a formal state guarantee or not. Since 2009, Russia has charged a high market price, while accepting large arrears from Ukraine, which have been the dominant theme of Ukrainian-Russian relations since 1991 (Balmaceda 2013).

An illustrative example of how this gas trade has undermined Ukraine's sovereignty was Viktor Yanukovych's extension of Russia's lease on the Sevastopol naval base for another 25 years in April 2010 in return for an alleged gas price discount. Another example was his agreement with Russian president Vladimir Putin on December 17, 2013, to abandon the European Association

---

5. David M. Herszenhorn, "At Request of U.S., Austria Arrests Ukrainian Businessman," *New York Times,* March 13, 2014.

Agreement again in exchange for a gas price discount of one-third; the Kremlin, however, suddenly withdrew this discount in early April 2014. Additional examples are Russia's cutting gas supplies to Ukraine twice during the Orange period in January 2006 and January 2009. Apparently, the Kremlin was more interested in corruption and in undermining Ukraine's sovereignty, or geopolitics, than in the commercial viability of Gazprom (Åslund 2010b).

Since 2010, gas rents have mostly been reaped within Ukraine, as Naftogaz has bought gas very cheaply from state-owned producers. It was supposed to pass these volumes on to consumers, but it diverted large amounts to the commercial market. "Since domestic prices for industrial users and budgetary institutions have been adjusted to import parity, the differential tariffs have created arbitrage opportunities for domestic gas sales (namely the possibility of siphoning of inexpensive gas for households and heating utilities to commercial sales), while also undermining the transparency of the energy sector and making it vulnerable to corruption" (IMF 2014c, 20).

Ukraine's energy inefficiency is stunning. The country "uses around 3.2 times more energy per unit of GDP [in purchasing power parities] than the average in OECD countries" (IEA 2012, 33). According to the IMF, "Ukraine is one of the least energy-efficient countries in Europe. Ukraine's energy intensity, defined as the ratio of total primary energy supply to GDP, is twice as large as that of Russia and ten times higher than the OECD average" (IMF 2014c, 20). Even so, the country's gas consumption has fallen by more than half since the Soviet era.

In 2013, Ukraine consumed 50.4 bcm of natural gas. The crisis in Ukraine has drastically cut gas demand. In 2014, gas consumption fell by 16 percent to 42.6 bcm.[6] Most of this decline was in industry (4.4 bcm) because steelworks and fertilizer factories in occupied Donbas have been standing still. If gas consumption falls by the same percentage in 2015 it would stop at 36 bcm. If gas consumption is further reduced to the Russian level through elementary energy savings, it could be cut to 25 bcm per year. On "the demand side, the potential for energy efficiency and energy savings is large, especially in the industry and residential sectors. This potential, however, remains largely untapped..." (IEA 2012, 9).

All Western initiatives to "help" Ukraine with energy saving have been meaningless, because the very low energy prices have not offered any incentives to invest in energy saving, nor to produce energy in Ukraine. As a consequence of the reduced consumption of gas in 2014, Ukraine imported only 46 percent of all the gas it consumed.[7] In the next five years, Ukraine should be able to cut

---

6. "Ukraina za god sokratila potreblenie gaza na 16%" ["Ukraine Cut Its Consumption of Gas by 16% in a Year"], *Ekonomichna pravda*, January 15, 2015.

7. "Dolya importa v postavkakh gaza Ukrainu upala nizhe 50%" ["The Import Share in the Gas Deliveries to Ukraine Fell to Less than 50%], *Ekonomichna pravda*, January 15, 2015.

its energy consumption by half relative to GDP, as Poland and Slovakia have done. Then, Ukraine would not need to import any natural gas.[8]

The low prices for domestic energy production effectively subsidize imports, boosting them to a higher level than Ukraine can afford. The country suffers from a persistent big balance-of-payments deficit with Russia, and the main reason is the excessively large gas imports. In 2013, Ukraine imported natural gas for $11.5 billion and oil for $7.0 billion, a total of $18.6 billion, about 10 percent of GDP.[9] By comparison, the current account deficit was $16.3 billion, or about 9.2 percent of GDP in 2013, according to the IMF (2014c; cf. Chow, Ladislaw, and Melton 2014). Given that Ukraine can be self-sufficient in energy within five years if it pursues serious reforms, this is a great opportunity. Furthermore, the country does not require anything very original, just decent practices as applied in many other countries.

In reality, the Ukrainian energy sector has substantial potential in both production and energy saving. The International Energy Agency (IEA 2012, 9) noted:

> On the supply side,... Ukraine can eliminate its natural gas import dependency in the foreseeable future by substantially increasing domestic gas production, both conventional and unconventional, developing the country's biomass potential and maximizing the energy efficiency gains... there is strong potential to attract investors to the modernisation of Ukraine's coal, electricity and heat generation sectors as well as heat and gas transmission sectors.

Ukraine has vast energy reserves. The government estimates the country's total hydrocarbon reserves at 9 billion tons of oil equivalent. Its conventional gas reserves are huge at 1.1 trillion cubic meters of proven reserves and 5.4 trillion cubic meters of potential reserves.[10] Its reserves of gas condensate exceed 400 million tons and its oil reserves amount to 850 million tons (IEA 2012, 82). Yet Ukraine's total production of primary energy dropped by 47 percent from 1990 to 2010, and its import dependency was 39 percent in 2010 (IEA 2012, 21). Many old wells and mines have been exhausted, but Ukraine possesses large energy resources, especially coal and natural gas. The cause of the decline in production has been persistent mismanagement and a hostile business environment, which has been so poor that even the hardened energy majors have found it impossible to work in Ukraine.

---

8. The costs and distributional consequences of Ukraine's gas pricing have been thoroughly studied, especially by the IMF (Mitra and Atoyan 2014, Parry et al. 2014, Ogarenko and Hubacek 2013).

9. State Statistics Service of Ukraine, 2014, http://ukrstat.org/uk/operativ/operativ2013/zd/tsztt/tsztt_u/tsztt1213_u.htm.

10. BP sets Ukraine's reserves at only 0.6 trillion cubic meters, 0.3 percent of the global total (*BP Statistical Review for Energy*, June 2014, www.bp.com/content/dam/bp/pdf/Energy-economics/statistical-review-2014/BP-statistical-review-of-world-energy-2014-full-report.pdf). BP is more cautious than the IEA and tends to use official figures. Since exploration has been neglected for long in Ukraine, I trust the higher figure more.

With better governance, Ukraine would be able to replace the exhausted energy sources, and it could be self-sufficient with energy for a century. At the 2013 level of gas consumption, its proven reserves would suffice for 22 years, and if gas consumption is halved Ukraine's proven reserves would last for 40 years, which is a great potential. If all the potential gas reserves turn out to be real Ukraine would have gas reserves for no less than 271 years.[11] Even after the loss of Crimea, which accounts for 2 bcm of gas production per year, the country still produces 18 bcm per year, and for years foreign energy experts have assessed that Ukraine could raise its production to 30 to 35 bcm per year of conventional gas (Pifer 2014). This potential includes large capacities of shale gas. In short, under normal market economic circumstances Ukraine would be a significant gas exporter. Instead, it has been a persistently large importer of gas.

Ukraine has repeatedly failed at energy reforms for three reasons. One is that the energy sector harbors powerful commercial and bureaucratic interests, those of the richest people of the land, who will defend their interests against any reform. Therefore, the new government needs to hit hard and fast to accomplish energy reform. Technical assistance is at hand. Numerous international agencies have engaged constructively with Ukraine on energy reform, each within its particular segment, because they all understand that energy reform is key to Ukraine's economic success.

Another reason for these reform failures is that the international agencies do not understand the political economy of reform very well. They think that the main threat is popular reaction, not understanding that the oligarchs are far more powerful. Because of this misunderstanding, the international agencies have persistently proposed too timid and gradual reforms. In its nine programs with Ukraine, the IMF has demanded multiple but gradual energy price increases. The government of the day has accepted to carry out one initial price increase, but stopped, contrary to its agreement with the IMF, because strong vested interests of the incumbent regime had seized control of the energy price arbitrage. Clearly, Ukraine needs to carry out a full-fledged liberalization of its energy prices to break out of its corruption trap.

The IMF and the other international organizations make the assumption that reforms have to be gradual. For example, the IEA (2012, 15) states: "Energy sector structural reform in Ukraine requires time to develop and take hold," arguing that "within three-to-four years the subsidy burden can be eased and progressively removed as prices are raised to market-based levels." But this is the policy that has failed.

Naftogaz CEO Kobolyev (2014) advocates early adjustment of all energy prices to a normal market level in one single step. Only then can corruption be defeated, whereas a gradual price increase is a vote for the maintenance of corruption. Nor can Ukraine afford to spend 10 percent of GDP on energy subsidies (IMF 2014d). The public reaction will not be greater if the prices are

---

11. Admittedly, some of these reserves are located on Crimea and in adjacent areas in the Black Sea.

quadrupled than if they are doubled, Kobolyev argues. A quick adjustment will convince the public of the need to save energy and entrepreneurs to produce more gas.[12]

The Coal Sector Is Also Bad

Ukraine's coal sector is also problematic. The maintenance of low state-controlled prices requires large state subsidies, while facilitating arbitrage by monopolists between state-controlled prices and much higher market prices. Inefficient and corrupt state companies incur unwarranted losses because of large arrears, which they regularly forgive. This is the result of wrong priorities, nontransparency, absence of clear guidance for state support, and no reform. The situation is well understood and extensively discussed.[13]

Ukraine has vast coal reserves and a viable private coal industry. Yet, the policy on coal mining has led to the most unsatisfactory financial and economic performance, with discretionary state regulation and excessive state ownership holding back the industry. Coal production has been stagnant. Labor productivity is low and falling, while costs are rising, because some very inefficient mines continue operating. Poor safety standards at many Ukrainian coal mines have led to the deaths of numerous miners. The security in Ukrainian coal mines, both private and state-owned, is weak, resulting in many serious accidents.

The only positive development is that most coal mines have been privatized, but otherwise the coal sector has never seen any real reform. The private coalmines have expanded their production because of better assets and management, while production in state-owned mines has continued to shrink. Like all murky industries in Ukraine, the coal industry is highly concentrated in the hands of a few major businessmen. The coal mines belong mainly to three groups: the state, Rinat Akhmetov (DTEK and Metinvest), and companies close to the Yanukovych family in the Donetsk and Luhansk regions.

The state has continuously paid large subsidies to loss-making coal companies, each year about 1 percent of GDP in direct budget subsidies. In 2013, the coal subsidies amounted to 13.2 billion hryvnia, that is, 0.9 percent of GDP (Vyshynsky 2014a). In 2003, Ukraine created a state intermediary company, Vuhillya Ukrainy (Coal of Ukraine), which was supposed to support state coalmines that produced low-quality coal at high costs by purchasing their coal at a subsidized high price. A more reasonable policy would have been to close down these unprofitable coal mines, but the political will was missing.

In 2013, the state-subsidized price of one ton of commercial coal was 480 hryvnia, whereas the production cost in a Donbas state mine was almost three times as high at 1,350 hryvnia. State subsidies covered the difference. When

---

12. Discussion with Kobolyev on January 20, 2015.

13. An outstanding source for most of this section is Vyshynsky (2014a).

Yanukovych was in power, a group from his family that controlled a large share of illegal (unofficial) coal mines in Donbas extracted these subsidies meant for loss making state mines, although their production cost was only about 500 hryvnia per ton (Vyshynsky 2014a). Their protector was Minister of Energy Eduard Stavytsky, who fled abroad after the ouster of Yanukovych and has been sanctioned by the European Union.[14] DTEK's private coalmines were both more resourceful and better run, able to produce coal at a cost of 500 to 550 hryvnia per ton. The same was true of other private mines, because the best mines had been privatized first.

Much of the coal is burnt by power stations, whose tariffs are controlled by the state far below cost. In addition, arrears to and from the public utilities have been chronic. Ironically, the lower the prices, the more obvious it seems to be to the consumers that they do not have to pay. As a consequence, the power distributors and generators have often suffered from large arrears to their suppliers, mainly coal producers. As long as the power utilities were publicly owned, the state tended to give away shares to the coal producers in intermittent debt settlements. Under Yanukovych, three big businessmen were allowed to buy a large share of the electricity sector in privileged privatizations with low prices.

Once most power stations were privatized, they turned the tables, running up arrears to the state coal trading company Coal of Ukraine, which buys coal that has not yet been produced on credit that it draws from state banks. However, it regularly restructures the arrears of the coal producers. This cost is shared by the state banks, which are regularly recapitalized by the state, and Coal of Ukraine, which receives a steady stream of subsidies from the state budget. Since power companies realize they might not have to pay, arrears naturally mount (Vyshynsky 2014a).

When I had lunch with Akhmetov in Donetsk in 2006, I asked him what he thought should be done to the coal industry. As a strategic businessman, he was prepared to work without any state subsidies if coal prices were freely set. Under such conditions, he would buy more coal mines, and has since done so.

It appears as if the government will abolish all coal subsidies in 2015 and liberalize the coal prices. This decision has been facilitated by coal production having plummeted and being concentrated to the occupied parts of Donbas, and it was controlled by Yanukovych cronies that have fled the country.

The Energy Sector Can and Must Be Reformed

The problems of the Ukrainian energy sector are as obvious as their solutions. The key reform is to unify energy prices at the market level. Then state energy subsidies would be superfluous, though a minor share could be allocated

---

14. "Council Regulation (EU) No. 208/2014 of 5 March 2014 concerning restrictive measures directed against certain persons, entities and bodies in view of the situation in Ukraine," *EUR-Lex*, April 15, 2014, http://eur-lex.europa.eu/legal-content/AUTO/?uri=CELEX:02014R0208-20140415&qid=1421953606327&rid=20 (accessed on January 22, 2015).

to fully compensate poor people for higher energy prices. Energy enterprises would be given normal price incentives to work efficiently for a profit and everybody would have an interest in saving energy. In addition, state corporations need to be disciplined through public audits, division mainly between production and transportation, and privatization. Private corporations should be offered normal conditions to produce energy.

This solution is known and has been tried in many East European countries, Poland, Estonia, and Georgia being outstanding successes. All these steps have been endorsed in manifold publications by the relevant organizations: the International Monetary Fund, World Bank, International Energy Agency, European Union, Organization for Economic Cooperation and Development, and European Bank for Reconstruction and Development.[15]

Unify Energy Prices and Abolish All Energy Subsidies Quickly

The most fundamental issue in economics is to get prices right. All energy prices—natural gas, coal, and electricity—should be unified and raised to a level that will cover the costs of production plus a competitive profit margin commensurate with an international market price. The tariffs on the transportation of gas are also too low and do not allow operators to modernize or even maintain underground storage facilities and gas pipelines. The whole infrastructure is neglected. All price subsidies and cross-subsidization should cease, and social compensation should be provided to truly needy groups.

Price hikes, therefore, must be radical, as was the case in Estonia and the late reformer Georgia (Laar 2002, Bendukidze and Saakashvili 2014). Poland raised energy prices by 220 percent in 1991 and by 1992, household gas tariffs were at a market level (Radeke and Walter 2012, 6). Ukraine needs to learn from the successes of these radical reformers and not repeat its old mistakes. Energy prices should be raised all the way to the market level in one single step, when there is a political window of opportunity. The new Naftogaz management favors an instant unification of gas prices for industry and households (Kobolyev 2014).[16] Over time, markets should evolve for natural gas and electricity, but initially their regulation appears necessary. The pipeline system and electricity grid should offer equal access to all at market-related prices.

Although private enterprises dominate the coal sector, prices remain regulated at too low a level. Coal products are priced on the basis of regulatory acts, not market forces. Here too price liberalization should be pursued and accompanied by the elimination of nontransparent subsidies that vary depending on their success in bargaining. Neither the distortion of coal prices nor the exten-

---

15. Recent policy papers are Clements et al. (2013), Gill et al. (2014), IEA (2012), Meissner, Naumenko, and Radeke (2012), OECD (2011), and World Bank (2012b).

16. "Ukraintsev predupredili o podorozhanii gaza srazu v 4 raza" ["Ukrainians Were Warned of Gas Price Increase Four Times"], *Ekonomichna pravda*, September 24, 2014.

sive state subsidies can be justified, as they do not encourage coal producers to produce more and become more effective. Since a coal market does exist, coal prices can simply be liberalized.

Reinforce a Unified Regulatory Agency for Natural Monopolies

Ukraine has had a National Energy Regulatory Commission (NERC), which was supposed to regulate natural monopolies in the power sector, the oil and gas complex, and heat generation (Energy Charter Secretariat 2013, 58) and a separate National Communal Services Regulatory Commission (Vashchenko 2013). Not surprisingly, related business interests had captured the NERC.

On August 27, 2014, President Poroshenko abolished both commissions and merged them into a new commission that will regulate both energy and utilities (communal) services. His intention was to reinforce the integrity and competence of the unified regulator.[17] The new national commission is supposed to be truly independent and strong. The best solution appears to be a well-paid board of independent and competent regulators, as for example Latvia has done. Their status would resemble that of an independent board of a central bank with fixed long terms. To make the independence more credible, it would be beneficial to invite some foreigners to serve on the commission.

To reinforce and unify the regulation of all natural monopolies this strong independent regulator should control pricing of services provided by all natural monopolies, that is, natural gas, electricity, the pipeline companies, the electrical grid, communal heating, and the railways. Its aim should be to ensure a balance of interests between producers, consumers, and state. It should guarantee reliable supply of high-quality services to consumers at fair prices, while making sure that the natural monopolies can make sufficient profits to develop (Golod 2014).

The national commission should propose and the parliament adopt laws and regulations for the Ukrainian natural gas market. They should include a gas network code with rules for access to gas pipelines and underground storage, and so on, in line with Ukraine's commitments as a party to the Energy Charter Treaty and its Transit Protocol.

Provide Social Cash Compensation

To render the desired energy price changes politically and socially possible, the World Bank is already providing Ukraine with assistance to give conditional cash transfers to households. In July 2014, the Ukrainian government started doing so after gas prices were hiked on May 1. It uses the country's

---

17. "Prezident ob'edinil NKRE i Natskomuslug v edinuyu natskomissiyu" ["The President United NERC and the National Commission for Communal Services in a Unified National Commission"], UNIAN, August 28, 2014, http://economics.unian.net/energetics/956198-prezident-obyedinil-nkre-i-natskomuslug-v-edinuyu-natskomissiyu.html (accessed on August 30, 2014).

well-developed system of 745 local social welfare bureaus that can provide cash transfers to 4.5 million households (IMF 2014a, 20). The Bank can extend this support to half the households. It has successfully implemented such schemes in more than 30 countries across the world, mainly in Latin America (Fiszbein and Schady 2009).

The current energy subsidies of prices and to energy companies not only breed corruption but also are socially unjust. According to the IMF (2014b, 88), the bottom quintile obtained 13.6 percent of total energy subsidies, while the top quintile received twice as much (26.5 percent). The government could expand its scheme to half the population. The cost would not be more than 2 percent of GDP, and the savings of the energy reform would be 8 percent of GDP. The losses would be borne by major corrupt operators.

Separate the State Energy Companies

A key target of energy reform must be Naftogaz Ukrainy. This large state holding company has never functioned acceptably. Nor has it been publicly audited. It contains many different kinds of companies. Some are fully state-owned, while others have large private minority shareholders. In either case, almost every company is controlled by one private business group, and the controlling interest for each company is well known. The four main Naftogaz subsidiaries are Ukrgazvydobuvannia, which produces gas, Ukrnafta, which produces oil and some gas, the gas trunk pipeline company Ukrtransgaz, and the oil trunk pipeline company Ukrtransnafta.[18]

Naftogaz, and all its subsidiaries, should be given proper governance with professional, competent supervisory boards, including independent directors. They should be subject to international auditing and their annual reports made public. Many old managers were replaced in 2014, but the management turnover should be complete. Two conditions for new managers should be that they are competent and that they do not have conflicts of interest, representing some related business interests.

Next, Naftogaz should be divided into separate companies. In December 2010, Ukraine ratified the protocol on its accession to the European Energy Community Treaty, and it joined the Energy Community in February 2011 (European Commission 2012b). By doing so, it has committed itself to specific reforms. The EU "third energy package," which the European Union adopted in July 2009, applies to Ukraine, which has thus committed itself to integrate its electricity and gas markets with the European Union, while separating transportation of natural gas from production as well as distribution.

Specifically, the gas transit system, that is, the company Ukrtransgaz, should be legally separated into an independent company. The same is true for Ukrtransnafta, the oil trunk pipeline company. The operation of underground

---

18. The main components of Naftogaz and their specializations are described in "Rada provalila reform 'Naftogaza'" ["Parliament Blocked Reform of Naftogaz"], *Zerkalo nedeli*, July 24, 2014.

gas storage should be divided from gas transportation. All enterprises should be guaranteed nondiscriminatory and transparent commercial access to the gas transmission systems and storage.

Members of the Energy Community can choose from three options for dealing with vertically integrated companies. The first option envisions compulsory separation of their property by selling pipelines to an independent operator without the right to any controlling interest. The second allows vertically integrated companies to remain the owner of their pipelines, provided they are managed by an independent operator appointed by the national government upon prior approval of the European Commission. The third choice foresees the retention of vertically integrated companies, monitored by a special supervisory authority, with an independent subsidiary in charge of daily operation of the pipelines. For Ukraine, the second option appears natural, since privatization by necessity will take some time and strong national security interests as well as current legislation oppose it, considering the risk that Russia will seize control of this strategic infrastructure.

The financial dissolution of Naftogaz must be handled with care. A careless liquidation could easily put Ukraine into default, and its debtors could find their debts written off. Presently, the corporation has liabilities on the order of $10 billion and would go bankrupt if it lost its state support. Its creditors need to be consulted and their interests considered before its liquidation.

Privatize Distribution and Production Companies, but Not Transportation

Enterprises in the energy sphere fall into four groups: producing companies, transportation companies, distributing or trading companies, and noncore assets. Each needs to be treated separately. Noncore assets are the easiest. They should be sold off as soon as the Ukrainian economy starts stabilizing.

State trading and distribution companies should be liquidated or sold off. In the electricity and gas industry, all regional and local distribution companies appear to have been privatized. Three groups own the regional electricity distributors: Akhmetov's DTEK, Konstantin Grigorishin's Energy Standard Group, and Aleksandr Babakov's VS Energy International.[19] Dmytro Firtash's GDF appears to have purchased all regional gas distributors. Refining has been largely privatized, but what remains should be sold off. The main remaining state asset is Coal of Ukraine, whose key function is to subsidize coal prices, which is no longer desired. However, when it is liquidated state claims on private companies should be maintained and collected. Naftogaz and several of

---

19. Babakov is a nationalist member of the Russian State Duma. In 2014, he was sanctioned by the European Union for having business investments in Ukraine and Crimea and voting in favor of Russian annexation of Crimea.

its subsidiaries are also distribution companies.[20] These functions should be liquidated or sold off.

The producing companies should be sold after energy prices have been liberalized and markets stabilized so that these companies can be reasonably valued. The most valuable is the gas-producing company Ukrgazvydobuvannia. Naftogaz's CEO Kobolyev (2014) has assessed that it could fetch a price above $12 billion, so its privatization has to be carefully done.

Ukrnafta, Ukraine's main oil-producing company, is the most problematic. For many years, the government has owned 50 percent plus one share and Privat Group[21] 42 percent, with the balance floating freely on the stock exchange. Although the state owns a majority of the shares, Privat Group has controlled Ukrnafta's management, letting it work in the interests of Privat Group. As Ukraine's leading brokerage, Dragon Capital, put it "the company's major shareholders have effectively stripped it of all profits generated... since 2010 despite the company suffering from heavy underinvestment in its upstream segment for years."[22] As the majority shareholder, the government needs to seize control of Ukrnafta, introduce proper governance, and impose new management. In January 2015, it passed such a law.[23] In due time, the state should sell its shares, but its shares must not be given as a bargain to Privat Group.

The main goal of coal sector reform needs to be a cardinal increase in efficiency and workers' safety. The best way of accomplishing that after liberalization of coal prices and the coal market would be to sell off the remaining state coal mines and introduce a competitive coal market. Ukraine can follow the successful Russian coal reform of 1998–99 that was spearheaded by the World Bank. The pillars of reform are privatization of the remaining public coal mines; liberalization of coal prices, which leads to the development of a normal coal market; simultaneous elimination of coal subsidies; and social support for restructuring (World Bank 2003). The private Russian coal industry has thrived since these reforms, developing a vibrant coal market, steadily expanding production, and generating substantial profits. Many loss-making Ukrainian state mines should be closed down, and social programs are required to take care of redundant miners and their communities.

The state sold off most of the electricity generating companies under Yanukovych, but Enerhoatom, which owns four large nuclear power stations producing 47 percent of Ukraine's electricity, remains fully state-owned. A mi-

20. "Rada provalila reform 'Naftogaza'" ["Parliament Blocked Reform of Naftogaz"], *Zerkalo nedeli*, July 24, 2014.

21. "Rada otobrala u Kolomoiskogo kontrol' nad 'Ukrnaftoi'" ["Parliament Took Control of Ukrnafta from Kolomoisky"], *Ukrainskaya pravda*, January 13, 2015.

22. Dragon Capital, *Dragon Daily*, September 4 and October 13, 2014.

23. "Rada otobrala u Kolomoiskogo kontrol' nad 'Ukrnaftoi'" ["Parliament Took Control of Ukrnafta from Kolomoisky"], *Ukrainskaya pravda*, January 13, 2015.

nor oligarchic group has controlled it, clearly benefiting financially. The state should recover control and sell off the nuclear power stations as separate entities when electricity prices have been liberalized and the market stabilized so that they can fetch reasonable market prices. A current proposal to sell off 40 percent of Enerhoatom makes no sense. The sale of a large minority post is a typical technique to scare off all bidders but the current controlling oligarchs because no other minority owner would be able to achieve control.[24]

The main transportation companies are the gas transit system Ukrtransgaz, the oil pipeline company Ukrtransnafta, the petroleum pipeline company Ukrspetstransgaz, and the electrical grid. Each of them should become an independent state corporation with proper governance, management, and audit, but for the sake of national security, they cannot be privatized in the near future. The risk of Russian interests taking them over is too great, as has happened in many other post-Soviet countries, notably Armenia, Belarus, and Moldova. No legal guarantees are strong enough in Ukraine to block such a development if private ownership is permitted. Therefore, the Ukrainian Parliament has prohibited the privatization of the gas transit system and the giant gas reservoirs.

Create Markets for All Kinds of Energy

Ukraine has an open and competitive market for gas tubes, oil, and petrol. After coal prices have been liberalized, a competitive coal market could arise without any further government intervention, and Coal of Ukraine should be liquidated. Natural gas and electricity, however, raise problems. In both cases, prices first have to be unified at the market level.

Ukraine has never had a gas market. The Cabinet of Ministers should develop a law on liberalization of the gas market to be adopted by parliament. It should be based on the principles of transparency and efficiency to stimulate competition. These principles should harmonize Ukrainian legislation with EU gas directives. This law should ensure legal and organizational independence of the gas transmission operators and prohibit cross-subsidization.

In the mid-1990s, the country undertook far-reaching structural reforms in the electricity sector with the support of the World Bank. The infrastructure for an electricity market was created. The power companies were restructured. A handful of generating companies were created, each region received its own distribution company, and the grid became a separate state company. A public wholesale market was organized, but since electricity tariffs remained regulated by the state at too low a level to recover costs, the wholesale market could not develop.

At present, the largely privatized generating companies incur chronic losses because of low consumer prices and massive nonpayments. They cannot generate profits for the maintenance and modernization of existing electricity

---

24. Yuriy Korol'chuk, "Privatizatsiya 'Energoatoma' yavlyaetsya nesvoevremennoi" ["Privatization of Enerhoatom Is Untimely"], *Ekonomichna pravda*, August 26, 2014.

generation or the grid, threatening the stable supply of electricity. These conditions offer no incentive to increase efficiency. The whole power sector suffers from excessive wear and tear on equipment. If electricity prices were liberalized, however, a market could easily evolve, as long as the state stays out of any role as an intermediary trader.

Save Energy and Reduce Pollution

The opportunities to save energy in Ukraine are truly enormous, which is a favorite topic of international organizations. Three sectors stand out: the steel industry, the chemical industry, and the heating sector. The World Bank (2013, 1) puts the situation in clear terms: "While Ukraine faces one of the highest average costs of gas supply, its gas and heating tariffs are among the lowest in Europe. The current low gas and heating tariffs are not targeted to the poor, adversely affect service delivery, impose a heavy fiscal burden, and result in inefficient use of energy." According to the Ukrainian Ministry of Regional Development, Construction, and Communal Services, about 3 bcm per year could be saved by modernizing the district heating systems, an amount worth $1.2 billion a year at a natural gas price of $400 per mcm (IEA 2012, 55).

The largest energy savings can presumably be achieved in the metallurgical sector. Among Ukraine's many steelworks, only one is newly built (Interpipe Steel in Dnipropetrovsk) and one fully modernized (Alchevsk Iron and Steel Works belonging to the Industrial Union of Donbas). All the others are old Soviet steel mills with varying degrees of modernization. The same is true of Ukraine's large fertilizer sector.

Although Ukraine has done little to save energy, both primary energy usage and greenhouse gas emissions fell by more than half from 1990 to 2000 and they have stayed at that level. Ukraine's gas consumption fell steadily from 110 bcm in 1989 to 42.6 bcm in 2013. Even if the energy sector has not been subject to much reform, Ukraine's economy as a whole has become a market economy, and private enterprises do economize. The most energy-inefficient Soviet factories were unprofitable even with very low energy prices and were forced to close down.

Since Ukraine is lagging so far behind in energy saving, it can easily accomplish great results. The most important lever is market-conform energy prices, which will convince private producers to save energy. If prices rise, effective collection and meters are likely to follow, because the economic interests have changed.

A favorite object of Western assistance to Ukraine has been energy saving devices, such as new technology or meters, presuming that energy saving is a technical issue, but it is a matter of economic interests. If meters would hinder powerful interests to divert gas and electricity for their own profits, they would not be installed even if given for free. Instead the Western donors should advocate instant energy price deregulation and assist with social cash compensation to the needy.

Figure 10.1   Production of natural gas in Ukraine, 1941–2012

billion cubic meters

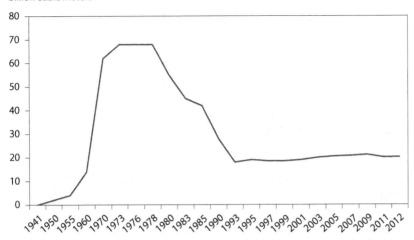

Source: Razumkov Center, *Ukraine's Gas Sector Development in the Context of European Integration*, 2014, www.razumkov.org.ua/upload/1392037862_file.pdf.

Stimulate Private Energy Production through a Good Business Environment

With its large reserves, Ukraine produced substantial amounts of natural gas, peaking at 68.7 bcm in 1975 (IEA 2012, 82). However, after the Soviet Union found its giant natural gas fields in West Siberia, it cut production prematurely in Ukraine. After the end of communism, the Ukrainian government failed to develop oil or gas production because of corrupt chaos. Although Ukraine has substantial oil and gas assets, its oil and gas production has been stagnating for more than two decades. The production of natural gas is almost constant at 20 bcm per year (of which 2 bcm in Crimea), while oil production at around 3 million tons a year is decreasing slowly (figure 10.1).

Ukraine possesses large known reserves of conventional gas, coal, and oil that can be commercially exploited. Vast gas assets are known to exist on the Ukrainian part of the Black Sea and Azov Sea shelves, but they have not been explored. Russia's annexation of Crimea deprives Ukraine of these assets and Chornomornaftogaz has been seized by Russia.[25] Ukraine has the third largest energy reserves in Europe after Russia and Norway.[26]

At present, only a few, small, private energy companies are producing oil

---

25. "Criminal Proceedings Against Seizure of Chornomornaftogaz's Station Launched," *Kyiv Post*, March 17, 2014.

26. *BP Statistical Review for Energy*, June 2014, page 20, www.bp.com/content/dam/bp/pdf/Energy-economics/statistical-review-2014/BP-statistical-review-of-world-energy-2014-full-report.pdf.

and gas in Ukraine besides subsidiaries of the state conglomerate Naftogaz. They are predominantly controlled by a handful of well-connected businessmen. Like coal and electricity production, oil and gas production in Ukraine is an inside ball game. Ukraine should set the not-very-ambitious target of doubling its production of oil and gas within a decade and become self-sufficient in energy.

The investment climate in the oil and gas sector in Ukraine must improve for both domestic and foreign investors so that they can be granted secure property rights, free market prices, and stable and reasonable rules of taxation. Price liberalization for production is the first condition, and prices of privately produced oil and gas are actually free today.

The second condition is trustworthy long-time licenses and permits. This is a great challenge, as the IEA (2012, 88) puts it: "Ukraine's upstream oil and gas industry remains complex and heavily regulated. State supervision in the upstream oil and gas sector has multiple layers and it remains challenging to fulfill the inconsistent requirements of the numerous legislative acts that are applicable to hydrocarbon exploration and production activities." The IEA lists 11 different authorities, each of which has to give its permission for any energy production to go ahead. This must be streamlined and simplified.

Finally, taxation must be stable, sensible, and predictable. Until the summer of 2014, private Ukrainian miners and energy producers paid small royalties on the natural resources. The Yatsenyuk government introduced or raised such resource taxes excessively, but taxation of all forms of energy production should be reasonable and coordinated.[27]

Ukraine adopted a law on product-sharing agreements (PSAs) in 1999, but it has not taken off. The Yanukovych government concluded PSAs with Chevron and Royal Dutch Shell on shale gas exploration and production in western Ukraine and Donbas, respectively. At the time of this writing, Shell has declared force majeure for some of its fields that were located in the worst war zone in Donbas, and Chevron has withdrawn.[28] ExxonMobil was intent on going ahead with PSAs for offshore blocks outside Crimea, but these plans have been stopped because of Russia's annexation of Crimea and the ensuing Western sanctions against Russia and Crimea.

The prospects for shale gas production in Ukraine are great. In 2012, the IEA (2012, 81) projected that Ukraine could produce 3 bcm of shale gas in 2020, rising to 20 bcm in 2035. Similarly, Chevron predicted that it could produce 5 to 10 bcm of shale gas a year in Ukraine within ten years after it starts, and Shell made similar projections. However, the Ukrainian energy bureaucracy is overwhelming even for these energy giants, and it will take years to sort out who is responsible for what in the energy sector.

---

27. "Uryad zbil'shue opodatkuvaniya velikogo biznesu—Yatsenyuk" ["Yatsenyuk: The Government Increases Taxation of Big Business"], *Ukrainskaya pravda*, July 27, 2014.

28. Conversations with the Ukraine managers for Chevron and Shell in September 2014.

End Gas Trade with Russia?

Ukraine has had no economic relation more important than its gas trade with and transit of Russian gas. But nor has any economic activity been more harmful to the Ukrainian economy, welfare, governance, and politics. Ukraine's main problem, apart from current Russian military aggression, is pervasive corruption, and its gas trade with Russia has been the kernel of its top-level corruption. Ukraine's gas trade with Russia can be seen as the nation's original sin. Should Ukraine stop trading gas with Russia?

In its trade with Ukraine, Gazprom has three objectives. Its first goal is the enrichment of Russian top officials, the second geopolitics, and only the third is the commercial interests of its shareholders. Gazprom should be treated as an organized crime syndicate, with which no links are advisable (Åslund 2010b). Given that Ukraine's main domestic problem is corruption, the country needs to isolate itself from this center of corruption. Gas is becoming abundant as production is expanding more than consumption worldwide, and prices are falling.

Ukraine's trade with Gazprom consists of its gas purchases from Russia and its transit of Russian gas to Europe. Both are plummeting. Ukraine has played a major role in Russia's transit of oil and gas to Europe. Its Gas Transit System has a transit capacity of 120 bcm and with minor repairs it could be expanded to 160 bcm,[29] but Russia's Gazprom uses ever less of it, only 62.2 bcm in 2014.[30] The current Russian policy is to bypass Ukraine altogether and close down the gas transit system. Gazprom has already built Nord Stream, which has a capacity of 55 bcm per year and has replaced nearly half of the Russian gas transit through Ukraine. Before the construction of Nord Stream between St. Petersburg and Germany, Ukraine accounted for 80 percent of Russia's gas exports to Europe, which has now fallen to about 40 percent.

An investigative article by Reuters revealed how the Russian-Ukrainian gas trade really functions. Since 2002, soon after Putin took over the control of Gazprom, the Ukrainian businessman Dmytro Firtash was the dominant intermediary in this trade. "Gazprom sold more than 20 billion cubic meters of gas well below market prices to Firtash" during the years 2010–13. "The price Firtash paid was so low, Reuters calculates, that companies he controlled made more than $3 billion on the arrangement. Over the same time period,... bankers close to Putin granted Firtash credit lines of up to $11 billion. That credit helped Firtash, who backed pro-Russian Viktor Yanukovich's successful

---

29. Joint EU-Ukraine International Investment Conference on the Modernisation of Ukraine's Gas Transit System, Joint Declaration of the Government of Ukraine, European Bank for Reconstruction and Development, European Commission, European Investment Bank, and the World Bank, March 23, 2009, www.naftogaz.com/files/DECLARATION-Ukraine-EC-engl.pdf (accessed on January 22, 2015).

30. "Tranzit rossiiskogo gaza cherez territoriyu Ukrainy upal na 28%" ["Transit of Russian Gas through the Territory of Ukraine Fell by 28%"], *Ekonomichna pravda*, January 15, 2015.

2010 bid to become Ukraine's president, to buy a dominant position in the country's chemical and fertiliser industry..." (Grey et al. 2014). "When Firtash was arrested in Vienna" a Russian businessman considered to be close to Putin "loaned the Ukrainian businessman $155 million for bail" (Ibid.). On the one hand, Firtash was widely seen as the second biggest and most powerful businessman in Ukraine under Yanukovych (after Rinat Akhmetov). On the other hand, *Forbes* assessed his net personal wealth at only $500 million (table 2.1). The question arises whether he merely operated on the basis of the $11 billion credit line from Gazprombank that Reuters revealed.

Russia's transit of natural gas through Ukraine has never functioned well. In hindsight, Ukraine would have been better off in terms of economic development, democracy, and governance if this gas transit had stopped with the end of the Soviet Union. Russia's oil transit through Latvia and Lithuania was the main source of high-level corruption in those two countries, and its end greatly helped both countries to check corruption. Both countries have flourished since they got rid of the dirty Russian energy trade.

In the long run, the Kremlin accepts gas and oil transit only through fully controlled pipelines. Joint ventures with 50-50 ownership have failed in many countries, such as Belarus and Moldova. The oil transit through the *Druzhba* (Friendship) pipeline in Ukraine functions well and attracts no attention. Even so, Russia appears intent on abandoning *Druzhba* within a few years. It is gradually diverting this oil transit to the Baltic Pipeline System, which transports oil entirely through Russia from West Siberia to St. Petersburg, where the oil is loaded on tankers. If the Kremlin is not satisfied with *Druzhba*, it will never be content with Ukraine's gas transit system. Gazprom's publicly announced policy is to reduce "the role of Ukraine as a transit country...to zero."[31] Ukraine is best advised to give up on both oil and gas transit from Russia until that country has cleaned up its top-level corruption. Ukraine has far too many serious problems to be concerned with Russia's sales of gas to Europe. The less time Ukrainian policymakers devote to this issue, the better for the country.

Similarly, the Ukrainian government should endeavor to manage without Russian gas supply. Prime Minister Yatsenyuk has set this as the goal for five years.[32] In the short term, Ukraine's gas supply challenges are somewhat difficult but manageable because internationally gas has become a normal traded commodity, global supply is ample, and prices are falling. Ukraine has three alternatives: to save energy, to import from Europe, or to make an agreement with Russia.

On June 16, 2014, Russia stopped delivering natural gas to Ukraine. Overtly, the dispute concerned the price and Ukrainian arrears, but Ukraine wanted

---

31. Gazprom, Russian Television Interview with Gazprom CEO Alexei Miller, Rossiya 24, December 6, 2014.

32. "Ukraina osvoboditsya ot 'gazovoi zavisimosti' ot RF cherez 5 let—Yatsenyuk" ["Yatsenyuk: Ukraine will free itself from gas dependence on Russia in 5 Years"], *Ekonomichna pravda*, September 8, 2014.

to cancel the unfavorable bilateral gas agreement of January 2009. Instead, it wanted an agreement on a lower price and smaller volume, not only a temporary unilateral decision by Russia. Russia complained about Ukrainian arrears of $4.5 billion, part of which depended on no agreement on the gas price in the second quarter of 2014. Ultimately, Russia appears to have been pursuing an act of war.

Russia's gas prices had nothing to do with economics. In the first quarter of 2014, Ukraine paid $268.50 per mcm in accordance with the Putin-Yanukovych agreement of December 17, 2013. On April 1, 2014, Gazprom raised the price to $385 per mcm, and two days later to $485 per mcm, with the motivation that since Russia had annexed Crimea it no longer needed to give a $100 per mcm discount for the lease of the Sevastopol naval base agreed with Yanukovych in April 2010 (Socor 2014).

Ukraine should say good riddance to Gazprom and meet it in court. It has proven to be a highly unreliable supplier. Unfortunately, on October 30, Russia, Ukraine, and the European Union concluded a short-term, provisional agreement on some Russian deliveries of gas to Ukraine in the winter. The European Union was the main advocate of this agreement, which ensured that gas would flow from Russia through Ukraine to Europe through the winter. For Ukraine, on the contrary, this agreement seemed unfortunate. It did not need the gas, the agreement deprived Ukraine of scarce cash, $3.1 billion, possibly prejudiced its arbitration case against Gazprom, and presumably made gas reform that much more difficult in Ukraine (Gregory 2014). Elementary decency would have requested that the European Union at least lend Ukraine the funds it forced the country to hand over to Gazprom on dubious legal grounds.

The best cure for Ukraine would be to swiftly raise all its domestic gas prices to the international market level of around $350 per mcm to stimulate both energy saving and production (Kobolyev 2014). Considering that Ukraine can both save energy and produce so much more relatively soon, major infrastructure investments for imports, such as a terminal for liquefied natural gas (LNG) importation and its gasification, hardly make sense.

The second objective should be to secure gas supplies from Europe. Ukraine can import this volume from Europe, through Slovakia, Poland, and Hungary. Since October 2014, Norway's Statoil has become Ukraine's largest gas supplier, offering gas at only $340 per mcm.[33] Admittedly, much of the gas from Poland, Slovakia, and Hungary could ultimately be delivered by Gazprom, and Gazprom has tried to block this reverse flow, but that should not be possible according to the rather strict EU competition rules (cf. Zachmann and Giucci 2014). In addition, Ukraine holds large gas reserves. Ukraine has many real problems, but its gas supply is the most exaggerated problem.

---

33. "Polovina reversnogo gaza v Ukrainu idet iz Norvegii" ["Half of the Reverse Gas to Ukraine Comes from Norway"], *Zerkalo nedeli*, October 8, 2014.

Recommendations

The Ukrainian energy sector can be reformed and turned highly profitable, rendering the country independent of energy imports within five years. To achieve these goals, the government needs to follow these recommendations:

1. Unify energy prices and abolish all energy subsidies as soon as possible.
2. Reinforce one unified regulatory agency for natural monopolies.
3. Provide social cash compensation to the poorest half of the population.
4. Improve governance and separate the state energy companies.
5. Privatize distribution and production companies, but not transportation.
6. Create markets for all kinds of energy.
7. Save energy and reduce pollution.
8. Stimulate private energy production through a good business environment.
9. Stop buying gas from Russia until it is cleansed of top-level corruption.
10. End gas transit from Russia to reduce Russia's corrupting Ukraine.

11

Social Policy Cannot Wait

The war should not justify the lack of real reforms.
—President Petro Poroshenko, July 9, 2014[1]

Few postcommunist countries have reformed their social system less than Ukraine. It maintains multiple forms of social assistance, with small payments to many, but substantial benefits to the privileged few. The correlation between payments and actual needs is poor, since the privileged are favored over the needy (Milanovic 1998). The system is overcentralized, highly politicized, corrupt, and unreliable.

Three shortcomings plague the Ukrainian social sector. First, social expenditures as a whole are far too large. Second, the population is greatly dissatisfied with the scope and quality of services delivered. Third, much of the social assistance is given to people not in great need, while those really suffering receive inadequate social support. Therefore, the three overall goals of social reforms should be trimming excessive pension expenditures, improving quality of healthcare and education, and targeting social support to those in true need.

The United Nations Development Program's *Human Development Report* (UNDP 2014) reflects the situation. Among 187 countries, Ukraine ranks 83 (p. 161), slightly better than its rank of 106 in terms of GDP per capita in purchasing power parities (IMF 2014e). The human development ranking is based on three factors—life expectancy, years of schooling, and GDP per capita. As other countries in the region, Ukraine is doing poorly on life expectancy, with an average at birth of only 68.5 years in 2013, placing it 122nd in the world (table 11.1; UNDP 2014, 161). Life expectancy at birth for women has

---

1. "Poroshenko schitayet, chto voyennyye deystviya ne dolzhny opravdyvat' otsutstviye reform" ["Poroshenko Believes That Military Action Should Not Justify the Lack of Reforms"], *Ukrainskaya pravda*, July 9, 2014.

Table 11.1   Life expectancy at birth in Ukraine, Poland, Russia, and Turkey, 2013 (years)

Country	Total	Male	Female	HDI world rankings for life expectancy	HDI world rankings overall	Gross national income per capita (2011 PPP dollars)
EU average	78.6	n.a.	n.a.	n.a.	n.a.	30,765
Poland	76.4	72.3	80.5	51	35	21,487
Russia	68.0	61.8	74.4	127	57	22,617
Turkey	75.3	71.8	78.7	62	69	18,391
Ukraine	68.5	62.8	74.4	122	83	8,215

n.a. = not available; HDI = Human Development Index; PPP = purchasing power parity

Source: UNDP (2014, http://hdr.undp.org/en/data).

risen to 74.4, but for men it is as low as 62.8. By contrast, Ukraine stands out with regard to years of education with an average of 11.3 years of schooling in 2012, putting it in 29th place in the world. Ukraine's achievement is even more impressive in higher education: No less than 80 percent of Ukrainian youth receive higher education (UNDP 2014, 161, 193). Hardly any country displays such a stark contrast between its international standing in health and education. In a very Soviet way, Ukrainians do not seem to care much about their health, while they are preoccupied with their education.

Since independence, Ukraine has not undertaken any significant social reforms. The dominant mood has been populist, to spend more on social benefits rather than improving the social systems. Social reforms require decentralization. The far-reaching centralization of funding has discouraged local authorities from spending more efficiently or improving the quality of social services. The absence of social reforms has cost Ukraine dearly. Usually social reforms generate swift visible benefits, such as greater social justice, better living standards, easier access to and better quality of social services, all of which increase the population's trust in the authorities. Therefore early social reforms should be a priority for the new government. It should focus on pension reform, healthcare reform, and modernization of the education system.

Ukraine Needs a Radical Pension Reform

The Ukrainian pension system costs far too much and is not financially sustainable. It rewards the old nomenklatura at the expense of the young, while the truly old and infirm receive insufficient financial support. Nor does the current pension system offer any incentives for private saving, and it does nothing for the development of capital markets. Ukraine needs a profound and radical pension reform based on clear principles. The Netherlands serves as an excellent example for Ukraine to follow.

The first and most fundamental problem is that Ukraine has the highest

Table 11.2   Public pensions as a percent of GDP, selected countries and Ukraine, 2000, 2005, and 2010

Country	2000	2005	2010
EU average	9.9	10.0	11.3
Estonia	6.6	5.9	8.9
Italy	14.3	14.6	16.0
Lithuania	7.8	6.5	8.5
Poland	12.6	12.7	12.0
Ukraine	7.5	16.5	17.9

Sources: Eurostat (2014); IMF, Article IV Consultations for Ukraine, 2000, 2005, and 2010.

pension expenditures as a share of GDP in the world—at 18 percent in 2010 (table 11.2). Poland and Italy have previously touched 16 percent of GDP. Old-age pensions account for approximately 80 percent of pension expenditures, about 14.5 percent of GDP. The OECD average for public expenditures on old-age and survivors' benefits was 7.8 percent of GDP (OECD 2013, 171). Italy has the highest public pension costs at 15.4 percent of GDP. Many wealthy countries have lower public pension costs. For example, in the Netherlands, which has one of the best pension systems in the world, public pension costs are only 5.1 percent of GDP, and its private pension costs are 5.6 percent of GDP, making its pension system financially and socially strong (OECD 2013, 171, 173).

For Ukraine, public pension expenditures of 8 percent of GDP would be appropriate, so pension costs should be cut by 10 percent of GDP.[2] In spite of the high unified social contributions, the Pension Fund of Ukraine is not financially sustainable and requires large annual additions from the state budget each year.

Contrary to widespread misperception, Ukraine's high pension costs are not a Soviet inheritance. Until Mikhail Gorbachev's pension reforms in 1985, pensions were minuscule and did not cover everyone (Åslund 1995). Pensions rose sharply in 1990 amid rampant populism preceding the collapse of the Soviet Union. In 1992-94, Ukraine's wild populism maintained high pensions, which contributed to hyperinflationary public expenditures. Until 2004, they were about 10 percent of GDP. In October 2004, in his populist attempt to win the presidential elections Prime Minister Viktor Yanukovych irresponsibly doubled pensions and tripled the minimum pension without additional financing. As a consequence, the cost of public pensions rose to 15 percent of GDP in

---

2. The concept of "pensions" is a bit confusing, because they encompass many different payments—old-age pensions, survivor benefits, early pensions, special pensions for certain professional groups, disability pensions, and sometimes family benefits.

2005. In 2009, amid plummeting output, Yanukovych and Yulia Tymoshenko boosted the cost of public pensions to 18 percent of GDP in populist competition, and it has stayed at that high level (Betliy and Giucci 2011, 6–7).

In 2011, Ukraine carried out a pension reform that seemed serious. The retirement age for women was increased by half a year each year, aiming to raise it from 55 to 60 in the course of a decade. Moreover, the minimum insurance period for receiving full pensions was increased from 20 to 25 years for women and from 30 to 35 years for men, but in the West 40 years of work is usually required for full pension. Certain restrictions were supposed to be introduced for special pensions and high pensions were to be capped, but that hardly happened. There were only limited improvements in the financial sustainability of the pension system. The second pillar of mandatory private saving was definitely not introduced (Betliy and Giucci 2011, Poteraj 2012).

One international report on this pension reform exclaimed: "The pension reforms in 2011 put the pension system on a sustainable path!" (European Centre 2012, 6). Alas, President Yanukovych eliminated such hopes by sharply increasing the minimum living standard and thus delivered an extraordinary pension hike in May 2012 (Tkachenko 2013). The pension system is highly sensitive to such arbitrary political interference, which has been frequent.

Needless to say, the public trust in the pension system is poor. Katerina Lisenkova (2011, 25) noted that because of "almost flat benefits, there is little incentive to participate in the system beyond minimal contributions. On top of this, the strong link between the level of pension benefits and the political cycle further decreases this motivation." She concluded that Ukraine needs a funded pillar in its pension system to establish confidence. One should be added to persuade people and companies to pay payroll taxes.

Unjustified extraordinary benefits to the old elite are being paid through the Pension Fund, such as the benefits of surviving Heroes of the Soviet Union. Sensibly, President Petro Poroshenko called for the elimination of excessive benefits of a few such groups, such as major privileges of former top government officials, their palatial residences at Koncha-Zaspa south of Kyiv, and the privileges of retired generals, but many more benefits should be eliminated.[3]

Numerous categories of professionals are entitled to early public pension, such as state officials, law enforcement, the military, and miners. Around 2010, the special pensions reached almost 4 percent of GDP (Betliy and Giucci 2011), and they have hardly decreased. The rules for special pensions should be tightened. They should not be paid from the general pension fund and most of them should probably not be paid at all.

---

3. "Poroshenko lishil l'got zhitelei Koncha-Zaspa iushcha-Voditsy" ["Poroshenko deprived residents of Koncha-Zaspa and Pushcha-Vodytsia of benefits"], *Ukrainskaya pravda*, August 1, 2014; "Prezident lishil l'got generalov v otstavke" ["President Deprived Retired Generals of Benefits"], *Ukrainskaya pravda*, August 4, 2014; "Poroshenko otmenil l'goty Yushchenko, Litvina, Azarova i drugikh" ["Poroshenko Cancelled Benefits of Yushchenko, Lytvyn, Azarov and Others"], *Ukrainskaya pravda*, August 4, 2014.

The retirement age must be raised. Soviet pensions were minuscule and therefore people usually continued working after having reached retirement age. Until 2011, Ukraine maintained the very low Soviet retirement age of 55 for women and 60 for men. Because of the low retirement and low birth rates for decades, Ukraine has an extraordinarily high number of pensioners, no fewer than 13.5 million out of a population of 45.4 million, or 30 percent, according to Ukraine's Pension Fund.[4] The share of pensioners is unsustainable and needs to be reduced through a hike in the retirement age. The 2011 increase in women's retirement age from 55 to 60 by 2021 was insufficient, as is obvious from Ukraine's pension costs having stayed at the same level as a share of GDP. The retirement age in most Western countries is 65, and many plan to raise it to 67 (OECD 2013, 9). Lisenkova (2011, 25) concluded on the basis of modeling that an increase in the retirement age to 65 for both sexes would be enough to sustain the first public pillar. Ukraine should aim at raising the retirement age for both men and women to 65 in the next few years.

Raising the retirement age is never popular. More than one-third of Ukrainian voters are pensioners and as elsewhere pensioners vote more than people who work. In 2014, Ukrainian populists, notably the Radical Party, even campaigned for the abolition of the minor pension reform of 2011 (Tkachenko 2013). But to oppose a higher retirement age is tantamount to advocating for Ukraine's financial default because the nation has no means to continue financing its current high pension costs. The high payroll taxes are insufficient and have driven a large share of the economy into the underground. Furthermore, the payroll taxes are being paid by young workers, who therefore cannot afford to have children, because they are financing parasitical young pensioners, who receive both pensions and salaries. The government needs to make it economically possible for Ukraine's young workers to start families without emigrating.

Male life expectancy at birth in Ukraine is only 63, and a common idea is that all should reach retirement age before they die. However, when German chancellor Otto von Bismarck introduced the first Old Age and Disability Insurance Law in Germany in 1889, it applied to workers who had reached the age of 70, although German life expectacy for men was 36 and 38 for women in the 1870s (Liedtke 2006). The Ukrainian retirement age of 60 for men and 55 for women was established in 1929, when life expectancy was 46 for men and 50 for women.

The purpose of old-age pension is that people should not live in poverty in their old age, but that is not true of the expensive Ukrainian system because such a large share of the pensions is spent not on the very poor but rather on healthy working pensioners, so that the truly old and infirm who can no longer work receive too little.

The eligibility for disability pensions needs to be checked. In Poland, a

4. Pension Fund of Ukraine, distribution of pensioners by category and size of pensions as of January 1, 2014.

large number of people received such pensions for not very good reasons and a tightening of the criteria for disability pensions sharply reduced pension costs. The same is undoubtedly true of Ukraine. It is just too easy to claim disability by buying a medical certificate from a corrupt doctor and thus becoming eligible for disability pension.

Finally, Ukraine needs to introduce a modern pension system with three pillars—a pay-as-you-go system for minimum pensions in line with the present system, a second pillar of mandatory private savings, and private pension savings (World Bank 1994). Such a system is financially sustainable. It offers the right incentives to work, save, and pay pension contributions, by relating pensions to contributions. It also boosts savings, stimulates the development of a financial market, and enhances security.

Reforming the Healthcare System

Ukraine's healthcare system stands out for its poor performance. It is costly, but it delivers little healthcare because of being wrongly structured and highly inefficient. The World Bank has aptly summarized it: "Ukraine's health system is weak and unable to perform the most basic functions.... [It] is complex, inefficient, highly inequitable, and of low quality. Ukraine lacks a comprehensive health reform implementation plan—though several reforms have been proposed and some have even been legislated, most have not been implemented" (Menon 2010, 1).

The average life expectancy at birth is 68.5 years as it was in 1989 (UNDP 2014, 161). Ukraine places last but one in Europe with regard to average life expectancy, at only 63 years for men, ahead of only Russia (by one year). At the same time Ukraine's fertility rate is only 1.2 children per woman. As a consequence of low birth rates, large emigration, and high death rates, Ukraine's population has shrunk from 52 million in 1991 to 45.4 million at present.[5]

The main reason for the low life expectancy, especially of middle-aged men, is an unhealthy lifestyle leading to early mortality caused by cardiovascular diseases (63 percent of deaths), cancer (12 percent), and trauma (8 to 9 percent). Each year, more than 100,000 Ukrainians die from smoking. About two-thirds of Ukrainian men, the highest rate in Europe, smoke. Every year over 20,000 Ukrainians die from injuries, including more than 10,000 in road accidents, and more than 40,000 from alcoholism. Life expectancy is most easily extended by limiting alcoholism, smoking, and road accidents. Many of the deaths could have been avoided if the healthcare system were more efficient, focusing more on primary healthcare than emergency care at hospitals.

Ukraine's healthcare system is expensive, poorly structured, and inefficient. At present, total healthcare expenditures are quite substantial at a total of 7.2 percent of GDP to compare with an EU average of 8.8 percent of GDP

---

5. This number includes Crimea, which had a population of 2.5 million at the time of the Russian annexation in March 2014, and Donbas.

Table 11.3   Total expenditure on health in Ukraine and Poland (percent of GDP)

Country	2000	2005	2010	2011
EU average	7.3	8.2	9.0	8.8
Poland	5.5	6.2	7.0	6.7
Ukraine	5.6	6.4	7.8	7.2

Source: UNDP (2014, http://hdr.undp.org/en/data).

in 2011 (table 11.3; UNDP 2014). Public healthcare expenditures, however, are only 4.2 percent of GDP (World Bank 2014a), reflecting that 45 percent of healthcare expenditures are private out of pocket. Nor is Ukraine suffering from any shortage of physicians. The Soviet pride was always the large number of physicians per capita, and Ukraine has 35 physicians per 10,000 people, slightly more than the EU average of 33 physicians (UNDP 2014).

Another Soviet pride was many hospital beds per population. The ratio has decreased marginally from 13 hospital beds per 1,000 people in 1989 to 9 in 2012, but today many hospital beds reflect inefficiency. Countries that have rationalized their healthcare, such as the United States, the United Kingdom, and Sweden, have less than 3 hospital beds per 1,000 people (World Bank 2014a). Ukraine maintains too many hospitals that cost much but are of poor standard. Their number has declined from 3,729 in 1989 to 2,369 in 2012, but that leaves Ukraine with three times more hospitals than desirable, while the country has too few primary care facilities.

A substantial literature has emerged on healthcare reforms in postcommunist countries. It is stronger on analysis of problems than on prescriptions for reform, reflecting the global confusion about what is a good healthcare system. Yet, Ukraine has done so poorly that without suggesting what would be the best system, we can propose nine directions of improvement. The key to success is to develop a clear reform strategy and pursue it (Reid 2009).

A first question is whether to introduce healthcare insurance or stick to direct state financing. In Europe, universal health insurance costs about 2 percent of GDP more in healthcare costs, and it is a more complex system without performing better (Leive 2010). Universal health insurance is neither necessary nor obviously beneficial. It would make sense for Ukraine to stay with a single payer state system, as the United Kingdom and the Scandinavian countries have done.

A second issue is centralization versus decentralization. The country inherited a highly centralized Soviet system, which has been largely unreformed. Formally, the Ministry of Healthcare is responsible for health policy, but managerially and financially regional and local authorities are responsible for healthcare facilities in their territory. Responsibilities need to be clarified and combined with authority to carry out the tasks (Lekhan, Rudiy, and Richardson 2010). Healthcare is an important part of the decentralization reform.

Third, Ukraine should close down substandard medium-sized hospitals and concentrate resources on primary healthcare as well as top-level hospital care. Today, government expenditure is largely directed to inpatient medical services, with private out-of-pocket payments financing most outpatient services. In 2007 only 30 percent of Ukraine's health facilities had main water supply and merely 21 percent had sewerage (Lekhan, Rudiy, and Richardson 2010, xvi–xviii). Ukrainian healthcare would be better off if these flawed clinics and hospitals were closed down.

Fourth, however difficult it is to get the incentive structure right in healthcare, Ukraine should be able to motivate healthcare managers and physicians to perform more work of improved quality and reduce costs.

Fifth, state financing is likely to prevail for the foreseeable future, but competition among providers of different ownership needs to develop. Fair competition is easy to facilitate among primary healthcare providers requiring little capital. State financing should be paid in return for services at fixed rates.

Sixth, the healthcare sector possesses far too much real estate, notably 1,600 obsolete hospitals in rural areas and small towns that provide insufficient services. The Ukrainian government should allow local authorities to sell these substantial assets to the benefit of the local or regional budget. That is usually the best incentive to get privatization done.

Seventh, the healthcare system has far too many employees. The government should encourage local authorities to lay off staff, especially administrative staff, by guaranteeing that they can reallocate that funding to other employees in the healthcare system and raise their meager salaries.

Eighth, the government should develop a comprehensive program to promote a healthy lifestyle, focusing on children and youth, and restrict advertising of alcohol and tobacco. The recent prohibition of smoking in most public places is an important step in this direction, as are the recently increased excise duties on tobacco and alcoholic beverages.

Ninth, Ukraine has a complex system of certification of medicines. As Georgia, it should accept the certification of the leading Western countries without unnecessary questions, which will greatly facilitate the introduction and imports of medicines to Ukraine (Bendukidze and Saakashvili 2014). Fortunately, the government program of December 2014 does exactly this.[6] Presumably this is a reflection of the appointment of the former Georgian minister of healthcare to Ukraine.

Finally, the government needs to design a reform strategy for the healthcare system to put all these elements together. There is no simple solution or optimal choice, but Ukraine has chosen the worst option, by not choosing. All the Central and East European countries have found solutions that have improved their healthcare systems and their health outcomes substantially. Ukraine needs to join them in their eclectic trial-and-error search. Healthcare reform is usually treated as a second generation reform, but it tends to come

---

6. Programma Deyatel'nosti kabineta ministrov Ukrainy [Action Program of the Cabinet of Ministers of Ukraine], Ukrainian government portal, December 9, 2014.

Table 11.4   Public expenditure on education in Ukraine and Poland (percent of GDP)

Country	1990	2000	2010	2012
EU average	4.4	5.0	5.4	5.5
Poland	n.a.	5.0	5.2	5.2
Ukraine	n.a.	4.2	n.a.	5.3

n.a. = not available

Source: UNDP (2014, http://hdr.undp.org/en/content/expenditure-education-public-gdp).

in many steps and the new government needs to work on it. Even if the whole reform will take time, some improvements can be accomplished fast, such as reallocation of resources and the installment of new allocation systems for public funding.

Modernizing the Education System

Since the collapse of the Soviet Union, the Ukrainian education system has fared much better than other parts of the social sector, offering a positive contrast to the pension and healthcare systems. Public funding of education has increased steadily, reaching the internationally high level of 5.3 percent of GDP by 2012. By comparison, the EU average was marginally higher at 5.5 percent of GDP (table 11.4; UNDP 2014). In addition, "grey" payments by parents through "charitable contributions," tuition for extra lessons, and other private payments have been extensive.

Ukrainian education suffers no lack of resources, while quality and efficiency are modest. The system of education has undergone a major expansion. According to the UNDP (2014, 193), no less than 80 percent of Ukrainians receive some kind of tertiary education, which puts Ukraine close to the top in the world, but only in quantitative terms. Ukrainians invest a lot of public and private money in education, but the returns are low.

In systemic terms, the main novelty is the emergence of many private educational institutions, especially in higher education, and some curriculum diversity has evolved, though vocational training has declined. Ukraine has too little vocational training, and many university graduates have recently experienced difficulties finding jobs.

In spite of minimal reforms, a clear idea of Europeanization of education has prevailed since the time of President Leonid Kuchma. In line with European standards, basic education was extended from 11 to 12 years. In 1999, the EU ministers signed the Bologna declaration on the standardization of higher education degrees. In 2005, Ukraine joined the Bologna process for "the harmonization of a European higher education's architecture via compatibility and comparability of the regional education systems," and it became the strategy for the development of Ukraine's higher education (Shemshuchenko 2011, European Commission 2012a).

Beginning in 2010, by contrast, Viktor Yanukovych's minister of education, Dmitry Tabachnyk, did whatever he could to turn the Ukrainian education system back to the Soviet model. For no apparent reason, he reduced basic schooling from 12 to 11 years. He returned to the old Soviet curriculum, cherishing the Soviet view of history. He abandoned the Bologna process in favor of the old Soviet degree system while Russia adopted the Western system. He also diminished the role of independent testing. As a result, he centralized both funding and power to the ministry of education.

Tabachnyk's aggressive pro-Russian agenda in the education ministry was widely despised by Ukrainian nationalists, and some activist groups compared him to Leonid Brezhnev, general secretary of the Central Committee of the Communist Party of the Soviet Union.[7] Remarkably he survived many government changes under Yanukovych until he was dismissed in February 2014.

One explanation for Tabachnyk's education policy is that he wanted to maximize the conditions for corruption, which thrived at the summit of the Ministry of Education and Science under his reign, since all powers over education were centralized to his ministry: the allocation of funds, procurement of textbooks, curriculum, and certification of educational institutions and degrees. The change of the number of school years necessitated a change of all textbooks, and the leadership of the Ministry of Education and Science was alleged to receive large kickbacks from the procurement of the new textbooks. Funding to education institutions was discretionary, facilitating kickbacks. The ministry itself was responsible for the issuing of degrees, involving more discretionary decision making and corruption. At local universities, black payments for acceptance and the awarding of degrees were all too common.[8] "The ministry of education with all its powers in the system of higher education was a monster of corruption. One organ regulated, controlled, and distributed financial resources."[9]

Needless to say, there is no contradiction between these two interpretations of Tabachnyk's reign. But it is clear that Tabachnyk was fully in charge of the country's education policy and whatever his motive he caused great damage to the education system (Likarchuk 2014, Kloshek 2014). The only advantage to his rule was that it made evident to all that Ukraine needed to go in the opposite direction and do so fast.

---

7. "Studenty Mogilyanki sravnili Tabachnika s Shapklyak, Brezhnevym I ZhEKom" ["Students at the Mohyla Academy Compared Tabachnik with Gibus, Brezhnev, and Communal Housing Office"], *Ukrainskaya pravda*, February 28, 2013; and "As Heads Roll In Kyiv, Few Tears Shed For Divisive Education Minister," Radio Free Europe/Radio Liberty, February 23, 2014, www.rferl.org/content/as-heads-roll-in-kyiv-few-tears-shed-for-divisive-education-minister/25274495.html.

8. "Ukraine's Real Problem: Rampant Corruption," *American Interest*, September 2, 2014.

9. "Osobennosti Reform Vysshego Obrazovania" ["Features of the higher education reform"], *Korrespondent*, August 13, 2014, http://korrespondent.net/ukraine/events/3405473-korrespondent-osobennosty-reformy-vyssheho-obrazovanyia (accessed on January 22, 2015).

The obvious goal of any government's education policy should be to raise the quality and efficiency of education by encouraging fruitful competition between private and public institutions, while ensuring high standards. Efficiency is best improved through decentralization and deregulation, and as in healthcare, state financing should be provided for services provided rather than to institutions for their existence. Standards can best be secured through independent testing. The state should finance universities and schools per student and for research rather than give lump sums to each institution. Internationalization is crucial for the success of higher education and research. Ukraine has opened up to multiple forms of international cooperation, but the overcentralized bureaucracy needs to be trimmed.

Reform of Higher Education

On July 1, 2014, Ukraine adopted a law on higher education that offers a profound transition from the old Soviet system of education to a modern Western system. It was widely seen as the first major systemic reform to be initiated by the new government after the fall of Yanukovych. It incorporates many sound principles, such as decentralization, internationalization, and transparency. Its aim is to raise the academic level and combat corruption. It will be introduced gradually.[10]

This law was a collective product, having been elaborated by a working group with the presidents of the best universities in Ukraine, parliamentarians and experts under the leadership of Minister of Education Serhiy Kvit, who was president of the Kyiv-Mohyla Academy during Euromaidan. This group had been working for years, so the proposal was well prepared and supported by key insiders.[11]

The heart of the reform is to give institutions of higher learning increased autonomy administratively, academically, and financially. Now universities can design and run their own academic programs without asking for the ministry's approval for each detail. State universities have finally gained some independence in their budgeting and payments, but they are also exposed to new demands on transparency, being required to publish their budget online and provide other key financial information. The universities have gained the authority to grant academic degrees, which was previously the monopoly of the ministry.

The new law on higher education returns Ukraine to the EU Bologna Process of standardization of European higher education with the recognition of

---

10. Law of Ukraine on Higher Education, no. 1556-VII, July 1, 2014, http://zakon4.rada.gov.ua/laws/show/1556-18/print1390875974587141 (accessed on January 22, 2015); Osobennosti Reform Vysshego Obrazovania [Features of the Higher Education Reform], *Korrespondent*, August 13, 2014.

11. Much of this account is based on a conversation with Minister of Education Serhiy Kvit in May 2014.

foreign degrees, standardization of licensing, accreditation, and certification of higher education. At long last, Ukraine is abandoning the Soviet system of degrees. The new system of academic degrees is basically the Western system: junior bachelor, bachelor, master, PhD, though the highest Soviet degree, doctor of science (*doktor nauk*), which corresponds to the old German *Habilitation*, is being retained, but the other Soviet degrees—junior specialist, specialist, and candidate of science—are being abolished.

An important intention of the reform is to make licensing and accreditation and other quality control of higher education independent from the ministry. A new body will be created, the National Agency for Higher Education Quality, which will be responsible for licensing and accreditation. Its 25 members will be elected by the universities' congress, the National Academy of Sciences, trade unions, and student unions. The law also introduces external independent testing. Previously, the minister of education was in charge of all testing and could change it at his whim, which he often did. Plagiarism is a serious concern in Ukrainian academia. It is all too easy to produce a master's thesis from the internet. The new law tries to combat it with transparency. All doctoral dissertations have to be published on university websites, and dissertation defenses are public, allowing anybody to attend.

Ukrainian universities also suffer from gerontocracy. All too often, old Soviet professors have stayed on as university presidents. The new law limits the tenure for all rectors, deans, and department heads to a maximum of two terms of five years. Previously, the requirements for being president of a Ukrainian university included being a Ukrainian citizen, with a Soviet *doktor nauk* degree, having taught for at least ten years at a Ukrainian university. These requirements, which effectively impeded any modernization or internationalization, have now been abolished.

Another concern has been that university teachers have only taught and not done much research, since teaching was the task of universities while research was delegated to the Academy of Sciences. Therefore, the maximum workload for a professor has been decreased from 900 hours per academic year to 600 hours. Similarly, the students have been spending too many hours in class rather than studying independently. Thus, the number of hours in class has also been decreased. Both professors and students are being given new incentives for academic mobility.

This law is a big step forward, but a few issues have been left aside for the time being. One is university governance. Ukrainian universities have boards, but their powers are minimal, being rather symbolic and advisory in their nature. They do not run the universities. The new law does not change this situation. The universities should become truly self-governing institutions governed by independent boards of trustees and with financial freedom from the state.

Another concern is that Ukraine has far too many institutions of higher learning, many of poor quality. Ideally, government funding should be distributed in a competitive fashion so that substandard institutions can be closed down. The requirements for licensing and accreditation should be enhanced as well so that third-rate institutions would be forced either to significantly improve their quality or close down. The danger, however, is that the bureaucrats eliminate new elite institutions instead.[12]

The law provides somewhat better opportunities for research at universities, but it ignores the large, stagnant Academy of Sciences. Incredibly, academician Borys Paton, who was born in 1918, when the Ukrainian Academy of Sciences was founded, has been its president since 1962. He is one of the most respected individuals in Ukraine, as was his father, who preceded him, but at 96 he should think about retiring.

Even if successful, Ukraine has a long way to go. Only a handful of Central and East European universities are among the 500 top 1,000 universities in the world on the Shanghai list or among the 400 top universities on the *Times Higher Education Supplement* list, and none of the Ukrainian universities (Shanghai Ranking Consultancy 2014, Times Higher Education 2014).

Ukraine needs to completely rethink its model for higher education. Online education will probably bring about a revolution in higher education, making it possible for students all over the world to benefit from lectures of the best American professors. This could be the greatest opportunity for Ukraine to leapfrog in terms of higher education. In the meantime, the best option remains education abroad at the best American and European universities, from which many Ukrainian students fortunately benefit. The latest count records more than 32,000 Ukrainians studying in Europe.[13]

Putting the School System in Order

The Ukrainian school system has been devastated by Tabachnyk's disorganization, cutting years of schooling from 12 to 11 years. A fundamental restructuring is necessary reforming the whole school system from the top down. A Western-style 12-year school system needs to be reintroduced to make the Ukrainian school system compatible with Western systems.

Ukrainians sensibly see Poland and Germany as models for their schools. In the 18th and 19th centuries, Eastern and Northern Europe adopted the German education system. Both Poland and Germany do well on the Organization for Economic Cooperation and Development's Program for International Student Assessment (OECD PISA) comparisons of school standards, and Poland performed better than Germany on all three sections (mathematics, science, and reading) in the most recent PISA (OECD 2014). Hundreds of thousands

---

12. I was the cochair of the board of directors of a small graduate school, the Kyiv School of Economics, from 2003 to 2012. One of my main preoccupations was to stop the Ukrainian government from closing it down for purely bureaucratic reasons. Needless to say, the government offered no help in any regard.

13. Oksana Onyshchenko, "Molodezh' vybiraet Evropu" ["Youth Chooses Europe"], *Zerkalo nedeli*, February 14, 2014.

of Ukrainians have lived and worked in Poland and thousands have attended university there. A sensible proposal is to divide the schools in a normal European fashion into a six-year primary school, a three-year secondary school and a three-year high school (Kloshek 2014).

Vocational training needs to be revitalized by engaging employers and professional associations, and the supply of vocational training needs to be adjusted to labor market demand. Germany, Austria, and Switzerland have well-functioning apprentice systems, which Ukraine could easily replicate (Aivazova 2013). Especially German companies have a habit of developing their apprentice systems wherever they are allowed to do so, even in the United States. The German government has been promoting vocational training "export" programs to companies operating in other countries. This may be an attractive option for Ukrainian companies looking for good quality apprenticeship training, as well as for Ukrainian policymakers who are looking for a way to better integrate vocational training to local labor market needs.[14]

The next task is to establish a modern curriculum. Once again, Poland could serve as a model. Ukraine could simply adopt its curriculum, adjusting for language and history. Specifically, English language learning must improve substantially, so that students learn to communicate internationally.

The big administrative change should be to transfer the responsibility for running primary and secondary education at the local level. The current over-centralization and petty tutelage must end. The central financing of education ought to change from its current arbitrary, discretionary form. Current budget funding of schools should be subject to unified norms of education costs per student, meaning that the government should grant a certain amount of financing for each student at a certain level of education. This money should be distributed to the institutions that attract students.

Ukraine needs to reintroduce centralized exams and tests for students. National and international standards and independent testing should be established for secondary schools. Specifically, all entry interviews should be prohibited, since those are the occasions when bribes are extorted and paid. The seemingly innocent initial question is: "Is an envelope required?" The follow-up question asks: "How much is there supposed to be in the envelope?"

From 1990 to 2013, the number of students plummeted by 41 percent, from 7.1 million students to 4.2 million, because of lower birth rates and emigration, but the number of schools declined by only 11.5 percent and the number of teachers by merely 5 percent. The student-to-teacher ratio dropped from 13.3 in 1990 to 8.3 in 2013, one of the lowest in Europe. This makes little sense and is not an efficient way of spending money on education (table 11.5).

These statistics make obvious what should be done. If Ukraine had wanted to keep the average number of students per school constant at 327 as in

---

14. Federal Ministry of Education and Research, *Berufsbildungskooperation: Erfolgreicher Export von Bildungsangeboten* [*International Vocational Training Cooperation: Successful Export of Educational Services*], June 2013, Berlin, Germany, www.bmbf.de/de/17127.php.

Table 11.5   Education in Ukraine

Year	Number of schools (thousands)	Number of students (thousands)	Number of teachers (thousands)	Number of students per school	Number of students per teacher
1990	21.8	7,132	537	327	13.3
1995	22.3	7,143	596	320	12.0
2000	22.2	6,764	577	305	11.7
2005	21.6	5,399	543	250	9.9
2010	20.3	4,299	515	212	8.3
2013	19.3	4,204	508	218	8.3

Source: State Statistics Service of Ukraine; author's calculations.

1990, the government should have closed 6,400 schools and sold off the real estate to the benefit of public finances. By and large, international research suggests that students do not benefit much from having a lower student-to-teacher ratio. If that ratio had been kept constant, 220,000 teachers could have been laid off. Their wage fund could have been distributed among the other teachers, who would have then received an acceptable salary, which could have attracted better teachers.

Some may harbor sentimental feelings for small village schools, but they are problematic for education. The test results in the rural schools are far worse than in urban schools. The state should not be steering pupils toward poor education (Likarchuk 2014). Few teachers want to work in villages, and rural education is very expensive. Given limited distances, the state should use the extensive school bus program to encourage pupils to attend good schools.

Primary and secondary education are in disarray, while resources are substantial. Elementary order in the curriculums is needed, and management needs to be decentralized, so that the substantial funds expended can be used much more efficiently.

Recommendations

1. Reduce pension costs to 8 percent of GDP in the medium term.

2. Cut excessive benefits for the old Soviet elite.

3. Tighten eligibility for early pensions and disability pensions.

4. Raise the retirement age for both men and women to 65 in the next few years.

5. Introduce a modern three-pillar pension system with both mandatory and voluntary private pension saving.

6. Close down substandard hospitals and concentrate resources on primary healthcare as well as top-level hospital care.

7. Introduce competition among healthcare providers of different ownership.

8. Sell unprofitable real estate in healthcare to the benefit of local budgets and raise salaries of healthcare employees by laying off superfluous administrative staff.

9. Finance universities and schools by stipends per student.

10. Make universities truly self-governing institutions governed by independent boards of trustees and with financial freedom from the state.

11. Restructure the school system by dividing the schooling period into six years of primary school, three years of secondary school, and three years of high school.

12. Revitalize vocational training by engaging employers and professional associations and adjust the supply of vocational training to labor market demand.

13. Transfer the running of primary and secondary education to the local level.

14. Establish a modern curriculum in schools following international experience (for example, Poland) and improve the teaching and learning of English.

15. Close down superfluous village schools and sell real estate in the school sector to ease public finances.

12

Conclusion

Ukraine faces the starkest choice of all: reform hard and fast to survive or cease to exist as a nation. The option of doing minimum reform to muddle through no longer appears feasible because it would only lead to a financial meltdown reminiscent of the Russian crash of August 1998; adding Russian military aggression, the future would look dire. The question today is whether Ukraine can save itself.

The fundamental problem with Ukraine is that the country never fully broke away from the old Soviet system. During the first three years of independence, 1991–94, the old establishment of party apparatchiki, state enterprise managers, and young communist league officials used their political power to extract substantial wealth through rent seeking, and they used that wealth to maintain their political power.

The consequence was a corrupt, rent-seeking society that was economically and politically unstable and produced little economic growth. On the one hand, Ukraine was quite an open society. On the other, it failed to build normal institutions, such as democracy and the rule of law. In 2014, Ukraine is as poor as it was in 1989, according to World Bank statistics. It has lost a quarter of a century, during which other postcommunist countries, such as Poland and Estonia, more than doubled their wealth.

This tension between the unsatisfactory social situation and considerable political openness has bred two popular movements, the Orange Revolution and the Euromaidan, or the Revolution of Dignity, as it is increasingly called. The reasons for the failure of the Orange Revolution were many, though it might suffice to say that economic growth was 12 percent the preceding year. At that time Ukraine experienced no economic or foreign policy crisis.

Today, virtually everything is different. Since February 2014, Ukraine has been subject to military aggression from its neighbor Russia, and for the time being the nation's best hope is that the ceasefire in eastern Ukraine holds. The economic situation is desperate. At the end of 2014, Ukraine's international reserves dwindled to a miserable $7.5 billion, five weeks of imports. Without additional financial assistance, Ukraine is likely to end up in a disorderly default a few months into 2015. Mainly because of the war, output fell by some 7 percent in 2014, while the consolidated budget deficit exceeded 10 percent of GDP and inflation reached 25 percent, after the exchange rate of the hryvnia dropped by 50 percent in a year.

To get out of this financial trap, the Ukrainian government needs to cut public expenditures by at least 8 percent of GDP and attract international financing for 2015 alone of no less than $27 billion, including funding from the International Monetary Fund. Given Ukraine's poor ranking in all corruption indexes, every potential creditor wants to see resolute measures against corruption before offering additional financial support to the country.

Ukraine should learn from more successful postcommunist countries such as Poland, the Czech Republic, Estonia, and more recently Slovakia and Georgia. The leading reformers in these countries shared the idea that sound democratic and market economic reforms required a sharp break with the past. These countries succeeded because reforms started from the top and focused on the key problems, and most were launched in the midst of severe crisis.

No country has managed to reform itself in isolation. For Central and Eastern Europe, the European Union was an anchor for their reforms. It offered support as a market, model, peer, and provider of assistance. Thanks to its conclusion of an Association Agreement with the European Union, Ukraine can now draw on the same EU resources as its more successful Western neighbors.

On the political front, Ukraine successfully conducted free and fair presidential elections in May 2014 followed by parliamentary elections in October. A majority of five parties formed a coalition government that resembles the early reform governments in Central and Eastern Europe with young professional technocrats and foreigners in prominent posts. The government swiftly presented a plausible reform program and the new parliament adopted it with a large majority.

On the economic front, the new government has no rational choice but to substantially cut public expenditures. The current budget deficit is not sustainable and reserves are running out. At the same time, the government needs to exploit the opportunity the crisis presents to eliminate the worst sources of corruption. One is arbitrage by a privileged few between low state-controlled energy prices and much higher market prices. The obvious solution is to unify all energy prices at the market level.

Another source of corruption is law enforcement and the judicial system. These systems need to be cleansed from the top down, which the law on lustration aims to do. The anticorruption law institutes a public electronic register of all banks, enterprises, and real estate with their beneficiary owners revealed.

Tax administration needs to be facilitated and made electronic as far as possible to prevent taxmen from contacting taxpayers at whim. The numerous inspection agencies should finally be abolished and inspection of enterprises reined in.

The goal of the reforms is primarily to salvage the public finances and check top-level corruption, but they should also let market forces free, which would lead to substantial economic growth of 5 to 7 percent a year, as has been customary for other countries in this part of the world at Ukraine's current level of economic development. In order to improve the standard of living of the population, the government also needs to decentralize power and render both health care and education more efficient.

The new Ukrainian government is facing a tall order. No reformer has succeeded in doing everything, but this government needs to accomplish a great deal if Ukraine is to continue to exist as an independent state.

References

Acemoglu, Daron. 2008. Oligarchic Versus Democratic Societies. *Journal of the European Economic Association* 6, no. 1: 1–44.

Adomeit, Hannes. 2012. *Putin's 'Eurasian Union': Russia's Integration Project and Policies on Post-Soviet Space*. Neighborhood Policy Paper 4 (July). Istanbul: Kadir Has University.

Aivazova, Natalia. 2013. *Role of Apprenticeships in Combating Youth Unemployment in Europe and the United States*. Policy Brief 13-20 (August). Washington: Peterson Institute for International Economics.

Åslund, Anders. 1995. *How Russia Became a Market Economy*. Washington: Brookings Institution.

Åslund, Anders. 2002. *Building Capitalism: The Transformation of the Former Soviet Bloc*. New York: Cambridge University Press.

Åslund, Anders. 2006. The Ancien Régime: Kuchma and the Oligarchs. In *Revolution in Orange*, eds. Anders Åslund and Michael McFaul. Washington: Carnegie Endowment for International Peace.

Åslund, Anders. 2007. *Russia's Capitalist Revolution: Why Market Reform Succeeded and Democracy Failed*. Washington: Peterson Institute for International Economics.

Åslund, Anders. 2009. *How Ukraine Became a Market Economy and Democracy*. Washington: Peterson Institute for International Economics.

Åslund, Anders. 2010a. Les élections présidentielles ukrainiennes. *Commentaire* 33, no. 130: 325–31.

Åslund, Anders. 2010b. Gazprom: Challenged Giant in Need of Reform. In *Russia after the Global Economic Crisis*, ed. Anders Åslund, Sergei Guriev, and Andrew Kuchins. Washington: Peterson Institute for International Economics and the Center for Strategic and International Studies.

Åslund, Anders. 2013a. *How Capitalism Was Built: The Transformation of Central and Eastern Europe, Russia, the Caucasus, and Central Asia*, 2d ed. New York: Cambridge University Press.

Åslund, Anders. 2013b. *Ukraine's Choice: European Association Agreement or Eurasian Union?* Policy Brief 13-22 (September). Washington: Peterson Institute for International Economics.

Åslund, Anders. 2013c. Sergey Glazyev and the Revival of Soviet Economics. *Post-Soviet Affairs* 29, no. 5 (September–October): 375–86.

Åslund, Anders. 2014a. Oligarchs, Corruption, and European Integration. *Journal of Democracy* 25, no. 3 (July): 64–74.

Åslund, Anders. 2014b. Marshall's Postwar Logic Holds True in Ukraine Today. *Financial Times*, October 2.

Åslund, Anders, and Georges de Ménil, eds. 2000. *Ukrainian Economic Reform: The Unfinished Agenda.* Armonk, NY: M. E. Sharpe.

Åslund, Anders, and Simeon Djankov, eds. 2014. *The Great Rebirth: Lessons from the Victory of Capitalism over Communism.* Washington: Peterson Institute for International Economics.

Åslund, Anders, and Valdis Dombrovskis. 2011. *How Latvia Came through the Financial Crisis.* Washington: Peterson Institute for International Economics.

Åslund, Anders, and Michael McFaul, eds. 2006. *Revolution in Orange: The Origins of Ukraine's Democratic Breakthrough.* Washington: Carnegie Endowment for International Peace.

Åslund, Anders, and Oleksandr Paskhaver, eds. 2010. *Proposals to Ukraine: 2010—Time for Reforms.* Kyiv: Independent International Experts Commission.

Åslund, Anders, and Andrew Warner. 2004. The EU Enlargement: Consequences for the CIS Countries. In *Beyond Transition: Development Perspectives and Dilemmas,* ed. Marek Dabrowski, Ben Slay, and Jaroslaw Neneman. Aldershot, UK: Ashgate.

Åslund, Anders, Peter Boone, and Simon Johnson. 2001. *Escaping the Under-Reform Trap.* IMF Staff Papers, Special Issue 48, no. 4: 88–108. Washington: International Monetary Fund.

Babenko, Mariya. 2014. Bogatye tozhe platyat. Chto poteryal Akhmetov iz-za voiny v Donbasse [The Rich Also Pay. What Akhmetov Lost because of the War in Donbas]. *Focus,* October 30. Available at focus.ua.

Balcerowicz, Leszek. 1992. *800 dni: Szok kontrolowany* [800 Days of Controlled Shock]. Warsaw: Polska Oficyna Wydawnicza BGW.

Balcerowicz, Leszek. 1994. Understanding Postcommunist Transitions. *Journal of Democracy* 5, no. 4: 75–89.

Balcerowicz, Leszek. 2014. Poland: Stabilization and Reforms under Extraordinary and Normal Politics. In *The Great Rebirth: Lessons from the Victory of Capitalism over Communism,* ed. Anders Åslund and Simeon Djankov. Washington: Peterson Institute for International Economics.

Baldwin, Richard E. 1994. *Towards an Integrated Europe.* London: Centre for Economic Policy Research.

Balmaceda, Margarita Mercedes. 1998. Gas, Oil and the Linkages between Domestic and Foreign Policies: The Case of Ukraine. *Europe-Asia Studies* 50, no. 2: 257–86.

Balmaceda, Margarita Mercedes. 2004. Ukraine's Persistent Energy Crisis. *Problems of Post-Communism* 51, no. 4: 40–50.

Balmaceda, Margarita Mercedes. 2013. *The Politics of Energy Dependency: Ukraine, Belarus, and Lithuania between Domestic Oligarchs and Russian Pressure.* Studies in Comparative Political Economy and Public Policy. Toronto: University of Toronto Press.

Banaian, King. 1999. *The Ukrainian Economy since Independence.* Cheltenham, UK: Edward Elgar.

Barro, Robert J., and Xavier Sala-i-Martín. 2004. *Economic Growth.* Cambridge, MA: MIT Press.

Barroso, José Manuel. 2014. Letter from President Barroso to President Putin. European Commission, Brussels, October 1. Available at http://europa.eu/rapid/press-release_STATEMENT-14-294_en.htm (accessed on January 22, 2015).

Bendukidze, Kakha, and Mikheil Saakashvili. 2014. Georgia: The Most Radical Catch-Up Reforms. In *The Great Rebirth: Lessons from the Victory of Capitalism over Communism,* ed. Anders Åslund and Simeon Djankov. Washington: Peterson Institute for International Economics.

Betliy, Oleksandra, and Ricardo Giucci. 2011. *Pension Reform in Ukraine: Comments on the Main Features of the Current Draft Law.* Policy Paper Series 01/2011 (February). Berlin/Kyiv: German Advisory Group, Institute for Economic Research and Policy Consulting.

Betliy, Oleksandra, Ricardo Giucci, and Robert Kirchner. 2013. *VAT in Ukraine: Would Other Indirect Taxes Perform Better?* Policy Paper Series 02/2013 (March). Berlin/Kyiv: German Advisory Group, Institute for Economic Research and Policy Consulting.

Bilak, Daniel. 2014. Ukraine Needs a Marshall Plan. *Kyiv Post,* February 11.

Bilenko, Sergey. 2014. Detsentralizatsiya: zemel'nye aspekty [Decentralization: Land Aspects]. *Ekonomichna pravda,* December 12.

Blanchard, Olivier, and Daniel Leigh. 2013. *Growth Forecast Errors and Fiscal Multipliers.* IMF Working Paper 13/01. Washington: International Monetary Fund.

Blinov, Andrei. 2014. Zakon o goszakupkakh: mezhdu iskliucheniyami i ravnymi sloviyami [Law on State Procurement: Between Exceptions and a Level Playing Field]. *Zerkalo nedeli,* August 8.

Blue Ribbon Commission for Ukraine. 2005. *Proposals for the President: A New Wave of Reform.* New York: United Nations Development Programme.

Bokros, Lajos. 2014. Regression: Reform Reversal in Hungary after a Promising Start. In *The Great Rebirth: Lessons from the Victory of Capitalism over Communism,* ed. Anders Åslund and Simeon Djankov. Washington: Peterson Institute for International Economics.

Brady, Rose. 1999. *Kapitalizm: Russia's Struggle to Free Its Economy.* New Haven, CT: Yale University Press.

Čábelková, Inna, and Jan Hanousek. 2004. The Power of Negative Thinking: Corruption, Perception and Willingness to Bribe in Ukraine. *Applied Economics* 36, no. 4: 383–97.

Cabinet of Ministers of Ukraine. 2014a. Concept of the Reform of the Local Self-Government and Territorial Organization of the Power in Ukraine, April 1, Kyiv.

Cabinet of Ministers of Ukraine. 2014b. Kontseptsiya reformirovaniya nalogovoi sistemy [Concept for Reform of the Tax System]. Kyiv. Photocopy (July).

Carlsson, Sten, and Jerker Rosen. 1961. *Svensk Historia (Swedish History),* 3d ed. Stockholm: Scandinavian University Books.

Carneiro, Francisco G. 2013. What Promises Does the Eurasian Customs Union Hold for the Future? *Economic Premise* no. 108 (February). Washington: World Bank.

Center for the Adaptation of the Civil Service to the Standards of the European Union. 2014. Twinning Project Status in Work Plan. Kyiv. Available at www.center.gov.ua/en/ (accessed on October 9, 2014).

Center for Political and Legal Reforms. 2014. Opinion by a Group of Researchers and Public Experts on the Draft Law on Amendments to the Constitution of Ukraine, June 26. Kyiv.

Chow, Edward C., Sarah O. Ladislaw, and Michelle Melton. 2014. *Crisis in Ukraine: What Role Does Energy Play?* Washington: Center for Strategic and International Studies.

Clements, Benedict, David Coady, Stefania Fabrizio, Sanjeev Gupta, Trevor Alleyne, and Carlo Sdralevich. 2013. *Energy Subsidy Reform: Lessons and Implications.* Washington: International Monetary Fund.

Collins, Susan M., and Dani Rodrik. 1991. *Eastern Europe and the Soviet Union in the World Economy.* Washington: Institute for International Economics.

Council of Europe. 1996. Measures to Dismantle the Heritage of Former Communist Totalitarian Systems. Resolution 1096, Parliamentary Assembly. Strasbourg.

Council of the European Union. 2009. Joint Declaration of the Prague Eastern Partnership Summit (May 7). Prague.

Dabrowski, Marek. 1994. The Ukrainian Way to Hyperinflation. *Communist Economies and Economic Transformation* 6, no. 2: 115–37.

Dabrowski, Marek. 2014. *Ukraine: Can Meaningful Reform Come Out of Conflict?* Bruegel Policy Contribution 2013/08. Brussels: Bruegel.

Dabrowski, Marek, and Svitlana Taran. 2012a. *Is Free Trade with the EU Good for Ukraine?* CASE Network Brief no. 06 (March). Warsaw: Center for Social and Economic Research.

Dabrowski, Marek, and Svitlana Taran. 2012b. *The Free Trade Agreement between the EU and Ukraine: Conceptual Background, Economic Context and Potential Impact.* CASE Network, CASE Studies and Analyses 437. Warsaw: Center for Social and Economic Research.

Dabrowski, Marek, Marcin Luczyński, and Malgorzata Markiewicz. 2000. The Phases of Budgetary Reform. In *Ukrainian Economic Reform: The Unfinished Agenda,* ed. Anders Åslund and Georges de Ménil. Armonk, NY: M. E. Sharpe.

Das, Udaibir S., Michael G. Papaioannou, and Christoph Trebesch. 2012. *Sovereign Debt Restructurings 1950–2010: Literature Survey, Data, and Stylized Facts.* IMF Working Paper 12/203. Washington: International Monetary Fund.

Davies, Norman. 1982. *God's Playground: A History of Poland.* Oxford: Oxford University Press.

Dawisha, Karen. 2014. *Putin's Kleptocracy.* New York: Simon & Schuster.

De Long, Bradford. 2002. Robber Barons. In *Ocherki o mirovoi ekonomiki: Vydayushchiesya ekonomisty mira v Moskovskom Tsentre Karnegie [Series of Lectures on Economics: Leading World Experts at the Carnegie Moscow Center],* ed. Anders Åslund and Tatyana Maleva. Moscow: Carnegie Endowment for International Peace.

Deloitte. 2014. *International Tax: Ukraine Highlights 2014.* Kyiv.

De Melo, Martha, and Stoyan Tenev. 1997. *Circumstance and Choice: The Role of Initial Conditions and Policies in Transition Economies.* World Bank Policy Research Working Paper 186. Washington: World Bank.

De Ménil, Georges. 1997. The Volatile Relationship between Deficits and Inflation in Ukraine, 1992–1996. *The Economics of Transition* 5, no. 2: 485–97.

De Ménil, Georges. 2000. From Hyperinflation to Stagnation. In *Ukrainian Economic Reform: The Unfinished Agenda,* ed. Anders Åslund and Georges de Ménil. Armonk, NY: M.E. Sharpe.

De Ménil, Georges, and Wing Thye Woo. 1994. Introduction to a Ukrainian Debate. *Economic Policy* 9 (supplement): 9–15.

Dovgan, Daria. 2014. Nalogam pred'yavili schet [Account of Taxes Presented]. *Zerkalo nedeli,* August 8.

Dragon Capital. 2014. Ukrainian Economy: Forecasts Revised to Factor in Protracted Military Conflict, October 2, Kyiv.

Dunn, Jonathan, and Patrick Lenain. 1997. The Role of Monetary Policy in Ukraine's Medium-Term Adjustment Strategy. In *Ukraine: Accelerating the Transition to Market,* eds. Peter K. Cornelius and Patrick Lenain. Washington: International Monetary Fund.

EBA (European Business Association). 2004. *Barriers to Investment in Ukraine.* Kyiv.

EBRD (European Bank for Reconstruction and Development). 1994. *Transition Report 1994.* London.

EBRD (European Bank for Reconstruction and Development). 1997. *Transition Report 1997.* London.

EBRD (European Bank for Reconstruction and Development). 1998. *Transition Report 1998.* London.

EBRD (European Bank for Reconstruction and Development). 1999. *Transition Report 1999.* London.

EBRD (European Bank for Reconstruction and Development). 2002. *Transition Report 2002.* London.

EBRD (European Bank for Reconstruction and Development). 2003. *Transition Report 2003.* London.

EBRD (European Bank for Reconstruction and Development). 2004. *Transition Report 2004.* London.

EBRD (European Bank for Reconstruction and Development). 2005. *Transition Report 2005.* London.

EBRD (European Bank for Reconstruction and Development). 2006. *Transition Report 2006.* London.

EBRD (European Bank for Reconstruction and Development). 2007. *Transition Report 2007.* London.

EBRD (European Bank for Reconstruction and Development). 2008. Online Database. London.

EBRD (European Bank for Reconstruction and Development). 2010. *Transition Report 2010: Recovery and Reform.* London.

EEAS (European External Action Service of the European Union). 2013. EU-Ukraine Association Agreement. Brussels.

Energy Charter Secretariat. 2013. In-Depth Review of the Energy Efficiency Policy of Ukraine. Brussels.

Eurasian Development Bank. 2012. *Ukraine and the Customs Union.* Report 1. St. Petersburg, Russia: Eurasian Development Bank Centre for Integration Studies. Available at www.eabr.org/general//upload/reports/Ukraina_doklad_eng.pdf (accessed on January 22, 2015).

Euromaidan Press. 2014. The Achievements of the New Government within 3 Months. Available at http://euromaidanpress.com/2014/05/25/the-achievements-of-the-new-government-within-3-months/ (accessed on May 28, 2014).

European Centre. 2012. *Strategy Paper for Pension Policy in Ukraine* (March). Kyiv.

European Commission. 2012a. *Higher Education in Ukraine.* Brussels.

European Commission. 2012b. Overview of the bilateral cooperation between EU and Ukraine. Brussels.

European Commission. 2014a. European Commission's Support to Ukraine. Memo (March 5). Brussels.

European Commission. 2014b. Joint Ministerial Statement on the Implementation of the EU Ukraine AA/DCFTA. Statement (September 12). Brussels. Available at http://europa.eu.

Eurostat. 2014. Eurostat Statistics Database. Available at http://epp.eurostat.ec.europa.eu/portal/page/portal/statistics/search_database (accessed on January 22, 2015).

Fiszbein, Ariel, and Norbert Schady. 2009. *Conditional Cash Transfers: Reducing Present and Future Poverty.* Washington: World Bank.

Freedom House. 2011. *Freedom in the World 2011.* Washington.

Freedom House. 2014. *Freedom in the World 2014.* Washington.

Freeland, Chrystia. 2000. *Sale of the Century: Russia's Wild Ride from Communism to Capitalism.* New York: Crown Business.

Frishberg, Alex. 2008. *The Steel Barons.* Logos.

Füle, Štefan. 2014. 2014 Enlargement Package (October 8). Brussels: European Commission.

Garbert, Folkert. 2013. *Belarus und die Zollunion—Eine Bestandsaufnahme* [*Belarus and the Customs Union—An Assessment*]. Newsletter 22 (March–April). Berlin: German Economic Team Belarus.

Gelpern, Anna. 2014. *Debt Sanctions Can Help Ukraine and Fill a Gap in the International Financial System.* Policy Brief 14-20 (August). Washington: Peterson Institute for International Economics.

Gill, Indermit, Ivailo Izvorski, Willem van Eeghen, and Donato de Rosa. 2014. *Diversified Development: Making the Most of Natural Resources in Eurasia*. Washington: World Bank.

Giucci, Ricardo. 2013. *Wie wichtig ist das DCFTA für die Ukraine? Eine Einschätzung* [*How Important is the DCFTA for Ukraine? An Assessment*]. Newsletter 57 (May). Berlin: Deutsche Beratergruppe.

Giucci, Ricardo, and Robert Kirchner. 2013. *Russische Zollschikanen gegen ukrainische Exporteure: Was tun?* (*Russian Customs Harassment against Ukrainian Exporters: What to Do?*). Newsletter 60 (August). Berlin: Deutsche Beratergruppe.

Global Witness. 2006. *It's a Gas: Funny Business in the Turkmen-Ukraine Gas Trade*. London.

Golod, Irina. 2014. Glava NKREKU: 'Ozhidat', chto pri rastushchikh tsenakh tarify ne budut rasti, - neskol'ko naivno [The Head of NKREKU: To Expect that Tariffs Would Not Rise with Prices Is Rather Naïve]. *RBK Ukraina*, October 30. Available at www.rbc.ua/rus/interview/economic/glava-nkreku-ozhidat-chto-pri-rastushchih-tsenah-tarify-ne-30102014182800 (accessed January 22, 2015).

Gorodnichenko, Yuriy, Jorge Martinez-Vazquez, and Klara Sabirianova Peter. 2009. Myth and reality of flat tax reform: Micro estimates of tax evasion and productivity response in Russia. *Journal of Political Economy* 117: 504–54.

Gorodnichenko, Yuriy, et al. 2014. Stravnenie program politicheskikh partii. *Ukrainskaya pravda*, October 21.

Gregory, Paul. 2014. A Bad Gas Deal for Ukraine As Europe Looks after Its Own Interests. *Forbes*, October 31.

Grey, Stephen, Tom Bergin, Sevgil Musaieva, and Roman Anin. 2014. Putin's Allies Channelled Billions to Oligarch Who Backed Pro-Russian President of Ukraine. Reuters, November 26.

Groisman, Volodymyr. 2014. Vladimir Groysman prizval soobshchestvo donorov sotrudnichat' v Plane vosstanovleniya i rosta dlya 2014-2016. Ukraine Government Portal, July 8.

Grygorenko, Yegor, Yuriy Gorodnichenko, and Dmytro Ostanin. 2006. *Relative Property Rights in Transition Economies: Can the Oligarchs Be Productive?* Economics Education and Research Consortium Working Paper 4. Moscow: Economics Education and Research Consortium.

Guriev, Sergei, and Konstantin Sonin. 2009. Dictators and Oligarchs: A Dynamic Theory of Contested Property Rights. *Journal of Public Economics* 93, no. 1-2: 1–13.

Hamilton, Carl B., and L. Alan Winters. 1992. Trade with Eastern Europe. *Economic Policy* 7, no. 14: 77–116.

Havrylyshyn, Oleh. 2014. Ukraine: Greatest Hopes, Greatest Disappointments. In *The Great Rebirth: Lessons from the Victory of Capitalism over Communism*, ed. Anders Åslund and Simeon Djankov. Washington: Peterson Institute for International Economics.

Havrylyshyn, Oleh, and Hassan Al-Atrash. 1998. *Opening Up and Geographic Diversification of Trade in Transition Economies*. IMF Working Paper 22. Washington: International Monetary Fund.

Havrylyshyn, Oleh, and Thomas Wolf. 2001. Growth in Transition Countries, 1990-98: The Main Lessons. In *A Decade of Transition: Achievements and Challenges*, ed. Oleh Havrylyshyn and Saleh M. Nsouli. Washington: International Monetary Fund.

Hay, Jonathan R., and Andrei Shleifer. 1998. Private Enforcement of Public Laws: A Theory of Legal Reform. *American Economic Review* 88, no. 2: 398–403.

Hellman, Joel S. 1998. Winners Take All: The Politics of Partial Reform in Postcommunist Transitions. *World Politics* 50, no. 2: 203–34.

Hoffman, David. 2002. *The Oligarchs*. New York: Public Affairs.

Hogan, Michael J. 1987. *The Marshall Plan*. Cambridge: Cambridge University Press.

Honkapohja, Seppo. 2009. *The 1990s financial crises in Nordic countries*. Bank of Finland Research and Discussion Papers 5. Helsinki: Bank of Finland.

Horne, Cynthia. 2012. Lustration and Trust in Central and East Europe: Assessing the Impact of Lustration on Trust in Public Institutions and National Government. *Comparative Political Studies* 45, no. 4 (June): 412–46.

IEA (International Energy Agency). 2012. *Ukraine 2012: Energy Policies beyond IEA Countries*. Paris.

IMF (International Monetary Fund). 1993. *Economic Review: Ukraine 1993*. Washington.

IMF (International Monetary Fund). 1995. *Economic Review: Ukraine 1994*. Washington.

IMF (International Monetary Fund). 2011. *Ukraine: First Review under the Stand-By Arrangement*. IMF Country Report 15/22 (February). Washington.

IMF (International Monetary Fund). 2012. *World Economic Outlook* database (October). Washington.

IMF (International Monetary Fund). 2014a. *Ukraine: Request for a Stand-By Agreement*. IMF Country Report 14/106 (April). Washington.

IMF (International Monetary Fund). 2014b. *Ukraine: 2013 Article IV Consultation and First Post-Program Monitoring*. IMF Country Report 14/145 (May). Washington.

IMF (International Monetary Fund). 2014c. *Ukraine: Ex Post Evaluation of Exceptional Access under the 2010 Stand-By Arrangement*. IMF Country Report 14/146 (May). Washington.

IMF (International Monetary Fund). 2014d. *Ukraine: First Review under the Stand-By Arrangement*. IMF Country Report 14/263 (September). Washington.

IMF (International Monetary Fund). 2014e. *World Economic Outlook* database (April). Washington.

Ivanova, Anna, Michael Keen, and Alexander Klemm. 2005. *The Russian Flat Tax Reform*. IMF Working Paper 05/16. Washington: International Monetary Fund.

Ivanter, Viktor, Valery Geets, Vladimir Yasinskiy, Alexander Shirov, and Andrey Anisimov. 2012. The Economic Effects of the Creation of the Single Economic Space and Potential Accession of Ukraine. In *Eurasian Integration Yearbook 2012*. Almaty, Kazakhstan: Eurasian Development Bank.

Iwulska, Aleksandra. 2012. *Golden Growth: Restoring the Lustre of the European Economic Model*. Washington: World Bank.

Karatnycky, Adrian. 2005. Ukraine's Orange Revolution. *Foreign Affairs* 84, no. 2: 35–52.

Kaufmann, Daniel. 1995. Diminishing Returns to Administrative Controls and the Emergence of the Unofficial Economy: A Framework of Analysis and Applications to Ukraine. *Economic Policy* 19 (supplement): 52–69.

Kaufmann, Daniel. 1997. Corruption: Some Myths and Facts. *Foreign Policy* 107: 114–31.

Kaufmann, Daniel, and Aleksander Kaliberda. 1996. Integrating the Unofficial Economy into the Dynamics of Post-Socialist Economies. In *Economic Transition in Russia and the New States of Eurasia Vol. 8*, ed. Bartlomiej Kaminski. New York: M. E. Sharpe.

Keen, Michael, Yitae Kim, and Ricardo Varsano. 2006. *The 'Flat Tax(es)': Principles and Evidence*. IMF Working Paper 218. Washington: International Monetary Fund.

Kindleberger, Charles P., and Robert Aliber. 2005. *Manias, Panics, and Crashes: A History of Financial Crises*, 5th ed. New York: Wiley.

Kirchner, Stephen. 2013. *Policy Reforms of Australia and What They Mean for Canada*. Vancouver: Fraser Institute.

Klaus, Václav. 2014. Czechoslovakia and the Czech Republic: The Spirit and Main Contours of Postcommunist Transformation. In *The Great Rebirth: Lessons from the Victory of Capitalism over Communism*, ed. Anders Åslund and Simeon Djankov. Washington: Peterson Institute for International Economics.

Klebnikov, Paul. 2000. *Godfather of the Kremlin: The Decline of Russia in the Age of Gangster Capitalism*. Orlando, FL: Harcourt.

Kobolyev, Andriy. 2014. Tsena gazovoi nezavisimosti [The Price of Gas Independence]. *Zerkalo nedeli*, August 21.

Kloshek, Grigory. 2014. Srednemu obrazovanie neobkhodimo shokovoe reformirovanie [Middle Education Needs Shock Reforms]. *Zerkalo nedeli*, July 18.

Kornai, János. 1992. The Postsocialist Transition and the State: Reflections in Light of Hungarian Fiscal Problems. *American Economic Review* 82, no. 2: 1–21.

Kornblum, John. 2014. Clowns Can't Save the Old World Order. *Die Welt am Sonntag*, September 7.

Koval, Yulia. 2014. Ukaz—ne zakon [A Decree Is Not a Law]. *Zerkalo nedeli*, August 8.

Kramar, Oleksandr. 2014. The Communist Party May Be on Its Last Legs, But Social Populism Is Still Alive. *Ukrainian Week*, October 23.

Kravchuk, Robert S. 1999. The Quest for Balance: Regional Self-Government and Subnational Fiscal Policy in Ukraine. In *State and Institution-Building in Ukraine*, ed. Taras Kuzio, Robert S. Kravchuk, and Paul D'Anieri. New York: St. Martin's Press.

Kravchuk, Robert S. 2002. *Ukrainian Political Economy: The First Ten Years*. New York: Palgrave Macmillan.

Krushelnycky, Askold. 2006. *An Orange Revolution: A Personal Journey through Ukrainian History*. London: Harvill Secker.

Kuchma, Leonid D. 2003. *Ukraina—ne Rossiia [Ukraine Is Not Russia]*. Moscow: Vremia.

Kuchma, Ostap. 2014. Urna NE dlya muzora: kak zastavit' rabotat' isbiratel'nuyu sistemu [The Urn Is NOT for Garbage: How to Make the Electoral System Work]. *Ukrainskaya pravda*, August 7.

Kudelia, Serhiy. 2014. The House that Yanukovych Built. *Journal of Democracy* 25, no. 3 (July): 19–34.

Kumar, Manmohan S., and Jaejoon Woo. 2010. *Public Debt and Growth*. IMF Working Paper 10/174. Washington: International Monetary Fund.

Kuzio, Taras. 1997. *Ukraine under Kuchma*. New York: St. Martin's Press.

Kuzio, Taras, and Andrew Wilson. 1994. *Ukraine: Perestroika to Independence*. Edmonton, AB: Canadian Institute of Ukrainian Studies.

Kuzio, Taras [and Andrew Wilson]. 2000 [1994]. *Ukraine: Perestroika to Independence*. Edmonton, Alberta: Canadian Institute of Ukrainian Studies.

La Porta, Rafael, Florencio Lopez-de-Silanes, Andrei Shleifer, and Robert Vishny. 1998. Law and Finance. *Journal of Political Economy* 106: 1113–55.

Laar, Mart. 2002. *Little Country That Could*. London: Centre for Research into Post-Communist Economies.

Laar, Mart. 2014. Estonia: The Most Radical Reforms. In *The Great Rebirth: Lessons from the Victory of Capitalism over Communism*, ed. Anders Åslund and Simeon Djankov. Washington: Peterson Institute for International Economics.

Leive, Adam. 2010. *Economic Transition and Health Care Reform: The Experience of Europe and Central Asia*. Working Paper 10/75. Washington: International Monetary Fund.

Lekhan, Valery, Volodymyr Rudiy, and Erica Richardson. 2010. Ukraine: Health System Review. *Health Systems in Transition* 12, no. 8: 1–183.

Leshchenko, Serhiy. 2014. The Media's Role. *Journal of Democracy* 25, no. 3: 52–57.

Lévy, Bernard-Henri. 2014. A Marshall Plan for Ukraine. *Huffington Post*, October 13.

Liedtke, Patrick. 2006. *From Bismarck's Pension Trap to the New Silver Workers of Tomorrow: Reflections on the New German Pension Problem*. European Papers on the New Welfare 4. Trieste, Italy: Risk Institute.

Likarchuk, Igor. 2014. Pora krichat' SOS! [Time to Shout SOS!] *Zerkalo nedeli*, August 15.

Linz, Juan J. 1990. The Perils of Presidentialism. *Journal of Democracy* 1, no. 1: 55–69.

Lisenkova, Katerina. 2011. *Pension Reform in a Rapidly Ageing Country: The Case of Ukraine*. Discussion Papers in Economics 11-26. Glasgow: University of Strathclyde.

Lovei, Laszlo. 1998. Gas Reform in Ukraine: Monopolies, Markets and Corruption. Note 169. Washington: World Bank.

Maliszewska, Maryla, Iryna Orlova, and Svitlana Taran. 2009. *Deep Integration with the EU and its Likely Impact on Selected ENP Countries and Russia*. CASE Network Report 88. Warsaw: Center for Social and Economic Research.

Marshall, George C. 1947. The Marshall Plan Speech (June 5). The George C. Marshall Foundation. Available at http://marshallfoundation.org/marshall/the-marshall-plan/marshall-plan-speech (accessed on January 22, 2015).

Meissner, Frank, Dmytro Naumenko, and Jörg Radeke. 2012. *Towards Higher Energy Efficiency in Ukraine: Reducing Regulation and Promoting Energy Efficiency Improvements*. Policy Paper 1/2012 (January). Kyiv: German Advisory Group.

Menon, Rekha. 2010. *Combating Ukraine's Health Crisis: Lessons from Europe*. Knowledge Brief 17 (January). Washington: World Bank.

Messerlin, Patrick A. 2001. *Measuring the Costs of Protection in Europe: European Commercial Policy in the 2000s*. Washington: Institute for International Economics.

Michalopoulos, Constantine, and David G. Tarr. 1996. *Trade Performance and Policy in the New Independent States*. Washington: World Bank.

Michalopoulos, Constantine, and Vladimir Drebentsov. 1997. Observations on State Trading in the Russian Economy. *Post-Soviet Geography and Economics* 38, no. 5: 264–75.

Miklos, Ivan. 2014. Slovakia: The Latecomer That Caught Up. In *The Great Rebirth: Lessons from the Victory of Capitalism over Communism*, ed. Anders Åslund and Simeon Djankov. Washington: Peterson Institute for International Economics.

Milanovic, Branko. 1998. *Income, Inequality, and Poverty during the Transition from Planned to Market Economy*. Washington: World Bank.

Milward, Alan S. 1984. *The Reconstruction of Western Europe 1945–51*. London: Methuen.

Mitra, Pritha, and Ruben Atoyan. 2014. *Ukraine Gas Pricing Policy: Distributional Consequences of Tariff Increases*. IMF Working Paper 12/247. Washington: International Monetary Fund.

Montesquieu, Charles de Secondat. 1748 (reprint 1977). *The Spirit of Laws*. Berkeley: University of California Press.

Morck, Randall, Daniel Wolfenzon, and Bernard Yeung. 2005. Corporate Governance, Economic Entrenchment, and Growth. *Journal of Economic Literature* 43 no. 3: 655–720.

Morris, Charles R. 2005. *The Tycoons: How Andrew Carnegie, John D. Rockefeller, Jay Gould, and J. P. Morgan Invented the American Supereconomy*. New York: Times Books.

Movchan, Veronika. 2011. *Ukraine's Trade Policy Choice: Pros and Cons of Different Regional Integration Options*. Analytical Report (December). Kyiv: Institute for Economic Research and Policy Consulting.

Movchan, Veronika, and Ricardo Giucci. 2011. *Quantitative Assessment of Ukraine's Regional Integration Options: DCFTA with European Union vs. Customs Union with Russia, Belarus and Kazakhstan*. Policy Paper 05/2011 (November). Kyiv: Institute for Economic Research and Policy Consulting.

Movchan, Veronika, and Volodymyr Shportyuk. 2012. *EU-Ukraine DCFTA: The Model for Eastern Partnership Regional Trade Cooperation*. CASE Studies and Analyses 445. Warsaw: Center for Social and Economic Research.

Movchan, Veronika, Ricardo Giucci, and Kateryna Kutsenko. 2010. *Trade Policy in the Ukraine: Strategic Aspects and Next Steps to Be Taken*. Policy Paper 02/2010 (April). Kyiv: Institute for Economic Research and Policy Consulting.

Neef, Christian. 2010. The Underbelly of Ukrainian Gas Dealings. *Der Spiegel*, December 30.

OECD (Organization for Economic Cooperation and Development). 2004. Improving the Conditions for Enterprise Development and the Investment Climate for Domestic and International Investors in Ukraine: Legal Issues with Regard to Business Operations and Investment. Washington and Kyiv. Photocopy.

OECD (Organization for Economic Cooperation and Development). 2011. Investment in Support of Energy Efficiency. In *OECD Investment Policy Reviews: Ukraine 2011*. Paris.

OECD (Organization for Economic Cooperation and Development). 2013. *Pensions at a Glance, 2013*. Paris.

OECD (Organization for Economic Cooperation and Development). 2014. *PISA 2012 Results: What Students Know and Can Do: Student Performance in Mathematics, Reading and Science*. Paris.

OHCHR (Office of the United Nations High Commissioner for Human Rights). 2014. *Report on the Human Rights Situation in Ukraine*. Geneva. Mimeo (November 15).

Ogarenko, Iuliia, and Klaus Hubacek. 2013. Eliminating Indirect Energy Subsidies in Ukraine: Estimation of Environmental and Socioeconomic Effects Using Input-Output Modeling. *Journal of Economic Structures* 2, no. 7: 1–27.

Olson, Mancur. 2000. *Power and Prosperity: Outgrowing Communist and Capitalist Dictatorships*. New York: Basic Books.

Olszański, Tadeusz A. 2012. After the parliamentary elections in Ukraine: A tough victory for the Party of Regions. Ośrodek Studiów Wschodnich, Warsaw (November 7).

OSCE (Organization for Security and Cooperation in Europe). 2014a. *Protocol on the Results of Consultations of the Trilateral Contact Group, Signed in Minsk, September 5, 2014*. Bern, Switzerland. Available at www.osce.org/ru/home/123258?download=true (accessed on November 4, 2014).

OSCE (Organization for Security and Cooperation in Europe). 2014b. *Memorandum of September 19, 2014, Outlining the Parameters for the Implementation of Commitments of the Minsk Protocol of September 5, 2014*. Bern, Switzerland. Available at www.osce.org/ru/home/123807?download=true (accessed on November 4, 2014).

Panchenko, Yuriy. 2014. Protivoyadie ot Rossii [Antidote against Russia]. *Yevropeiska pravda*, October 7.

Parry, Ian, Dirk Heine, Eliza Lis, and Shanjun Li. 2014. *Getting Energy Prices Right: From Principle to Practice*. Washington: International Monetary Fund.

Pifer, Steven. 2004. Ukraine's Future and US Interests. Testimony before the House International Relations Committee, Subcommittee on Europe. US Department of State. Available at www.state.gov (accessed on July 10, 2008).

Pifer, Steven. 2014. Taking Stock in Ukraine. *American Interest*, October 24.

Pirian, Armenuhi. 2003. Bulgarian Brady Bonds and the External Debt Swap of Bulgaria. University of Sofia, Bulgaria, Bratislava: Network of Institutes and Schools of Public Administration in Central and Eastern Europe. Mimeo. Available at http://unpan1.un.org/intradoc/groups/public/documents/NISPAcee/UNPAN009285.pdf (accessed on January 22, 2015).

Plank, Christina. 2013. Land Grabs in the Black Earth: Ukrainian Oligarchs and International Investors. Heinrich Böll Stiftung, October 30. Available at http://www.boell.de/de/node/280169 (accessed on January 22, 2015).

Poroshenko, Petro. 2014. Obrashchenie Prezidenta Ukrainy po povodu dosrochnykh parlamentskikh vyborov 26 oktyabrya [Declaration of the President of Ukraine on Early Parliamentary Elections on October 26]. Official Website of the President of Ukraine, August 25.

Poteraj, Jaroslaw. 2012. Pension System in Ukraine. *International Journal of Business Management and Economic Research* 3, no. 4: 598–606.

Prizel, Ilya. 1997. Ukraine between Proto-Democracy and 'Soft' Authoritarianism. In *Democratic Changes and Authoritarian Reactions in Russia, Ukraine, Belarus and Moldova*, eds. Karen Dawisha and Bruce Parrott. Cambridge: Cambridge University Press.

Prytula, Olena. 2006. The Ukrainian Media Rebellion. In *Revolution in Orange*, ed. Anders Åslund and Michael McFaul. Washington: Carnegie Endowment for International Peace.

Puglisi, Rosaria. 2003. The Rise of the Ukrainian Oligarchs. *Democratization* 10, no. 3: 99–123.

Putin, Vladimir. 2005. Annual Address to the Federal Assembly of the Russian Federation. April 25. Available at www.kremlin.ru.

Putin, Vladimir. 2014a. Address by President of the Russian Federation. March 18. Available at www.kremlin.ru.

Putin, Vladimir. 2014b. Direct Line with Vladimir Putin. April 17. Available at www.kremlin.ru.

Radeke, Jörg, Ricardo Gucci, and Dmytro Naumenko. 2012. *Adjusting Gas Prices to Unlock Ukraine's Economic Potential*. Policy Paper 2/2012 (March). Kyiv: German Advisory Group.

Radeke, Jörg, and Woldemar Walter. 2012. *How to Adjust Ukraine's Energy Tariffs? International Experience of Energy Reform and Social Protection*. Policy Briefing Series 8/2012 (November). Berlin: German Advisory Group.

Reforms in Ukraine. 2014. *Strategy of Ukraine 2020* (English translation). Available at http://reforms.in.ua/2020/strategy2020eng.pdf (accessed on January 22, 2015).

Reid, T. R. 2009. *The Healing of America: A Global Quest for Better, Cheaper, and Fairer Health Care*. New York: Penguin.

Reinhart, Carmen, and Kenneth Rogoff. 2009. *This Time Is Different: Eight Centuries of Financial Folly*. Princeton, NJ: Princeton University Press.

Remington, Thomas F., Steven S. Smith, and Moshe Haspel. 1998. Decrees, Laws, and Inter-Branch Relations in the Russian Federation. *Post-Soviet Affairs* 14, no. 4: 287–322.

Rose-Ackerman, Susan. 1999. *Corruption and Government: Causes, Consequences, and Reform*. Cambridge: Cambridge University Press.

Rustow, Dankwart. 1970. Transitions to Democracy: Toward a Dynamic Model. *Comparative Politics*. 2, no. 3: 337–64.

Sachs, Jeffrey D. 1993. *Poland's Jump to the Market Economy*. Cambridge, MA: MIT Press.

Sachs, Jeffrey D. 1994. Life in the Economic Emergency Room. In *The Political Economy of Policy Reform*, ed. John Williamson. Washington: Institute for International Economics.

Sadowski, Rafał. 2014. Russia Is Blocking a Free Trade Area between the EU and Ukraine. Analyses (September 17). Warsaw: Centre for Eastern Studies.

Sarna, Arkadiusz. 2014. Transformation of Ukrainian Agriculture: From Kolkhozy to Agro-holdings. Commentary 127 (February 6). Warsaw: Centre for Eastern Studies.

Schadler, Susan. 2014. *Ukraine: Stress at the IMF*. Policy Brief 49 (October). Waterloo, Canada: Centre for International Governance Innovation.

Semak, Ihor. 2014. The Stumbling Stones on the Lustration Path. VoxUkraine, December 9.

Shanghai Ranking Consultancy. 2014. Academic Ranking of World Universities. Available at www.shanghairanking.com/ARWU2014.html (accessed on January 22, 2015).

Shemshuchenko, Yuriy. 2011. Trends in the Development of the Higher Education System in the Ukraine in the Context of the Bologna Process. In *Dialogue of Cultures under Globalization*, eds. A. S. Zapesotsky and S. R. Abramov. St. Petersburg, Russia: St. Petersburg University of the Humanities and Social Science.

Shepotylo, Oleksandr. 2010. A Gravity Model of Net Benefits of EU Membership: The Case of Ukraine. *Journal of Economic Integration* 25, no. 4 (December): 676–702.

Shepotylo, Oleksandr. 2013. *Export Potential, Uncertainty, and Regional Integration: Choice of Trade Policy for the Ukraine.* Working Paper. Kyiv: Kyiv School of Economics.

Shevchenko, Natalya, and Thomas Otten. 2014. *Tax Code of Ukraine: Development, Impact and Application Issues.* Policy Paper Series 08/2014 (June). Kyiv: German Advisory Group and Otten Consulting LLC.

Shleifer, Andrei, and Robert W. Vishny. 1998. *The Grabbing Hand: Government Pathologies and Their Cures.* Cambridge, MA: Harvard University Press.

Shleifer, Andrei, and Daniel Treisman. 2000. *Without a Map: Political Tactics and Economic Reform in Russia.* Cambridge, MA: MIT Press.

Sidorenko, Sergey. 2014. Prezident VK: 'Lyustratsiya byvshei vlasti, kak takovaya, vpolne priemlema' [President of the Venice Commission: 'Lustration of the Former Power As Such Is Fully Acceptable']. *Ekonomichna pravda*, December 12.

Snyder, Timothy. 2013. A Way Out for Ukraine. *New York Review of Books*, December 5.

Snyder, Timothy. 2014a. Don't Let Putin Grab Ukraine. *New York Times*, February 3.

Snyder, Timothy. 2014b. Crimea: Putin vs. Reality. *New York Review of Books*, March 7.

Snyder, Timothy. 2014c. Fascism, Russia, and Ukraine. *New York Review of Books*, March 20.

Socor, Vladimir. 2014. Russia Suspends Natural Gas Supplies to Ukraine. *Eurasia Daily Monitor*, June 19.

Soros, George. 2014. Sustaining Ukraine's Breakthrough. Project Syndicate, February 26.

Speck, Ulrich. 2014. Postponing the Trade Agreement with Ukraine: Bad Move, EU. Carnegie Europe, September 30.

Staats, Johann-Friedrich. 2011. Lustration—oder die Überprüfung der Richter und Staatsanwälte aus der DDR. In *Die Einheit: Juristische Hintergründe und Problems. Deutschland im Jahr 1990*, ed. Klaus Bästlein. Berlin: Landesbeauftragter f. d. Unterlagen d. Staatssicherheitsdienstes d. ehemaligen DDR.

Staats, Johann-Friedrich. 2012. Die Überprüfung der Richter und Staatsanwälte aus der DDR und die Strafverfahren wegen Rechtsbeugung. In *Von der SED-Diktatur zum Rechtsstaat: Der Umgang mit Recht und Justiz in der SBZ/DDR*, eds. Andreas Apelt, Robert Grünbaum, and Martin Gutzeit. Berlin: Metropol Verlag.

Stan, Lavinia. 2009. *Transitional Justice in Eastern Europe and the Former Soviet Union: Reckoning with the Communist Past.* New York: Routledge.

Stanisławski, Wojciech. 2005. *The Orange Ribbon. A Calendar of the Political Crisis in Ukraine (Autumn 2004).* Warsaw: Centre for Eastern Studies.

Stecklow, Steve, Elizabeth Piper, and Oleksandr Akymenko. 2014. Special Report: How Scams and Shakedowns Brought Ukraine to Its Knees. Reuters, August 7.

Stiglitz, Joseph E. 2002. *Globalization and Its Discontents.* New York: Norton.

Stubenhoff, Heinz. 2011. Fällt das Moratorium auf den Kauf landwirtschaftlicher Flächen. Newsletter (March). Berlin: Deutsche Beratergruppe.

Sushko, Oleksandr, Olga Zelinska, Robert Khorolskyy, Veronika Movchan, Iryna Solonenko, Viktoria Gumeniuk, and Vadym Triukhan. 2012. *EU-Ukraine Association Agreement: Guideline for Reforms*, KAS Policy Paper 20. Kyiv: Konrad-Adenauer-Stiftung (Ukraine Office) and Institute for Euro-Atlantic Cooperation.

Tanzi, Vito. 2011. *Government versus Markets: The Changing Economic Role of the State.* New York: Cambridge University Press.

Tanzi, Vito, and Hamid Davoodi. 1997. *Corruption, Public Investment, and Growth.* IMF Working Paper 139. Washington: International Monetary Fund.

Tanzi, Vito, and Ludger Schuknecht. 2000. *Public Spending in the 20th Century.* Cambridge: Cambridge University Press.

Tarr, David. 2012. *The Eurasian Customs Union among Russia, Belarus and Kazakhstan: Can It Succeed Where Its Predecessor Failed?* Working Paper. Moscow: New Economic School.

Thiessen, Ulrich. 2001. *Presumptive Taxation for Small Enterprises in Ukraine.* Working Paper 6. Kyiv: Institute for Economic Research and Policy Consulting.

Tilly, Charles. 1992. *Coercion, Capital and European States, AD 990–1992.* Hoboken, NJ: Wiley-Blackwell.

Times Higher Education. 2014. World University Rankings. Available at www.timeshighereducation.co.uk/world-university-rankings/2013-14/world-ranking (accessed on January 22, 2015).

Timoshenko, Viktor. 1998. Vse bogatye lyudi Ukrainy zarabotali svoy capital na rossiyskom gaze [All Rich People in Ukraine Made Their Capital on Russian Gas]. *Nezavisimaya Gazeta*, October 16.

Tkachenko, Lidia. 2013. Posledstviya vozmozhnoi otmeny pensionnoi reformy [Consequence of a Possible Cancellation of the Pension Reform]. *Zerkalo nedeli*, April 19.

Transparency International. 2013. Corruption Perceptions Index 2013. Berlin.

Treisman, Daniel. 2014. The Political Economy of Change after Communism. In *The Great Rebirth: Lessons from the Victory of Capitalism over Communism*, eds. Anders Åslund and Simeon Djankov. Washington: Peterson Institute for International Economics.

UNDP (United Nations Development Programme). 2014. *Human Development Report: Sustaining Human Progress: Reducing Vulnerabilities and Building Resilience.* New York.

UNECE (United Nations Economic Commission for Europe). 2000. *Economic Survey of Europe 2000*, no. 1. New York.

UNECE (United Nations Economic Commission for Europe). 2004. *Economic Survey of Europe 2004*, no. 2. New York.

Vashchenko, Yuliya. 2013. National Regulatory Authorities in the Energy Sector of Ukraine: Problems of the Legal Status in the Context of the European Integration and the Administrative Reform. *Jurisprudence* 20, no. 3: 1231–48.

Volkov, Vadim. 2002. *Violent Entrepreneurs: The Use of Force in the Making of Russian Capitalism.* Ithaca, NY: Cornell University Press.

Von Cramon-Taubadel, Stephan, Sebastian Hess, and Bernhard Bruemmer. 2010. *A Preliminary Analysis of the Impact of a Ukraine-EU Free Trade Agreement on Agriculture.* Policy Research Working Paper 5264 (April). Washington: World Bank.

Von Hirschhausen, Christian. 1999. Gas Sector Restructuring in Ukraine: Import Dependence, Price Formation, and Socio-Economic Effects. In *Ukraine at the Crossroads: Economic Reform in International Perspective*, ed. Axel Siedenberg and Lutz Hoffmann. Heidelberg, Germany and New York: Physica-Verlag.

Vorozhbyt, Olha. 2014. The Ex-President's Baggage. *The Ukrainian Week*, September 18.

Vyshynsky, Andriy. 2014a. Akhmetov i 'Ugol Ukrainy:' skhema vremen ATO [Akhmetov and Ukraine Coal: A Scheme during the Anti-Terrorist Operation]. *Ekonomichna pravda*, August 5.

Vyshynsky, Andriy. 2014b. Kak Yatsenyuk i Khomenko prikrylis' Yevrosoyuzom [How Yatsenyuk and Khomenko Used the European Union As Their Cover]. *Zerkalo nedeli*, August 22.

Weber, Max. 1922 (reprint 1980). *Wirtschaft und Gesellschaft [Economy and Society].* Tübingen: Mohr.

Williamson, John. 1990. *Latin American Adjustment: How Much Has Happened?* Washington: Institute for International Economics.

Williamson, John, ed. 1994. *The Political Economy of Policy Reform.* Washington: Institute for International Economics.

Williamson, Oliver E. 1975. *Markets and Hierarchies.* New York: Free Press.

Wilson, Andrew. 2000. *The Ukrainians. Unexpected Nation.* New Haven, CT: Yale University Press.

Wilson, Andrew. 2002. *The Ukrainians. Unexpected Nation,* 2d ed. New Haven: Yale University Press.

Wilson, Andrew. 2005. *Ukraine's Orange Revolution.* New Haven, CT: Yale University Press.

Wolczuk, Roman. 2002. *Ukraine's Foreign and Security Policy 1991–2000. Basees/Curzon Series on Russian and East European Studies.* New York: RoutledgeCurzon.

World Bank. 1994. *Averting the Old Age Crisis: Policies to Protect the Old and Promote Growth.* Oxford and Washington: Oxford University Press and World Bank.

World Bank. 2003. *Empowerment Case Studies: Russian Federation: Coal Sector Adjustment Loans.* Washington.

World Bank. 2012a. *Assessment of Costs and Benefits of the Customs Union for Kazakhstan.* Report 65977-KZ. Washington.

World Bank. 2012b. *Europe and Central Asia Balancing Act: Cutting Subsidies, Protecting Affordability, and Investing in the Energy Sector in Eastern Europe and Central Asia Region.* Report 69447-ECA (June). Washington.

World Bank. 2013. *Residential Gas and District Heating Tariffs in Ukraine* (October). Washington.

World Bank. 2014a. *World Development Indicators.* Washington. Available at http://data.worldbank.org/data-catalog/world-development-indicators (accessed on September 18, 2014).

World Bank. 2014b. *Ukraine: Special Focus: Structural Reforms,* October 2. Washington.

Yatsenyuk, Arseniy. 2014a. Vstupitelnoye slovo Premyer-Ministra Ukrainy Arseniya Yatsenyuka na zasedanii Pravitel'stva 3 Sentyabrya 2014 goda [Introductory Words of Ukraine's Prime Minister Arseniy Yatsenyuk at the Government Meeting, September 3, 2014]. Ukraine Government Portal, September 3.

Yatsenyuk, Arseniy. 2014b. Vstupitelnoye slovo Premyer-Ministra Ukrainy Arseniya Yatsenyuka na zasedanii Pravitel'stva 9 dekabrya 2014 goda [Introductory Words of Ukraine's Prime Minister Arseniy Yatsenyuk at the Government Meeting, December 9, 2014]. Ukraine Government Portal, December 9.

Yatsenyuk, Arseniy. 2014c. Vstupitelnoye slovo Premyer-ministra Ukrainy Arseniya Yatsenyuka na zasedanii Pravitel'stva 9 aprelya 2014 g [Opening Remarks by Prime Minister of Ukraine Arseniy Yatsenyuk at a meeting of the Government on April 9, 2014]. Ukraine Government Portal.

Zachmann, Georg, and Ricardo Giucci. 2014. *Short-Term Gas Supply Options for Ukraine.* Policy Briefing Series 06/2014 (June). Berlin/Kyiv: German Advisory Group, Institute for Economic Research and Policy Consulting.

Notable Politicians
and Businessmen

Abromavičius, Aivaras. Businessman and state official. Born in 1976. Partner and fund manager of East Capital (2002–14), minister of economy and trade (since December 2014).

Akhmetov, Rinat L. Businessman and Ukraine's richest man, based in Donetsk. Born in 1966. Major owner of System Capital Management (founded in 2000), member of the Supreme Rada for the party of Regions (2006–12), owner of Shakhtyar Donetsk soccer club.

Arbuzov, Serhiy. State official. Born in 1976. Director of PrivatBank and Ukreximbank (2000s), governor of the National Bank of Ukraine (2010–12), and first deputy prime minister (2012–14).

Azarov, Mykola Y. State official. Born in 1947. Deputy director of Research Institute for Mining Geology (1984–95), head of the State Tax Administration (1996–2000), minister of finance and first deputy prime minister (2002–05; 2006–07), minister of finance (2006–07), prime minister under Yanukovych (2010–14).

Bakai, Ihor M. Gas trader. Born in 1963. Head of Naftogaz Ukrainy (1998–2000) and of the presidential administration's property management (2003–04). Russian citizen since 2005.

Bilous, Ihor. State official. Born in 1978. Investment banker at UBS (2005–13), chairman of the State Fiscal Service of Ukraine (2014–15).

Boholiubov, Hennadiy B. Businessman and one of Ukraine's richest men, based in Dnipropetrovsk. Born in 1962. Cofounder and coowner of Privat Group and PrivatBank (since 1992).

Boyko, Yuriy A. Businessman and state official. Born in 1958. Chair of Lysychansk Oil Refinery (1999–2001), UkrTatNafta (2001–02), and Naftogaz Ukrainy (2002–05); minister of fuel and energy (2006–07), minister of energy and coal industry (2010–12), and vice prime minister (2012–14).

Chernomydrin, Viktor S. Russian state official. Born in 1938, died in 2010. Minister of gas industry of the Soviet Union (1985–89), transformed the Ministry of Gas Industry into Gazprom (1989). Deputy prime minister of Russia (1992) and prime minister (1992–98). Russia's ambassador to Ukraine (2001–09).

Firtash, Dmytro V. Gas trader. Born in 1965. Coowner of RusUkrEnergo since its creation from Eural Trans Gas (in 2004), head of the board of directors of Group DF (since 2007), and owner of Ukraine's Inter TV channel (since 2013).

Groisman, Volodymyr B. Politician. Born in 1978. Mayor of Vinnytsia (2006–14), minister of regional policy (2014), deputy prime minister (February–November 2014), chair of the Supreme Rada (November 2014).

Hontareva, Valeriya A. Banker. Born in 1964. Chair of Investment Capital Ukraina (2007–14), head of the Supervisory Board of Bank Avangard (2013–14), chair of the National Bank of Ukraine (since 2014).

Jaresko, Natalie A. Businesswoman and state official. Born in 1965. Head of the economics section of the US Embassy in Ukraine (1992–95), executive vice president (1998–2001) and then president and CEO of Western NIS Enterprise Fund (2001–14), minister of finance (since December 2014).

Klitschko, Vitaliy V. Heavyweight boxing champion and politician. Born in 1971. Founder of the political party "Punch" (Ukrainian Democratic Alliance for Reform, UDAR) (2010), with his party coming in third with 42 seats in the 2012 parliamentary elections; elected mayor of Kyiv (in 2014).

Kliuev, Andriy P. Businessman and politician from Donetsk. Born in 1964. Worked in regional leadership positions in Donetsk (1994–2002) before becoming vice prime minister for energy under Yanukovych (2003–04); minister of economic development and trade and first vice prime minister (2010–12), secretary of the National Security and Defense Council (2012–14).

Kobolyev, Andriy. Businessman. Born in 1978. Worked at PricewatehouseCoopers (1999–2002), specialist in the Economy and Price Policy Department of Naftogaz (2002–10), CEO of Naftogaz (since 2014).

Kolomoiskiy, Ihor V. Businessman and one of Ukraine's richest men based in Dnipropetrovsk. Born in 1964. Major owner of Privat Group, cofounder of PrivatBank and head of its board of directors (since 1992), owner of Dnipr and KrivBass soccer clubs, governor of Dnipropetrovsk Oblast (since 2014).

Kravchuk, Leonid M. President. Born in 1934. Various positions in the Ideological Department of the Central Committee of the Communist Party of Ukraine (1960-88), chair of the Supreme Rada (1990-91), and president of Ukraine (1991-94).

Kuchma, Leonid D. President. Born in 1938. Was a professor, engineer at Baikonur space center (1960-82) and manager of Pivdenmash company, the giant rocket factory in Dnipropetrovsk (1986-92); prime minister (1992-93) and president of Ukraine (1994-2004).

Kvit, Serhiy M. Academic and state official. Born in 1965. Doctoral degree in journalism at Kyiv National Taras Shevchenko University (1997), and defended his thesis at the Ukrainian Free University in Munich (2001). Worked in Ukrainian press (1991-2001), dean of the Faculty of Social Sciences and Social Technologies at the Kyiv-Mohyla Academy (2001-07) and its president (2007-14), minister of education and sciences (since February 2014).

Kvitashvili, Aleksandre. State official. Born in 1970. Director of the East-West Institute (since 2004) and minister of Labor, Health and Social Affairs of Georgia (2008-10), minister of Health of Ukraine (December 2014).

Lazarenko, Pavlo I. Businessman and state official. Born in 1953. Driver and senior agronomist at a kolkhoz (1970-85), representative of the president in Dnipropetrovsk (1992-95), first deputy prime minister (1995-96) and prime minister (1996-97). In jail in the United States for money laundering (since 1999).

Lutsenko, Yuriy V. Politician. Born in 1964. Engineer and constructor at Rivne GazTron plant (1989-96), leader of the popular movement Ukraine without Kuchma (2001), a leader of the Orange Revolution, minister of interior affairs (2005-06, 2007-10), leader of Poroshenko Bloc in parliament (since October 2014).

Lyashko, Oleh V. Politician. Born in 1972. Political magazine editor (1992-2006), deputy of Tymoshenko Bloc (2006-07). Formed the Radical Party (2011), was its presidential candidate (May 2014), and leads his party faction in parliament (since October 2014).

Lytvyn, Volodymyr M. Politician. Born in 1956. Professor of history at Kyiv State University (1978-90 and since 2006), head of the presidential administration (1999-2002), chair of the Supreme Rada (2002-06 and 2008-12).

Moroz, Oleksandr O. Politician. Born in 1944. Head of the Socialist Part of Ukraine (since 1991), presidential candidate (1999 and 2004), and speaker of the Supreme Rada (1994–98 and 2006–07).

Petrenko, Pavlo D. State official. Born in 1979. Worked in private law (2001–10) before becoming a deputy of the SupremeVerkhovn Rada (2012–14). Minister of Justice (since 2014).

Pinchuk, Victor M. Businessman and one of Ukraine's richest men, based in Dnipropetrovsk. Born in 1960. Engineer at various pipe plants (1981–83), founder and major owner of the Interpipe Group (in 1990; renamed EastOne in 2007).

Poroshenko, Petro O. Businessman and president. Born in 1965. Held top management positions at various industrial companies (since 1990). Major owner of UkrPromInvest Group (founded in 1993), secretary of the National Security and Defense Council (2005), chair of the Council of the National Bank of Ukraine (since 2007), minister for foreign affairs (2009–10), and minister of trade and economic development (2012). Elected president of Ukraine (May 2014).

Pynzenyk, Viktor M. Politician and economist. Born in 1954. Minister of economy and deputy prime minister for economy (1992–93), deputy prime minister for economic reforms (1994–96 and 1996–97), minister of finance (2005–06, 2007–09), deputy of the Supreme Rada for UDAR (2012–14), and the Poroshenko Bloc (since 2014).

Rybachuk, Oleh B. State official and civil activist. Born in 1958. Head of the foreign affairs department of the National Bank of Ukraine (1992–99), chief of staff of Prime Minister Viktor Yushchenko (1999–2001), deputy prime minister for European integration (2005) and chief of staff of President Yushchenko (2005–06). Now civil activist.

Semerak, Ostap M. Politician. Born in 1972. Deputy of the Tymoshenko Bloc (2007–12), minister of the Cabinet of Ministers of the Yatsenyuk government (in 2014), deputy for the People's Front (since October 2014).

Sheremeta, Pavlo M. Academic. Born in 1971. Founding dean of Kyiv-Mohyla Business School (1999–2008), director of MBA program at International Institute of Management in Kyiv, president of Kyiv School of Economics (2013–14), minister of economic development and trade (in 2014).

Taruta, Serhiy O. Businessman. Born in 1955. Held various top management positions at AzovStal factory (1979–95), coowner of Industrial Union of Donbas (founded in 1995), governor of Donetsk Regional State Administration (in 2014).

Turchynov, Oleksandr V. Politician. Born in 1964. First deputy prime minister under Tymoshenko (2007–10), chair of the Supreme Rada (2014), secretary of the National Security and Defense Council of Ukraine (since December 2014).

Tyhypko, Serhiy L. Businessman and politician. Born in 1960. Chair of Privat-Bank (1992–97), deputy prime minister for economy (1997–99), minister of economy (1999–2000), chair of the National Bank of Ukraine (2002–04), head of Viktor Yanukovych's presidential campaign (2004), deputy prime minister (2010–11).

Tymoshenko, Yulia V. Politician. Born in 1960. CEO and coowner of United Energy Systems of Ukraine (1995–97), deputy prime minister for fuel and energy (1999–2001), prime minister (2005, 2007–10), leader of the Fatherland party in the Supreme Rada since the 2014 elections.

Yanukovych, Viktor F. President. Born in 1950. Electrician (1972), senior manager in various transportation companies in Yenakiyeve and Donetsk (1976–96), governor of Donetsk oblast (1997–2002), prime minister (2002–05 and 2006–07), president of Ukraine (2010–14) until the Supreme Rada voted to remove him from his post (in February 2014).

Yarosh, Dmytro A. Born in 1971. Founder of the nationalist organization Trident (1994) and joined other nationalist groups such as Stephan Bandera Organization (1994), which later became a main part of the Right Sector party (2014). Right Sector deputy in the Supreme Rada (since 2014).

Yatsenyuk, Arseniy P. State official. Born in 1974. Senior partner in a law firm (1992–97), minister of economy of Crimea (2001–03), first deputy chair of the National Bank of Ukraine (2005), minister of economy (2005–06), minister for foreign affairs (2007), speaker of parliament (2007–08), prime minister of Ukraine (since February 2014).

Yekhanurov, Yuriy I. State official. Born in 1948. Various positions in the construction industry (1967–91), head of the State Property Fund (1994–97), minister of economy (1997), first deputy prime minister (1999–2001), prime minister (2005–06), minister of defense (2007–09), and first deputy head of the Presidential Secretariat (2009–10).

Yushchenko, Viktor A. President. Born in 1954. Accounting associate at a kolkhoz (1975), top manager of various banks (1976–93), chair of the National Bank of Ukraine (1993–99), prime minister (1999–2001), and president of Ukraine (2005–10).

Chronology of Events

1990

March 4   Ukrainian parliamentary elections; communists retain power

July 16   Ukrainian parliament adopts Declaration of State Sovereignty

1991

March 17   Referendum on the future of the USSR

August 1   US President George H. W. Bush makes "Chicken Kiev" speech in the Ukrainian parliament

August 19–21   Abortive Moscow coup

April 24   Ukraine declares independence

August 30   Communist Party of Ukraine is prohibited

December 1   National referendum supports Ukrainian independence; Leonid Kravchuk is elected Ukraine's first president

December 8   Treaty between Belarus, Russia, and Ukraine dissolves the USSR

December 21   Eleven Soviet republics form the Commonwealth of Independent States in Alma-Ata

1992

January 2	Russia liberalizes prices, forcing Ukraine to do the same
September 3	Ukraine joins the International Monetary Fund (IMF)
October 13	Leonid Kuchma is confirmed as prime minister
November 18	Kuchma receives special powers on economic policy for six months

1993

January 26	Viktor Yushchenko is appointed chair of the National Bank of Ukraine (NBU)
February 7	Parliament ratifies Kuchma's economic reform program
June	Ten-day strike by coal miners in Donbas
June 23	Parliament rejects Kuchma's improved economic reform program
June 24	Russia and Ukraine conclude bilateral free trade agreement
August 31	Kuchma resigns
September	Ruble zone finally ends
September 22	Yuhym Zviahilsky is appointed acting prime minister
September 24	Kravchuk and parliament agree to hold early parliamentary and presidential elections
October	Kravchuk attempts to return to command economy

1994

January 14	Presidents Boris Yeltsin, Bill Clinton, and Leonid Kravchuk sign Trilateral Accord on Ukraine's denuclearization
April 10	Second round of parliamentary elections
June 16	Kravchuk appoints Vitaliy Masol prime minister
July 10	Second round of presidential election; Kuchma defeats Kravchuk
October 11	Kuchma's presidential address on radical market economic reform
October 26	First IMF agreement is approved

November	Parliament approves freeing of the exchange rate and liberalizing prices
November 22	The Rada ratifies the Nuclear Non-Proliferation Treaty (NPT)
December 5	Ukraine signs the Budapest memorandum on the country's denuclearization with security assurances from the United States, United Kingdom, and Russia

1995

March 1	Masol resigns and First Deputy Prime Minister Yevhen Marchuk is appointed acting prime minister
April 4	Kuchma holds his second annual address on "correction" of reforms
June 8	Kuchma appoints Yevhen Marchuk prime minister
October 11	Parliament approves Marchuk's economic program of "corrected reforms"

1996

April 19–20	G-7 meeting in Moscow on closure of Chernobyl nuclear power plant
May 27	Kuchma fires Marchuk and appoints Pavlo Lazarenko prime minister
June 28	New constitution is adopted
June	Ukraine frees itself of nuclear weapons
September 2–16	New Ukrainian currency hryvnia replaces karbovanets

1997

May 28	Ukraine and Russia sign agreement on the division of the former Soviet Black Sea Fleet
May 31	Kuchma and Yeltsin sign a friendship treaty between Russia and Ukraine
June 19	Kuchma dismisses Lazarenko
July 9	Kuchma signs NATO-Ukraine special partnership charter at Madrid summit

| July 16 | Valeriy Pustovoitenko is confirmed as prime minister |
| August 25 | IMF approves one-year stand-by credit for Ukraine |

1998

March 1	Treaty on partnership and cooperation between Ukraine and the European Union comes into effect
March 29	Parliamentary elections
August 17	Russian financial crisis leads to sharp hryvnia devaluation
September 4	IMF approves a three-year credit for Ukraine under the Extended Fund Facility
November	Kuchma rejects IMF advice to combat financial crisis, calling for currency controls, monetary expansion, and limits on NBU independence

1999

February 17	Parliament strips Lazarenko's immunity, and he is arrested in the United States three days later
July	Parliament agrees to deploy 800 soldiers for peacekeeping in Kosovo
November 14	Second round of presidential election; Kuchma is reelected
December	Kuchma abolishes collective farms; land to be divided among farm workers with the right to rent the land but not to sell it
December 22	Viktor Yushchenko replaces Pustovoitenko as prime minister

2000

March	The IMF accuses Ukraine of manipulating its currency reserves
April 6	Parliament adopts big economic reform package
September 16	Journalist Heorhiy Gongadze is murdered
November 28	Socialist Party leader Oleksandr Moroz publicizes a tape recording from Kuchma's office of illegal actions against Gongadze
December 15	Chornobyl nuclear power plant is shut down

2001

January 19	Kuchma dismisses Deputy Prime Minister Yuliya Tymoshenko
February	Large demonstrations call for Kuchma's impeachment
February 13	Tymoshenko is arrested on charges of tax evasion
March 27	Tymoshenko is released from detention
April 26	Parliament sacks Yushchenko's government through a no-confidence vote
May 29	Anatoliy Kinakh is confirmed as prime minister

2002

March 31	Parliamentary elections
September 16	Large demonstration in Kyiv demands Kuchma's resignation
November 16	Kuchma dismisses Kinakh's government
November 21	Viktor Yanukovych becomes prime minister

2003

May	Ukraine reforms tax code, introducing 13 percent flat income tax
October	Border dispute with Russia erupts on the island of Tuzla

2004

June	Viktor Pinchuk and Rinat Akhmetov buy steelworks Kryvorizhstal
July 26	Russian president Vladimir Putin meets Kuchma and Yanukovych in Yalta
September 5	Presidential candidate Viktor Yushchenko is poisoned
October 26–29	Putin meets Kuchma in Kyiv and campaigns for Yanukovych
October 31	First round of presidential election; Yushchenko wins with slight margin
November 12–13	Putin meets Kuchma
November 21	Second round of presidential election; Yanukovych wins; Yushchenko claims election rigged

November 22	Mass demonstrations in Kyiv against rigged election start Orange Revolution
December 2	Kuchma meets Putin in a Moscow airport (12th meeting in 2004)
December 3	Ukraine's Supreme Court recognizes massive electoral fraud and orders a rerun of the second round
December 8	Parliament passes constitutional amendments and other legislative measures to resolve the presidential election crisis
December 26	Rerun of the second round of presidential election; Yushchenko wins

2005

January 23	Yushchenko is sworn in as Ukraine's new president
January 24	Yuschenko nominates Yuliya Tymoshenko as prime minister; he makes first trip abroad to Moscow
February 21	The European Union and Ukraine sign action plan as part of the European Neighborhood Policy
March 19	Putin meets Yushchenko in Kyiv
September 8	Yushchenko sacks both Tymoshenko's government and Secretary of National Security Petro Poroshenko
September 22	Yuriy Yekhanurov is approved as prime minister
October 24	Kryvorizhstal is reauctioned
December 1	The European Union grants Ukraine market economy status

2006

January 1	New constitution comes into force transforming Ukraine into parliamentary-presidential republic; Russia cuts gas supply to Ukraine
January 4	Ukraine signs agreement on gas supply with Gazprom and RosUkrEnergo
February 17	The United States recognizes Ukraine's market economy status
March 26	Parliamentary elections
August 4	Parliament confirms Yanukovych as prime minister

2007

March 21	Parliament approves Yushchenko's choice for foreign minister Arseniy Yatsenyuk
April 2	Yushchenko issues a decree to dismiss parliament and calls a snap election
May 27	Agreement is reached between Yushchenko, Yanukovych, and Moroz to hold early parliamentary election
September 30	Extraordinary parliamentary elections
December 18	Tymoshenko is appointed prime minister

2008

January 15	Yushchenko, Tymoshenko, and Yatsenyuk sign a letter to NATO secretary general asking for membership action plan (MAP) for Ukraine
April 3–4	NATO summit in Bucharest does not offer MAP to Ukraine
May 16	Ukraine becomes 152nd member of the World Trade Organization
August 8–12	Russia-Georgia war in South Ossetia and Georgia
September 3	Our Ukraine faction withdraws from a coalition with Tymoshenko's Bloc
October 26	Agreement between government and IMF on economic program supported by a $16.5 billion loan
October 31	Parliament passes anticrisis legislation
November 5	IMF approves a two-year Stand-By Arrangement for $16.5 billion to help Ukraine restore financial and economic stability

2009

January 1	Russia cuts off gas supplies again to Ukraine
January 18–19	Tymoshenko and Putin reach a deal, resulting in gas delivery from Russia restarting the next day
May 7	The EU officially launches its Eastern Partnership with six post-Soviet countries, including Ukraine

2010

January 1 — The customs union between Russia, Belarus, and Kazakhstan comes into existence

February 7 — Yanukovych wins the second round of Ukraine's presidential elections

August 11 — The IMF approves a $15.1 billion stand-by agreement with Ukraine

October 1 — The Constitutional Court abolishes the parliamentary-presidential constitution of 2004 and restores the constitution of 1996

December 9 — Yanukovych announces a major cabinet change, reducing the number of ministries and appointing members of his "family"

2011

July 8 — Parliament passes a pension reform bill, moderating government spending and increasing the retirement age

August 5 — Tymoshenko arrested on charges of abuse of power and sentenced to seven years in prison

October — Several CIS countries, including Ukraine, conclude a multilateral CIS free trade agreement

2012

July 19 — Yanukovych and the EU presidents initial the association agreement in Brussels

October 28 — The Party of Regions wins parliamentary elections

2013

November 21 — The Ukrainian Cabinet of Ministers decides "to stop the process of preparation for the signing of the association agreement," causing demonstrators to rally in Maidan, Kyiv's Independence Square

November 28–29 — Yanukovych attends the Eastern Partnership summit in Vilnius but does not sign the association agreement

November 30 — Nighttime crackdown by the government's riot police on 300 peaceful protesters in Maidan triggers a large rally in Kyiv the next morning

| December 1 | Protesters establish a tent camp on Maidan, and occupy Kyiv City Hall as well as two nearby public buildings. The protest rallies swell to numbers as large as 800,000, demanding the signing of the EU Association Agreement and early elections |
| December 17 | Putin agrees with Yanukovych that Russia will buy $15 billion of Ukrainian government bonds and cut its price for natural gas |

2014

January	Massive protests continue and spread to other regions of Ukraine; clashes with police lead to the killing of several protesters
January 16	Yanukovych forces the parliament to adopt nine harsh anti-protest laws
January 25–26	Yanukovych loses control over Ukraine as protesters occupy government buildings in the western half of the country
January 28	Prime Minister Mykola Azarov resigns and the antiprotest laws that stoked the protests are repealed
February 18–20	Riot police storm the Maidan; 100 protesters are killed
February 20	Mass defections occur in the Party of Regions in parliament, disintegrating one of the main foundations of Yanukovych's power
February 21	Yanukovych and opposition leaders sign a deal calling for the formation of an interim government, constitutional changes, and early presidential elections by December. Parliament reinstates the 2004 Constitution, and Tymoshenko is freed from jail
February 22–23	Yanukovych flees Kiev. The parliament votes to oust him from office, and sets early presidential elections for May 25. Oleksandr Turchynov is appointed acting president
February 27	Interim government is formed, led by Prime Minister Yatsenyuk; Russian "small green men" occupy the Crimean parliament in Simferopol
March 6	The United States sets its first round of sanctions against Russia in response to Russia's intervention in Crimea
March 17	European Union sanctions are announced
March 18	Russia annexes Crimea

April 7	Donetsk and Lugansk government buildings come under occupation by separatists
April 15	Turchynov announces the start of the government's antiterrorist operation (ATO) in eastern Ukraine
April 28	The United States announces new sanctions against 7 Russian officials and 17 companies linked to Putin
April 30	IMF approves a $17 billion stand-by loan for Ukraine
May 2	Serious unrest in Odessa; 52 people, mainly pro-Russian protesters, die in a building fire
May 25	Presidential elections held in Ukraine; Petro Poroshenko wins with 54.7 percent of the vote
May 29	Russia, Belarus, and Kazakhstan sign an agreement founding the Eurasian Economic Union
June 7	Poroshenko is sworn in as president of Ukraine
June 12	First reports of tanks and heavy armor entering eastern Ukraine from Russia
June 16	Russia cuts off gas supplies to Ukraine
June 27	Ukraine signs the EU Association Agreement and the Deep and Comprehensive Free Trade Agreement (DCFTA)
July 5	Ukrainian military forces retake Slovyansk
July 16	The United States introduces sectoral sanctions, notably financial sanctions, against Russia
July 17	Separatists in eastern Ukraine shoot down Malaysian Airlines flight MH17; all 298 people are killed
July 24	The majority coalition collapses and Yatsenyuk resigns, giving Poroshenko the opportunity to dissolve parliament
July 31	The European Union adopts sectoral sanctions against Russia, targeting banks, oil and military industries
August	Russia begins massive buildup of military forces at Ukrainian border; Ukrainian security forces surround the separatist strongholds of Donetsk and Luhansk
August 22	Russian regular forces "on vacation" pursue major offensive causing the Ukrainian forces heavy losses
August 25	Poroshenko dissolves parliament and calls for snap parliamentary elections on October 26

August 26	Putin meets Poroshenko in Minsk for closed-door talks
September 5	Ceasefire agreement signed in Minsk between Ukraine, Russia, and the Organization for Security and Cooperation in Europe (OSCE)
September 12	The European Union and Ukraine agree to postpone implementation of the association agreement until January 1, 2016
September 16	Parliament ratifies the EU Association Agreement/DCFTA, and legislates self-rule in the separatist-held regions
September 16	Parliament passes lustration law
September 19	Another agreement in Minsk between Ukraine, Russia, and the OSCE calls for a buffer zone and the removal of heavy weapons
September 25	Poroshenko outlines "Strategy 2020," a political and economic reform program to put Ukraine on the road toward applying for EU membership
October 9	Poroshenko signs the lustration law
October 14	Parliament adopts package of anticorruption laws
October 26	Parliamentary elections are held; the pro-European parties win big
November 21	Five-party coalition is formed and adopts a coalition agreement
November 27	Yatsenyuk is reappointed prime minister
December 2	The Cabinet of Ministers is appointed
December 9	The Cabinet of Ministers presents its program

Sources: Åslund (2009); Center for Strategic and International Studies, Ukraine Crisis timeline, 2014, http://csis.org/ukraine/index.htm#111; Dragon Capital, Ukrainian economy: Forecasts revised to factor in protracted military conflict, October 2, 2014.

Abbreviations

CEE	Central and Eastern Europe
CEE-10	ten CEE countries that joined the European Union in 2004 and 2007
CES	Common Economic Space (CIS)
CIS	Commonwealth of Independent States
CMEA	Council of Mutual Economic Assistance (also called COMECON)
CPSU	Communist Party of the Soviet Union
DCFTA	deep and comprehensive free trade agreement
EBRD	European Bank for Reconstruction and Development
ECB	European Central Bank
ECE	Economic Commission for Europe (United Nations)
EIB	European Investment Bank
ENP	European Neighborhood Policy
ENPI	European Neighborhood and Partnership Instrument
EU	European Union
EU-15	15 countries that were members of the European Union before 2004
FDI	foreign direct investment
FSR	former Soviet republic
FSU	former Soviet Union

FTA	free trade agreement
GATT	General Agreement on Tariffs and Trade
GDP	gross domestic product
GNP	gross national product
IFI	international financial institution
IMF	International Monetary Fund
MAP	membership action plan (to NATO)
NATO	North Atlantic Treaty Organization
NBU	National Bank of Ukraine
NERC	National Energy Regulatory Commission
OECD	Organization for Economic Cooperation and Development
OSCE	Organization for Security and Cooperation in Europe
PPP	purchasing power parities
SES	Single Economic Space (CIS)
SOE	state-owned enterprise
TACIS	Technical Assistance for the CIS
UNDP	United Nations Development Program
USAID	United States Agency for International Development
USSR	Union of Soviet Socialist Republics
VAT	value-added tax
WTO	World Trade Organization

Index

composition, 50
ignorance of, 62
slow transition to, 4
Martynenko, Mykola, Yushchenko support from, 71
medicine, Ukraine certification system, 214
Medvedev, Dmitry, meeting with Azarov, 9
Merkel, Angela, 9
metallurgical sector, energy savings in, 200
ministries, staff cuts, 142–43
Ministry of Education and Science, 216
Ministry of Finance, 175
Ministry of Information, 135
Ministry of Infrastructure, 135
Ministry of Regional Development, Construction, and Communal Services, 135, 200
Ministry of Revenues and Charges, 135
Ministry of Youth and Sports, 135
Mizsei, Kálmán, x
Moldova, 25
DCFTA with EU, 44
Eastern Partnership and, 42
financial crisis, 164
parliamentary elections, 116
parliamentary system, 128
poor economic performance in 1990s, 7
Russian trade sanctions, 48
Ukraine exports, 2005–13, 49t
money laundering, legislation against, 143
Montesquieu's principle of division of power, 129

Naftogaz, 84, 92, 187, 188
oil rig purchases, 93–94
Naftogaz Ukrainy, 186, 196
National Agency for Higher Education Quality, 218
national agency for the state service, 137
National Anti-Corruption Bureau, 144
National Bank of Ukraine (NBU), 36, 62, 85, 148, 179
estimates on condition of banks, 176
and exchange rate, 158–59
National Commission for the Struggle against Corruption, 144
national commission on information, 135
National Communal Services Regulatory Commission, 195
National Energy Regulatory Commission (NERC), 195
National Front, 118
national security, 41
of Ukraine, 188

nationalists
"historical compromise" with communists, 60
and Ukrainian independence, 147
nationality, Putin's definition by language and ethnicity, 19
natural gas, 92–93
domestic trade of, 28
as imports from Russia, 65
market for, 199
prices, 82, 84, 205
production, 186–87, 201
Russia cutoff to Ukraine and Europe, 76–77, 204–05
transit from Russia to Europe, 203–04
Ukraine as market for Europe, 205
Ukraine conflicts with Russia, 75–78
Ukraine consumption, 189
Ukraine reserves, 191
natural resource royalties, 174
Netherlands, public pension costs, 209
Nord Stream, 203–04
North Atlantic Treaty Organization (NATO), 41, 55, 70
Putin statements at Bucharest summit (2008), 19–20
tension between Putin and Ukraine over, 77
Ukraine conflicts with Russia, 75–78
Novinsky, Vadim, 29
"Novorossiya" (New Russia), 20
nuclear power stations, 198–99
nuisance taxes, 167

obshchak, 121
Odessa, military clashes, 18
oil
production, 201
transit from Russia to Europe, 203–04
oligarchs, 8, 10, 59, 61–67, 78
damage to assets, 23
decline in power, 26–32
and land ownership, 154
power of, 18
and reform failure, 191
in Ukraine, 30t
Yanukovych and, 80–82
open party lists, 126
Opposition Bloc, 117–18
Orange government, EU accession as goal, 43
Orange Revolution (2004), 42, 60, 68–72, 78, 223
avoiding mistakes of, 111–12
Orange Revolution, after parliament, 116

Other Publications from the
Peterson Institute for International Economics

* = out of print

POLICY ANALYSES IN INTERNATIONAL ECONOMICS Series

America in the World Economy: A Strategy for the 1990s* C. Fred Bergsten
1988 ISBN 0-88132-089-7

Managing the Dollar: From the Plaza to the Louvre* Yoichi Funabashi
1988, 2d ed. 1989 ISBN 0-88132-097-8

United States External Adjustment and the World Economy* William R. Cline
May 1989 ISBN 0-88132-048-X

Free Trade Areas and U.S. Trade Policy*
Jeffrey J. Schott, ed.
May 1989 ISBN 0-88132-094-3

Dollar Politics: Exchange Rate Policymaking in the United States* I. M. Destler and C. Randall Henning
September 1989 ISBN 0-88132-079-X

Latin American Adjustment: How Much Has Happened?* John Williamson, ed.
April 1990 ISBN 0-88132-125-7

The Future of World Trade in Textiles and Apparel* William R. Cline
1987, 2d ed. June 1999 ISBN 0-88132-110-9

Completing the Uruguay Round: A Results-Oriented Approach to the GATT Trade Negotiations* Jeffrey J. Schott, ed.
September 1990 ISBN 0-88132-130-3

Economic Sanctions Reconsidered (2 volumes)
Economic Sanctions Reconsidered: Supplemental Case Histories Gary Clyde Hufbauer, Jeffrey J. Schott, and Kimberly Ann Elliott
1985, 2d ed. Dec. 1990 ISBN cloth 0-88132-115-X/
paper 0-88132-105-2
Economic Sanctions Reconsidered: History and Current Policy Gary C. Hufbauer, Jeffrey J. Schott, and Kimberly Ann Elliott
December 1990 ISBN cloth 0-88132-140-0
ISBN paper 0-88132-136-2

Pacific Basin Developing Countries: Prospects for the Future* Marcus Noland
January 1991 ISBN cloth 0-88132-141-9
ISBN paper 0-88132-081-1

Currency Convertibility in Eastern Europe*
John Williamson, ed.
October 1991 ISBN 0-88132-128-1

International Adjustment and Financing: The Lessons of 1985-1991* C. Fred Bergsten, ed.
January 1992 ISBN 0-88132-112-5

North American Free Trade: Issues and Recommendations* Gary Clyde Hufbauer and Jeffrey J. Schott
April 1992 ISBN 0-88132-120-1

Narrowing the U.S. Current Account Deficit*
Alan J. Lenz
June 1992 ISBN 0-88132-103-6

The Economics of Global Warming
William R. Cline
June 1992 ISBN 0-88132-132-X

US Taxation of International Income:
Blueprint for Reform Gary Clyde Hufbauer, assisted by Joanna M. van Rooij
October 1992 ISBN 0-88132-134-6

Who's Bashing Whom? Trade Conflict in High-Technology Industries Laura D'Andrea Tyson
November 1992 ISBN 0-88132-106-0

Korea in the World Economy* Il SaKong
January 1993 ISBN 0-88132-183-4

Pacific Dynamism and the International Economic System* C. Fred Bergsten and Marcus Noland, eds.
May 1993 ISBN 0-88132-196-6

Economic Consequences of Soviet Disintegration* John Williamson, ed.
May 1993 ISBN 0-88132-190-7

Reconcilable Differences? United States-Japan Economic Conflict* C. Fred Bergsten and Marcus Noland
June 1993 ISBN 0-88132-129-X

Does Foreign Exchange Intervention Work?
Kathryn M. Dominguez and Jeffrey A. Frankel
September 1993 ISBN 0-88132-104-4

Sizing Up U.S. Export Disincentives*
J. David Richardson
September 1993 ISBN 0-88132-107-9

NAFTA: An Assessment Gary Clyde Hufbauer and Jeffrey J. Schott, rev. ed.
October 1993 ISBN 0-88132-199-0

Adjusting to Volatile Energy Prices
Philip K. Verleger, Jr.
November 1993 ISBN 0-88132-069-2

The Political Economy of Policy Reform
John Williamson, ed.
January 1994 ISBN 0-88132-195-8

Measuring the Costs of Protection in the United States Gary Clyde Hufbauer and Kimberly Ann Elliott
January 1994 ISBN 0-88132-108-7

The Dynamics of Korean Economic Development* Cho Soon
March 1994 ISBN 0-88132-162-1

Reviving the European Union*
C. Randall Henning, Eduard Hochreiter, and Gary Clyde Hufbauer, eds.
April 1994 ISBN 0-88132-208-3

China in the World Economy Nicholas R. Lardy
April 1994 ISBN 0-88132-200-8

Greening the GATT: Trade, Environment, and the Future Daniel C. Esty
July 1994 ISBN 0-88132-205-9

Western Hemisphere Economic Integration*
Gary Clyde Hufbauer and Jeffrey J. Schott
July 1994 ISBN 0-88132-159-1

Currencies and Politics in the United States, Germany, and Japan C. Randall Henning
September 1994 ISBN 0-88132-127-3

Estimating Equilibrium Exchange Rates
John Williamson, ed.
September 1994 ISBN 0-88132-076-5

Managing the World Economy: Fifty Years after Bretton Woods Peter B. Kenen, ed.
September 1994 ISBN 0-88132-212-1

Reciprocity and Retaliation in U.S. Trade Policy
Thomas O. Bayard and Kimberly Ann Elliott
September 1994 ISBN 0-88132-084-6

The Uruguay Round: An Assessment* Jeffrey J. Schott, assisted by Johanna Buurman
November 1994 ISBN 0-88132-206-7

Measuring the Costs of Protection in Japan*
Yoko Sazanami, Shujiro Urata, and Hiroki Kawai
January 1995 ISBN 0-88132-211-3

Foreign Direct Investment in the United States,
3d ed.   Edward M. Graham and Paul R. Krugman
January 1995   ISBN 0-88132-204-0

The Political Economy of Korea-United States
Cooperation*   C. Fred Bergsten and
Il SaKong, eds.
February 1995   ISBN 0-88132-213-X

International Debt Reexamined*
William R. Cline
February 1995   ISBN 0-88132-083-8

American Trade Politics, 3d ed.   I. M. Destler
April 1995   ISBN 0-88132-215-6

Managing Official Export Credits: The Quest for
a Global Regime*   John E. Ray
July 1995   ISBN 0-88132-207-5

Asia Pacific Fusion: Japan's Role in APEC*
Yoichi Funabashi
October 1995   ISBN 0-88132-224-5

Korea-United States Cooperation in the New
World Order*   C. Fred Bergsten and
Il SaKong, eds.
February 1996   ISBN 0-88132-226-1

Why Exports Really Matter!*
   ISBN 0-88132-221-0
Why Exports Matter More!*   ISBN 0-88132-229-6
J. David Richardson and Karin Rindal
July 1995; February 1996

Global Corporations and National Governments
Edward M. Graham
May 1996   ISBN 0-88132-111-7

Global Economic Leadership and the Group of
Seven   C. Fred Bergsten and C. Randall Henning
May 1996   ISBN 0-88132-218-0

The Trading System after the Uruguay Round*
John Whalley and Colleen Hamilton
July 1996   ISBN 0-88132-131-1

Private Capital Flows to Emerging Markets after
the Mexican Crisis*   Guillermo A. Calvo, Morris
Goldstein, and Eduard Hochreiter
September 1996   ISBN 0-88132-232-6

The Crawling Band as an Exchange Rate
Regime: Lessons from Chile, Colombia, and
Israel   John Williamson
September 1996   ISBN 0-88132-231-8

Flying High: Liberalizing Civil Aviation in the
Asia Pacific*   Gary Clyde Hufbauer and
Christopher Findlay
November 1996   ISBN 0-88132-227-X

Measuring the Costs of Visible Protection
in Korea*   Namdoo Kim
November 1996   ISBN 0-88132-236-9

The World Trading System: Challenges Ahead
Jeffrey J. Schott
December 1996   ISBN 0-88132-235-0

Has Globalization Gone Too Far?   Dani Rodrik
March 1997   ISBN paper 0-88132-241-5

Korea-United States Economic Relationship*
C. Fred Bergsten and Il SaKong, eds.
March 1997   ISBN 0-88132-240-7

Summitry in the Americas: A Progress Report
Richard E. Feinberg
April 1997   ISBN 0-88132-242-3

Corruption and the Global Economy
Kimberly Ann Elliott
June 1997   ISBN 0-88132-233-4

Regional Trading Blocs in the World Economic
System   Jeffrey A. Frankel
October 1997   ISBN 0-88132-202-4

Sustaining the Asia Pacific Miracle:
Environmental Protection and Economic
Integration   Andre Dua and Daniel C. Esty
October 1997   ISBN 0-88132-250-4

Trade and Income Distribution
William R. Cline
November 1997   ISBN 0-88132-216-4

Global Competition Policy   Edward M. Graham
and J. David Richardson
December 1997   ISBN 0-88132-166-4

Unfinished Business: Telecommunications after
the Uruguay Round   Gary Clyde Hufbauer and
Erika Wada
December 1997   ISBN 0-88132-257-1

Financial Services Liberalization in the WTO
Wendy Dobson and Pierre Jacquet
June 1998   ISBN 0-88132-254-7

Restoring Japan's Economic Growth
Adam S. Posen
September 1998   ISBN 0-88132-262-8

Measuring the Costs of Protection in China
Zhang Shuguang, Zhang Yansheng, and Wan
Zhongxin
November 1998   ISBN 0-88132-247-4

Foreign Direct Investment and Development:
The New Policy Agenda for Developing
Countries and Economies in Transition
Theodore H. Moran
December 1998   ISBN 0-88132-258-X

Behind the Open Door: Foreign Enterprises
in the Chinese Marketplace   Daniel H. Rosen
January 1999   ISBN 0-88132-263-6

Toward A New International Financial
Architecture: A Practical Post-Asia Agenda
Barry Eichengreen
February 1999   ISBN 0-88132-270-9

Is the U.S. Trade Deficit Sustainable?
Catherine L. Mann
September 1999   ISBN 0-88132-265-2

Safeguarding Prosperity in a Global Financial
System: The Future International Financial
Architecture, Independent Task Force Report
Sponsored by the Council on Foreign Relations
Morris Goldstein, Project Director
October 1999   ISBN 0-88132-287-3

Avoiding the Apocalypse: The Future of the
Two Koreas   Marcus Noland
June 2000   ISBN 0-88132-278-4

Assessing Financial Vulnerability: An Early
Warning System for Emerging Markets
Morris Goldstein, Graciela Kaminsky, and
Carmen Reinhart
June 2000   ISBN 0-88132-237-7

Global Electronic Commerce: A Policy Primer
Catherine L. Mann, Sue E. Eckert, and Sarah
Cleeland Knight
July 2000   ISBN 0-88132-274-1

The WTO after Seattle   Jeffrey J. Schott, ed.
July 2000   ISBN 0-88132-290-3

Intellectual Property Rights in the Global
Economy   Keith E. Maskus
August 2000   ISBN 0-88132-282-2

The Political Economy of the Asian Financial Crisis   Stephan Haggard
August 2000   ISBN 0-88132-283-0

Transforming Foreign Aid: United States Assistance in the 21st Century   Carol Lancaster
August 2000   ISBN 0-88132-291-1

Fighting the Wrong Enemy: Antiglobal Activists and Multinational Enterprises
Edward M. Graham
September 2000   ISBN 0-88132-272-5

Globalization and the Perceptions of American Workers   Kenneth Scheve and Matthew J. Slaughter
March 2001   ISBN 0-88132-295-4

World Capital Markets: Challenge to the G-10
Wendy Dobson and Gary Clyde Hufbauer, assisted by Hyun Koo Cho
May 2001   ISBN 0-88132-301-2

Prospects for Free Trade in the Americas
Jeffrey J. Schott
August 2001   ISBN 0-88132-275-X

Toward a North American Community: Lessons from the Old World for the New
Robert A. Pastor
August 2001   ISBN 0-88132-328-4

Measuring the Costs of Protection in Europe: European Commercial Policy in the 2000s
Patrick A. Messerlin
September 2001   ISBN 0-88132-273-3

Job Loss from Imports: Measuring the Costs
Lori G. Kletzer
September 2001   ISBN 0-88132-296-2

No More Bashing: Building a New Japan–United States Economic Relationship   C. Fred Bergsten, Takatoshi Ito, and Marcus Noland
October 2001   ISBN 0-88132-286-5

Why Global Commitment Really Matters!
Howard Lewis III and J. David Richardson
October 2001   ISBN 0-88132-298-9

Leadership Selection in the Major Multilaterals
Miles Kahler
November 2001   ISBN 0-88132-335-7

The International Financial Architecture: What's New? What's Missing?   Peter B. Kenen
November 2001   ISBN 0-88132-297-0

Delivering on Debt Relief: From IMF Gold to a New Aid Architecture   John Williamson and Nancy Birdsall, with Brian Deese
April 2002   ISBN 0-88132-331-4

Imagine There's No Country: Poverty, Inequality, and Growth in the Era of Globalization   Surjit S. Bhalla
September 2002   ISBN 0-88132-348-9

Reforming Korea's Industrial Conglomerates
Edward M. Graham
January 2003   ISBN 0-88132-337-3

Industrial Policy in an Era of Globalization: Lessons from Asia   Marcus Noland and Howard Pack
March 2003   ISBN 0-88132-350-0

Reintegrating India with the World Economy
T. N. Srinivasan and Suresh D. Tendulkar
March 2003   ISBN 0-88132-280-6

After the Washington Consensus: Restarting Growth and Reform in Latin America   Pedro-Pablo Kuczynski and John Williamson, eds.
March 2003   ISBN 0-88132-347-0

The Decline of US Labor Unions and the Role of Trade   Robert E. Baldwin
June 2003   ISBN 0-88132-341-1

Can Labor Standards Improve under Globalization?   Kimberly Ann Elliott and Richard B. Freeman
June 2003   ISBN 0-88132-332-2

Crimes and Punishments? Retaliation under the WTO   Robert Z. Lawrence
October 2003   ISBN 0-88132-359-4

Inflation Targeting in the World Economy
Edwin M. Truman
October 2003   ISBN 0-88132-345-4

Foreign Direct Investment and Tax Competition
John H. Mutti
November 2003   ISBN 0-88132-352-7

Has Globalization Gone Far Enough? The Costs of Fragmented Markets   Scott C. Bradford and Robert Z. Lawrence
February 2004   ISBN 0-88132-349-7

Food Regulation and Trade: Toward a Safe and Open Global System   Tim Josling, Donna Roberts, and David Orden
March 2004   ISBN 0-88132-346-2

Controlling Currency Mismatches in Emerging Markets   Morris Goldstein and Philip Turner
April 2004   ISBN 0-88132-360-8

Free Trade Agreements: US Strategies and Priorities   Jeffrey J. Schott, ed.
April 2004   ISBN 0-88132-361-6

Trade Policy and Global Poverty
William R. Cline
June 2004   ISBN 0-88132-365-9

Bailouts or Bail-ins? Responding to Financial Crises in Emerging Economies   Nouriel Roubini and Brad Setser
August 2004   ISBN 0-88132-371-3

Transforming the European Economy   Martin Neil Baily and Jacob Funk Kirkegaard
September 2004   ISBN 0-88132-343-8

Chasing Dirty Money: The Fight Against Money Laundering   Peter Reuter and Edwin M. Truman
November 2004   ISBN 0-88132-370-5

The United States and the World Economy: Foreign Economic Policy for the Next Decade
C. Fred Bergsten
January 2005   ISBN 0-88132-380-2

Does Foreign Direct Investment Promote Development?   Theodore H. Moran, Edward M. Graham, and Magnus Blomström, eds.
April 2005   ISBN 0-88132-381-0

American Trade Politics, 4th ed.   I. M. Destler
June 2005   ISBN 0-88132-382-9

Why Does Immigration Divide America? Public Finance and Political Opposition to Open Borders   Gordon H. Hanson
August 2005   ISBN 0-88132-400-0

Eclipse: Living in the Shadow of China's
Economic Dominance   Arvind Subramanian
September 2011   ISBN 978-0-88132-606-2
Flexible Exchange Rates for a Stable World
Economy   Joseph E. Gagnon with
Marc Hinterschweiger
September 2011   ISBN 978-0-88132-627-7
The Arab Economies in a Changing World,
2d ed.   Marcus Noland and Howard Pack
November 2011   ISBN 978-0-88132-628-4
Sustaining China's Economic Growth After the
Global Financial Crisis   Nicholas R. Lardy
January 2012   ISBN 978-0-88132-626-0
Who Needs to Open the Capital Account?
Olivier Jeanne, Arvind Subramanian, and John
Williamson
April 2012   ISBN 978-0-88132-511-9
Devaluing to Prosperity: Misaligned Currencies
and Their Growth Consequences   Surjit S. Bhalla
August 2012   ISBN 978-0-88132-623-9
Private Rights and Public Problems: The Global
Economics of Intellectual Property in the 21st
Century   Keith E. Maskus
September 2012   ISBN 978-0-88132-507-2
Global Economics in Extraordinary Times:
Essays in Honor of John Williamson
C. Fred Bergsten and C. Randall Henning, eds.
November 2012   ISBN 978-0-88132-662-8
Rising Tide: Is Growth in Emerging Economies
Good for the United States?   Lawrence Edwards
and Robert Z. Lawrence
February 2013   ISBN 978-0-88132-500-3
Responding to Financial Crisis: Lessons from
Asia Then, the United States and Europe Now
Changyong Rhee and Adam S. Posen, eds
October 2013   ISBN 978-0-88132-674-1
Fueling Up: The Economic Implications of
America's Oil and Gas Boom
Trevor Houser and Shashank Mohan
January 2014   ISBN 978-0-88132-656-7
How Latin America Weathered the Global
Financial Crisis   José De Gregorio
January 2014   ISBN 978-0-88132-678-9
Confronting the Curse: The Economics and
Geopolitics of Natural Resource Governance
Cullen S. Hendrix and Marcus Noland
May 2014   ISBN 978-0-88132-676-5
Inside the Euro Crisis: An Eyewitness Account
Simeon Djankov
June 2014   ISBN 978-0-88132-685-7
Managing the Euro Area Debt Crisis
William R. Cline
June 2014   ISBN 978-0-88132-678-1
Markets over Mao: The Rise of Private Business
in China   Nicholas R. Lardy
September 2014   ISBN 978-0-88132-693-2
Bridging the Pacific: Toward Free Trade and
Investment between China and the United
States   C. Fred Bergsten, Gary Clyde Hufbauer,
and Sean Miner. Assisted by Tyler Moran
October 2014   ISBN 978-0-88132-691-8
The Great Rebirth: Lessons from the Victory of
Capitalism over Communism
Anders Åslund and Simeon Djankov, eds.
November 2014   ISBN 978-0-88132-697-0

Ukraine: What Went Wrong and How to Fix It
Anders Åslund
April 2015   ISBN 978-0-88132-701-4

SPECIAL REPORTS

1   Promoting World Recovery: A Statement on
    Global Economic Strategy*
    by 26 Economists from Fourteen Countries
    December 1982   ISBN 0-88132-013-7
2   Prospects for Adjustment in Argentina,
    Brazil, and Mexico: Responding to the Debt
    Crisis*   John Williamson, ed.
    June 1983   ISBN 0-88132-016-1
3   Inflation and Indexation: Argentina, Brazil,
    and Israel*   John Williamson, ed.
    March 1985   ISBN 0-88132-037-4
4   Global Economic Imb alances*
    C. Fred Bergsten, ed.
    March 1986   ISBN 0-88132-042-0
5   African Debt and Financing*   Carol
    Lancaster and John Williamson, eds.
    May 1986   ISBN 0-88132-044-7
6   Resolving the Global Economic Crisis:
    After Wall Street*   by Thirty-three
    Economists from Thirteen Countries
    December 1987   ISBN 0-88132-070-6
7   World Economic Problems*   Kimberly Ann
    Elliott and John Williamson, eds.
    April 1988   ISBN 0-88132-055-2
    Reforming World Agricultural Trade*
    by Twenty-nine Professionals from
    Seventeen Countries
    1988   ISBN 0-88132-088-9
8   Economic Relations Between the United
    States and Korea: Conflict or Cooperation?*
    Thomas O. Bayard and Soogil Young, eds.
    January 1989   ISBN 0-88132-068-4
9   Whither APEC? The Progress to Date and
    Agenda for the Future*   C. Fred Bergsten, ed.
    October 1997   ISBN 0-88132-248-2
10 Economic Integration of the Korean
    Peninsula   Marcus Noland, ed.
    January 1998   ISBN 0-88132-255-5
11 Restarting Fast Track*   Jeffrey J. Schott, ed.
    April 1998   ISBN 0-88132-259-8
12 Launching New Global Trade Talks: An
    Action Agenda   Jeffrey J. Schott, ed.
    September 1998   ISBN 0-88132-266-0
13 Japan's Financial Crisis and Its Parallels to
    US Experience   Ryoichi Mikitani and
    Adam S. Posen, eds.
    September 2000   ISBN 0-88132-289-X
14 The Ex-Im Bank in the 21st Century: A New
    Approach   Gary Clyde Hufbauer and
    Rita M. Rodriguez, eds.
    January 2001   ISBN 0-88132-300-4
15 The Korean Diaspora in the World
    Economy   C. Fred Bergsten and
    Inbom Choi, eds.
    January 2003   ISBN 0-88132-358-6
16 Dollar Overvaluation and the World
    Economy   C. Fred Bergsten and
    John Williamson, eds.
    February 2003   ISBN 0-88132-351-9